# CINEMA AND CLASSICAL TEXTS

Apollo was the ancient god of light and the divine patron of the arts. He is therefore a fitting metaphor for cinematography, which is the modern art of writing with moving light. This book interprets films as visual texts and provides the first systematic theoretical and practical demonstration of the affinities between Greco-Roman literature and the cinema. It examines major themes from classical myth and history such as film portrayals of gods, exemplified by Apollo and the Muses; Oedipus, antiquity's most influential mythic-tragic hero; the question of heroism and patriotism in war; and the representation of women like Helen of Troy and Cleopatra as products of male desire and fantasy. Covering a wide range of European and American directors and genres and of classical authors, this study provides an innovative perspective on the two disciplines of classics and cinema and demonstrates our most influential medium's unlimited range when it adapts ancient texts.

MARTIN M. WINKLER is Professor of Classics at George Mason University.

# CINEMA AND CLASSICAL TEXTS

*Apollo's New Light*

MARTIN M. WINKLER

CAMBRIDGE
UNIVERSITY PRESS

CAMBRIDGE UNIVERSITY PRESS
Cambridge, New York, Melbourne, Madrid, Cape Town, Singapore, São Paulo, Delhi

Cambridge University Press
The Edinburgh Building, Cambridge, CB2 8RU, UK

Published in the United States of America by Cambridge University Press, New York

www.cambridge.org
Information on this title: www.cambridge.org/9780521518604

First published 2009

Printed in the United Kingdom at the University Press, Cambridge

*A catalogue record for this publication is available from the British Library*

*Library of Congress Cataloguing in Publication data*
Winkler, Martin M.
Cinema and classical texts : Apollo's new light / Martin M. Winkler.
p.   cm.
Includes bibliographical references and index.
ISBN 978-0-521-51860-4 (hardback)
1. Motion pictures and literature.   2. Classical literature – History and criticism.   I. Title.
PN1995.3.W56   2009
791.43′6 – dc22      2008037147

ISBN 978-0-521-51860-4 hardback

# Contents

# Illustrations

vii

# Acknowledgments

Some chapters or parts of chapters in this book were published separately when they had been completed, not always in readily accessible places. But my individual studies had always been intended to form a coherent whole. All material published earlier appears in this book in thoroughly revised, updated, and expanded form. Part of Chapter 1 is based on a section of "Altertumswissenschaftler im Kino; oder: *Quo vadis, philologia?*" *International Journal of the Classical Tradition*, 11 (2004): 95–110, and on some observations made in my "Introduction" to *Classical Myth and Culture in the Cinema* (New York: Oxford University Press, 2001): 3–22. Chapter 2 appeared as "Neo-Mythologism: Apollo and the Muses on the Screen" and Chapter 4 as "*Dulce et decorum est pro patria mori?* Classical Literature in the War Film," both in the *International Journal of the Classical Tradition*, 11 (2005): 383–423 and (2000): 177–214. A condensed version of Chapter 3 appeared as "Oedipus in the Cinema" in *Arethusa*, 41 (2008): 67–94. The first section of Chapter 6 was published as "Chronotope and *locus amoenus* in *Daphnis and Chloe* and *Pleasantville*" in Michael Paschalis and Stavros Frangoulidis (eds.), *Ancient Narrative*, Supplementum 1: *Space in the Ancient Novel* (Groningen: Barkhuis / University Library Groningen, 2002): 27–39; the second as "Seduction by Luxury: Antony and Cleopatra at Tarsus and in Hollywood" in Ulrich Müller, Margarete Springeth, and Michaela Auer-Müller (eds.), *Paare und Paarungen: Festschrift für Werner Wunderlich* (Stuttgart: Heinz, 2004): 362–372. Occasional recourse to other published work is identified in my notes.

For helpful advice and information I am indebted to Thomas Mann at the Library of Congress in Washington, DC, and to Horst-Dieter Blume, Eleonora Cavallini, Wolfgang Haase, and Joachim Latacz. I am particularly grateful to Frederick Ahl and David Konstan, who have closely followed and supported my work on classics and cinema for many years. At the press my editor, Michael Sharp, deserves my thanks for his ready interest in and support of this project. I am also grateful to Jodie Barnes and Paul Stevens for their practical help during the production process and especially to Rose Bell for her careful copy-editing. I am, of course, solely responsible for any errors of fact or judgment.

I should also acknowledge one further debt, my most substantial one. Since my early teens I have been fascinated by ancient literature and by the cinema. The works of classical authors and of film directors, first separately and then in conjunction, have given me countless hours of emotional and intellectual pleasure. Many, but by no means all, of the ancient and modern works and their creators are dealt with in the present book, which is meant to stand as a small tribute to their companionship over the years.

# ΦΟΙΒΩΙ ΑΠΟΛΛΩΝΙ ΦΩΤΟΚΙΝΗΤΗΙ

*Apollo, the god of* light.

— Theodoros Angelopoulos

*Light: the gentle, dangerous, dreamlike, living, dead, clear, misty, hot, violent, bare, sudden, dark, springlike, falling, straight, slanting, sensual, subdued, limited, poisonous, calming, pale light. Light.*

— Ingmar Bergman

*Cinema is the art of light.*

— Abel Gance

*There are so many ways you can use light to tell a story.*

— Sven Nykvist

*A film is writing in images.*

— Jean Cocteau

*The task I'm trying to achieve is above all to make you see.*

— D. W. Griffith

*There are so many things our eyes don't see. But the camera sees everything.*

— Robert Bresson

*The camera has X-ray eyes. It penetrates into your soul.*

— Douglas Sirk

*"Do you know what transforms night to light?" — "Poetry."*

— Jean-Luc Godard, *Alphaville*

*A film is never really good unless the camera is an eye in the head of a poet.*

— Orson Welles

*I am not a poet.*

— John Ford

ΚΟΣΜΟΝ ΑΝΤΙΣΤΑΘΜΟΝ ΑΛΛΑ
ΤΑΙΣ ΕΠΙΘΥΜΙΑΙΣ ΗΜΩΝ ΟΜΟΛΟΓΟΝ
ΔΗΛΟΙ ΤΗΙ ΟΨΕΙ Ο ΚΙΝΗΜΑΤΟΓΡΑΦΟΣ

# Introduction: *The god of light and the cinema eye*

To the ancient Greeks and Romans Apollo was the patron of arts and sciences like music, poetry, medicine, and prophecy. Apollo also came to be the god of light, literally in his identification with the sun and figuratively as bringer of culture and enlightenment.[1] His most common epithet attests to his essence: *Phoibos* or *Phoebus* ("Shining, Brilliant"). The word expressed the god's nature so well that the ancients came to regard it as practically a second name. As representative of civilization Apollo was also the *Mousagetês*, the leader of the nine Muses, his half-sisters who were themselves guardians of arts and sciences. Apollo's half-sister Athena – Minerva to the Romans – was associated with culture and the arts as well.

Apollo is the first god to make a personal appearance in the history of classical literature. At the opening of Homer's *Iliad* he brings a devastating plague upon the camp of the Greeks by means of his far-reaching arrows. The first Homeric epithet for Apollo is therefore *hekêbolos*: "hitting his mark" but subsequently understood to mean "hitting from afar."[2] Related to this word is another adjective frequently found in Homer and later authors to characterize Apollo: *hekaergos* – "working from afar."[3]

For the purpose of the present book the meaning of this latter term will be understood beyond the range that was open to the ancients. The reach of

---

[1] Apollo has been attested as god of light since the fifth century BC: Aeschylus, *Suppliants* 213–214 and Fragm. 83 Mette (from the lost play *The Bassarids*, in which the singer Orpheus worships Helios-Apollo and rejects Dionysus); Euripides, *Phaethon* 224–226 (in Fragm. 781 Kannicht). The great *Homeric Hymn to Apollo* already indicates the association of Apollo and the sun. Cahn 1950: 198 note 65 lists additional sources. The identification of Apollo with the sun extends through Greek and Roman antiquity and is regularly attested. Overviews of the variety of Apollonian myths and images in antiquity may be found in standard books on Greek myth and, with greater detail, in Graf 2009 and Solomon 1994. For Apollo's importance in the later Western tradition, especially in the Renaissance, cf., e.g., Seznec 1953 and Bull 2005: 301–343 and 418–419 (notes). The works here listed are valuable starting points and provide additional references.

[2] Homer, *Iliad* 1.14.

[3] It appears for the first time at Homer, *Iliad* 1.147. The etymological meaning of *hekê-* or *heka-* seems to have been different from what it came to mean in association with *hekathen* ("from afar").

Apollo as god of light exceeds that of Apollo the archer. In antiquity the rays of the sun could be captured and focused only to a limited degree – if very effectively, as Archimedes demonstrated to the Romans with spectacular success in 212 BC during the siege of Syracuse.[4] Now, however, the light of the sun can be combined with other kinds of light. It can be preserved on film or digitally, and it can be exhibited, either unchanged or after technical manipulation, by means of a projector or comparable device onto a screen or monitor. Consequently, from a modern quasi-mythological perspective Apollo may be linked to the new light that makes cinema possible. The shining god now takes on another important function and becomes the patron of the art of painting with light. Our term *photography* means "light-writing," while *cinematography* is "movement-writing" (and strictly speaking should be *photocinematography*: "light-movement-writing"). The cinema is a modern Apollonian art form, the most important heir of painting, sculpture, and literature. D. W. Griffith's *Intolerance* (1916), one of the most famous and influential epic films of the silent era, was advertised as "A Sun-Play of the Ages." Film theaters and production or distribution companies frequently feature the god's name.[5] We may even apply another ancient Greek term to Apollo which expresses, quite literally, this new area of his responsibilities. This word is *phôtokinêtês*: "light mover." It refers to both of the crucial features that make film possible: the light, without which the camera could not record anything and without which the projector or

---

[4] Archimedes was killed during the Romans' capture of the city. Epic cinema has paid tribute to his invention of giant convex mirrors to focus the rays of the sun onto the Roman fleet only twice: in an episode of Giovanni Pastrone's epoch-making *Cabiria* (1914) and in the almost entirely fanciful plot of Pietro Francisci's *Siege of Syracuse* (1960). Howard Hawks's sophisticated comedy *Ball of Fire* (1941), co-written by Billy Wilder, contains a clever and witty tribute to Archimedes at its climax.

[5] *ApolloMedia* is a German film and television production company; the two l's in its name are in the shape of abstract Ionic columns. Various production and technical companies have been called *Apollo Film*. (A large one is now operating in Poland.) *Apollo Cinema* is the name of a Los Angeles-based distribution company; *Apollo Cinemas* are a large theater chain in Great Britain. ("Apollo" is a standard name for film theaters.) A "supreme motion picture" is being advertised as playing "at the Apollo Theatre" in Harold Lloyd's silent comedy *Speedy* (1928). In Agostino Ferrente's *The Orchestra of Piazza Vittorio* (2006) the eponymous musicians endeavor to save the Apollo on Rome's Esquiline, one of Italy's oldest and most attractive theaters, from being turned into a bingo parlor after it already suffered the indignity of being a venue for pornographic films. The *Apollo Film Festival* regularly takes place in the Apollo Theatre in Victoria West, South Africa. An *Atelier Apollo* had been established in Finland in 1889. The protagonist of Brian de Palma's political-conspiracy thriller *Blow Out* (1981) works for a sleazy film production company in a seedy part of Philadelphia; appropriately for the film's context but regrettably for lovers of antiquity, the company's offices are above an Apollo theater that shows only hardcore pornography. The electronic *Apollo Movie Guide* (www.apolloguide.com) promises "intelligent reviews online." (The level of this intelligence varies.) *Apollo* is also the name of a line of projection screens. *Delos-Film*, a minor German production company that released a few romantic melodramas and comedies in the mid-1950s, had a stylized Ionic column for its logo. The island of Delos is Apollo's birthplace.

monitor could not show anything, and the motion that distinguishes film as a series of moving images from static ones. In Greek director Theodoros Angelopoulos's *Ulysses' Gaze* (1995) Apollo has indeed become the god of cinema, as we will see in Chapter 2. Angelopoulos regards the classical god of light as the spiritual guardian of the most powerful modern medium of art and communication. Apollo's ties to cinema had, however, been established much earlier through his function as *Mousagetês*. French poet, painter, and filmmaker Jean Cocteau repeatedly hailed the cinema as a new Muse: "FILM, the new Muse"; "the Muse of Cinema, whom the nine sisters have accepted into their close and strict circle"; and: "The Muse of Cinema is the youngest of all Muses."[6] Early French cinema even had a star who paid specific tribute to these classical ladies: actress and later screenwriter, producer, and director Jeanne Roques assumed the name Musidora ("Muses' Gift"). She became immortal to film buffs as Irma Vep in Louis Feuillade's crime serial *Les vampires* (1915) and as the screen's first vamp. The god who leads the Muses is even better known. Actress Barbara Apollonia Chalupiec (spellings vary) became one of the silent screen's greatest stars as Pola Negri. Her name is doubly appropriate: "Pola" from Apollo, "Negri" after Italian poetess Ada Negri.

It is a fitting serendipity that the name of the French founding fathers of film should have meant *Light*. The brothers Auguste and Louis Lumière began making short films lasting about fifty to fifty-two seconds in 1895.[7] A modern scholar comments:

Photography, as its name implies, is inscription by light, light that the camera receives from its subjects and retains in its pictures. And out of light the film image is twice made: light inscribes the image in the camera and light projects the image

---

[6] Quoted from Cocteau 1992: 23, 123, and 56 (with slight corrections). That ancient poets invoked their Muse for inspiration is well-known; Homer, *Iliad* 1.1 and *Odyssey* 1.1, and Virgil, *Aeneid* 1.8, are the most famous instances. Ahl and Roisman 1996: 27 point out the pre-eminence of the Muse even over the poet: "As the *Odyssey* opens, the poet asks the Muse . . . to sing in him . . . Once the appeal is completed, the Muse's voice takes over, we are invited to believe. The poet, who appears to know the story he is prompting the Muse to recite through him, vanishes from view and does not intervene again." So, at least in traditional cinematic storytelling, the film's creator may seem to retreat in comparable fashion behind the narrative on the screen, which unfolds as if by superhuman power or magic. (Cf. my quotations from André Bazin in connection with Cocteau's *Orphée* in Chapter 6.) That there still *is* such a creator, though, I argue in detail in Chapter 1.

[7] A number of the Lumière brothers' "actualities" from 1895 to 1897 are collected on the DVD *The Lumière Brothers' First Films*. A useful anthology of very early films, including the Lumières', is on the five-DVD set *The Movies Begin: A Treasury of Early Cinema, 1894–1913*. Louis Lumière's famous verdict that the cinema has no future and no business potential whatever is one of the most endearing misjudgments ever made, especially poignant for coming from one of the fathers of the new medium.

on the screen . . . Lumière's original movie camera doubled as a movie projector: light went into the machine and light came out.[8]

The light of cinema, discovered, harnessed, and presented by the Lumière brothers and their successors, instigated a profound change in Western culture – from reading stories to viewing stories, from literature to image, from linguistic text to cinematic text. As much as this was a radical break with the past, it was also a continuation of the entire tradition of human civilization. I address this topic in greater detail in Chapter 1, but it is appropriate here to quote a knowledgeable if rather rhapsodic witness who testifies to this continuity. French film pioneer Abel Gance had begun writing and acting in films in 1909 and had directed his first film in 1911. He published an article with the prophetic title "The Time of the Image Has Come" in 1927, the year that also saw the release of his six-hour historical epic *Napoleon*. In his encomium to cinema Gance wrote:

> In truth, the Time of the Image has come!
> All the legends, all mythology and all the myths, all founders of religion and all religions themselves, all the great figures of history, all objective gleams of people's imaginations over millennia – all of them await their resurrection to light, and the heroes jostle each other at our gates in order to enter . . . and it is not just a Hugoesque [i.e. flippant] joke to think that Homer would have published there [i.e chosen the new medium for] the *Iliad* or, perhaps even better, the *Odyssey*.
> The Time of the Image has come!
> . . .
> Look well! Adorable blue shadows are playing on the figure of Sigalion: they are the Muses, who are dancing around him and celebrating him, vying with each other.
> The Time of the Image has come![9]

With his references to myths and to Homer's *Iliad* and *Odyssey*, the very beginnings of Western literature, Gance was not simply bragging about the cinema or showing off his classical erudition but rather pointing to an ongoing development in the creative arts from antiquity to his own day. His conjuring up of Sigalion and the Muses makes the point more vivid.

---

[8] Perez 1998: 336.

[9] Quoted, in my translation, from Gance 1927: 96 and 98. For background information about this essay see King 1984: 61. King 1984: 62–79, reprints excerpts in translation of Gance 1929 (as "The Cinema of Tomorrow"), which incorporates material from the earlier essay, including the main part of the first passage quoted here (cf. King 1984: 78). Throughout the 1927 essay, Gance repeats its title phrase in an incantatory manner, thereby not only stating his argument as emphatically as possible but also revealing his love for the still young medium. Who could resist him when he exclaims in the same article: "Shakespeare, Rembrandt, Beethoven will make films"?

Sigalion is the ancient god of silence.[10] Gance names him as a reminder that films at his time are silent, if with the exceptions of the intertitles that provide narration and dialogue and of the music regularly accompanying the screenings.

An ancient Greek novelist with a highly developed sense of the visual corroborates Gance's perspective when he emphasized the visual (and aural) attractions that stories held for ancient listeners or readers. Heliodorus, probably writing around 360 AD, includes a moment in *An Ethiopian Story* when Kalasiris, one of the novel's major characters, recounts his adventures to Knemon, a curious young man. He mentions the ritual procession which he had witnessed at Delphi, Apollo's sanctuary, as part of the Pythian Games held in the god's honor. Kalasiris omits details of the festival from his account since they are not important, but Knemon interferes:

"When the procession and the rest of the ceremony of propitiation had come to an end – "

"Excuse me, Father," interrupted Knemon, "but they have not come to an end at all. You have not yet described them so that I can see them for myself. Your story has me in its power, body and soul, and I cannot wait to have the pageant pass before my very eyes. Yet you hurry past without a second thought."

On Knemon's insistence Kalasiris describes the festivities and mentions a hymn that he heard sung. When he neglects to quote from it, Knemon again insists on being told more:

"For a second time, Father, you are trying to cheat me of the best part of the story by not giving me all the details of the hymn. It is as if you had only given me a view of the procession, without my being able to hear anything."[11]

Kalasiris is forced to yield; he quotes part of the hymn and describes its musical performance. The words Heliodorus puts in Knemon's mouth are revealing. Knemon sees and hears in his mind a story he is being told only verbally, as expressions like "see for myself," "before my very eyes," and "a view of the procession" indicate. This is how all readers mentally imagine what they read. Roughly a century before Heliodorus, Lucian of Samosata had made this point in a comparison of the work of the historian and that of the sculptor:

---

[10] See Ausonius, *Epistles* 29.26–28.
[11] Heliodorus, *An Ethiopian Story* 3.1–3. Both excerpts are taken from the translation by J. R. Morgan in Reardon 1989: 349–588; quotations at 409 and 410. I have examined Heliodorus' novel in Winkler 2000–2001, with references to earlier scholarship on Heliodorus' visual narrative style.

The historian, we may say, should be like Phidias, Praxiteles, Alcamenes, or any great sculptor . . . When . . . a hearer [we might add: or a reader] feels as though he were looking at what is being told him, and expresses his approval, then our historical Phidias's work has reached perfection, and received its appropriate reward.[12]

What Heliodorus tells us about Knemon's psychological fascination with the visual and aural sides of narrative applies to other forms of storytelling as well. In the cinema we see and hear literally and not, as in Knemon's case, only with our mind's eyes and ears. But our imagination is as strongly engaged as Knemon wants to be involved in Kalasiris' account. Modern terminology like *imagination* (from Latin *imago*, "image"), *fantasy* (from Greek *phainesthai*, "to appear"), *idea* (Greek for "mental picture, perception," from *idein*, "to see"), and *aesthetics* (from Greek *aisthanesthai*, "to perceive visually") all attest to the highly visual nature of understanding, to visual and mental ways of perception. Our expression "I see what you mean" expresses the same idea. What Knemon sees and hears while listening to Kalasiris are moving images and sequences of sound – after all, Kalasiris is describing to him something in motion, a procession. Greeks and Romans could not *make* motion pictures, but they could *imagine* them by visualizing motion in progress. In the first century BC the Roman poet Lucretius described just such a thing. His lines about visions that come to us in our dreams today reads like an ancient account of cinema – the "dream factory," as it is often called – with its forms and figures succeeding each other through dissolves or cuts:

> it is not wonderful that images move
> And sway their arms and other limbs in rhythm –
> For the image does seem to do this in our sleep.
> The fact is that when the first one perishes
> And a new one is born and takes its place,
> The former seems to have changed its attitude.
> All this of course takes place extremely swiftly,
> So great is the velocity and so great the store
> Of them, so great the quantity of atoms
> In any single moment of sensation
> Always available to keep up the supply . . .
> And what when we see in dreams the images
> Moving in time and swaying supple limbs,
> Swinging one supple arm after the other

---

[12] Lucian, *How to Write History* 51; quoted from *The Way to Write History* in Fowler and Fowler 1905: 109–136; quotation at 132.

In fluid gestures and repeating the movement
Foot meeting foot, as eyes direct? Ah, steeped in art,
Well trained the wandering images must be
That in the night have learned such games to play! . . .
     It sometimes happens also that the image
Which follows is of a different kind: a woman
Seems in our grasp to have become a man.
And different shapes and different ages follow.
But sleep and oblivion cause us not to wonder.[13]

The film camera records fixed images at such a rapid pace that they can be projected onto a screen in a manner that makes them appear to be moving. Earlier, the photographer's still camera, reproducing what was put before it in usually black-and-white images and with absolute fidelity, had irreversibly changed the way modern man saw the world. But the camera did not present a completely new way of seeing. That had occurred in the Renaissance, when artists prominently turned to perspective in drawing and painting. Critic John Berger comments:

Today we see the art of the past as nobody saw it before. We actually perceive it in a different way.
This difference can be illustrated in terms of what was thought of as perspective. The convention of perspective, which is unique to European art . . . , centres everything on the eye of the beholder. It is like a beam from a lighthouse – only instead of light travelling outwards, appearances travel in. The conventions called those appearances *reality*. Perspective makes the single eye the centre of the visible world. Everything converges on to the eye as to the vanishing point of infinity. The visible world is arranged for the spectator as the universe was once thought to be arranged for God.
According to the convention of perspective there is no visual reciprocity . . . The inherent contradiction in perspective was that it structured all images of reality to address a single spectator who, unlike God, could only be in one place at a time.[14]

Berger is correct in his observation that perspective is unique to European art, but he might have pointed out that its origins are ancient, a fact not as widely known as it deserves to be. The earliest perspectival paintings were the architectural representations on the backdrop of the Athenian stage, the *skênographia* that had been introduced by Sophocles in the fifth century BC. The first painter of perspectival *skênographia* is said to have

---

[13] Lucretius, *On the Nature of Things* 4.768–776, 788–793, and 818–822; quoted from Melville 1997: 122–124.
[14] Berger 1972: 16; with typography slightly altered, as also in the following quotations.

been Agatharchus.[15] The camera is both new as an advanced technical instrument and traditional in its reproduction of perspective and in the artistic composition of images that perspective demands. The film camera is the best means to put before our eyes realistic-looking images that tell stories and are at the same time artistic compositions.

The perspective in a painting or photograph, at which a viewer is gazing from a distance, literally by being placed at some remove from the image itself and figuratively by being completely removed from the scene being presented, prepares the way for a quasi-divine perspective that is to come with images that move and tell stories. The film camera can show us everything either subjectively from the point of view of characters or (apparently) objectively. It may be detached from individual characters or from the story, appearing to be omniscient as from God's – or a god's – superior position. Hence the recourse in films to the device of the omniscient narrator, who serves a function parallel to that of the divinely positioned camera. The perspective in painting and still photography prepares us for the power of perspective in motion pictures, which also work through a single-eyed gaze. But since film images move, the quasi-divine power to change the place of looking by means of camera movements, dissolves, and cuts introduces a new element, that of time passing. About the still camera as an intermediate stage between painted and moving images Berger goes on to observe:

> After the invention of the camera this contradiction gradually became apparent.
> The camera isolated momentary appearances and in so doing destroyed the idea that images were timeless . . . the camera showed that the notion of time passing was inseparable from the experience of the visual (except in paintings). What you saw depended upon where you were when. What you saw was relative to your position in time and space. It was no longer possible to imagine everything converging on the human eye as on the vanishing point of infinity . . . Every drawing or painting that used perspective proposed to the spectator that he was the unique centre of the world. The camera – and more particularly the movie camera – demonstrated that there was no centre.
> The invention of the camera changed the way men saw. The visible came to mean something different to them.[16]

In 1928 Abel Gance had already commented on the novelty of moving images and their impact on people's ways of perception:

---

[15] Vitruvius, *On Architecture* 7 Preface 11, attributes the discovery of fifth-century painting in perspective to Agatharchus, a somewhat problematical dating. Pollitt 1974: 236–247, collects and discusses the ancient sources on *skēnographia* and gives further references. See especially White 1956 and Richter 1970b.

[16] Berger 1972: 17–18.

The most familiar objects have to be seen as if for the first time, producing a transmutation of all our values. This transformation of our way of looking, in an absolutely new domain unfamiliar to our senses, is in my opinion the most wonderful of modern miracles.[17]

The technical, artistic, and psychological impact on traditional ways of seeing that arrived with the film camera led to the kind of exuberance that we can observe in Gance's words and in early filmmaking. The gleeful trickery to be found at the beginning of cinema, for instance in the films of Georges Méliès, is the best example. But the intellectual and artistic challenges that the cinema brought with it had been expressed a few years before Gance's enthusiasm for his medium in an even more ecstatic hymn to cinema and the technical potential of the camera, the essential tool to capture and project light and to inspire the filmmaker's creativity. Russian writer, director, editor, and theoretician Dziga Vertov wrote in 1923:

> The main and essential thing is:
> The sensory exploration of the world through film.
> We therefore take as the point of departure the use of the camera as a kino-eye, more perfect than the human eye, for the exploration of the chaos of visual phenomena that fills space.
> The kino-eye lives and moves in time and space; it gathers and records impressions in a manner wholly different from that of the human eye . . .
> I am kino-eye, I create a man more perfect than Adam, I create thousands of different people in accordance with preliminary blueprints and diagrams of different kinds . . .
> I am kino-eye, I am a mechanical eye. I, a machine, show you the world as only I can see it.
> Now and forever, I free myself from human immobility, I am in constant motion, I draw near, then away from objects, I crawl under, I climb onto them. I move apace with the muzzle of a galloping horse, I plunge full speed into a crowd, I outstrip running soldiers, I fall on my back, I ascend with an airplane, I plunge and soar together with plunging and soaring bodies. Now I, a camera, fling myself along their resultant, maneuvering in the chaos of movement, recording movement, starting with movements composed of the most complex combinations . . .
> My path leads to the creation of a fresh perception of the world. I decipher in a new way a world unknown to you.[18]

Vertov's views of cinema are exemplified in his masterpiece, *The Man with the Movie Camera* (1929).[19] This film shows the reality of the cinema eye

---

[17] Gance 1928: 197–209; quoted from the translation by King 1984: 56.

[18] Quoted from Vertov 1984: 14–15 and 17–18. *Kino* is Russian for *cinema*. Berger 1972: 17 quotes parts of this text in a different translation.

[19] For an analytic introduction to this seminal film see Roberts 2000. On Vertov and the cinema eye see now also Hicks 2007, with updated bibliography. Master cinematographer Nestor Almendros pays tribute to Vertov with the title of his autobiography (Almendros 1984).

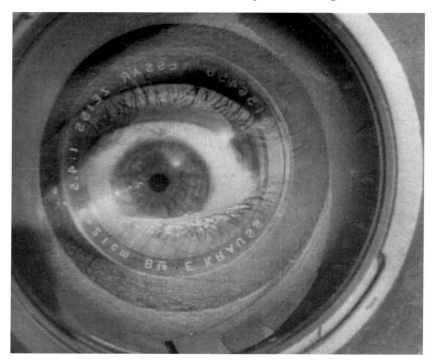

**Fig. 1.** *The Man with the Movie Camera.* Dziga Vertov's Cinema Eye, the film's final image. (VUFKU-Image)

in a famous image when a camera lens appears superimposed on a close-up of a human eye; it is impossible to separate the one from the other (Fig. 1). Decades later director Federico Fellini was to observe: "the camera is just my eye."[20] In 1924 Vertov made a series of four documentaries which he titled *Kino Glas*: "Cinema Eye." The sensory exploration of the world that Vertov mentions is the chief purview of art, as it has always been. In antiquity such exploration was often but not always divided: either word or image, but not both simultaneously – except in the theater, which combined the visual and the verbal. Our word *theater* comes from the Greek *theatron* ("viewing space") and is based on the verb *theân* ("to see" or "look at"); our term *drama* is a Greek noun and derives from *drân* ("to do," "act"), a reference to the actors' movements on stage. (Latin *actor* literally means "doer.") The chief modern viewing space for actions is the cinema with its theater (and now home theater). It combines the visual

---

[20] Quoted from Stevens 2006: 638.

and the verbal arts into one, incorporating yet others like music, song, and dance – all forms of expression that were crucial for the development of archaic and classical Greek culture.[21] The cinema provides artists with the ultimate means to achieve a previously elusive goal, the presentation or representation of the world of human experience in a *Gesamtkunstwerk*, a creation that encompasses all the arts.

Decades after Abel Gance wrote the words quoted above, a distinguished classical scholar confirmed that the time of the image has come. J. B. Hainsworth observes about the time of Homer, the change from oral to written storytelling, that "at the beginning of literature, when heroic poetry reached society as a whole . . . society *listened*; in the twentieth century society *views*." In between listening and viewing, society has been reading. For better or worse, society's viewing now seems to edge out society's reading. Hainsworth further comments that "the modern heroic medium is film, and not necessarily the productions that are held in highest critical regard."[22]

Among the productions that are not generally held in high regard are western films. The western is the one genre of cinema that comes closest to expressing the essence of classical myth.[23] One specific moment in a well-known western epic illustrates Hainsworth's point, for we view (and hear) how stories or myths used to originate when society listened. In John Sturges's *The Magnificent Seven* (1960) a hero-worshiping youngster, who himself aspires to heroic stature and will eventually be accepted into the titular group, comments on the exploits of its leader after a day of fighting: "You know what? They'll make up a song about you . . . villagers like this, they'll make up a song about every big thing that happens, sing 'em for years." Here the cinema recalls the pre-literate age when epic songs were performed orally by singers or bards. The Homeric epics, which combine features of the oral tradition of composition and performance with the beginnings of literacy, are our greatest examples of this stage of storytelling. Homer, the father of Western literature, is also the godfather of film. His Odysseus has inhabited the land of cinema since 1905, when Georges Méliès made *L'île de Calypso: Ulysse et le géant Polyphème*. The title of this film, abbreviated to *Ulysses and the Giant Polyphemus* in English, carries an archetypal meaning. Its three proper names point to the nature of popular narrative: a beautiful woman of supernatural allure is in love with a handsome and clever hero who is himself the vanquisher of a savage

---

[21] We may note in passing that the Italian term for a film studio's "sound stage" is *teatro*.
[22] Hainsworth 1991: 148.    [23] I have addressed this topic in Winkler 1985 and 1996.

monster. The birth of cinema reincarnates Homeric epic. Or, to look at it from the opposite perspective: Homeric epic, chiefly the *Odyssey*, is the precursor of a new technological medium of storytelling in images, just as it had provided the impulse for a new art form in the seventeenth century. Claudio Monteverdi's and Giacomo Badoaro's *Il ritorno d'Ulisse in patria* came near the birth of opera in 1640.

Hainsworth's point about the variable nature of epic cinema is important. It indicates that the traditional disdain that literary and classical scholars used to evince for the cinema has become anachronistic. But it is worth recalling what that attitude was like. No less a figure than Gilbert Highet of Columbia University, a widely read (in both senses of the term) scholar and a dedicated teacher and propagator of classical culture in and beyond the academy, could write in 1949 in his best-known and most frequently reprinted book:

> The difference between an educated man and an uneducated man is that the uneducated man lives only for the moment, reading his newspaper and watching the latest moving-picture, while the educated man lives in a far wider present, that vital eternity in which the psalms of David and the plays of Shakespeare, the epistles of Paul and the dialogues of Plato, speak with the same charm and power that made them immortal the instant they were written.

Yet Highet was aware, if condescendingly, that the cinema was not solely of and for the uneducated. In his chapter on Renaissance drama he commented, if only in a note buried at the end of his long book:

> It has been interesting to watch the gradual self-education of the films (largely through experiment, but to a considerable extent also by tutelage from the stage and by criticism) from the early crudity when they produced nothing but farces, serial melodramas, and spectacles, towards something like a real understanding of the power of drama.[24]

Echoes of Highet's position toward cinema survive. Five and a half decades later Charles Martindale, a scholar well-known for openness toward modern critical approaches to antiquity, wrote in his introduction to a collection of scholarly essays on the reception of classical literature, art, and culture:

> I fear . . . that, if we abandon a serious commitment to the value of the texts we choose for our attention and those [*sic*] of our students, we may end by trivializing reception within the discipline; already a classics student is far more likely to spend time analysing *Gladiator* than the *Commedia* of Dante. I find this trend worrying. This is not to decry the study of a wide range of cultural artefacts (there

---

[24] The quotations are from Highet 1949: 545 and 598 note 3.

are many more good things in the world than the canon knows), and certainly not to criticize the study of film or even of popular culture. It is simply to say that we form ourselves by the company that we keep, and that in general material of high quality is better company for our intellects and hearts than the banal or the quotidian (often we use the latter, archly and somewhat cheaply, merely to celebrate our own cultural superiority). We need to believe in the value of what we do, and whatever we do we need to do it in full seriousness, not in any spirit of cynicism or condescension.[25]

Disingenuity is palpable in these lines, which despite protestation to the contrary archly reveal (celebrate?) the writer's own superiority. The adverb "even" that accompanies Martindale's reference to popular culture is the giveaway. Martindale appears not to apply to himself his exhortation to others, for if he did why should he be afraid of *Gladiator*? And is it an expression of a spirit of condescension that this film, which Martindale had mentioned on his second page, does not rate an entry in the book's index, just as the cinema as a whole is conspicuous by its absence from almost the entire volume?[26]

In their different ways across half a century, Highet's and Martindale's words, taken together with all the other quotations given above, are my justification for the present book. It presents thematically related essays on the affinities between classical and cinematic narratives. The book interprets films as visual "texts" that are capable of the close analysis that classical philologists are trained to carry out. I call this *classical film philology*, an important new branch on the venerable tree of traditional classical scholarship that addresses the links between texts and images. As none other than Johann Wolfgang Goethe had emphasized in 1816, "philology without an understanding of the [visual] arts is only one-eyed."[27] Chapter 1 lays the foundation for this kind of endeavor from specific theoretical and historical points of view. Obviously, several other approaches to film, to film and literature, and to classics and cinema are possible. These exist alongside and complement mine, but they are not my subject here. Instead I have set myself the task to develop, for the first time, a system that combines a reaffirmation of classical philology and the study of ancient literature,

---

[25] Martindale 2006: 11.

[26] Exceptions are a mention in passing of the documentary *Paris Is Burning* (1990) and a brief discussion of Wolfgang Petersen's *Troy* (2004) at Martindale and Thomas 2006: 31 and 190.

[27] Goethe wrote this in a letter dated January 15, 1816. He specifically referred to the new study of ancient art as revolutionized by Johann Joachim Winckelmann. The original sentence reads: "Seit Winckelmanns und seiner Nachfolger Bemühungen ist Philologie ohne Kunstbegriff nur einäugig." Shortly after, Goethe adds that the different branches of scholarship advance each other ("so fördern die verschiedenen Zweige der Wissenschaften einander"). My quotations are taken from Goethe 1902: 221.

culture, and history for their own sake and in their own right with an exhortation to integrate film into such work. A perspective like this enables us to view the ancients as important and even fundamental contributors to an ever-evolving and never-ending cultural continuity. Diachronic study necessitates considerations of new aspects, in our case of a technology that did not yet exist in antiquity but whose roots go back to a pre-technological past. André Bazin, one of the most influential critics and theoreticians of film, explicitly made this point in 1946:

> The cinema is an idealistic phenomenon. The concept men had of it existed, so to speak, fully armed in their minds, as if in some Platonic heaven, and what strikes us most of all is the obstinate resistance of matter to ideas rather than of any help offered by techniques to the imagination of the researchers.

Bazin illustrates this observation with an analogy from Greek myth: "the myth of [Daedalus and] Icarus had to wait for the internal combustion engine before descending from the Platonic heavens. But it had dwelt in the soul of every man since he first thought about birds."[28]

Subsequent chapters apply the perspective proposed in Chapter 1 to specific representative cases of ancient literary and modern visual texts. Chapter 2 addresses filmic portrayals of the divine, exemplified by Apollo, the patron god of cinema, and the Muses. Chapter 3 deals with Oedipus, antiquity's most influential mythic-tragic hero and a figure directly connected to Apollo by means of the Delphic oracle. Through Sigmund Freud, his modern champion, as it were, Oedipus is also crucial for the nature of cinema, as we will see in the same chapter. Chapter 4 starts with Horace's famous if controversial line that it is "sweet and fitting to die for your country" and discusses heroism and patriotism. This, the most serious topic in the book, is of special significance in the present age of imperial warfare. To emphasize the importance and the unbroken tradition of the theme of individual heroism and glibly invoked patriotism I examine in this chapter a considerable amount of modern literature in conjunction with ancient literature and film; in this way I hope to make evident how important the cinema is for our culture and how closely it is connected to the classical tradition. Like the Muses discussed in Chapter 2, women as objects or products of male desires and fantasies are the topic of Chapters 5 and 6. A brief epilogue returns us to Homer and Apollo. The book as a whole has something to say about the variability and adaptability of ancient literature and myth, the nature of creativity and commercialism

---

[28]  Bazin 1967a: 17 and 22, slightly altered and corrected.

in the progression from texts to images, the persistence of antiquity in a global society that is becoming increasingly unfamiliar with and even alienated from its classical origins, and the dual importance of the study of antiquity for its own worth and for its importance today, not least in view of its wide dissemination in our mass media. By examining the filmic reconstructions of and variations on certain fundamental ancient themes the book hopes to contribute something to our understanding of ourselves. Its individual topics are meant to be regarded as representatives of other related and interrelated themes and approaches that are wider than those encountered here.

One aspect of modern representations of classical themes that the book deals with repeatedly deserves a brief theoretical consideration at the outset. Most of the ancient stories and figures that will be examined are taken from myth, so the films that recreate or adapt them are also mythic, if in their own ways. In antiquity the concept of myth was fluid enough to accommodate a wide range of divergent, even contradictory, versions of the same story. This tradition continues in modern times: myths, whether ancient or later, preserve their Protean nature. Classical antiquity has always played a major part in film history, but screenwriters and directors as a rule take extensive liberties with their source materials. Archetypal figures recur with almost infinite changes in films based on Greek and Roman literature, especially epic and tragedy, and in films with invented historical, pseudo-historical, or modern settings. The same concept applies to other subjects, for instance history.[29] What film scholar Pierre Sorlin has deduced about historical films applies equally to literary and mythical subjects, as my parenthetical additions to his words here quoted will make evident:

An historical film [or a film based on a work of literature] can be puzzling for a scholar: everything that he considers history [or important for the plot and style in a literary work] is ignored; everything he sees on the screen is, in his opinion, pure imagination. But at the same time it is important to examine the difference between history [or the scholarly study of literature] as it is written by the specialist and history [or the original text] as it is received by the non-specialist.

Sorlin sees the most important aspect of historical film in "the use of historical understanding in the life of a society" – that is to say, in the society that makes such films.[30] The same goes for literary adaptations, which

[29] Regarding films set in classical antiquity cf. Winkler 2004a: 16–24 (section entitled "Film and Historical Authenticity").
[30] Both quotations are from Sorlin 1980: ix.

illuminate the life of the society that produces them. So the conclusion becomes unavoidable that, as far as cinematic recreations of times past are concerned either in historical settings or in literary adaptations, scholars' understandable demands for authenticity are beside the point.[31] They fail to take into account the nature of film as a narrative medium which needs creative freedom in order to tell its stories. For this reason the cinema cannot be solely or chiefly indebted to or dependent on principles of historical or philological authenticity. This observation is not meant to denigrate historical accuracy or literary faithfulness in a visual adaptation. On the contrary, concern for authenticity in the recreation of the past is a sign that creative artists such as directors, screenwriters, set decorators, or costume designers take their task seriously. But correctness in the representation of the past is neither a necessary nor a sufficient condition to assure the quality of the result.

In the area of mythology the tradition of imagining alternatives to well-attested and even canonical versions of myth goes back to antiquity itself. Our surviving texts reveal that different or mutually exclusive variants of certain parts or individual moments in a myth existed in antiquity, and we have visual evidence of myths or versions of a myth that are unattested in any text – a kind of visual equivalent to textual *hapax legomena*, words occurring only once in our surviving literature. It is therefore difficult, not to say impossible, to maintain that certain accounts of a myth are the correct ones and that others are false. Alternative versions used to circulate far and wide throughout ancient literature and the visual arts, as the works of playwrights, mythographers, and epic and lyrical poets on the one hand and those of sculptors and painters on the other attest.[32] This tradition has continued uninterrupted. Today, in an age of advanced technology, myths can be told or retold chiefly or entirely in images, moving ones at that. Cinema and its offspring, television, have proven fertile grounds for re-imagining and re-inventing stories from classical antiquity. Film and television are now followed by video and computer games with often sophisticated levels of "interactivity." Italian director Vittorio Cottafavi, who made several cinema and television films set in Greece and Rome, aptly described his and his fellow filmmakers' approach to their subject matter as "neo-mythologism."[33] Chapters 2, 3, and 5 in particular demonstrate the validity of film-philological examinations of such neo-mythologism.

---

[31] Cf. Solomon 2006. Bertelli 1995 examines errors in a large variety of historical films.

[32] A case in point are the ancient portrayals of Odysseus as hero in epic and as villain in tragedy. Stanford 1954 is the classic account.

[33] On Cottafavi and his term "neo-mythologism" see Leprohon 1972: 174–179. Cf. further Winkler 2007b.

The present book interprets several if by no means all possible approaches to ancient subjects that filmmakers can adopt. More than any other means of creative and commercial expression, film as a narrative medium encompasses all the ranges of high and low culture. My own preferences – if not, I hope, prejudices (except very occasionally) – will quickly become apparent, although I have taken pains not to let them color my arguments. While the films I examine differ considerably in their artistic qualities, they all present in their own and sometimes unique ways noteworthy examples of the continuing vitality of the classical past in today's culture. At the same time it is worth remembering that classical and biblical antiquity has always conferred social acceptability and cultural prestige on a new medium whose origins and early history made it suspect to most of the members of good society.[34] An anecdote from the silent days of cinema that is as amusing as it is charming illustrates this fact. British film pioneer Cecil Hepworth recounts the following story from his days as presenter of film shows:

I was giving my lecture once in a large hall built underneath a chapel. My apparatus was set up as usual in the heart of the audience, and while I was waiting beside it for the hour to strike when I was to begin, the dear old parson came and sat down beside me. He said he was quite sure that my entertainment was everything that it ought to be, but he knew I would understand that, as shepherd of his little flock, it was his duty to make doubly certain and would I let him see my list of pictures. So I handed him the list and watched him mentally ticking off each item until he came to the pick of the whole bunch, a hand-coloured film of Loie Fuller in her famous serpentine dance. He said at once that he could not allow that – a vulgar music-hall actress. I said rather indignantly that there was nothing vulgar about it; that it was indeed a really beautiful and artistic production, but he was adamant and insisted that it must be omitted. Then I had to begin. Apart from my reluctance to leave out my best picture, I was faced with the practical difficulty of how to do it. For this was the last picture but one on the spool. There was no earthly means of getting rid of it except by running it through in darkness, and I didn't think the little flock would stand for that. Then, just as I came to the danger-point, I had a sudden brainwave. I announced the film as "Salome Dancing before Herod". Everyone was delighted. Especially the parson. He said in his nice little speech afterwards that he thought it was a particularly happy idea to introduce a little touch of Bible history into an otherwise wholly secular entertainment.

And he added that he had no idea that the cheenimartograph had been invented so long![35]

---

[34] I examine a specific case and refer to related examples in Winkler 2007a.

[35] Hepworth 1948; quoted from *The Penguin Film Review* 1977–1978, vol. 2: 33–39, at 38–39. Hepworth was himself a filmmaker and writer on cinema; as early as in 1897 he published *Animated Photography: The ABC of the Cinematograph* (cf. Hepworth 1900). On then famous dancer Loie Fuller see Current and Current 1997.

Antiquity and the cinema are inseparable, and their interactions today ought to be part of anybody's assessment of modern culture. But if antiquity is important for cinema, cinema is also important for antiquity and the presence of classical Greece and Rome in our culture and education.

While it is true that the ancients did not actually know the "cheenimar-tograph," it is equally true that the idea of progressive storytelling, if in static images, was anything but alien to them. And their verbal narratives exhibited a variety of what we would now call filmic techniques as we already saw in Lucretius.[36] So the cinematic nature of much of ancient art and literature is itself sufficient justification for classical scholars to engage in research and teaching of film in connection with their work on the Greeks and Romans. The present book, written by someone who has been equally in thrall to the nine ancient Muses and the tenth cinematic Muse for many years, is intended to give classical scholars interested in similar endeavors a theoretical foundation and a number of practical examples to broaden the reach of their field beyond its established boundaries. But the book addresses a considerably wider audience: those who work in film studies, comparative literature, cultural studies, European and American history and culture, and related fields in the humanities and social sciences. Far from being meant for academics only, the book also hopes to reach readers who love both antiquity and the cinema – amateurs in the literal and best sense of the term. For this reason my book requires no expert knowledge of either antiquity or film. I have avoided all specialized terminology, which in academic circles tends to degenerate into jargon so obscure as to be unhelpful to all except true believers. Specific vocabulary is accompanied by explanations except when familiarity may be taken for granted. All passages from the classical languages are quoted in transla-tion, as are those from modern sources that were originally published in languages other than English. The book provides extensive references to recent and current scholarship on all topics covered for those interested in finding out more.

Although I point to the cinema's almost limitless possibilities to adopt and adapt classical literature, my book is not and cannot be exhaus-tive in demonstrating the variety of ties between ancient literature, art, thought, and history on the one hand and film on the other. No sin-gle author could undertake such an endeavor, not even in a series of

---

[36] I discuss examples of these aspects of Greek and Roman culture in Winkler 2000–2001, 2001b: 11–14, and Winkler 2006b: 48–63. For other examples see especially Newman 2001 and Mench 2001.

books.[37] But I hope that readers will take the very absence of a particular topic, figure, film, or literary work which they would have liked to see included as an incentive to pursue their own lines of enquiry, to take my chapters as starting points for further professional work on or private pursuit of cinematic variations of classical themes. They are also welcome to take issue with my arguments or conclusions. Intellectual engagement between writers and readers is at the heart of literature, and the same goes for films and their viewers. This principle applies to classical film philology in equal measure. If my discussions send readers back to particular films or classical works, if they encourage them to read a text or to view a film again or for the first time, this book will have achieved its goal.

[37] Particularly desirable, to mention just one instance, is a systematic overview of the connections between ancient philosophy, both in general and in regard to ancient views of the visual arts as forms of representation (*mimesis*), on the one hand and the philosophy of film on the other, with emphasis on the ontological and phenomenological aspects of cinema. If modern philosophers can fruitfully turn to cinema – I mention, as only one prominent example, Deleuze 1986 and 1989 – why not also scholars of ancient philosophy?

# CHAPTER I

# A certain tendency in classical philology

This chapter provides a theoretical overview of the similarities between classical scholarship and scholarship on the cinema. It is not my goal, nor would it serve any practical purpose, to delineate either the one or the other in its entirety or to discuss their obvious differences. Rather, I intend to provide those engaged in classical scholarship with a justification to turn to the cinema as an important complement to their work and as a means to illuminate classical texts from a contemporary perspective. Various modern approaches to antiquity in such areas as comparative literature, art history, political theory, feminism, psychoanalysis, history, and anthropology have yielded significant insights into ancient works and their cultural, aesthetic, and social contexts. There is then no reason to assume that the cinema could not also increase our understanding of the past and of its continuing influence on the present. Film, together with related media like television and the production of digital images, is now our chief means of storytelling and the most important heir to textual narrative; it also has a greater reach than any other medium of high and popular culture. The reception of classical art and literature has by now become inseparable from the ancient works themselves. Translations and creative adaptations of ancient texts have given strong impulses to the entire history of Western culture. In striking ways, the cinema exemplifies the continuing importance of classical works. So professionals who interpret the past ought to be knowledgeable about the history of this past's influence at different times and in different media.

The cinema presents traditional literary scholars with what may at first seem a bewildering variety of quality and quantity, ranging from large numbers of crassly commercial products to rarefied art-house films, with great variability between these extremes. Films also have a complex production process that involves dozens and often hundreds or even thousands of people in the creation of one single work. In literature, more often than not the process of production is considerably simpler. We refer to a poem, play, novel, or essay as the work of a creative individual whom we call an author. Classicists might therefore be tempted to argue that films cannot be compared to literature because they appear not to have authors. Two well-known classical scholars have recently advanced just such an argument. The cinema, they write, is

so *different* from everything they [classicists] regularly have to do with . . . The product cannot be reduced to the intention of an individual "author" – simply too many people are decisively involved in the process of production – nor can we adduce the public's understanding as a standard . . . Film is the postmodern medium *par excellence*. The "death of the author," frequently adduced, does here not remain merely a decorative slogan but turns into visible and audible reality and forces on us different ways of approaching and working with film than we are accustomed to.[1]

This perspective is demonstrably wrong. The idea of authorship, as we will see, applies just as readily to the cinema as it does to literature. Not all films have authors in any serious sense of the term (nor does every written work), but most good films and all of the very best films do. So we need a greater measure of clarity about the concept of literary and cinematic authorship and a working definition of the term *author* as applicable to both literature and film. But we first need an understanding of film as a narrative medium that is analogous to that of textual narratives. We can then proceed to a consideration of cinema as a modern form of visual poetry. Lastly, we need a broader understanding of what constitutes legitimate areas of classical scholarship in an ever-changing world that has considerably expanded the ways and means of creative expression and that provides us with new ways to engage with ancient Greece and Rome. A wider comprehension of what classical scholarship entails fits the parameters of classicists' intellectual responsibilities that had been established in antiquity itself. With the framework provided in this chapter we can apply principles of classical philology to the cinema, as Chapters 2–6 will demonstrate.

---

[1] The quotations, in my translation, are taken from the editors' preface ("Vorwort") to Korenjak and Töchterle 2002: 7–11, at 7 and 8. The original text reads: "[. . . das Kino] so *anders* ist als alles, womit sie sonst zu tun haben . . . Weder lässt sich das Produkt auf die Absicht eines einzelnen 'Autors' zurückführen – dazu sind einfach zu viele Personen massgeblich in den Entstehungsprozess involviert – , noch können wir das Verständnis des Publikums als Massstab heranziehen . . . Film ist das postmoderne Medium *par excellence* . . . Der vielbeschworene 'Tod des Autors' bleibt hier kein dekoratives Schlagwort, sondern wird sicht- und hörbare Realität und zwingt uns andere Zugangs- und Arbeitsweisen auf, als wir es gewohnt sind." On the death of the author cf. especially Roland Barthes's essay "Death of the Author" from 1968, in Barthes 1977: 142–148 or Barthes 1986: 49–55. For a detailed study of the entire question with extensive bibliography see Benedetti 2005 (with a title changed rather infelicitously from the original, Benedetti 1999). Schmitz 2007: 50–55 and 124–127 provides an overview.

With the exception of abstract or non-narrative works, literature and film are forms of storytelling in good Aristotelian fashion: with a beginning, middle, and end, if not always in that order. Literary and filmic narratives have specific ways in which they present and develop their plots and in which readers and viewers follow them. Gerald Mast, a film scholar trained in literary studies, observes:

A movie contains all six of Aristotle's elements of the drama – plot, character, thought, diction (in two senses: the diction of dialogue and the cinematic "diction" of the movie's visual style), melody, and spectacle. Yet a movie has as much in common with narrative fiction as with the drama. Like the novel it uses a focused narration (lens parallels narrator); like the novel it is freer in its manipulation of time and space than . . . realist drama.[2]

Films therefore are kinds of texts. Among the fundamental tasks of all literary scholarship are interpretations of content and form (plot and style) of an individual text, of its place in its author's life and work, and, beyond this, of its importance for literary and cultural history. The same is true for film scholarship.

Literary storytelling is limited to words or to words supported by visuals as in drama, while cinematic storytelling occurs primarily but not exclusively in images. The close affinities between verbal and visual narratives were well known in antiquity, best expressed in the famous saying by Simonides of Keos that painting is silent poetry while poetry is painting that speaks. In Rome, Horace restated the idea in his influential *Art of Poetry* in a phrase that has sometimes been misunderstood: *ut pictura poesis* ("like painting, poetry").[3] The prologue to Longus' novel *Daphnis and*

---

[2] Mast 1977: 18.

[3] The most important classical sources are Plutarch, *Moralia* 17f–18a (in "How the Young Man Should Study Poetry") and 346f–347c (in "Were the Athenians More Famous in War or in Wisdom?" = "On the Fame of the Athenians"); Plato, *Phaedrus* 275d and *Republic* 595a–608b; Cicero, *On Invention* 2.1 (painting and rhetoric); Vitruvius, *On Architecture* 5.6.9; Horace, *Art of Poetry* 361 (*ut pictura poesis*; on this see primarily Lee 1967, a fundamental work; cf. also Brink 1971: 368–372); Philostratus the Elder, *Imagines* 1.1–2; Philostratus the Younger, *Imagines*, preface; Dio Chrysostom, *Olympicus* (*Oration* 12), 26, 44–46, and 61–72: sculptor (Phidias) as rival to poet (Homer); Demetrius, *On Style* 14 (writing analogous to scupture). Cf. also Aristotle, *Poetics* 1447a8–1448a18 (in Chapter 1), 1450a24–28 and 1450a37–b3 (both passages in Chapter 6), and Quintilian, *Institutes of Oratory* 12.10.1–9 (comparison of painters and sculptors with orators in the context of the *genus orationis*). Cf. Zanker 2000 on Aristotle's *Poetics*; further Benediktson 2000: 12–30 and 197–202 (notes), and A. Ford 2002: 96–101 (section entitled "Singing, Painting, and Speaking" in chapter "Song and Artifact"). See further Finkelberg 1998: 100–130 (chapter "Song and Artefact"). As late as the eleventh century AD, Byzantine philosopher Michael Psellus refers to Simonides: "according to Simonides, the word is the image of the thing"; quoted from David A. Campbell 1991: 363. – Also valuable,

*Chloe*, which dates to the late second century AD, demonstrates that one and the same story can be told equally well in images as in words. The narrator explains how he came to write his novel:

I saw the most beautiful sight I have ever seen . . . : a painting that told a story of love . . . combining great artistic skill with an exciting, romantic subject . . . I gazed in admiration and was seized by a yearning to depict the picture in words.

I searched out an interpreter of the picture and produced the four volumes of this book.[4]

with extensive references, is Kristeller 1951–1952, rpt. in Kristeller 1990: 163–227. The comparison of poetry and painting is fundamental to literature and the arts. As Kristeller 1952: 36 (= Kristeller 1990: 217) observes in connection with Gotthold Ephraim Lessing's *Laocoon* (1766): "the parallel between painting and poetry was one of the most important elements that preceded the formation of the modern system of the arts." For theoretical affinities of Lessing's *Laocoon* to cinema see especially Sergei Eisenstein's monograph-length essay "Laocoön" in Eisenstein 1988: 109–202.

[4] Quoted from Longus, *Daphnis and Chloe*, tr. Christopher Gill, in Reardon 1989: 285–348; quotation at 288–289. I have examined examples of the inherently filmic quality of ancient literature in Winkler 2000–2001 and 2006b. Malissard 1974 and 1982 examines parallels between historical narrative in ancient sculpture and epic and principles of narrative film. Cf. Ann Steiner 2007 on "reading" images on Greek vases. – The first technical handbook on cinematography by a film cameraman had an appropriate title: *Painting with Light* (Alton 1949). Cf. such technical terms as *prises de vue* ("captures of images") for cinematographic shots and *direttore delle luci* ("director of lights") for the cinematographer. The title of a recent monograph on Italian director Enrico Guazzoni rightly calls him a "director-painter" (Bernardini, Martinelli, and Tortora 2005). See also Bordwell 2005. An instance of non-narrative film in which a painter literally paints with light (and with brush and paints) is Henri-Georges Clouzot's *The Mystery of Picasso* (1956). Picasso drew and painted on a transparent surface that allowed Clouzot to film him from behind it in such a way as to make it appear to viewers that Picasso was painting directly onto the screen. (The film had to be reversed in the laboratory to present the correct left-right view when screened.) Non-narrative and experimental cinema has a long-standing tradition of filmmakers painting, drawing, or even scratching lines and shapes directly onto the filmstrip; Canadian filmmaker Norman McLaren was a pioneer of this. For a number of years, director Martin Scorsese has used the phrase "A Martin Scorsese Picture" (rather than "A Martin Scorsese Film") in his screen credits to emphasize the painterly aspects of his work. Cf. Ingmar Bergman on *The Seventh Seal* (1957): "The whole film is based on medieval pictures in a Swedish church. If you go there, you will see death playing chess, sawing a tree, making jokes with human souls . . . . I have the feeling simply of having painted a canvas . . . . I said, 'Here is a painting; take it, please.'" Quoted from Samuels 1972: 204. German Expressionism of the 1920s embraced three art forms simultaneously: literature, painting, and film. Cubist and surrealist art also found its way onto the screen; the classic instances are, for the former, Fernand Léger's *Le ballet mécanique* (1924) and, for the latter, *An Andalusian Dog* (1929) and *Age of Gold* (or *The Golden Age*, 1930), both directed by Luis Buñuel and written by him in collaboration with Salvador Dalí. Jean Renoir's *A Day in the Country* (1936) is one of the most painterly films ever made, reminiscent of the work of his father Pierre Auguste Renoir. Three later films consciously evoke the light and color of his father's paintings: *French Cancan* (1955), *Elena and Her Men* (or *Paris Does Strange Things*, 1956), and, primarily, *Picnic on the Grass* (1959). The cinematographer on *A Day in the Country* and *Elena and Her Men* was Jean Renoir's nephew Claude Renoir, one of the most distinguished French cameramen. In general cf. Andrew 1984. Director Robert Bresson once compared a particular aspect of filmmaking to a particular procedure of painters: "Several takes of the same thing, like a painter who does several pictures or drawings of the same subject and, each fresh time, *progresses towards rightness*." Quoted from Bresson 1977: 53. Director King Vidor reports that in preparation for his first color film (*Northwest Passage*, 1940) he studied painting and himself started painting. He learned

Compare the words of film director Jean Renoir:

I'm a storyteller . . . I feel . . . an urge to tell the story, and I tell the story. Now I tell the story with the camera, or with a pen, or with a typewriter – well, to me it doesn't make very much difference. The main thing is to tell the story.[5]

Any modern reader of Longus can only agree with Renoir.[6] Equally, film viewers will immediately agree with Longus' perspective, even if they are aware that the situation described in his Prologue is fictional: an author's or narrator's set-up for the story that will follow.

The affinities common to reading and viewing were well established in antiquity. The Latin word *legere* ("to read") can mean "to see" because its original meaning is "to pick up" something piece by piece, first literally and then figuratively. (Its Greek cognate *legein* has the same original meaning but then comes to mean "to say, speak" rather than "to read.") So picking up the meanings of words and picking up those of images are related mental activities, both carried out initially with our eyes. An explanatory example in Roman literature occurs in Book Six of Virgil's *Aeneid*. Before Aeneas descends to the Underworld, he and his companions look at the images on the doors of Apollo's temple. Virgil uses the expression *perlegere oculis*: "to read through with their eyes." The ancient commentary by Servius gives *perspectare* as a synonym of *perlegere* and adds: "like a picture." Servius then observes: "Nor does he say inappropriately that a picture can be read since in Greek *grapsai* means 'to paint' [Latin *pingere*] and 'to write'."[7]

---

from Picasso about forced perspective for the most famous shot in *The Crowd* (1928); see Stevens 2006: 52 and 43–44.

[5] Quoted from Part Two ("Hollywood and Beyond") of *Jean Renoir* (1993), a BBC documentary directed by David Thompson. After retiring from filmmaking, Renoir wrote several novels and some non-fiction books.

[6] The parallel (if not identical) nature of literary and filmic storytelling appears to especially telling effect in the case of Eric Rohmer's *Six Moral Tales*. Rohmer had written them years before filming them. The series of six films, two short and four feature-length films, however, were to him the definitive versions: "It is only on the screen that the form of these tales is fully realized." Quoted from Rohmer's "Preface" to *Six Moral Tales* in Rohmer 1980: v–x; quotation at x. Its 2006 reprint is included in the DVD boxed set of the films released by the Criterion Collection (and carries the company's logo). In his "Preface" Rohmer discusses similarities, differences, and interactions between his written and filmed tales, but he begins with two questions that reinforce the affinity of both to each other: "Why film a story when one can write it? Why write it if one is going to film it?" (v). Rohmer also reveals that the written tales were somewhat changed for publication after they had been filmed (ix) – an additional layer of composition: writing, filming, rewriting. Rohmer, it should be added, is one of the most learned and literate of filmmakers. A look at some of his essays and reviews as collected in Rohmer 1989 is instructive. Cf. also the brief remarks on Japanese writer and director Yasujiro Ozu in Mast 1977: 57.

[7] Virgil, *Aeneid* 6.33–34: *quin protinus omnia / perlegerent oculis*; Servius on *Aeneid* 6.34. Servius then quotes Horace, *Art of Poetry* 52–53, as his authority for comparing Greek and Latin usages. Similar situations and expressions using *perlegere* occur at Ovid, *Fasti* 1.591, and Statius, *Thebaid* 3.500.

When we call verbal narratives "texts," we describe them with an imaginative metaphor, one that equally fits visual storytelling. A text is, etymologically, a product of weaving: the Latin *textum* or *textus* (from *texere*, *textum*: "to weave") indicates that literary authors put their words and lines together just as weavers do with their threads and so produce a "web" of words.[8] Quintilian, for instance, once uses the expression "fabric of speaking" (*dicendi textum*).[9] More important for our context, however, is the phrase with which Virgil characterizes the scenes on Aeneas' shield in Book Eight of the *Aeneid*. They make for an art work of such great beauty that the narrator has the difficult task to do the near-impossible in his attempt to describe the scenes in words: they represent a *non enarrabile textum*, a "fabric impossible to describe in words."[10] But since we *are* reading what he then does manage to describe in great detail in a passage that is one of Virgil's (and Roman literature's) most famous, we are in fact encountering an *enarrabile textum*, a fabric that *is* capable of verbal description. The juxtaposition of *textum* and an adjective derived from the verb *narrare* ("to tell") is one of the best instances in ancient literature to point us back to the affinities between the verbal and the visual. The prefix *e-* ("out") specifies and reinforces both sides: *enarrabile* is something that can be spoken out loud, as in a recital of poetry, and that can be told in sequence, as is appropriate for the individual scenes that are listed in the order of their appearance on the shield. The result is a kind of verbal sculpture. The narration in images and the narration about images works through text and context simultaneously.[11]

In Greek, the image of weaving also underlies the word *rhapsôdos* ("weaver of song") for the archaic poet-performer and regularly appears, for instance, in lyric poetry.[12] Simultaneously it refers us to Simonides: ancient weavers could, and did, put pictures and whole stories into their

---

[8] On this see the *Oxford Latin Dictionary* s. vv. *texo* 1.e ("to represent in tapestry"), 3.a ("put together or construct") and b (regarding "writings and other mental constructs"), *textum* 1.b (on "rhetorical style"), and *textus* 3 ("fabric made by joining words together"), with the ancient sources cited there.

[9] Quintilian, *Institutes of Oratory* 9.14.17, about the Greek orator Lysias.    [10] Virgil, *Aeneid* 8.625.

[11] The rendition of Virgil's *textum* as "texture and context" by Ahl 2007: 204 is therefore both apt and felicitous.

[12] The metaphor goes back to an Indo-European tradition; cf. Durante 1960. Jane McIntosh Snyder 1981 gives a concise introduction to this aspect of ancient literature, which is far too large a topic to be dealt with or summarized here. See especially Scheid and Svenbro 1996, with detailed discussions of primary sources and extensive references to scholarship. On *textus* see Scheid and Svenbro 1996: 111–155 and 204–214 (notes). Jane McIntosh Snyder 1981: 195 notes that "the image of the poet as weaver has clearly become an important means of self-description" by the time of Pindar. On Roman culture cf. now Bergmann 2006 and Corbier 2006.

tapestries, carpets, or cloaks. Several famous descriptions of woven images occur in classical literature.[13]

Films provide viewers with only a minimum of non-visual information about characters, about their thoughts, emotions, or motivations, and about the atmosphere prevailing in a given scene or sequence. So viewers must draw the appropriate conclusions chiefly from the images on the screen; that is to say, they must pay close attention to what they are watching and hearing and interpret a film with the help of the visual and verbal clues which director, writer, editor, and cast provide through action and dialogue. Music and sound effects give supporting aural clues.[14] An interpretive approach is also required for our understanding of literature. Anyone who has studied the classical languages knows that the closest attention to every detail, to each word and even to a word's ending or one single letter in it, is necessary. All classical literature and each meaningful film call on us to pay this kind of attention if we wish to appreciate its artistic quality. Rigorous training in philology of the kind classical scholars undergo, first in their undergraduate language courses and then in graduate school, is the best conditioning for any kind of analysis, "close reading," or *explication de texte*.[15] It works equally well for the analysis and interpretation

[13] Here are some of the best known: the images woven on Jason's cloak in Apollonius of Rhodes, *Argonautica* 1.721–767; those woven by Minerva and Arachne in Ovid, *Metamorphoses* 6.70–128 (with phrase *Pallas . . . pingit* at 70–71: "Athena paints"). Instances of images and stories told visually on artifacts and reported textually (in *ecphrases*, "descriptions") are numerous. The tradition goes back as far as the earliest work of ancient literature; most famously, Homer gives a detailed description of the scenic and narrative decorations on the shield of Achilles in Book 18 of the *Iliad*. I explain the cinematic nature of this *ecphrasis* and of Homeric similes in Winkler 2006b: 48–63. On Longus cf. Mittelstadt 1967. Brilliant 1984 is a useful introduction to the subject of visual narratives; cf., among much other work, Stansbury-O'Donnell 1999, Zanker 2004, and Ann Steiner 2007. Cf. the words of master cinematographer William Daniels: "You see, *we try to tell the story with light as the director tries to tell it with his action.*" Quoted from Higham 1970: 72. – The modern novel with its cinematic aspects of storytelling continues the tradition of mutual influence; see especially Magny 1972 and Spiegel 1976. On earlier novelists see especially Fell 1986: 1–86, with additional references.

[14] A more detailed description of this process is at Mast 1977: 18–19.

[15] For brief and non-technical definitions of "philology" see, e.g., Jan Ziolkowski 1990b: 5–7 and Thomas 1990: 69–70. A simple exercise may serve as a reminder to those who only dimly remember their Latin or as an elementary demonstration to those without any Latin (or Greek) how decisive even a single letter in a given text can be. Here is an elementary Latin example, with minimal changes from sentence to sentence: *Quid egit Marcus?* ("What did Marcus do?") – *Quid agit Marcus?* ("What is Marcus doing?") – *Quid aget Marcus?* ("What will Marcus do?") – *Quid agat Marcus?* ("What can Marcus do?"). Even on this level philologists need to *look* carefully; far more is required for works of great literature. Concerning literature in general and classical literature in particular, we have the following concise summary: "Good reading is a matter of paying attention, of observing the effects of adding one detail to another and of watching how the new details build on, qualify, refine, elaborate, or contradict what has gone before . . . The ancient critics insist on the importance of individual syllables, clusters of consonants, sequences of vowels . . . We tolerate this microscopic

of films. In analogy to the well-established philologies we might call such an approach to visual texts the philology of film.[16] Like the words on the page, the images on the screen are only the outer manifestation of a work's meaning, which lies below the surface. "The camera," director Elia Kazan has observed, "is more than a recorder, it's a microscope. It penetrates, it goes into people and you see their most private and concealed thoughts."[17] To this we could add: and their emotions, as director John Ford once said: "The camera photographs your innermost thoughts and picks them up. If you concentrate, the camera can look into your innermost feelings."[18] The camera becomes "an instrument for photographing the invisible."[19] Therefore viewers must carefully look at the visible to be able to reach and interpret the invisible, such as characters' thoughts, emotions, and

scrutiny of language for lyric poetry, rarely for other genres. But in prose too, of course, minor details of phrasing make a difference... Appreciation of the verbal texture of language is one of the most important objects of the teaching and study of literature" (Segal 1985; rpt. in revised form in Segal 1986: 359–375; here quoted from this reprint at 363–364). – The inflections in Greek and Latin morphology are analogous to the visual compositions in a film's individual shot; the morphological changes of nouns, adjectives, or words in a sentence or clause parallel the movements of camera, actors, or objects within a shot. A cut in a film may then be regarded as functioning like the punctuation marks (commas, periods, etc.) modern editors introduce into classical texts. The ancients did not generally use – and did not need to use – such conventions, just as editing in classical cinema was mostly meant to be unobtrusive or unnoticeable, even invisible, to viewers. In the words of writer-director Richard Brooks: "You shouldn't be aware of the director. If anybody at any time says, 'Wow, what a shot,' then you've lost the audience. They should never know there's a director in it. They should never know where the music starts or ends. They should never see the camera move... They should be lost in the story. That's all you're telling them. That's where the camera is." Quoted from Stevens 2006: 547.

[16] The term (as *Filmphilologie*) was previously applied to classical literature by Sütterlin 1996: 173.

[17] I quote Kazan from Scorsese and Wilson 1997: 148. Cf. Bresson 1977: 39: "Your camera passes through faces... Cinematographic films [are] made of inner movements *which are seen*." And: "Your camera catches... certain states of soul... which it alone can reveal" (53). The kind of films Bresson refers to are films of an artistic and creative nature, not commercial films. As actress Louise Brooks wrote: "The great art of films does not consist of descriptive movement of face and body, but in the movements of thought and soul, transmitted in a kind of intense isolation." Quoted from Kenneth Tynan, "Louise Brooks," in Tynan 1990: 483–525; quotation at 524.

[18] Quoted from McBride 2001: 158.

[19] Geoffrey O'Brien 1993: 87. He mentions (87–88) the work of Robert Bresson, Carl Theodor Dreyer, Kenji Mizoguchi, and Roberto Rossellini as examples. Other directors' names could be added. On the subject cf. the study by future screenwriter and director Paul Schrader (Schrader 1972). A comparable perspective informs Kawin 1978. Earlier, and on a significantly larger scale, Kracauer 1947 had made the case for German cinema between World War I and 1933. As he states: "Inner life manifests itself in various elements and conglomerations of external life, especially in those almost imperceptible surface data which form an essential part of screen treatment. In recording the visible world – whether current reality or an imaginary universe – films therefore provide clues to hidden processes" (7). Those he analyzes "expos[e] the German soul" (1). A more recent individual example is the description by Michael Chapman, director of cinematography on Martin Scorsese's *Taxi Driver* (1976), of this film being "a documentary of the mind"; quoted from *Making Taxi Driver*, written and directed by Laurent Bouzereau (1999), a documentary included on the "collector's edition" DVD of the film.

motivations or the structure and meaning of the story that is being watched. After all, as Christian Metz has pointed out: "A film is difficult to explain because it is easy to understand."[20]

The analogy between literary, especially classical, texts and films extends even further. Digital technology now makes it possible for philologists of the cinema to have easy access to a particular film and to work with it as traditional philologists have always worked with *their* materials. In ways comparable to how we can consult books, we can now view a film again and again at any time we wish, go from any scene or sequence to any other within seconds, concentrate on a scene or an individual moment for particular scrutiny by putting it into slow motion, or even pause a film to look at single frames. In other words, we are now in the position to "read" a filmic work in ways similar to those in which we read a literary one. The literary term *chapters* for a film's individual sequences or scenes in DVD editions is entirely appropriate.

Since the arrival of digital technology an increasing number of films have begun to receive critical attention that is no less philological than the kind accorded literary texts. Just as practically all works of ancient literature exist in scholarly editions, DVDs of films are now appearing in comparable form. Editors of classical texts consult the manuscript traditions of the works they are editing and weigh the importance of textual variants in the manuscripts and those proposed by earlier scholars; they emend and restore the text to come as closely as possible to the original work as its author intended it. Frequently an extensive commentary accompanies such a critical edition; a case in point is Eduard Fraenkel's monumental three-volume edition, translation, and commentary of Aeschylus' *Agamemnon*.[21] All serious readers of classical Greek or Latin literature, including scholars, rely on such an expert's introduction, commentary, or both. Now films, too, exist in critical editions alongside earlier incomplete, re-edited, or variant prints. For example, several different versions of Fritz Lang's *Die Nibelungen* (1924) or Sergei Eisenstein's *Battleship Potemkin* (1925) which had circulated for decades have now been superseded. A "director's cut" DVD of a film originally released in a different form or severely cut by a studio gives its maker a chance to restore deleted scenes or even to provide a different ("alternate") but more appropriate ending. In addition we are now frequently able to view different camera takes or outtakes of a scene. In some cases individual moments or whole scenes intended for television

---

[20] Quoted from Stephenson and Phelps 1989: 28.
[21] Fraenkel 1950. His commentary takes up two volumes.

broadcasts as alternatives to those shown theatrically, especially if sex and violence are an issue, are included alongside their original versions. Roughly, all these are the equivalents of the "variant readings" (*variae lectiones*) of ancient texts. Washed-out colors and faded black-and-white images are restored to their original appearance through recourse to the camera negative when it survives or to an exceptionally well-preserved print, often in combination with digital image enhancement. Widescreen films are restored to their original aspect ratio, which is sometimes accompanied by the older – and compositionally ruinous – "pan and scan" format. Unlike the preservation and editing of ancient texts, however, the process of film restoration today can involve the original creator, usually the director. Terry Gilliam's cooperation on the three-DVD set of his film *Brazil* (1985) is just one representative example of many. A number of DVD editions of modern films are therefore being presented as "director-approved" versions. An individual DVD or boxed set may even offer different versions of an entire film for scholarly study, as is the case with *Brazil*. Even greater complexity is evinced by the three-DVD set of Orson Welles's *Mr. Arkadin* (1955), which has three versions under two titles. A somewhat different case is Howard Hawks's *The Big Sleep*. For the first time in decades we can now compare the film's original pre-release version of 1944 with the general-release version of 1946. Some scenes were either shortened or expanded by reshooting, the placement of a few scenes was changed, and some footage was dropped altogether. Hawks was in charge of filming and incorporating all changes, which are substantive enough to affect the narrative itself. The film's second version has the reputation of presenting to viewers a plot of such labyrinthine complexity as to be nearly impenetrable; the earlier version is noticeably clearer. And Hawks's epic western *Red River* (1948) exists in two versions of which one uses a voice-over narration, the other a written on-screen text; the versions also differ in the way the film's climax is edited. Film scholars have been debating the merits of either version much in the same manner in which textual scholars compare and evaluate different manuscripts or editions of a play, poem, or novel.[22]

Other films may exist in versions that differ in their very format, as when director Raoul Walsh simultaneously made a widescreen and a standard version of his epic western *The Big Trail* (1930) and reshot dialogue

---

[22] For instructive examinations of the "book version" vs. the "voice version" of this film see especially Mast 1982: 337–346 ("A Note on the Text of *Red River*") and 381–382 (additional information and references in notes), and McCarthy 1997: 440–442. The conclusions they reach and the chain of reasoning they employ to reach them are instructive – and familiar to textual scholars. (Mast was a professor of English.)

scenes and close-ups with a different cast for the film's release in Germany, Italy, and Spain. Before dubbing films for foreign markets became the standard way, many films had different actors in other-language versions. An example is *The Testament of Dr. Mabuse* (1933), which director Fritz Lang shot in German and French, using different casts in the main parts and somewhat different camera set-ups. As late as 1953 Jean Renoir filmed *The Golden Coach* in no fewer than three different languages. In Renoir's case we know which of these versions he preferred, in Lang's case it is immediately obvious which version represents his true intentions, and in Walsh's case it is easy to decide which screen format is preferable. But in the case of Hawks and the two versions of *The Big Sleep* the question of authorship and of what constitutes the best "text" of this work becomes more difficult (and fascinating) to answer. Textual scholars and classical philologists have dealt with such problems for centuries. But *Brazil, The Big Sleep*, or even *Mr. Arkadin* are far from being the most complex cases. Mainly for financial reasons Francis Ford Coppola edited his two-part epic *The Godfather* (1972, 175 mins.) and *The Godfather: Part II* (1974, 200 mins.) into *The Godfather Saga* (1977, 434 mins.) for television: one continuous version with rearranged chronology, added footage, and cuts of the most violent moments. *The Godfather: Part III* (1990) had different running times for its theatrical release (162 mins.) and its "Final Director's Cut" video release (170 mins.). As if this were not enough, *The Godfather DVD Collection* (2001) expands the entire trilogy to a running time of 545 minutes and contains yet additional footage. In a kind of reverse process, in 1991 director Jacques Rivette edited outtakes and other unused footage from his four-hour film *La belle noiseuse* into a version (*La belle noiseuse: Divertimento*) of just over half the original's length, thereby achieving not just a shorter but, according to some critics, quite a different work. For Rivette, however, this is nothing extreme. In 1972 he had released *Out 1: Spectre* with a running time of four and a quarter hours. This film was edited down from *Out One* (or *Out One: Noli me tangere*), his film of the year before. The earlier version had run to no fewer than twelve hours and forty minutes and was once characterized by Rivette in analogy to the modern *roman fleuve* as a *film fleuve*.[23] (*Out One* was based on Honoré de Balzac's novel *Histoire des treize* and deals with two theater companies that are in rehearsals for Aeschylus' *Seven against Thebes* and *Prometheus Bound*.)

More recently, and perhaps closer to classicists' hearts, writer-director Oliver Stone agreed to a truncated version of *Alexander* (175 mins.) for

---

[23] Rosenbaum 1977: 39, in an interview first published in *La nouvelle critique* 63 (April, 1973).

its theatrical release in 2004 and re-edited it in 2005 for a "director's cut" on DVD that was marketed alongside the DVD edition of the theatrical version. The new version is seven or eight minutes shorter than the earlier one because Stone removed and added footage and tampered with existing scenes. Is this then the real *Alexander*? Not at all. Stone prepared a third version, called *Alexander Revisited: The Final Cut*, for release in 2007 on DVD only. It is a little over three and a half hours long. Stone has said about it:

Over the last two years I have been able to sort out some of the unanswered questions about this highly complicated and passionate monarch – questions I failed to answer dramatically enough. This film represents my complete and last version, as it will contain all the essential footage we shot. I don't know how many filmmakers have managed to make three versions of the same film, but I have been fortunate to have the opportunity because of the success of video and DVD sales in the world, and I felt if I didn't do it now, with the energy and memory I still have for the subject, it would never quite be the same again. For me, this is the complete *Alexander*, the clearest interpretation I can offer.[24]

Stone elaborated on this in a video introduction to this last version, in which he said in part:

This third version . . . was undertaken in an entirely different way. It was done only for DVD home use . . . The structure has been changed, in some cases radically. We start the movie on a wholly different note . . . Part of this process of going through three cuts is of course wrestling with the idea of making it clearer to the public. It was always a difficult film to understand and difficult to do. This is a breakthrough for me, to give me complete freedom to break the constraints of theatrical, commercial filmmaking, to go and make a film at any length that was required by the material itself, without studio interference, without critics, without even having to satisfy an audience except ourselves. In so doing we would create a film that was undiluted, untampered with, uncensored. This would be a freedom for me that I've never had, and I took it.

Whether Stone succeeded in making a difficult film and its complex protagonist clearer to the public in this third cut, which relentlessly switches back and forth in time throughout its entire length, is debatable. But Stone's various comments and the availability of three editions of one and the same film afford us an opportunity to become aware of some of the quandaries and vagaries inherent in commercial epic filmmaking today.

[24] Quoted from the descriptive announcement of this release at http://www.thedigitalbits.com/ mytwocentsa132.html#alex.

But this is nothing in comparison with a cult favorite like Ridley Scott's *Blade Runner* (1982). Its *Ultimate Collector's Edition* on five DVDs contains no fewer than five versions, beginning with a work print (a preview cut) and ending with a 2007 Final Cut. Intermediate stages are the 1982 theatrical American cut, the 1982 international cut that also appeared on cable television and home video, and a 1992 director's cut. There are three commentary tracks, one by the director, one by the writers and producers, and one by the film's art directors, designers, and special-effects crew. Nine hours' worth of bonus materials include trailers, teasers, and TV spots, several deleted and alternate scenes, an alternate title sequence, two different endings, and a few completely new scenes. Modern digital effects were used to alter some of the existing scenes. A long documentary features dozens of participants, and there are several memorabilia, including a note from Scott. The film is available in standard and in competing higher-quality (HD, Blu-Ray) DVD transfers. By contrast, Scott's *Gladiator* (2000) exists in "only" two different cuts.[25]

If Scott could revisit a work a quarter-century after its initial release and Stone had the chance to present a complete *Alexander* in his final cut, there never has been and never will be a complete or final widescreen-and-color *Cleopatra*. The ill-fated version of 1963, written and directed by Joseph L. Mankiewicz, never even came to exist in anything close to its intended form: a two-part epic of between three and four hours' running time for each part, to be shown in theaters on alternate days. Instead, the film was ruthlessly truncated and survives today at a maximum length of 243 minutes, roughly two thirds to half of what it should have been. Shorter cuts exist as well. Since Mankiewicz was never allowed to assemble his own cut and since additional footage seems to have been irretrievably lost or destroyed, we are left with an epic in ruins, whose state resembles that of numerous ancient texts.[26] They survive in fragments that give us a good idea of what the entire work may have been like, and they make us hope against hope for the missing parts still to turn up. So both literature and film scholars speculate, present more or less imaginative ideas for reconstructions, comment on the gaps they know or suspect to exist, evaluate what we have against what we

[25] By contrast, the pretentiously named "Imperial Edition" of *Caligula* (1979), directed by Tinto Brass and then changed by producer Bob Guccione, contains on its three DVDs two versions of the film, deleted and alternate scenes, three audio commentaries, a documentary, and assorted other tidbits. Bottom's up.

[26] On the production and cutting history of *Cleopatra* cf. especially Geist 1978: 302–345, Beuselink 1988, Bernstein 1994: 343–386 and 429–431 (notes), and the documentary film *Cleopatra: The Film That Changed Hollywood* (2001), directed by Kevin Burns and Brent Zacky and included in the DVD edition of *Cleopatra*. I give a brief appreciation of the film in Winkler 2002a. A section of Chapter 6 below deals with one of its episodes.

could have had, and express their views in articles, book chapters, and, in the case of films, audio commentaries and documentaries. But sometimes even the most dedicated scholarship can take us only so far.

Analogous to the scholarly editions of ancient texts, DVDs of significant films now regularly include continuous audio commentaries by film historians and, for more recent films, by directors, screenwriters, or others involved in their making. Documentaries, behind-the-scenes footage, production stills, and other materials round off these editions – just as classical editors include all available historical and textual information or at least references to it in theirs. *Blade Runner* may be an extreme case, but then the entire *Godfather DVD Collection* runs to 725 minutes for the films and their supplements. The DVD edition of *The Testament of Dr. Mabuse* includes a specialist's commentary on the visual comparison not only of the differences and discrepancies between the German and French versions but also of a later version, altered and dubbed in English for the American market. Images from two of these versions often appear on the screen side by side and make exact comparison and analysis possible.[27] Beyond such work on their texts, literature and films have come to share a tradition of extensive interpretation in books and scholarly journals. And just as scholarly editions and commentaries of texts are subject to revision, expansion, correction, or entirely new editions, so apparently definitive editions of films are subject to later improvement. For example, after appearing in what was considered a definitive edition on DVD some years ago, Akira Kurosawa's *Seven Samurai* (1954) was re-issued in an elaborate three-DVD set in 2005. One disc contains the film itself ("All-new, restored high-definition digital transfer"), the other two contain supplemental material: not, as before, one but two complete audio commentaries on a film 206 minutes long; two documentaries on its making and on its cinematic and cultural background; a two-hour video conversation with its director; behind-the-scenes photographs and production stills; a booklet with various kinds of testimony to the film and an interview with its star; and several other pieces. The three-DVD set of *Mr. Arkadin* includes audio commentary, alternate scenes, outtakes, rushes, stills, and various other pieces of information, a booklet, and even the original novel on which Welles had loosely based his film. The director's commentary on the standard DVD of *Alexander Revisited* is different from the one Stone recorded for the same cut of the film's DVD in HD (High Definition), which furthermore contains a commentary by Oxford scholar Robin Lane Fox, Stone's historical advisor

---

[27] The same scholar provides a full audio commentary to the film itself. He is the author of a study of Mabuse films and novels (Kalat 2001).

(and one of Alexander's generals in the film). These and comparable editions of other films should silence any doubts about the nature of films as texts or the necessity of film philology.[28]


AUTHORSHIP: ANCIENT *AUCTOR* AND CINEMATIC *AUTEUR*

If it is sensible to regard films as visual narratives, the question immediately arises: Do films then have authors? By *author* we usually mean the individual who is the sole and original creator of a literary work. But this narrow understanding of what constitutes an author did not arise until the eighteenth century and did not exist in antiquity.[29] The Latin word *auctor* (pl. *auctores*) carries the basic meaning of "furtherer, promoter" (from the verb *augêre*, "to increase") or "guarantor" (e.g. in historical contexts as "predecessor," "informant," or "source").[30] This is true throughout the history of Greek and Roman literature, although ancient writers never developed a precise terminology. Classical literature – that is, written works – derived from an oral tradition which had been largely anonymous.[31] Names of individual authors from the age of oral performance

---

[28] Sometimes such accumulation of details may become excessive; cf. Rafferty 2003, rpt. in Noël Carroll and Choi 2006: 44–48. Rafferty's main point of criticism is the "interactive" nature of DVDs, which does not affect our subject. If film scholars can be excessive in their hunt after each and every surviving scrap of film, they only follow the example of traditional scholars, who have long been a target of ridicule for their dry-as-dust bookishness and obsession with trivialities. Robert Browning's poem "A Grammarian's Funeral Shortly After the Revival of Learning in Europe" (1855) is a, well, classic example: "This man decided not to Live but Know" (line 139). The grammarian, of course, was a scholar of Greek. For the Latin side we have the school teacher in Anton Chekhov's *Three Sisters*.

[29] On this see, e.g., Abrams 1953: 272–285 and Lieberg 1982: 159–173. Cf. Kristeller 1983, rpt. in Kristeller 1990: 247–258.

[30] Cf. the definition in Lewis and Short, *A Latin Dictionary*, s. v. *auctor*: "he that brings about the existence of any object, or promotes the increase or prosperity of it, whether he first originates it, or by his efforts gives greater permanence or continuance to it." Cf. the *Oxford Latin Dictionary* s. v. *auctor*, especially 2.a and c, 4.d, 7–9, 13.b–c and g, with the ancient sources cited there. Cf. also Pollitt 1974: 311–318 (on *auctoritas*). Wetzel 2000 surveys the subject from a modern perspective, with extensive additional references. Cf. Wetzel 480–481 (on the etymology of *auctor*), 481 (on the death of the author), and 502–509 (on the concept of authorship from antiquity [502–503] to the early modern age).

[31] Nilsson 1932, a classic study, demonstrates that Greek myths, the fundamental subject matter of classical literature, were already fully formed before the advent of writing and depended on oral retellings. Artifacts from before the introduction of the alphabet do not reveal names of storytellers or authors. On oral composition and performances see, e.g., Nagy 1989: 38: "the pan-Hellenic tradition of oral poetry appropriates the poet, potentially transforming even historical figures into generic ones who merely represent the traditional functions of their poetry. The wider the diffusion and the longer the chain of recomposition, the more remote the identity of the composer will become. Extreme cases are Homer and Hesiod." Nagy has published numerous other studies of this and related subjects.

of narratives did not survive into the age of writing except for Homer's. Homer and after him Hesiod, the earliest Greek authors who survive in name and work, are near or on the border of oral and written composition. While Hesiod speaks about himself in his *Theogony* and *Works and Days*, specific knowledge about Homer the man was as good as nonexistent.[32] With the introduction of writing, authors could ensure their remembrance by mentioning their names in their works as a kind of signature or seal (*sphragis*).[33]

Medieval and early modern authors followed the ancient *auctores* and regarded themselves primarily as mediators. A poet was still the same kind of author as his ancient predecessor. To use Latin terms, he was an *inventor* (i.e. "finder"; from *invenire*, "to come upon, find"): someone who finds an existing theme or topic for his composition, who takes up and reshapes old material according to his own ingenuity (in Latin, *ingenium*: "set of innate qualities"), and who gives it new life in his retelling.[34] A film scholar once said almost the same thing about plot content and visual appearance in the cinema: "the normal function of a director," wrote V. F. Perkins, is "not to devise stories and not to construct painterly patterns but to realize given material and organize it into significant form."[35] This organization, of course, represents a new synthesis based on pre-existing kinds of content and form and ideally achieves a work that transcends but does not wholly disregard generic, formulaic, or stylistic principles.

Complete originality and creative autonomy, the very qualities we expect from and attribute to our authors today, were impossible throughout antiquity, as such central terms of ancient literary theory and history as *exemplum* ("model, exemplar"), *imitatio* ("artistic imitation" of a model; *mimêsis* in Greek), and *aemulatio* ("artistic competitiveness") attest. For the ancients, knowledge of a text always included an awareness of its contexts, usually other texts by earlier *auctores* who in turn depended on *their* predecessors.[36] As mentioned, Homer, the first *auctor* in the history of Western literature whose works survive because they came to be written down, had his roots in the anonymous oral tradition. He did not invent or create the subject matter of the *Iliad* or *Odyssey*.[37] As has been said appropriately about later

---

[32] Cf. in this context Danek 1998.   [33] On this see Kranz 1961, rpt. in Kranz 1967: 27–78.

[34] On *ingenium* cf. Pollitt 1974: 382–389.   [35] Perkins 1972: 79.

[36] This also applies to authors who consciously turned away from their precursors. Examples are discussed in Chapter 5. For detailed studies of the subject in Greek and Roman literature, with additional references, see Rosenmeyer 1992 and Conte 1986.

[37] The subject of Homer's authorship, generally called the "Homeric question," was first broached in Friedrich August Wolf's *Prolegomena in Homerum* of 1795, a study that revolutionized Homer scholarship. For a modern annotated translation see Wolf 1985.

ages of antiquity: "One of the most striking features of Latin and later Greek literature is the pervasive imitation (*mimêsis*) of previous authors. Originality is found within an awareness of a past tradition, authors name and adapt their predecessors, and audiences are expected to recognise these allusions."[38]

The basis of cinema is a technology far more complex in its processes of production, distribution, and consumption than the technology required for printed literature. Even so, the most conspicuous and artistically decisive contributor to a film is generally its director, as the very term and its equivalents in other languages (*Regisseur, regista, metteur en scène*, etc.) indicate. In the words of American critic William Pechter, ideally a film is "demonstrably stamped with an identifiable directorial style" and with "the imprint of an authorial imagination" on the part of a director "whose work, in its totality, seems both to be encompassed by a controlling vision and to encompass the kind of imaginative world one finds in the work of the first-rank creators of literary or dramatic fiction."[39] As early as 1913, American director D. W. Griffith, one of the greatest pioneers of the new medium, took out a full-page advertisement in *The New York Dramatic Mirror* to claim personal authorship for the films he had been making since 1908 and to take credit for "revolutionizing motion picture drama and founding the modern technique of the art."[40] Griffith was justified to do so. As Jean Renoir remarked, individual creativity applies to all forms of art:

---

[38] Quoted from Innes 1989: 246. The phenomenon of *mimêsis* or homage to great and revered predecessors is standard in the cinema. It is helpful here to keep in mind the points raised by Bloom 1997, even if "anxiety of influence" is probably too strong or neurotic-sounding a term to characterize the majority of ancient authors and modern filmmakers. An illustrative example of non-anxious influence are these words by Federico Fellini about Ingmar Bergman: "he confesses candidly that he has seen all my films and cites them in his own. Being a rich, an authentic artist, he can borrow from others without being guilty of plagiarism." Cf. Bergman about himself: "I have never been scared of being influenced. I like to use others' styles. I don't want to be unique. I am a cinemagoer. I have no complexes on this subject." The quotations are from Samuels 1972: 135 and 196.

[39] Pechter 1982: 59. Cf. Pechter 152 on Michelangelo Antonioni's film *L'Avventura* (1960): "a work whose importance lies . . . in its giant appropriation for the film medium of a territory of psychological subtlety and emotional nuance previously thought exclusively to belong to the novel." On the immediacy of film style cf. the following words by director King Vidor: "I'm a firm believer in the fact that you put your individual stamp on your work . . . I went into a projection room at MGM at one time and sat down waiting for some dailies to end, and said, 'Oh, that's George Stevens.' I spotted his style in that footage. Another time I went in and – with no name on it or anything – knew it was [Josef] von Sternberg. I spotted that because of the photography." Quoted from Stevens 2006: 52.

[40] Quoted from Henderson 1970: 158, where the full text of the ad may be found. Cf. Gunning 1991.

All works of art bear the artist's signature. If there is no signature, there is no work of art. And by "art," I don't mean only paintings, sculpture, films, plays; I mean anything in life that is done well and carefully. In my opinion, our age commits its greatest crime when it kills the author or makes him disappear.[41]

In the first century AD Pliny the Elder used the term *auctor* equally for the painter and the sculptor.[42] The work of either bears the artist's signature. The true signature is not the name written on a work but its artistic quality, its style, as we will see soon.

Filmmaking involves any number of participants in artistic, technical, administrative, and many other functions. But this is no reason to deny films their authorship. Ancient terms can again help us understand the situation better. Romans used *auctor* or *artifex* for the man who functions as a sovereign creative artist. By contrast, a *faber* or *opifex* was the technician, the mere workman. In the *Art of Poetry* Horace clearly distinguishes between these two kinds of people involved in the collaborative production of works of art. The *faber*, Horace emphasizes, is subordinate because he does not know how to design or compose (*componere*: "to put together") an artistic whole.[43] If we apply Horace's perspective to the cinema, such craftsmen are, primarily, the entire technical staff engaged in the process of making a film. All filmmaking depends on the creative and technical expertise of many people and is often so highly collaborative as to make it impossible or at least difficult for us to identify individual contributions to the finished work that appears on our screens, let alone to find proof of one particular person's creative intelligence that gives it its final shape. This circumstance applies to the largest quantity of films made: commercial works meant purely for spectacle, thrills, superficial entertainment, and the highest profits possible. It applies far less frequently to art cinema. But on either level the artist and the technician depend on each other. Art historian Erwin Panofsky once expressed the complexity of the creative process in a memorable comparison. The conclusions he drew are worth remembering:

---

[41] Quoted from Samuels 1972: 210.

[42] Pliny the Elder, *Natural History*, preface 23 and 34.19.93. It is worth remembering that Plutarch, *Moralia* 747–748 ("Table Talk: Question 15"), especially at 748a, widens Simonides' saying about poetry and painting to apply it to poetry and dancing. Evidently some of the ancients were readier to take broad and comparative views than some of the moderns.

[43] Horace, *Art of Poetry* 32–35; cf. 45–46. Robert Bresson accordingly did not consider himself a *metteur en scène* (the common French term for a film director) but as someone who arranges the order of his work: *metteur en ordre*. On originality in ancient literature in connection with cinema cf. Dehon 1994.

It might be said that a film, called into being by a cooperative effort in which all contributions have the same degree of permanence, is the nearest modern equivalent of a medieval cathedral; the role of the producer corresponding, more or less, to that of the bishop or archbishop; that of the director to that of the architect in chief; that of the scenario writers to that of the scholastic advisers establishing the iconographical program; and that of the actors, cameramen, cutters, sound men, makeup men, and the divers technicians to that of those whose work provided the physical entity of the finished product, from the sculptors, glass painters, bronze casters, carpenters, and skilled masons down to the quarry men and woodsmen . . .

This comparison may seem sacrilegious, not only because there are, proportionally, fewer good films than there are good cathedrals, but also because the movies are commercial. However, if commercial art be defined as all art not primarily produced in order to gratify the creative urge of its maker but primarily intended to meet the requirements of a patron or a buying public, it must be said that noncommercial art is the exception rather than the rule, and a fairly recent and not always felicitous exception at that. While it is true that commercial art is always in danger of ending up as a prostitute, it is equally true that noncommercial art is always in danger of ending up as an old maid . . .

It is [the] requirement of communicability that makes commercial art more vital than noncommercial, and therefore potentially much more effective for better or worse . . . in modern life the movies are what most other forms of art have ceased to be, not an adornment but a necessity.[44]

A more modern analogy, frequently employed by film directors themselves, is that of the orchestra conductor. It is equally enlightening and worth juxtaposing with Panofsky's. In the words of director Fred Zinnemann:

there is a good deal of similarity between a conductor and a director, in the sense that you work with a large number of people. What you have to do is persuade them of your own vision so that they form one body working together for one purpose – to the ideal result.[45]

Only in their anonymity do the medieval artists and craftsmen differ from those of the cinema. But it is often just as difficult sharply to distinguish between the artists and *fabri* of cathedrals as between those of the cinema. Screenwriters, cinematographers, actors, producers, and editors, for example, can participate in creative decisions and in some cases decisively shape the completed work. They can even become *auctores* in their own

---

[44] Erwin Panofsky, "Style and Medium in the Motion Pictures" (1947); rpt. in Panofsky 1995: 91–125 and 210 (notes); quotation at 119–120. Panofsky adduces Georges Seurat's "Grande Jatte" and Shakespeare's sonnets as examples of noncommercial, Albrecht Dürer's prints and Shakespeare's plays as examples of commercial art. A shorter version of Panofsky's essay had appeared in 1936 under the title "On Movies."

[45] Quoted from Stevens 2006: 412.

right.[46] Some time ago British film scholar Roger Manvell summarized the situation with memorable concision:

> unlike the novel which is written by one man or the picture which is painted in seclusion, the film is the result of conferences and staff work in which it might be thought that the sensitive artist would become lost among a welter of executives. But this is not so. The twentieth-century artist of the film – the director – is a man who combines sensitiveness with leadership, who can convey to his cameramen, his electricians, his scenic designers and builders, his costumiers and his property-men, the spirit of the film as a whole and of the sequence on which they are working in particular. The film is a co-operative art, but, as in all creative work, a single mind with a single purpose must dominate the whole. The names on the credit titles are the names of those who have served under the leadership of the director to create the unified though composite achievement of the film.
>
> Behind every large-scale film there lies, therefore, the financial conference, the staff work for camera, lighting, sets, costumes, make-up and finally cutting, together with the discussions of producer, director, scenarist, cameraman, editor and actors. Collectively they stand or fall.[47]

When a film's production proceeds in the harmonious collaboration of an artistic designer or *auctor* with his staff of *fabri*, both sides stand to gain. As Jean Renoir observed: "The more you help your partners to express themselves, the more you express yourself . . . I believe that we should feel the presence of the author in a film."[48] American director Frank Capra was especially outspoken on this matter, summarizing his view in the

---

[46] Well-known if random examples: it is a cliché about film history that screenwriters have complained about being neglected as the true creators of the films they write; cf. McMurtry 1987: 13: "If one were to make a misery graph of Hollywood, screenwriters would mark high on the curve . . . in terms of steady, workaday, year-in-year-out dolorousness, the writers have no near rivals." See also Goldman 1983 and 2000 and Dunne 1997. Orson Welles repeatedly drew attention to the importance of cinematographer Gregg Toland for *Citizen Kane* (1941) and to the fact that he learned everything about the camera from Toland on this film, which is frequently cited as the best ever made. Actors with star power and producers with strong personalities decisively shaped the films even of well-known writers and directors, usually without screen credit. For an illuminating account of the importance of film editing on the part of an editor who is not otherwise creatively involved in a film's production see the cases described by Rosenblum and Karen 1979. Cf. Welles's 1964 comment on American technical crews: "You are side by side with men who don't feel themselves to be workers but who think of themselves as very capable and very well paid artisans. That makes an enormous difference [to a director] . . . And it is not only a question of technique, it essentially concerns the human competence of the men with whom I worked . . . they do not think of themselves as belonging to another class." Quoted from the reprint of Cobos, Rubio, and Pruneda 1966 in Estrin 2002: 96–125, at 120.

[47] Quoted from Manvell 1950: 26.

[48] Quoted from Samuels 1972: 210 and 214. The working method of Alfred Hitchcock is the best-known example of such an approach; Hitchcock gives a concise and illuminating description at Samuels 1972: 234.

concise phrase "one man, one film."[49] As Italian filmmaker Michelangelo Antonioni described it:

Only one person has the film clearly in mind, insofar as that is possible: the director. Only one person fuses in his mind the various elements involved in a film, only one person is in a position to predict the result of this fusion: the director.[50]

The collective nature of filmmaking has a parallel in literature. While a lone individual may autonomously create a novel, poem, or play, the process of printing, publishing, marketing, and selling it involves many others. So direct correspondences between literature and film exist in this regard, too. Nevertheless nobody is likely to deny that the collaborative or collective nature of the publishing industry has caused the death of the author. The argument about the absence or death of an author cannot hold true for cinema or any other creative medium. In antiquity, too, authors depended on collaborators, for how else could a written work that started as one single manuscript have found its readers or have survived? An even better illustration is Greek drama. In ancient Athens the performances of tragedies and comedies depended on the city's involvement in the festivals during which the plays were produced and in their financing, on skilled craftsmen for building the stage, on actors and singers for performing, and on judges to award prizes. These are only the most obvious kinds of involvement by people other than the author. But no one will deny Aeschylus, Sophocles, Euripides, Aristophanes, or any of the other Greek playwrights their authorial status. Since the ancient playwright also functioned as producer and director of his own works, he is comparable to a modern filmmaker – a "hyphenate" like a producer-director, writer-director, or, ideally, writer-producer-director-actor. The best-known example of this is Charles Chaplin, who sometimes composed the music for his films as well. Or we may think of Orson Welles, who in 1941 and 1942 directed, acted in, co-wrote, and co-produced *Citizen Kane* and directed, wrote, and co-produced *The Magnificent Ambersons*. Or we might consider Jean Cocteau alongside Sophocles. Both were poets, playwrights, and stage directors. Sophocles introduced set painting (*skênographia*) to the classical theater, Cocteau was a painter and draughtsman. Unlike Cocteau, Sophocles also

---

[49] See on this Stevens 2006: 77–79 and 87–89; cf. the words of King Vidor at Stevens, 50 and 52.

[50] Quoted from Billard 1996: 144 in an interview conducted and first published in French in *Cinéma 1965*, 100 (November, 1965). See further Antonioni's more detailed comments in Labarthe 1996: 136–137 (originally in Labarthe 1960).

composed the music for his plays.[51] Unlike Sophocles, Cocteau also acted.[52] Small wonder that on numerous occasions he called the cinema a modern Muse or "the tenth Muse."[53]

Filmmakers have known all along that the cinema is by no means a radically new medium of artistic creativity – not even in its dependence on modern technology – but that it is firmly anchored in the entire tradition of literature and the visual arts. Sergei Eisenstein, a screenwriter, director, editor, theoretician of cinema, and cultural critic, long ago pointed to the ancient Greeks as the earliest models and precursors of the art of cinema:

our cinema is not altogether without parents and without pedigree, without a past, without the traditions and rich cultural heritage of the past epochs. It is only very thoughtless and presumptuous people who can erect laws and an esthetic for cinema, proceeding from premises of some incredible virgin-birth of this art! . . . Let Dickens and the whole ancestral array, going back as far as the Greeks and Shakespeare, be superfluous reminders that both Griffith and our cinema prove our origins to be not solely as of Edison and his fellow inventors, but as based on an enormous cultured past; each part of this past in its own moment of world history has moved forward the great art of cinematography.[54]

[51] Cocteau did, however, compose the music for Harry Kümel's *Anna la bonne* (1958), an experimental short film based on Cocteau's poem.

[52] And he adapted Sophocles for the modern stage. *Oedipe Roi*, a short play based on Cocteau's work for Igor Stravinsky's oratorio *Oedipus Rex*, and *The Infernal Machine* are adaptations of the most famous and influential of Sophocles' plays and indeed of all Greek tragedies. Oedipus, Antigone, and the Sphinx briefly appear in Cocteau's film *The Testament of Orpheus* (1959). Cocteau also wrote an *Antigone*.

[53] For examples see Cocteau 1992: 23, 123, and 56 (with slight corrections); cf. also 176–177 and 192–193. Three of Cocteau's best-known films are on or related to classical subjects: *The Blood of a Poet* (1930), *Orphée* (1949), and *The Testament of Orpheus*. I discuss *Orphée* in Chapter 6 below. – The metaphor used to appear regularly, often in more or less loose usage; cf., e.g., director Anthony Asquith's now little-known article "The Tenth Muse Climbs Parnassus" (Asquith 1946; rpt. in *The Penguin Film Review* 1977–1978, here vol. 1, 10–26, a brief survey of film history), and this advice to aspiring filmmakers by Orson Welles from 1982: "give your attention to the charms of the most perverse of muses." Quoted from Boujut 2002: 175. Cf. also the quotation from Abel Gance in the Introduction to this book.

[54] Eisenstein, "Dickens, Griffith, and the Film Today" (1944) in Eisenstein 1949: 195–255, at 232–233. The literal translation of the title of Eisenstein's essay is "Dickens, Griffith, and Us"; cf. Eisenstein 1949: 267. Aristotle's influence on Eisenstein in regard to the concept of *mimêsis* appears, e.g., in Eisenstein's 1929 essay "Imitation as Mystery," tr. Richard Taylor, now in Eisenstein 2006: 11–19. Literature on the artistic prehistory of cinema is extensive; the *locus classicus* is the 1933 essay by Rudolf Arnheim, "The Thoughts That Made the Pictures Move," now in Arnheim 1957: 161–180. For additional discussion and references cf. Winkler 2001b: 14–17. Cf., on a smaller scale, early French film director, screenwriter, and critic Louis Delluc, "From Orestes to Rio Jim" (Delluc 1921; now in Abel 1988, vol. 1: 255–258). Despite its amusing title, this brief article makes a number of serious points about the continuity of Greek tragedy and its connections to film. Delluc's title refers to *Two-Gun Hicks* (1914), an American western directed by and starring William S. Hart and released in France as *Le serment de Rio Jim* ("Rio Jim's Oath").

Eisenstein referred to the ancients on numerous occasions in his writings. In his essay "Laocoön," for example, he prominently discusses Homer and Virgil; in another he turns to the Parthenon and its environs.[55] The Greeks in particular are a living presence in Eisenstein's thinking about cinema. So is the entire tradition of Western art and literature, which derives from antiquity. As early as 1915, about twenty years after the birth of cinema, American poet Vachel Lindsay, who had been trained as a painter, had examined the various ways in which the cinema and the traditional arts are connected.[56]

As already indicated, there are also films whose creative authorship is unknowable or unclear, films that are unworthy of serious concern or too shallow to make any interpretation possible. But in this, cinema is again comparable to literature. In the history of narrative prose, which is the kind of writing most closely analogous to the cinema, there exists a plethora of mediocre products for every immortal masterpiece. The genre of the novel

---

[55] Eisenstein, "Laocoön" in Eisenstein 1988: 157–163, and "Montage and Architecture" in Eisenstein 1988: 59–81 at 60–67, with the following conclusion: "In the 'montage plan' of the Athenian Acropolis we find, of course, the same unsurpassed artistry as in other monuments of antiquity" (67).

[56] Lindsay 1915. For examples of German-speaking writers dealing with early cinema cf. Kaes 1978; authors include Alfred Döblin, Hugo von Hofmannsthal, Bertolt Brecht (who worked on screenplays during his exile in Hollywood), Gerhart Hauptmann, and Heinrich and Thomas Mann. Cf. playwright and soon-to-be screenwriter and director Marcel Pagnol, "The Talkie Offers the Writer New Resources," in Abel 1988, vol. 2: 55–57; originally Pagnol 1930. Elie Faure, "The Art of Cineplastics," tr. Walter Pach, in Abel 1988, vol. 1, 258–268 (originally published as "De la cinéplastique" in Faure 1922: 277–304); and Panofsky, "Style and Medium in the Motion Pictures," are examples of how prominent art historians have judged the cinema. His correspondence shows that Panofsky took cinema seriously. In a letter of September 11, 1944, to American film historian Parker Tyler he speaks of the "literary factor in cinematic art" and remarks on French cinema: "the French actors, directors and possibly even producers are . . . imbued with a humanistic tradition." In a letter of February 13, 1948, to James B. Conant, president of Harvard University, Panofsky looks into the academic future: "I do not see any reason why a university should not deal with the motion pictures on the same critical and historical level as it does with the productions of painting, sculpture or literature and thereby try to raise critical standards." Both letters, here quoted in my translation, are now in Wuttke 2003: 484–485 (no. 953; quotation at 485), and 904 (no. 1194). For another famous art historian's take on the cinema see Arnheim 1957. Perkins 1972 is a kind of riposte to early critics like Lindsay and Arnheim; cf. especially Perkins 9–27 (chapter entitled "The Sins of the Pioneers"). But it is well to remember as telling an example of mainstream cinema as American director Henry Hathaway, who observed in connection with his film *Peter Ibbetson* (1935), in which he took his lighting cues from works by Rembrandt: "I was influenced more by paintings than anything . . . You learn about photography from these people" (i.e. Hogarth, Brueghel, Dufy, and Vermeer, whom he had just named). Quotation from Behlmer 2001: 116–117. Cf. master cinematographer Lee Garmes on Rembrandt as quoted in Higham 1970: 35–36. Rembrandt's "north light" technique is clearly evident in Garmes's body of work. The influence of Rembrandt on cinema is greater than art historians tend to realize. Still valuable on this topic is Manvell 1950, especially its first part ("The Film as a New Art Form"): "Introduction: The Peculiarities of the Fine Arts Generally" (22–23) and "The Peculiarities of the Film in Particular" (24–26). On style and content in film cf., e.g., Perkins 1972: 116–133 (chapter entitled "'How' Is 'What'").

is the best illustration: it encompasses the greatest works of psychological realism and the modern *nouveau roman* all the way down to predictable romances and pornography, with formulaic or stereotypical fiction coming somewhere in between. Still, even if the amount of trash far exceeds that of genuine achievement, no one denies the novel its status as a literary art form. It is only fair to apply the same perspective to film. Jean Cocteau put it succinctly:

Cinematography is an art. It will free itself from the industrial bondage whose platitudes no more condemn it than bad pictures and bad books discredit painting and literature.[57]

That even the traditional Hollywood studio system worked for commerce and profit but at the same time also fostered individual talents is obvious to anyone familiar with film history. Andrew Sarris's book *The American Cinema* provides ample if by no means exhaustive evidence.[58] We should keep in mind that the arts have always depended on commerce. Distinguished writer and filmmaker Marcel Pagnol rather vividly observed on behalf of cinema in 1933:

a work of art must not only be conceived; its creator must realize it. A ton of marble is needed to sculpt the Venus de Milo; ten pounds of gold for a cup by Cellini... That's why, in order for its works first of all to be realized and then to be distributed, an art needs to be nurtured by a world of commerce: it needs people to buy the books, paintings, statues, theater or cinema seats. So as to make the idealists happy, let's say that this commerce is the manure which nurtures the flower. But the prosperity of this commerce is indispensable to the brilliance, vigor, and diffusion of any art whatsoever.[59]

Serious studies of cinematic authorship began in the silent era and have proliferated enormously in the last few decades since the advent of academic

---

[57] Cocteau 1967: 49 (in an essay entitled "On the Marvels of Cinematography").

[58] For a recent introduction to current Hollywood filmmaking, see, e.g., Maltby 2003. For a first orientation in regard to the question "studio or individual filmmaker?" see, e.g., Durgnat 1967: 61–86 (chapter entitled "Auteurs and Dream Factories"); Bordwell, Thompson, and Staiger 1985; and Schatz 1988. Among innumerable other works see Luhr and Lehman 1977, with case studies mainly of films by John Ford, who was and is famous for his genre films, especially westerns, and who nevertheless (or for that very reason) has the reputation of being one of the most important cinematic *auteurs*. That as ritualistic and formulaic a genre as the western indeed admits of, even encourages, serious films by *auteurs* is demonstrated in the classic study of Kitses 1969, especially 7–27 (chapter entitled "Authorship and Genre"). The recent new edition of this book (Kitses 2004) exemplifies the difference between the qualities of traditional scholarship and current academic trends. The old version was written with clarity and evident love for its subject and was pleasurable to read; the new edition's added material, illuminating to the patient readers, is marred by jargon.

[59] Marcel Pagnol, "Cinematurgy of Paris," in Abel 1988, vol. 2: 129–136; quotation at 130. The article first appeared in Pagnol 1933.

film studies. But the most influential answer to the question of who is a film's true creator, its *author*, as it were, came with an essay written by young French critic and soon-to-be director François Truffaut, published in 1954 in the journal *Cahiers du cinéma*: "A Certain Tendency of the French Cinema."[60] Truffaut's essay was rather polemical, but theorists, historians, critics, and many filmmakers adopted, if not without lively debates about its pros and cons, what Truffaut called *la politique des auteurs*, an expression generally rendered in English as "the *auteur* theory."[61]

According to this view, the *auteur* or author of a film is in most cases its director, the one who puts a personal stamp on the finished work. Anticipating much of what later came to be called reader-response criticism and the idea of the reader's presence in the text, the *auteur* theory introduced, indeed demanded, an equivalent viewer response. From this derives the claim, often made explicitly, that *auteur* cinema is as important for the life of a culture and for the culture of life as literature and all the other arts. The rejection of the counter-claim that cinema is a mere commodity is implied in this. As has been well said, the *auteur* theory

> insists on a *personal* relationship between filmmaker and film viewer. Movies must no longer be alienated products which are consumed by mass audiences; they are now intimate conversations between the people behind the camera and the people in front of the screen.[62]

---

[60] Truffaut 1954. An English version is readily available in Nichols 1976: 224–237. Cf. Tredell 2002: 101–130 and 243–244 (notes; chapter entitled "The Birth of the *Auteur*: *Cahiers du cinéma*"). For different approaches to the question of authorship in film see, e.g., Stillinger 1991: 174–181 (in chapter entitled "Plays and Films: Authors, Auteurs, Autres"; close to the position of Korenjak and Töchterle) and Benedetti 2005: 78–82. Marie 2003 provides a first orientation about the state of French cinema and culture at the time of Truffaut's writing. For additional information see Monaco 1977 and Neupert 2002.

[61] Cf., e.g., Caughie 1981, reprinting Barthes, "The Death of the Author" (208–213); Naremore 1999, and Casetti 1999: 76–82. Cf. further Sarris 1968 and Sarris 1977; rpt. in Wexman 2002: 21–29; further Wollen 1998. Gerstner and Staiger 2003 presents valuable introductions to the topic by the editors and examines a number of case studies. A modern assessment of the *auteur* theory, with brief discussion of the death of the author, is to be found in Perez 1998: 3–9. Truffaut was by no means the first to use the term "author" for the filmmaker; a much earlier example is film director (and *auteur*) René Clair, "Film Authors Don't Need You," tr. Stanley Appelbaum, in Abel 1988, vol. 2: 57–60; Clair speaks of "the true film author, who has been able to dominate the author of [a literary] original . . . and . . . has been able to recreate, for a new form of expression, a subject that was not intended for it" (58). The original, a short salvo aimed at Pagnol's article on the talking film, is Clair 1930. On the necessity of the ideal director as *auteur* to be a veritable polyhistor see Kazan 2006. Kagan 2006 has insights into filmmaking from script to postproduction, but not all of the directors interviewed can be regarded as major *auteurs*. Earlier, if more briefly, director King Vidor had made similar observations, including points about the director as writer and painter; see Vidor 1972: 35–37. On the related question of a film canon, which runs parallel to critical disputes about literary canons, cf. Schrader 2006.

[62] Monaco 1977: 8.

Crystallizing earlier views about filmic authorship, resurrecting and empha-
sizing the traditional Romantic view of the individual creator, and propos-
ing what at the time appeared to be an almost radically new view of
authorship in the cinema, Truffaut provided a strong impulse for, among
other countries, France, Britain, and West Germany in the 1950s and 1960s:
the *nouvelle vague* (New Wave), the British New Wave, and the "young
German film." The last of these was often referred to as *Autorenkino*: "cinema of authors."[63] Even before Truffaut film scholars had applied principles
of literary scholarship to the cinema. Research into what is usually called
"the language of film" – its grammar, semiotics, or semantics – illustrates
the affinities between literary and filmic storytelling. Once again we find
corroboration that films, as coherent narratives, are visual texts.[64] One of
the most influential statements of this perspective is an article by French
critic and filmmaker Alexandre Astruc, who asserted the importance of language over the image and coined the arresting term *caméra-stylo* ("camera
pen"):

---

[63] Not to be confused with the earlier German term *Autorenfilme* ("authors' films") which goes back
to 1913 and denotes films based on literature or involving literary authors or stage actors.

[64] Spottiswoode 1935 is the pioneering study. Clifton 1983 examines filmic analogies to literary tropes;
his chapter headings consist of or contain such basic rhetorical terms as symbol, simile, metaphor,
anadiplosis, antithesis, hyperbole, ellipsis, metonymy, synecdoche, and allegory. Harrington 1973:
144–158 gives a brief introductory survey. For exemplary demonstrations of how greatly principles
of literary scholarship can deepen our understanding of films and their *auteurs* see Mast 1982 and
Wood 2002 on Howard Hawks and Alfred Hitchcock, two directors who were fully integrated
into the studio system but created highly personal bodies of work. Mast was Professor of English
before turning to film studies, Wood studied under F. R. Leavis. On the death of the author
see further Wood 1998a, especially 27–28 (section entitled "L'Auteur est Mort – Vive l'Auteur!").
Wood's essay deals with *auteur* Anthony Mann. In general cf. also the following: Richardson 1969,
Chatman 1978, Beja 1979, Browne 1982, Branigan 1984, and Bordwell 1985. David Bordwell in
particular has examined filmic narration and narrative in several studies. The title of Phillips 2000
and the main title of Monaco 2000 are telling. (That of Ann Steiner 2007 is analogous to the
latter.) Cf. also Thompson 1999, Bordwell 2006, and Cahir 2006: 44–71 (chapter entitled "The
Language of Film and Its Relation to the Language of Literature"). Robert Bresson once gave an
elegant definition of the fundamental nature of cinema: "CINEMATOGRAPHY IS A WRITING WITH
IMAGES IN MOVEMENT AND WITH SOUNDS." Quoted from Bresson 1977: 2. Cf. the main titles
of George M. Wilson 1986 and Bernardi 2001. On differences and analogies of literary and filmic
points of view and for an overview of various analytical positions see Branigan 2006: 39–54 and
235–241 (notes). On film semiotics see especially Metz 1994 and 1986 and Metz 1982b. Only earlier
versions of Metz's books exist in English (Metz 1974a, 1974b, and 1982a). Metz concluded that the
language of cinema is significantly different from all other languages. Cf. Mast 1977: 16: "the cinema
has no language. It has, rather, many languages." See also Wollen 1998 and John M. Carroll 1980 on
film language, linguistics, and grammar. There is extensive further literature. Soviet film theoretician
Dziga Vertov anticipated this with great concision when he noted in 1928 about his approach to film
(which he named *kino glas*: "cinema eye"): "Kino-eye's new experimental work aims to create a truly
international film-language, *absolute writing in film*, and the complete separation of cinema from
theater and literature." Quoted from Vertov 1984: 283. Vertov made this observation in connection
with his next film, *The Man with a Movie Camera* (1929), which he called "A Visual Symphony."

the cinema is quite simply becoming a means of expression, just as all the other arts have been before it, and in particular painting and the novel . . . it is gradually becoming a language. By language, I mean a form in which and by which an artist can express his thoughts, however abstract they may be, or translate his obsessions exactly as he does in the contemporary essay or novel. That is why I would like to call this new age of cinema the age of *caméra-stylo* (camera-pen). This metaphor has a very precise sense. By it I mean that the cinema will gradually break free from the tyranny of what is visual, from the image for its own sake, from the immediate and concrete demands of the narrative, to become a means of writing just as flexible and subtle as written language.[65]

Alongside this consider the following statement by French *auteur* Robert Bresson, one of the greatest cinema artists, about his own approach to filmmaking:

each shot is like a word, which means nothing by itself, or rather means so many things that in effect it is meaningless. But a word in a poem is transformed, its meaning made precise and unique, by its placing in relation to the words around it: in the same way a shot in a film is given its meaning by its context, and each shot modifies the meaning of the previous one until with the last shot a total, unparaphrasable meaning has been arrived at.[66]

Bresson's words are a clear, elegant, and immediately understandable description of how a film artist proceeds. His reference to poetry is illuminating and appropriate. For Truffaut (under Astruc's influence) and contemporary theorists and critics writing in *Cahiers du cinéma*, several of whom later became influential directors, the analogy of film to literature and of the literary author to the film director was a matter of course. Terms like Astruc's *caméra-stylo* and, more generally, *écriture* ("writing") emphasize the quasi-literary nature of filmmaking and filmic storytelling. French writer-director Agnès Varda, who coined the word *cinécriture* ("filmwriting"), has described her conception of it in the following terms:

I invented the word and now I use it to mean the filmmaker's work. It puts the work of the scriptwriter who writes but does not film, and of the director who does the mise-en-scène, back in their respective boxes. The two may be the same person, but there's often lasting confusion . . .

    A well-written film is also well filmed, the actors are well chosen, so are the locations. The cutting, the movement, the points-of-view, the rhythm of filming

---

[65] Quoted from Astruc 1968: 17–18. The original (Astruc 1948) is now also in Astruc 1992: 324–328; original of text quoted at 325. On Astruc see Neupert 2002: 45–49 and especially Monaco 1977: 3–12 ("Introduction: The Camera Writes"). In 1948 Astruc directed *Ulysse ou les mauvaises rencontres* ("Ulysses, or Bad Encounters"), a short film now lost.

[66] Cf. the following brief statement in Bresson 1977: 15: "Cinematography: new way of writing, therefore of feeling."

and editing have been felt and considered in the way a writer chooses the depths of meaning of sentences, the type of words, number of adverbs, paragraphs, asides, chapters which advance the story or break its flow, etc.

In writing it's called style. In the cinema, style is *cinécriture*.[67]

So screenplay credits of Varda's films say *cinécrit* ("filmwritten") instead of the common credit *écrit par . . .* ("written by . . .").[68] In 1971 a number of German directors had organized their own distribution under the name *Filmverlag der Autoren*. A *Verlag* is primarily a publishing house, so the choice of the term for films came with the immediately evident claim that films are comparable to literature and that their directors are their authors. Long before this, Russian pioneer Vsevolod Pudovkin had spoken of the *kinopisatel* ("cinemawriter"), who is not identical with the screenwriter, and Dziga Vertov, another influential Russian filmmaker and theoretician, had written about what he called *kino glas* ("cinema eye"):

Kino-eye = kino-seeing (I see through the camera) + kino-writing (I write on film with the camera) + kino-organization (I edit).[69]

Varda's concept of *cinécriture* reminds us of Roland Barthes's parallel term concerning literature: *écriture*. It is worth recalling that Barthes and the *auteur* theorists and New Wave filmmakers have more in common than those who attribute Barthes's idea of the death of the author to cinema seem to be aware of. The matter has been summarized with admirable concision:

At about the same time that Alexandre Astruc wrote his essay on the Caméra-Stylo, Roland Barthes . . . was beginning to work out a theory of literature which is not dissimilar to the New Wave vision of film. Barthes suggests a subtle and variegated critical theory that places emphasis not on the historical dimension of literature (what he calls its "language"), nor on the personal dimension (the "style") but on a third thing, the product of the two – what Barthes calls *écriture* ("a mode of writing") . . . this is a useful way to approach the cinema of the New Wave: as a tertium quid – a cinematic *écriture* that combines "language" and "style" and is "written" with a Caméra-Stylo.[70]

---

[67] Quoted from Alison Smith 1998: 14 note 3. The original French appears on the same page. On style in film cf. below.

[68] Vsevolod Pudovkin, "On the Language of the Script: A Conversation," in Pudovkin 2006: 179–184. The conversation dates to 1928.

[69] Quoted from Vertov 1984: 87.

[70] Monaco 1977: 8–9. Monaco quotes a passage from Barthes 1968: 14 here omitted, as are further similarities between Barthes's *écriture* and the *cinécriture* of the New Wave, important as these are.

So filmmakers are best regarded as authors of their works, and many great directors understand themselves as such.[71] The common and familiar international custom of identifying a film by its director's name indicates such authorship. Credits and advertisements indicate the same: "Alfred Hitchcock's *Psycho*," for instance, or *Un film de* . . . , *Ein Film von* . . . , *Un film di* . . . , etc., with the director's name appearing in place of my ellipses.[72] Jean-Luc Godard – like Truffaut first a film critic and then a screenwriter and director and like Truffaut one of the most important *auteurs* in the history of cinema – once expressed this perspective in an essay about a film by Swedish *auteur* Ingmar Bergman:

The cinema is not a craft. It is an art. It does not mean teamwork. One is always alone; on the set as before a blank page. And . . . to be alone means to ask questions. Nothing could be more classically romantic.[73]

With this we may compare Bergman's own assessment of writing and editing his films. He identifies

a fundamental truth – that editing occurs during filming itself, the rhythm created in the script . . .
    The rhythm in my films is conceived in the script, at the desk, and is then given birth in front of the camera. All forms of improvisation are alien to me . . . Filming for me is an illusion planned in detail, the reflection of a reality.[74]

Orson Welles, another acknowledged *auteur*, seems to concur. Three years after Godard's mention of the blank page, Welles said: "Film is a very personal thing, much more than theatre, because the film is a dead thing – a ribbon of celluloid – like the paper on which one writes a poem. Theatre is a collective experience; cinema is the work of one single person – the director."[75] Repeatedly Welles stressed the importance of writing. About his own approach he has said, for example:

---

[71] Cf. King Vidor on the term *auteur*: "Of course, the meaning of the word in French is 'author' but with a broader meaning than its English equivalent. Its connotations include much more than simply the authorship of original, written material. It means the control of screenplay, casting, decor, editing, acting, with a dynamic emphasis on the supervision of photography." Quoted from Vidor 1972: 109.

[72] Contrast, however, the words of writer-director Carol Reed: "it's stupid to write, as they do in Europe, a film by so-and-so. The English or American terminology is much better: written by – – , from a play by – – , adapted by – – , produced by – – , directed by – – . Then you know – approximately – who did what." But note his immediately following statement about his own films: "In my case, the film is really mine." Quotations from Samuels 1972: 79. Reed's distinction between (continental) European and English-language practice is too rigid.

[73] Godard 1958, quoted from Narboni and Milne 1972: 76.        [74] Quoted from Bergman 1988: 73.

[75] Quoted from Cowie 1973: 108, originally in Bogdanovich 1961.

I always begin with the dialogue. And I do not understand how one dares to write action before dialogue. It's a very strange conception. I know that in theory the word is secondary in cinema but the secret of my work is that everything is based on the word. I do not make silent films. I must begin with what the characters say. I must know what they say before seeing them do what they do.[76]

And:

the various technical jobs [of filmmaking] can be taught, just as you can teach the principles of grammar and rhetoric. But you can't teach writing, and directing a picture is very much like writing, except that it involves 300 people and a great many more skills . . . So it's partly a question of personality, which isn't so easy to acquire as a skill.[77]

The words of a filmmaker who was also a literary author and painter may carry special weight in this context. Jean Cocteau once said about film language and his own work in cinema:

The cinematograph requires a syntax. This syntax is obtained through connection and the clash between images. No wonder that the peculiarity of such a syntax (our style) expressed in visual terms seems disconcerting to spectators accustomed to slapdash translations and to the articles in their morning paper . . . Before film art can be worthy of a writer, the writer must become worthy of film art. I mean, he should . . . work hard at building an object in a style equivalent to his written style . . . I am a draughtsman. It is quite natural for me to see and hear what I write, to endow it with a plastic form. When I am shooting a film, every scene I direct is for me a moving drawing, a painter's grouping of material . . . I work in close collaboration with my assistants. Consequently, as my unit itself admits, the film becomes a thing of my very own to which they have contributed by their advice and skill.[78]

The "classic" that Godard had in mind is, of course, not a reference to classical antiquity but to the tradition and influence of Romanticism and

---

[76] Quoted from Cobos, Rubio, and Pruneda 1966 in Estrin 2002: 102. Welles often stressed the importance of the writer over the director; cf., e.g., this comment: "I'm sure I can't make good films unless I also write the screenplay." Quoted from Bazin and Bitsch 2002: 46 (originally Bazin and Bitsch 1958). Cf. Cocteau's words: "It is probably true that an author's text is the very foundation of a spoken film, but no more than the foundation. The real syntax of a film remains silent, wordless. Its style is visual. It is that 'writing' – the mechanism of the photographing of the scenes and the rhythm with which they are put together – that is the hallmark of the film-maker's language." Quoted from Steegmuller 1986: 483; source reference at 558.

[77] Quoted from Kenneth Tynan: "*Playboy* Interview: Orson Welles," in Estrin 2002: 126–145; quotation at 136. The interview first appeared in *Playboy* (March, 1967). Cf. writer-director Abraham Polonsky on directing: "It's almost as good as writing because it is a form of writing. . . . The set is a live thing – a more complex writing experience." Quoted from Pechter 1971: 153. Pechter 274 observes: "just as a film's editing corresponds to the writer's final act of revision, the analogue to the original act of literary creation is filming."

[78] Quoted from Cocteau 1954/1972: 16 and 21–22.

its conception of the artistic individual who independently creates a work of art through his own ingenuity.[79] The reference to writing seems to have occurred to Godard as the obvious point of departure for the creative artist in the medium of film. The elective affinity, as it were, between filmmakers and literary authors could scarcely have been expressed more elegantly. The same affinity, if to a lower degree, applies to less accomplished and even to crassly commercial films. The author, often prematurely pronounced dead, has been and continues to be alive and well in the cinema and is likely to enjoy good health in the future.[80] So the only way in which the claim that films do not have authors makes any sense is to restrict the term "author" to literature and to deny its applicability to all other forms of art. We have already seen that the ancients were far from taking this narrow view, and no one today is likely to feel comfortable with such a rigidly limited understanding of authorship. Films, we conclude, are created, either exclusively or chiefly, by their directors, who function as their *auctores* or *auteurs*, if with varying degrees of artistry. On the highest level of film as a modern art form we find directors whose status as cinematic *auteurs* it is pointless to question or deny.[81]

### THE CINEMA OF POETRY

Style is one of the most important aspects of literature, particularly significant in poetry. If films are texts whose narratives can be presented in specific styles, can there then also exist a kind of poetry in the cinema? Can visual images be said to be analogous to literary poetry or actually to *be* poetic? We are likely to answer this question negatively if we apply the word "poetry" in the strictest sense, i.e. exclusively to literature. But as we have seen in the case of the term "author," such limitation is not helpful. Style is fundamental to all visual arts, and poetic qualities may be inherent in nonliterary forms of art as well, for instance in music. Etymology points

---

[79] McGann 1991 and Stillinger 1991, however, adduce ample evidence of the collaborate nature even of Romantic poetry production. McGann, editor of Lord Byron's poetry, speaks of "the hidden features of textual media" (10) and observes: "texts are produced and reproduced under specific social and institutional conditions . . . every text, including those that may appear to be purely private, is a social text" (21). And: "authorship is a social and not a solitary act or set of acts" (64).

[80] On Barthes and the death of the author in cinema see especially Colin MacCabe, "The Revenge of the Author," in MacCabe 1999: 33–41; rpt. in Wexman 2002: 30–41. Cf. the perspectives of various directors in Littger 2006.

[81] Sarris 1968: 39 famously grouped the greatest artists together as "Pantheon Directors" who "have transcended their technical problems with a personal vision of the world" and created "a self-contained world with its own laws and landscapes. They were also fortunate enough to find the proper conditions and collaborators [we might say, their *fabri*] for the full expression of their talent."

us in the right direction: "poetry" derives, via Latin *poesis*, from Greek *poiêsis*, a word whose literal meaning (from the verb *poieîn*, "to make") fits all acts of creation: those of craftsmen who create something tangible with their hands – cf. above on *fabri* – and those who create through ingenuity: poets, painters, sculptors, composers, and others.

Consideration of style is a useful way for literary scholars to approach the question of textual authorship and to deepen their appreciation of an author's work.[82] The same is true for visual storytelling, and film scholars regularly examine the question of cinematic style and poetry in their studies of a director's body of work, even if the term "poetry" is often applied as loosely to a film as it is to other works of art. The subject is too large to be dealt with systematically here, but some observations are appropriate.[83] In 1948 Roger Manvell made the following fundamental points:

The use of the word "poetry" is always ambiguous, even when applied solely to the literary medium. To use it of the film is to imply that the motion picture is capable of intense emotional concentration as well as prolonged periods of narrative and character presentation which are rich in human understanding and illuminate the experience of life. It implies that the medium is flexible and eloquent under the control of the artist, and that it offers him resources of expression which will win his devotion and excite his genius. It implies also that these resources are not available in the same form in the other narrative arts, and that the film becomes a speciality and the film artist a specialist. It implies that the film is not a mere substitute for the drama or the novel, but an art with its own peculiar properties to arouse the aesthetic susceptibilities of artist and audience.[84]

---

[82] Cf. the comments by two directors, the former an *auteur* (Fritz Lang), the latter (Edward Dmytryk) not: "Every picture has a certain rhythm which only one man can give it. That man is the director. He has to be like the captain of a ship." Quoted from Rosenberg and Silverstein 1970: 347. And: "He must know how to use the various members of the production company to play them as a composer plays the keys of a piano." Quoted from Dmytryk 1984: viii.

[83] Specific instances of philological approaches to film and classical literature are Newman 2001 and Mench 2001.

[84] Manvell 1948, quoted from *The Penguin Film Review* 1977–1978, vol. 2: 111–124, at 112–113. Cf. there Manvell 121 on films that "rise . . . from the higher levels of emotional narrative to the degree of poetry itself" and 112: "Many men and women who would otherwise have been the poets of the twentieth century have found their medium of expression in the motion picture. To them is due our right to speak of the poetry of the cinema." About two decades earlier, André Maurois, well-known author and future member of the Académie française, had made the same case in Maurois 1927; cf. also Levinson 1927. Russian Formalists had expressed the analogy of poetry and film at the same time; I cite, as an example representative of numerous other works, Viktor Shklovsky, "Poetry and Prose in Cinematography," tr. T. L. Aman, in Bann and Bowlt 1973: 128–130 (originally published in a book on the poetics of cinema in 1927). Cf. Galan 1984: 95–104. For a more recent theoretical view cf. Bordwell 1989. A specific test case of how far one may wish to go applying the idea of poetry to cinema may be one's response to Kael 1976; rpt. in Kael 1980: 112–119 and Kael 1994: 668–674. Kael's subject is Sam Peckinpah's film *The Killer Elite* (1975).

Orson Welles, whose work is regularly called poetic, has confirmed the critic's view from a practicing filmmaker's perspective:

What is marvelous about the cinema . . . is that it has many elements that may conquer us but may also enrich us, offer us a life impossible anywhere else. The cinema should always be the discovery of something. I believe that the cinema should be essentially poetic; that is why, during the shooting and not during the preparation, I try to plunge myself into a poetic development, which differs from narrative development and dramatic development . . . the cinema, the true cinema, is a poetic expression.[85]

Basically, poetic expression in great cinema affects viewers' sense of aesthetics. Ideally, it also acquires a philosophical or moral dimension. Director Andrei Tarkovsky expressed this point in Platonic terms:

Cinema is a high art . . . It seems to me that the purpose of art is to prepare the human soul for the perception of good. The soul opens up under the influence of an artistic image . . . I could not imagine a work of art that would prompt a person to do something bad . . . My purpose is to make films that will help people to live, even if they sometimes cause unhappiness . . . Art can reach to the depths of the human soul and leave man defenceless against good.[86]

Filmmakers' emphasis on the poetic nature of their medium goes back to the silent era. Abel Gance, for instance, whom I discussed in my Introduction, spoke of the "poetry of images and light" in 1929.[87] But poetry in cinema received a strong theoretical impulse in 1965 from Italian poet, dramatist, essayist, screenwriter, and director Pier Paolo Pasolini. His theory of the *cinema of poetry* is worth examining in some detail because Pasolini made the case for the poetry of film concisely and convincingly. For this reason it may serve as an exemplary illustration, not least since Pasolini points out similarities and dissimilarities of film and literature.[88] Influenced by the aesthetics of Benedetto Croce and the psychoanalysis of Sigmund Freud, among others, Pasolini applies a semiotic approach. Language, he observes, regularly encompasses abstraction, but cinema cannot

---

[85] Quoted from Cobos, Rubio, and Pruneda 1966 in Estrin 2002: 99–100. Cf. director Vittorio de Sica on Italian neorealist cinema: "neorealism is not shooting films in authentic locales; it is not reality. It is reality filtered through poetry, reality transfigured." Quoted from Samuels 1972: 144.

[86] Quoted from Turovskaya 1989: xiv–xv (in Ian Christie's introduction). On Tarkovsky and poetic cinema cf. also Bureau 2006 (1962 interview).

[87] Quoted from King 1984: 65 (in Gance's essay "The Cinema of Tomorrow").

[88] Pier Paolo Pasolini, "The 'Cinema of Poetry'," in Pasolini 1988: 167–186; the following quotations are from pages 171–178, 182, and 184. A different translation appeared in Nichols 1976: 542–558. On Pasolini's theory of cinema see Greene 1990: 92–126 (chapter entitled "Theory: Toward a Poetics of Cinema"), Viano 1993: 93–98 (on Pasolini's *Mamma Roma* of 1962), Ward 1994, and Wagstaff 1999. Cf. Baranski 1999b (on Pasolini's 1964 film *The Gospel According to St. Matthew*).

do so: "The linguistic or grammatical world of the filmmaker is composed of images, and images are always concrete, never abstract." Since narrative films are concerned with plots, the language of cinema has predominantly resembled that of literary prose. But as a "new 'technique' or 'genre' of expression," the cinema is characterized by "irrational, oneiric, elementary, and barbaric elements" that "were forced below the level of consciousness." (We may be reminded of the common description of Hollywood as a dream factory.) The cinema's "narrative convention belongs without question, by analogy, to the language of prose communication, but it has in common with such a language only the external manifestation – the logical and illustrative processes – while it lacks one fundamental element of the 'language of prose': rationality. Its foundation is that mythical and infantile subtext which, because of the very nature of cinema, runs underneath every commercial film which is . . . fairly adult aesthetically and socially." From this Pasolini deduces that cinema, with its "language of [image]-signs, has a double nature: it is both extremely subjective and extremely objective" to an extent that the two sides become inseparable.[89] By contrast, literature also has a dual language (prose and poetry), but both sides are separable and often separate. Due to its lack of "a conceptual, abstract vocabulary," cinema is "powerfully metaphoric."[90]

For Pasolini this aspect of film leads to the heart of the matter. He poses the following question: "how is the 'language of poetry' theoretically explicable and practically possible in cinema?" He approaches the answer by first turning to a related question: "is the technique of free indirect discourse possible in cinema?" With this procedure Pasolini implicitly asks if film can adopt and express one of the most sophisticated techniques of literature.[91] As expected, he answers in the affirmative: "free indirect cinematographic discourse" is "the immersion of the filmmaker in the mind of his character [most commonly, a film's protagonist] and then the adoption on the part of the filmmaker not only of the psychology of his character but also of his language." While a filmic narrative that appears objective or neutral is analogous to prose narrative, direct discourse in literature corresponds to the point-of-view shot in film. The filmic equivalent of free

---

[89] We may compare Pasolini's term "image-sign" to Abel Gance's earlier "image-text"; in 1921 Gance had addressed the "literature" and "philosophy" of moving images. Cf. the quotations and discussion in King, 1984: 56, with source references at 222.

[90] Cf., in the context of more traditional filmmaking, the exhortation to future filmmakers by screenwriter and author Ray Bradbury on the importance of metaphor for both poetry and film at Stevens 2006: 382.

[91] Cf. on this the 1977 essay by Eric Rohmer, "Film and the Three Levels of Discourse: Indirect, Direct, and Hyperdirect," in Rohmer 1989: 84–92.

indirect discourse in literature is the "free indirect point-of-view shot," but whereas literature is capable of interior monologues, cinema is not, "since cinema does not have the possibilities of interiorization and abstraction that the word has. It is an 'interior monologue' of images." So complete correspondence between literature and film is not possible. A writer who recreates a character's speech "immerses himself in his psychology" (as does the filmmaker) and "in his *language*. Free indirect discourse is therefore always linguistically differentiated when compared to the language of the writer." In this, filmmakers, restricted as they are to image-signs for their language of communication, cannot follow or imitate writers: "They cannot take into consideration, because they don't exist [in image-signs], special languages, sublanguages, slang – in short, social differences."

From this, Pasolini reaches his conclusion about the importance of cinematic style as the decisive factor to create visual poetry:

In practice, therefore, on a possible common linguistic level predicated on "gazes" at things, the difference that a director can perceive between himself and a character is only psychological and social. *But not linguistic.* He therefore finds himself in the complete impossibility of effecting any naturalistic *mimesis* of this language, of this hypothetical "gaze" at reality by others.

Thus, if he immerses himself in his character and tells the story or depicts the world through him, he cannot make use of that formidable natural instrument of differentiation that is language. *His activity cannot be linguistic; it must, instead, be stylistic.*

Moreover, a writer, too . . . can differentiate his psychology from that of his character . . . by means of a style – that is . . . through certain characteristic traits of the "language of poetry." Thus the fundamental characteristic of the "free indirect point-of-view shot" is not linguistic but stylistic. And it can therefore be defined as an interior monologue lacking both the explicit conceptual element and the explicit abstract philosophical element. This . . . causes the "free indirect point-of-view shot" in cinema to imply the possibility of an extreme stylistic articulation . . . In short, it is the "free indirect point-of-view shot" which establishes a possible tradition of the "technical language of poetry" in cinema.

For illustrations of such stylistic articulation Pasolini turns to two specific films – Michelangelo Antonioni's *The Red Desert* (1964) and Bernardo Bertolucci's *Before the Revolution* (1964) – and, more generally, to the cinema of Jean-Luc Godard. These films reveal that the cinema of poetry is "profoundly based, for the most part, on the practice of style as sincerely poetic inspiration." This in turn means that "a common technical/stylistic tradition is taking form [in early 1960s cinema]; a language, that is, of the cinema of poetry." This new kind of cinema makes viewers fully aware of camera techniques, whereas classic cinematic narratives had adhered to the principle of keeping camera movements largely out of viewers' consciousness – in Pasolini's phrase: "the camera was not felt." Traditional films were not made "according to the canons of the 'language of poetry.'" Even so Pasolini calls the works of earlier directors like Charles Chaplin, Kenji Mizoguchi, and Ingmar Bergman "great film poems" and refers to "the classical 'cinema of poetry.'"[92] Overall, he characterizes this poetic tradition as being analogous to great prose literature:

The poetic nature of classical films was . . . not obtained using a specifically poetic language. This means that they were not poems but stories. Classical cinema was and is narrative. Its language is that of prose. Poetry is internal to it, as, for example, in the tales of Chekhov or Melville.

Just as prose writers can be highly poetic, creating an "art prose . . . whose real protagonist is style," so classical filmmakers imbue their prosaic narratives with cinematic style, if not to the extent Pasolini postulates for the cinema of poetry.[93]

Pasolini's theory, here presented only in outline, is sophisticated and attractive. Still, not all scholars of literature or the cinema and not all filmmakers are likely to follow Pasolini in each and every point of his argument.[94] Traditional filmmaking can be far more poetic than Pasolini might have allowed for. In fairness to him we should remember that his theory is meant specifically to account for the new and liberating advances in technology and for filmmakers' approaches to their medium that originated in European cinema in the wake of Italian Neorealism and

---

[92] That the cinema of Bergman is related to the cinema of poetry, especially in regard to style and subjectivity, becomes evident, for instance, in Kawin 1978. Cf. Sontag 1967a; rpt. in Michaels 2000: 62–85. The collaboration of Jacques Prévert as author of film scripts, original or adapted, or as author of film dialogue with directors Jean Renoir and especially Marcel Carné is a particularly telling example of how decisively a literary poet can influence the work of earlier cinematic poets. On the "poetic realism" associated with Prévert, Carné, Renoir, and other French directors, especially Jean Vigo, René Clair, Julien Duvivier, and Jacques Feyder, see Andrew 1995. On the films of Andrei Tarkovsky, who is regularly called a film poet, cf., e.g., Turovskaya 1989 and, if with a different artistic metaphor, Tarkovsky's own book (Tarkovsky 1986). Cf. further Ruiz 1995. Instructive in this context are the contributions to "Poetry and the Film: A Symposium" of 1953, in which authors Arthur Miller and Dylan Thomas discussed cinema with filmmaker Maya Deren and film scholar Parker Tyler; most remarkable is the literary authors' lack of comprehension and their condescension. The symposium was published in *Film Culture*, 29 (Summer, 1963), and is now easily accessible in Sitney 1970: 171–186.

[93] Cocteau's film *Orphée*, dealt with in Chapter 6, is an especially striking instance of cinema of poetry from an earlier time.

[94] A noteworthy exception is British poet, dramatist, and filmmaker Tony Harrison, who refers to his work in cinema as "film/poems." He describes his views on poetry and cinema at Tony Harrison 1998: xxiii–xxvii, with several references to Pasolini. Harrison begins the introduction to the text edition of his film/poem *Prometheus* (1998) with a quotation from Pasolini: "To make films is to be a poet" (Tony Harrison 1998: vii). Cf. also Tony Harrison 2007.

the French New Wave. But it is entirely appropriate to the entire history of film that scholars and critics should fall back on analogies to literature – as Pasolini himself does in the last few passages quoted above – and, beyond this, should describe or analyze the works of any great filmmaker in terms derived from the interpretation of poetry. I adduce just one example of how a sensitive critic, here William Pechter, may assess the work of an important director. John Ford was for decades a popular traditional filmmaker, an acknowledged *auteur*, and, to critics and historians alike, a visual poet. Pasolini would regard him as an artist in the classical mold to whose filmic narratives poetry is internal. But even so the visual poetry of Ford and its style are clearly visible on screen. The influence on Ford of German Expressionist cinema as exemplified by one of its masters, Friedrich Wilhelm Murnau, has long been familiar to film scholars. Together with the cinema of montage of great Russian directors like Sergei Eisenstein, Dziga Vertov, Vsevolod Pudovkin, and others, Expressionism was one of the most influential ways that brought the cinema into the realm of modern art in the 1920s. As Ford biographer and scholar Tag Gallagher put it, under Murnau's influence "Ford's cinema became totally stylized . . . Ford found cinema could be completely poeticized."[95]

Looking back on Ford's career after Ford retired from filmmaking, Pechter expressed his summation of Ford in literary terms:

John Ford has been making films since 1917, and his work has come, in its entirety, to resemble one vast fiction of such breadth and limpidity as virtually to make it seem a creation of the art of another age . . . but for Chaplin and Keaton, Ford is the only American director of films whose body of work has the formal beauty, richness of imagination, thematic unity, and wholeness of vision which we associate with artistic greatness as it is commonly understood with respect to the traditional arts. In order to see this, I believe one has to accept and reject several things; to accept, for instance, the Hollywood system in which Ford has had to function and which required his continually having to buy again the freedom to make a film of his own choosing with others that were commercial successes (a system, however, in which Ford . . . could thrive because of having by nature the gifts of a truly popular artist); and accept also Ford's imperfections of nature – his penchant for low comedy and his occasional inclinations toward sentimentality (good Shakespearean and Dickensian faults, respectively). I believe one has to reject, or at least have serious reservations about, such a textbook classic as *The Informer* . . . And one must reject as well the cult of Ford . . . or of thirty years of "Fordolatry" restricted to gauzily impressionistic tributes to his masterly visual style; both, in their insularity, confining to the dimensions of a ghetto an art whose

---

[95] Quoted from Gallagher 1984: 54. On Murnau and Ford cf. Gallagher 1984: 49–54 and McBride 2001: 158–163.

reach encompasses a world . . . The finest of Ford's films remain among the few great Apollonian in the art of this century.[96]

Further comments on the literary and cinematic concepts examined here are not required for our purposes.[97] We have seen that the cinema, a narrative medium, is closely related to literature, that films are or can be visual texts created by individual authors, and that scholarly interpreters of narratives and poetry ought to approach films philologically and often do. We now turn to a demonstration of how and why classical philology may be conceived to encompass film philology as an aspect integral to its nature. This implies the justification for those who practice the former also to engage in the latter.

## PHILOLOGIA CLASSICA ET CINEMATOGRAPHICA: FROM CLASSICAL PHILOLOGY TO FILM PHILOLOGY

Academic departments of film studies train future scholars to deal with filmic texts, to teach courses on them, and to research specific aspects of cinema. Alongside such film scholars those trained in any of the modern

[96] Pechter 1971: 234–235 and 240 (in a piece entitled "A Persistence of Vision"). Sarris 1975 examines Ford's work as visual poetry. With characteristic grumpiness, Ford always denied that he was a poet and maintained that he did not know what such an expression meant. Here is an example from 1973, when Ford could look back on his entire career: "I am not a poet . . . I'm just a hard-nosed, hardworking, run-of-the-mill director." Quoted from Wagner 1975: 54, rpt. as Wagner 2001 in Peary 2001: 159. Ford deceived few if any. He also often denied being the *auteur* of his films and compared himself to an architect, but cf. this answer from 1965 to the question "How would you define yourself?": "John Ford, author of westerns, war stories where men count more than events, and comedies where the strength of feelings counts. Heroism, laughter, emotion: the rest is just the rest." Quoted from Leguèbe 2001: 72. On the cult of film directors see Pechter 1971: 52, with mention of Ford. Caughie 1981: 68–120 devotes an entire section to a "Dossier on John Ford."

[97] Except, perhaps, to note that belief in the death of the author in literary studies predictably resurrected belief in the death of cinematic authors and of the *auteur* theory, thus returning us to the older and rather unhelpful view that consideration of the collaborative nature of filmmaking can lead to more important insights into the medium than consideration of authorship. The former approach is more fruitful for our understanding of cinema from commercial or sociological points of view, the latter for that of cinema as art, if on various levels of achievement. Ford himself can serve as an illustration even today. Sharrett 2006, a recent article on *The Searchers* (1956), Ford's greatest work, elicited the following responses from a reader and, in return, the writer: "Apparently, news of the demise of the *auteur* thesis has not reached [Sharrett's] film studies department." – "On the demise of the *auteur* theory, it is manifest that cinema is a collaborative art form . . . but 'death of the author' claptrap is at least as dubious as the staunchest defenses of *auteur*ism . . . Theories aside, I consider *The Searchers* to be a film by John Ford. Ford's films are always very recognizable . . . For me, he is the principal author of his work . . . one of Hollywood's most acknowledged (justifiably so) *auteurs*." Quoted from Ceplair and Sharrett 2006. Apparently, Truffaut and Barthes stirred up quite a hornets' nest in their different ways. While siding more with Sharrett than with Ceplair, I do not think that the former's reappraisal does justice to the complexity of *The Searchers*, although I doubt that any one critic can.

philologies like English, French, German, or Italian have shown themselves
to be equally capable of the serious study and explication of visual texts.
A large amount of analytical writing about cinema is the work of such
philologists, of scholars originally trained in literature who during their
academic careers began to incorporate films into their courses or added
entire film courses to their teaching, to write about literature and film side
by side, or to turn exclusively to the cinema. Classical scholars have begun
to follow suit.[98] But many are still skeptical about combining classics with
cinema, the old with the modern. To show that such skepticism is beside
the point I quote in this section a larger number of older and contemporary
classicists than would otherwise be necessary.

One of the latter has pointed out "the value of cinema to classicists (and
the value of classicists to cinema)" and concluded:

> It readily reveals connections and differences between antiquity and modern soci-
> eties, and exposes the mechanisms whereby modern cultures use the classical past
> to interrogate the present; its study can illuminate classical cultures and their lit-
> eratures . . . cinema brings classics out into a very public domain and makes the
> interrogation of antiquity and the classical tradition available globally.[99]

Classical scholarship is based on rigorous training that encompasses detailed
and thorough knowledge of ancient literature in terms of linguistics, morphology, syntax, aesthetics, and literary history in addition to yet other
aspects. Classical philology is the best training ground for interpretive
approaches to all and any texts, literary or visual. Classical philologists are
uniquely prepared to contribute exemplary work to the study of cinema
and to give major impulses to this newer field.[100] At the same time classicists can enhance, from a new perspective, their own understanding and
appreciation of classical culture and its modern reception and continuing
influence. When classicists are prepared to regard their own scholarly discipline as a source of never-ending research – that is to say, when they adhere
to the idea of *philologia perennis* (more on this below) – and engage in

---

[98] They are now beginning to teach and research cinema, primarily the reception of ancient Greece
and Rome on the screen and the adaptations of classical themes or archetypes in films not ostensibly
connected with or referring to antiquity. There is, however, no systematic theoretical engagement
by classicists concerning their discipline and film. For brief early examples cf. Wyke 1998 and 2003
and Winkler 1991b and 2001b: 18–22.

[99] Wyke 2003: 445. Cf. in general Martindale 2006: 5–6: "Antiquity and modernity, present and past,
are always implicated in each other, always in dialogue – to understand either one, you need to
think in terms of the other."

[100] Winkler 2003 is an example of how the editorial practice of classical texts may be applied to a
cinematic text. Following the model of editors' prefaces to their critical editions of classical texts,
this short article is in Latin.

film philology alongside their other work, they are in a much better position to furnish the modern or postmodern world, which more and more
often takes a dim view of the significance of classical teaching and research,
with exemplary proof that such scholarship is anything but outdated or
"irrelevant" – today's favorite term for the facile consignment of something
insufficiently understood to disdain or oblivion.[101] As one classical and
medieval scholar has put it:

> philologists must realize that making their texts relevant to a modern audience,
> which necessitates asking new questions of their texts, is not inherently mere-
> tricious; on the contrary, it is an urgent desideratum . . . Just as knowledge will
> be lost if old standards are dropped, so too fields will die if their representatives
> cannot find meaning for today's readers and today's new questions in the texts. At
> a time when literature in printed form has taken a back seat to television, film, and
> music, it is extremely important that scholars be able to articulate why students
> and colleagues should care about the books with which they work . . . we cannot
> allow our profession to be split into two castes, one of which devotes itself wholly
> to conceptual work, the other to textual or technical work.[102]

A moment spent on a brief recapitulation of the history of film criticism
may be instructive at this point. Gerald Mast, whom I quoted earlier in
this chapter, has summarized the two main phases of serious film criticism
in terms that will immediately be familiar to literary scholars, not least
classicists:

> While the roots of empirical-phenomenological film theory lie in the humanities
> (in literature, philosophy, art history, aesthetics) the roots of the new poststruc-
> turalist film theory lie in the social sciences (anthropology, sociology, psychology,
> economics). While the humanist film theorist-critic seeks to understand the work
> of art in its own terms and in its effect on the viewer, the poststructuralist film
> theorist-critic wishes to understand in so far as it reveals (and conceals) the cultural
> attitudes that produced it and the cultural interests which it serves.[103]

These words were written a quarter-century ago, but they apply today
virtually without any change. So my call to classical scholars to turn to
the cinema is anything but radical. Film philology is already being practiced in modern philologies and by theorists-critics whose roots are in the

---

[101] Unthinkable as it may have been only a few decades before, alarm about the relevance of their
discipline and the ways classics, classical studies, and classical philology have been and continue
to be pursued and taught in the academy has periodically led to much anguish and soul-searching
on the part of professionals. I cite only Culham and Edmunds 1989, Hanson and Heath 2000,
Wiseman 2002, and Pearcy 2005 – books from different places and perspectives whose titles speak
for themselves.

[102] Jan Ziolkowski 1990b: 9 and 11.

[103] Quoted from the "Preface (1983)" to Mast 1977: vii–xii; quotation at x.

humanities and who turn to the modern social sciences alongside their traditional empirical-phenomenological studies. (Cf. the beginning of the present chapter.) But most importantly, my call accords with the spirit of the entire history and tradition of classical scholarship. I adduce a number of past and present scholarly authorities in support of this claim; to make it as convincing as possible, I quote them at some length.

What Rudolf Pfeiffer, both an influential classicist and one of the greatest historians of classical scholarship, wrote about the scholarly practice in Hellenistic Alexandria is fully applicable to all of today's scholarship in the humanities and social sciences. Pfeiffer defined textual scholarship in the following terms:

> Scholarship is the art of understanding, explaining, and restoring the literary tradition. It originated as a separate intellectual discipline in the third century before Christ through the efforts of poets to preserve and to use their literary heritage, the "classics". So scholarship actually arose as "classical" scholarship.[104]

At least in the Western hemisphere all scholarship was originally classical scholarship. In the preface to the book whose first chapter opens with the quotation just given, Pfeiffer had called the Alexandrians "our ancestors" as scholars. He concluded:

> it was in the course of time and the succession of peoples and generations that the full nature and the many forms of scholarship were revealed. The history of classical scholarship, therefore, is classical scholarship in the making . . . it is obvious that . . . we want to explore the continuity of knowledge, the *philologia perennis*.[105]

Keeping these observations in mind, classicists can broaden their understanding of the reach of classical philology to encompass new areas for their work, not least those which did not exist in antiquity but which the Alexandrians would have been unlikely to disdain. What Pfeiffer said about the Alexandrian origins of scholarship in the words to be quoted next applies equally to the Alexandrians' successors in the twenty-first century; we need only understand terms like "cultural" or "artistically created" alongside Pfeiffer's "literary" and "written," hardly a radical interference:

> Now for the first time we find wide literary knowledge being acquired for the sake of the literary tradition itself, that is, for the works to be written in the present age and for the preservation and understanding of the works written in past ages. This is the new separate discipline of scholarship.[106]

---

[104] Pfeiffer 1968: 3.     [105] Pfeiffer 1968: x and vii. For more on this see Pfeiffer 1961.
[106] Pfeiffer 1968: 134.

There can be little doubt that the Alexandrian scholars were interested in each and any text, art work, or artifact in any available medium which had some connection to the classic works they prized. The roots of modern reception studies are to be found in Alexandria. Nor can we doubt that the Alexandrians did not hesitate to include any detail of the survival of the past in their scholarly endeavors.[107] Callimachus, the greatest of them, was famous for the far ranges of his interests and knowledge.[108] Hellenistic scholars did not limit themselves to working on literature; those at Pergamon, another great center of learning with its own major library, "were primarily interested in the visual arts."[109] The Alexandrians were interested in acquiring encyclopedic knowledge. The environment that made their endeavors possible has been characterized as

"a place for the Muses", a centre for all the kinds of intellectual activity which require imaginative inspiration...The Alexandrian Museum was an academy...devoted to creative work (in both arts and sciences), to research, learning and scholarship and with some emphasis too on education.[110]

If the Alexandrians were in principle ready and willing to regard anything new that was not trivial as an object worthy of curiosity, study, and preservation, then a wide interest commensurate with theirs is rightly to be expected from their modern successors in the same discipline. This is especially true in an age such as ours, in which scholars in the humanities and social sciences have begun to expand the traditional boundaries of their fields of study and to consider related areas of enquiry as legitimate objects for their own research and teaching. So the idea of a *philologia perennis*, a continuing and by necessity ever-increasing kind of philology, inevitably comes closer and closer to being a kind of all-encompassing undertaking,

[107] Cf. the chapter on the Mouseion and the library of Alexandria in P. M. Fraser 1972, vol. 1: 305–335 and vol. 2: 462–494 (notes), especially vol. 1: 317–319 (on the range of scholarly activities in the Mouseion) and 455–456 (on the *Laterculi Alexandrini*, inventories which include lists of painters, sculptors, and architects). The Stoic philosopher Chrysippus, too, dealt with poetry and painting, as Diogenes Laertius, *Lives of Eminent Philosophers* 7.200–201, reports in his listing of Chrysippus' works: *On Poems* (one book), *On the Right Way to Read Poetry* (two books), *Against Touching Up Paintings* (one book). None survives. On Alexandrian scholarship cf. further P. M. Fraser 1972, vol. 1: 447–479 and vol. 2: 647–692 (notes), Canfora 1989, a general introduction, and Blum 1991; the last includes detailed studies of Callimachus' and other Alexandrian scholars' lists of authors and artists. Cf. Hopkinson 1988: 83 on the variety of Callimachus' works resulting from his "omnivorous reading": his catalogues (*Pinakes*, in 120 volumes) on authors' biographies, the authenticity of their works, stylistic and other criticism, and studies of "topography, ethnography, natural history, language and etymology."

[108] See especially P. M. Fraser 1972, vol. 1: 717–793 and vol. 2: 1004–1102 (notes), a chapter entitled "The Horizon of Callimachus" (i.e. as poet, scholar, and human).

[109] Green 1990/1993: 169. On Pergamene scholarship cf. Esther V. Hansen 1971: 397–433.

[110] Bulloch 1985: 542.

a *philologia perennis et universalis*. It is in the nature of their discipline that classicists are virtually required to expand the horizons of their work. As Ulrich von Wilamowitz-Moellendorff, perhaps the most famous classicist of his day, wrote in 1921 as the conclusion to his overview of the field's history:

> What classical scholarship is, and what it should be, are clear from its history. Has this long [preceding] parade of its worthies taught us what a scholar should be? All those mentioned have been selected because they served the cause of learning, but they differed greatly in intellectual power and character, in interests and abilities. So the most modest definition will probably be the best. A scholar may do any number of things, and may do them in any number of ways; but there is one thing he must *be* if he is to achieve anything that will endure, and that is *vir bonus, discendi peritus*.[111]

*Vir bonus, discendi peritus*: "a good man, experienced in learning" – this definition of the scholar as someone with a sense of intellectual responsibility and the capacity for broadmindedness can hardly be improved on. Some time earlier, John Edwin Sandys, the eminent British historian of classical scholarship, had observed:

> The true scholar, though in no small measure he necessarily lives in the past, will make it his constant aim to perpetuate the past for the benefit of the present and the future . . . "Classical Scholarship" may be described as being . . . "the accurate study of the language, literature, and art of Greece and Rome, and of all that they teach us as to the nature and the history of man".[112]

Decades later American classicist Moses Hadas concurred:

> Classical philology in its broader sense . . . is not a subject but a complete curriculum.
>
> Nor can the student of antiquity blind himself to other knowledge. The political significance of Caesar, for example, was first appreciated by a scholar who had studied Napoleon, and of Demosthenes by one who had direct experience of the diplomatic problems of the 19th century. The student of ancient religion must today be grounded in the findings of modern psychology, and the student of literature in the new techniques of criticism. But for fruitful applications of new knowledge and techniques to ancient problems, a full knowledge of antiquity itself is essential.[113]

---

[111] Wilamowitz-Moellendorff 1982: 178. The Latin is a clever variation – *discendi* ("learning") for *dicendi* ("speaking publicly") – of Cato the Elder's famous definition of the Roman orator (Fragm. 370 Schönberger).

[112] Sandys 1920: 1–2.

[113] Hadas 1954: 120–121. Classics has always been an "interdisciplinary" area of intellectual enquiry; cf., e.g., Galinsky 1981a = 1981b. For examples of classicists' engagement with modern aspects of scholarship and theory cf. the various (and varied) essays collected in de Jong and Sullivan 1994, in

The same perspective applies today. The "other knowledge" that Hadas mentioned as being important for scholars, however, has expanded well beyond any limits he and earlier generations of classicists may have been able to envision. American classicist Charles Segal wrote in 1985:

Literary study today is consequently less definitely literary than at any time in the past. It is extraordinarily hospitable to a wide range of extraliterary influences. Indeed, these are perhaps the most powerful determinants of current critical directions.[114]

That this applies specifically to classical – and classic – literature, perhaps more importantly so than to other kinds, had been shown a decade earlier when Frank Kermode observed in his study *The Classic*: "the books we call classics possess intrinsic qualities that endure, but possess also an openness to accommodation which keeps them alive under endlessly varying dispositions."[115]

Some contemporary classicists have restated these positions forcefully, if independently of the scholars quoted above. The words in my next quotation on continuity and change by two scholars writing jointly are worthy of our consideration:

The aim of *Classics* [as academic discipline] is not only to *discover* or *uncover* the ancient world...Its aim is also to define and debate *our* relationship to that world...Over the centuries classical texts and commentaries have changed enormously, like every other aspect of *Classics*...Most striking of all is the range of what has been deemed to count as *Classics*, and how boundaries between *Classics* and other disciplines have been defined and redefined. Over the centuries questions brought to *Classics* and to classical texts have included (and still do) most of the core issues in subjects that we commonly think of as far removed from the study of Greece and Rome, but which arose directly out of work on the ancient world and its literature... *Classics* cannot ever be a subject safely locked away in a past, 2,000 years distant. For *Classics* continually finds richer texture in its works of art and literature – its meanings changed and renewed – from the multiplications of reactions and re-workings among its vast community of readers across the millennia... So much of Western culture turns on centuries of exploration of the legacy of the classical world that it lies *somewhere* at the roots of pretty well all we can say, see, or think.[116]

which especially Sullivan 1994; and Falkner, Felson, and Konstan 1999, in which especially Segal 1999 and Konstan 1999 on *Arethusa*, a classics journal founded as a kind of counter-traditional venue, which has now become mainstream. Sullivan 1994: 22–26 provides an introductory bibliography; cf. also the "General Bibliography" in de Jong and Sullivan 1994: 282–288. Since then, work on these and comparable lines of critical engagement has proliferated.

[114] Segal 1985: 360.    [115] Kermode 1983: 44.

[116] Beard and Henderson 2000: 6–7, 61, 104, and 122. Cf. also the following two statements: "the interpretation of texts is inseparable from the history of their reception. It follows that the classical

German classicist Friedrich Nietzsche had anticipated much of this in 1874–1875. In *Wir Philologen*, a work characterized as "the most radical critique of classical scholarship ever made from within the profession," Nietzsche had called for a new approach to classical studies that should emphasize the undiminished importance of antiquity for later generations.[117] He observed, if in a somewhat contrarian spirit:

Classical studies as knowledge of the ancient world can't, of course, last forever; their material is exhaustible. What can't be exhausted is the always-new adjustment every age makes to the classical world, measuring itself against it. If we set the classicist the task of understanding *his own* age better by means of antiquity, then his task has no end. – This is the antinomy of philology. *The ancient world* has in fact always been understood only *in terms of the present* – and will *the present* now be understood *in terms of the ancient world*? More accurately: men have explained the ancient world from their own experience; and from what, by so doing, they have acquired of the classical world, they have *appraised* and evaluated their own experience.[118]

We may juxtapose Nietzsche's words with Ernst Vogt's recent assessment of F. A. Wolf's fundamental work on Homer, the *Prolegomena in Homerum* of 1795. Vogt sees Wolf's chief merit in the fact that he was the first to conceive of a comprehensive kind of scholarship on the ancient world that unites *all* individual disciplines dealing with antiquity into one meaningful whole.[119]

The endless tasks of the classicist require constant adjustments of perspective – in cinematic terms, ranging from close-ups on individual details to extreme long-shots of vast fields of knowledge.[120] In this context programmatic, if brief, statements made in 1982, 1987, and 2001 by different

world cannot be coherently studied in isolation, if we are to try to articulate the history and status of our current goals and assumptions." Quoted from Martindale 1993: xiii. And: "If Classics is to find a purpose and role in the third millennium, it needs to ask questions about its purpose and role in past centuries. 'Classics' needs to understand the history of Classics as practiced and enjoyed both within and outside the confines of academic institutions and published scholarship." Quoted from the editors' "Preface" to Hall and Macintosh 1995: vii–xxii, at ix.

[117] My quotation is from the "Introduction" by classicist William Arrowsmith to his translation of *Wir Philologen* as *We Classicists* in Nietzsche 1990: 307–320, at 307; the text is at Nietzsche 1990: 321–387. Arrowsmith notes in his introduction (Nietzsche 1990: 307) that Nietzsche's "critique of philology is coherent, consistent, and radical" and that "it is topical" today.

[118] Nietzsche 1990: 339–340.

[119] "Wolfs Hauptverdienst liegt in der von ihm entwickelten Konzeption einer umfassenden, alle [!] auf die alte Welt bezüglichen Einzeldisziplinen zu einer Einheit zusammenschließenden Altertumswissenschaft." Quoted from Vogt 1997: 125.

[120] Cf. Thomas 1990: 69 and 72: "philology . . . is as broad as the questions that its texts generate . . . Philology takes what it wants from wherever it wants – from theory, from technology, from a number of other, evolving disciplines – and brings it to bear on the text."

editors of the *American Journal of Philology* are representative of and instructive about changes in classical philologists' responsibilities.[121] But regardless of any individual scholar's preferences or areas of expertise, it should be evident to all that classical scholarship engages in and depends on a back-and-forth interaction between past and present. The same is true for all studies of the arts and humanities. If Sandys could extol the value of Greece and Rome for "all that they teach us as to the nature and the history of man" across time and space, then modern classical philologists may safely turn to the cinema, for it is an artistic medium whose aims and effects, at least where its highest levels are concerned, are closely related to the nature and history of man. What Robert Bresson once observed about the artistic potential of the cinema echoes rather closely what Sandys had written about antiquity: "I believe in a Muse of Cinema . . . I firmly believe in the cinema as a serious art . . . as a means of taking a deeper look at things, a kind of aid to the deepening of man, a means for the discovery of man."[122]

A significant new area of classical philology then ought to be classical film philology, a *philologia classica et cinematographica*. Antiquity has played a major part in film history since the earliest days of the medium.[123] Through films about ancient Greece and Rome the classical world has stayed alive in the awareness of a larger percentage of the world's population than would otherwise have been possible. Therefore all classical philologists and historians who are concerned with the reception and survival of the ancient cultures in our rapidly changing age are called upon to take seriously the cinema and its digital-media offshoots, which preserve films and disseminate them more easily and more rapidly than ever before, and to make them a part of their professional work. The reception of the great classics of *their* antiquity was close to the Alexandrian scholars' hearts; the reception of antiquity in the entire history of civilization from their time to ours

---

[121] Cf. Clay 1982 and Luck 1987 (with reference to "an ever-broadening profession"). See especially Gold 2001: iii, describing her editorial aim as proceeding "by preserving [the journal's] venerable traditions and its strong roots in classical philology and by continuing to open up the journal to the exciting interdisciplinary and contemporary developments that now characterize some of the best work done in our field . . . I am interested in publishing work that stands at the intersections of various aspects of our discipline, that incorporates new and innovative approaches, and that opens up classical philology to different ways of thinking." In the spring of 2003 she restated this position in a four-page brochure mailed to prospective journal subscribers. A testimonial in this flyer by another scholar says that the journal "has evolved to embrace the more diverse approaches to the ancient world that are currently revitalizing the discipline" (4).

[122] Quoted, with some adaptations, from the subtitles to "Un metteur en ordre: Robert Bresson," a 1966 French television discussion with Bresson about his film *Au hasard Balthazar*.

[123] French film pioneer and *auteur* Georges Méliès was especially interested in classical subjects. (His two-minute-long *Cleopatra* of 1899 was recently rediscovered.) Cf. Solomon 2001: 3–4 on Méliès and on other early films on ancient themes.

should be – and now is becoming – a prominent area of modern classicists' interests.[124] This field is wide, even daunting in its ramifications.[125] The cinema is an integral and major part of it. Even the two classicists cited at the beginning of this chapter state about the cinema "that it may well represent the most powerfully effective medium of the reception of antiquity that has ever existed."[126]

There is also the other side: classical scholars' engagement with their own contemporary culture, their interpretations of modern artists' works and of current social, intellectual, political, and other trends. This includes classicists' interpretations of cinema, for instance in pointing out archetypal ancient themes in individual films or film genres whose plots are not set in antiquity or, beyond this, analyses of the body of work by a particular filmmaker. Examples of the former approach will appear in subsequent chapters of this book. An example of the latter is classicist William Arrowsmith's book on Michelangelo Antonioni. Arrowsmith's understanding of Antonioni as an *auteur* and exemplar of the cinema of poetry indicates how fruitfully classical training can be applied to cinema as a modern poetic art. Arrowsmith is quite forceful about the importance of his subject's work and about its place in film history and in the history of modern literature:

Let me be clear about what I think: that Antonioni is one of the greatest living artists, and that, as a director of film, his only living peer is Kurosawa; and that he is unmistakably the peer of the other great masters in all the arts. As an innovator and manipulator of images, he is the peer of Joyce in the novel; in creating a genuine cinematic poetry, he stands on a level with Valéry and Eliot in poetry proper; and that his artistic vision, while perhaps no greater than that of Fitzgerald or Eliot or Montale or Pavese, is at least as great and compelling.[127]

---

[124] Proof is the existence of the International Society for the Classical Tradition, founded in 1991 and affiliated with the Institute for the Classical Tradition at Boston University, and of its journal, the *International Journal of the Classical Tradition*, which began publication in 1994. *Der Neue Pauly: Enzyklopädie der Antike*, the modern successor to the nineteenth-century *Realenzyclopädie der classischen Altertumswissenschaft* (Pauly-Wissowa), devotes five of its eighteen volumes to reception and the history of classical scholarship. For an overview see Cancik and Mohr 2002.

[125] For a first orientation see, e.g., the essays collected in Dummer and Kunze 1983.

[126] Korenjak and Töchterle 2002: 8 (in their "Vorwort"); my translation. The original reads: "dass es [das Kino] das vielleicht wirkungsmächtigste Rezeptionsmedium der Antike darstellt, das je existiert hat." Cf. Paul 2005: 688 (in a review of Winkler 2004b): "successfully – and fruitfully – the study of classics and cinema has asserted itself as a leader in the field of reception studies." It is appropriate that schools and universities should begin offering their students the opportunity to learn about antiquity and cinema in conjunction. King's College London offers a three-year full-time "Classical Studies with Film Studies BA" program; an outline is at http://www.kcl.ac.uk/ugp07/programme/131.

[127] Quoted from the editor's "Introduction" to Arrowsmith 1995: 3–19, at 4. Arrowsmith died in 1992. For a different approach to Antonioni on the part of a classical scholar and poet see Carson 2005: 43–57 ("FOAM [Essay with Rhapsody]: On the Sublime in Longinus and Antonioni"). Besides

These words may stand as an eloquent piece of evidence in support of my claim that classical scholars are justified to work on cinematic and literary authors. Decades earlier, however, Arrowsmith had already made a passionate case for the importance of cinema in education:

In humanistic education the future lies with film. Of this I am firmly convinced . . . This conviction rests upon a faith that human society cannot do without the humanities, cannot forsake its faith in the project of making men more fully human, helping men to "become the thing they are." If real education – and not merely the transmission of knowledge – is to take place, a curriculum is required which corroborates and exemplifies moral discovery, the making of a fate, the hunger for identity. Literature and the arts have always been at the heart of the humanities because they provided just such corroboration; our most enduring use for art has been precisely in education – and it is an end worthy of art, this "expansion of love beyond ourselves," as Nietzsche called education.[128]

Frequently in the past, however, and occasionally in the present, as we have seen, classical scholars have disdained cinema, particularly films set in ancient Greece or Rome, pointing to their inaccuracies as the basis for value judgments. I have here attempted to show the narrowness of such a view. The cinema may not be one of the "media of salvation" for classical studies, as classicist George Hadzsits memorably called it almost nine decades ago in his plea to classical scholars not to ignore film.[129] But a critical interpretation of all aspects of popular adaptations of ancient literature illuminates these texts' influences on modern culture. This process is nothing new. It is already evident in the Homeric epics at the birth of Western literature. As George Steiner has put it, the *Iliad* as we have it is "the product of an editorial recension of genius, of a wonderfully formative act of combination, selection and editing of the voluminous oral material" that existed before it and that served as its source. This in turn set the pattern for the "perennial ubiquity of translations from Homer, of Homeric variants, re-creations, pastiches and travesties." Steiner appropriately refers to "the complexity of modulation" that is found in English-language adaptations of Homer.[130] Steiner refers only to literary texts, but we may also think

being a filmmaker, Antonioni was also a film critic, literary author, and painter. For his perspectives on cinema see especially Antonioni 1996 and Cardullo 2008.

[128] Arrowsmith 1969: 75 (opening paragraph). Carr 2006 is a recent example of such an approach from an educator's perspective. Cf. Cavell 2005c.

[129] Hadzsits 1920. I omit quoting and discussing this article and its implications here because I have already done so in Winkler 2001b: 3–9 and 2007a: 202–204 (section entitled "Classical Educators and the Cinema"). I refer readers to these *loci*.

[130] "Introduction" to George Steiner 1996: xv–xxxiv; my quotations are from xxviii, xvii, and xvi. – Genette 1997 has developed the concept of the *hypotext*, a literary work that shapes subsequent

of visual narratives told in the complex language of film. Classical scholar
Eleonora Cavallini extends Steiner's view beyond textual narratives:

The idea that antiquity conveys to us of Homeric epic is . . . that of an "open work,"
continually susceptible of re-readings, re-interpretations, transformations: a kind
of work in progress, destined to perpetuate itself across the centuries until it has
availed itself of new, sophisticated media made available by modern technological
society.[131]

One ancient author provides us with the best justification for the kind
of tradition described by Steiner and Cavallini and encountered in the
present book. He can speak with particular authority because he was both
a practicing poet and a literary theorist, highly influential in both aspects.
Concerning those who disdain recent versions of works by revered and
usually long-dead authors like Homer, he unequivocally states that those
who judge nothing to be comparable to the old masters are in serious
error. Their judgment is wrong because it is no more than a prejudice
against anything modern. "I find it offensive," he says, "when something is
criticized . . . merely because it is new." The ultimate problem with blind
adherence to everything ancient and with quick condemnation of everything modern is that this attitude denies the great authors of the past one
of their most important achievements – their creation of a never-ending
tradition of influence. Or, in this author's words: "If the Greeks had hated
anything new as much as we do now, what would now be old?" Our poet
had previously observed about the ancient Greeks that their earliest works
are the greatest of all, so the attitude with which he takes issue, had it pre-
vailed, would have stopped any literary creativity since the time of Homer
dead in its tracks.

But who is this author who is so outspoken in his attack on the diehard
traditionalists, the precursors of some of today's critics and scholars? It
is none other than Horace, whom we already encountered earlier on the
subject of text and image. In an open letter addressed to Emperor Augustus
Horace anticipated much of the seventeenth-century *Querelle des Anciens*

---

*hypertexts* by exerting strong influences on their authors. To Genette the most powerful hypotext
of all is the *Odyssey*. The essays collected in Erhart and Nieberle 2003 take Homer and Stanley
Kubrick's film *2001: A Space Odyssey* (1968) for their starting points.

[131] Eleonora Cavallini, "Introduzione" to Cavallini 2007: 1–6; quotation at 5 (my translation). The
original reads: "L'idea che l'antichità ci trasmette dell'epica omerica è . . . quella di un' 'opera
aperta,' continuamente suscettibile di riletture, reinterpretazioni, trasformazioni: una sorta di *work
in progress*, destinato a perpetuarsi nei secoli fino ad avvalersi dei nuovi, sofisticati *media* messi a
disposizione dalla moderna civiltà tecnologica."

*et des Modernes.*[132] Horace firmly came down on the side of the Moderns, among whom he numbered himself, but without being in the least disdainful of the Ancients or denying them their high standing. Virtually all his works, most famously his *Odes*, demonstrate how sensible Horace's position is in balancing the old and the new and in finding praiseworthy qualities in both. Horace's view on "the folly of archaism" applies not only to poetry but also to all creative endeavors in literature and the visual arts.[133]

I close this chapter with a quotation from a modern scholar who possessed a virtually Alexandrian breadth and depth of interests and who eloquently restates Horace's view. Looking back over the history of aesthetics from antiquity to the eighteenth century, a history that continues to our day, Paul Oskar Kristeller refers to the cinema. His judgment is applicable to classical film philology, and all scholars working in the humanities today can only profit from heeding it:

There were important periods in cultural history when the novel, instrumental music, or canvas painting did not exist or have any importance . . . the moving picture is a good example of how new techniques may lead to modes of artistic expression for which the aestheticians of the eighteenth and nineteenth century had no place in their system. The branches of the arts all have their rise and decline, and even their birth and death, and the distinction between "major" arts and their subdivisions is arbitrary and subject to change . . . historical understanding might help to free us from certain conventional preconceptions and to clarify our ideas on the present status and future prospects of the arts and of aesthetics.[134]

---

[132] Horace, *Epistles* 2.1, especially lines 45–49, 63–65, 76–77 (quoted above), and 90–91 (quoted above); my translations. On these lines and their contexts see especially Brink 1982: 57–132.

[133] The quotation is from Brink 1982: 74. The preceding discussion is expanded from Winkler 2007c: 84–85.

[134] Kristeller 1951–1952: 45–46 (= Kristeller 1990: 227). This passage concludes his essay.

# CHAPTER 2

# Divine epiphanies: Apollo and the Muses

Filmic representations of classical texts are adaptations either set in Greece or Rome or updated to modern times, or they are modern stories in which figures from ancient history, literature, or myth play a part. Most of the films deviate from or contradict our sources, for they are highly inventive rather than faithful, authentic, or accurate. This phenomenon goes back to the earliest days of cinema, which has made possible the greatest variety in modern resurrections of ancient literature, especially myth. As representative and at the same time thematically focused examples of filmmakers' approaches to ancient myth this chapter examines the screen appearances of Apollo and the Muses, whom we encounter both in artistically significant films and in crassly commercial products. The very differences between and among these films make a comprehensive enquiry rewarding.

My intentions in this chapter are twofold. The first is to demonstrate the validity of the neo-mythological approach outlined in my Introduction. I have therefore chosen as a test case the subject of Apollo and the Muses, a topic that is especially suitable because it remains manageable for the purpose of such an enquiry (and because, as we have already seen and will see again, the god of light is also the god of cinema). The films involved are few enough to make a reasonably complete survey possible. Traditional philologists strive to demonstrate familiarity with all ancient texts relevant to their topics; by the same token, I discuss or at least mention most of the occurrences of Apollo and the Muses on the screen that I have been able to find. (I omit a few negligible instances.) On the other hand, films featuring Apollo or the Muses are numerous enough to present us with a surprising breadth of themes, settings, and levels of artistic achievement. But even crass works of commercialism, some of which will be encountered below, may contain aspects worthy of attention. As a result, the broad range of artistic and commercial works, of genre films and art-house cinema, reveals the vitality of ancient myth in today's culture. My second intention is to illustrate through descriptions and analyses how classical scholarship may approach and intellectually engage with modern neo-mythologism in a popular medium. Like others, this chapter may provide an impulse for all those who wish to bridge the distance between today's culture and ancient myth.

## GOD OF LIGHT, GOD OF CINEMA

Apollo, the god of prophecy, has the power to bring hidden things to light and reveal the future to mortals or to withhold such knowledge. The name of the island of Delos, on which Apollo had been born and which held his most important sanctuary after Delphi, means "Visible, Conspicuous, Clear" and points to these aspects of the god.[1]

The most profound recourse to Apollo and Delos occurs in a film in which the god plays a rather unusual but crucial part although he does not appear on screen. Theodoros Angelopoulos's film *Ulysses' Gaze* (1995), with its epic running time of almost three hours, tells a story set in the Balkan wars of the late twentieth century. The film is a modern reworking of themes of Homer's *Odyssey*.[2] The film's fictional protagonist is a famous expatriate Greek film director, who remains unnamed – in the script he is called "A" – and stands in for all filmmakers, not least Angelopoulos himself.[3] This director has returned to Greece for showings of his latest film. He receives a request through the Athens Film Archive to search for three unexposed reels of film shot by the brothers Miltos and Yannakis Manaki, actual pioneers of Balkan cinema at the beginning of the twentieth century. Their 1905 film *The Weavers*, brief excerpts of which appear in

[1] The name "Delos" is etymologically related to the verb *dêloun* ("to make visible, disclose, reveal"). In Greek legend the island is so named because it suddenly became visible after having been hidden below the sea.

[2] Vöhler 2002 examines classical and Homeric aspects of the film. Létoublon and Eades 2003 give a more detailed interpretation. I am indebted to Françoise Létoublon for making the original French version of their article ("Des mythes antiques à celui du premier regard et de la parole originelle chez Angelopoulos") available to me. Cf. also the chapter on this film in Horton 1999: 181–201. Rollet 1995 gives an introduction to *Ulysses' Gaze* and Odyssean overtones in earlier films by Angelopoulos. On Angelopoulos's cinema, with brief discussions of *Ulysses' Gaze*, cf. Bordwell 2005: 140–185 and 286–289 (notes; the chapter is entitled "Angelopoulos, or Melancholy").

[3] This is so despite Angelopoulos's statement that "'A' is not me, not Angelopoulos!" in Horton 1997b: 103. A film directed by "A" that is screened early in *Ulysses' Gaze* is never seen, but its soundtrack is that of Angelopoulos's own film *The Suspended Step of the Stork* (1991). In his *Voyage to Cythera* (1983), Angelopoulos had provided the voice for the actor who plays the protagonist, a film director "who resembles a younger Angelopoulos" (Horton 1999: 127).

*Ulysses' Gaze*, is considered to have been the "first known Greek film."[4] The Manaki brothers had brought the cinema to Greece, but their film for which the director is searching has remained completely unknown. On his journey to discover its whereabouts the director travels deep into the heart of darkness of south-eastern Europe, the very region that had once provided the cradle of European civilization. His quest is also a journey of self-discovery. *Ulysses' Gaze* is Angelopoulos's homage to cinema as a modern art form and as witness to contemporary history. He pays tribute to the Manaki brothers and to the nature of film as an artistic medium whose technology can be mastered but whose essence remains elusive. Early on, the director meets a young woman who works in a film archive and is herself a preserver of cinema and culture. He tells her the story of an eerie and almost supernatural experience he once had on Delos. The presence and power of Apollo had made itself felt to him in a kind of mythic epiphany:

Two years ago, mid-summer, I was on Delos location-hunting for a film; the sun blazed white on the ruins. I wandered around amongst the broken marble, fallen columns. A frightened lizard slithered into hiding under a tombstone. Invisible cicadas droned away, adding a note of desolation to the empty landscape. And then I heard a creaking sound, a hollow sound, as if coming from the depths of the earth. I looked up, and on the hill I saw an ancient olive tree slowly toppling over, an olive tree on a hill slowly sinking to its death on the ground, a huge, solitary tree, lying. A gash made by the fallen tree revealed an ancient head, the bust of Apollo . . . I walked on further, past the row of lions, the columns of the row of phalloi, till I reached a small secret place, the birthplace of Apollo according to tradition. I raised my polaroid [camera] and pressed the button. And when the photograph slid out, I was amazed to see it hadn't registered a thing. I shifted my position and tried again. Nothing. Blank negative pictures of the world, as if my glance wasn't working. I went on taking one photograph after another, clicking away – the same empty squares, black holes. The sun dipped into the sea, as if abandoning the scene. I felt I was sinking into darkness. And when the Film Archives suggested this [current] project, I was only too eager; it was a way out. I'd have given up soon enough, only I discovered something: three reels of film not mentioned by any film historian. I don't know what came over me then; I was strangely disturbed. I tried to shrug the feeling away, to – to break free, but I couldn't. Three reels, perhaps a whole film, undeveloped. The first film, perhaps the first glance, a lost glance. A lost innocence. It turned into an obsession, as if they were my own work, my own first glance, lost long ago.

---

[4] Quotation from Georgakas 2002–2003: 2.

The director finds Apollo – or rather, Apollo reveals himself to him – but loses his gaze, his ability to record, realistically as well as artistically, the world around him.[5] Or does Apollo take his creativity away, symbolically protecting the mysterious nature of art in an age of advanced technology and political abuses of art? As Angelopoulos put it when he was writing the film's screenplay: "The filmmaker tries to take a picture of this event, but when he develops it, he sees that nothing appears. You see, the head had emerged from the spot where Apollo, the god of *light*, had first appeared. The light at such a spot, the source of light, was too strong for the camera!"[6]

The way in which Angelopoulos presents the film director's account of his experience with Apollo to the viewers of his own film is significant, too, for it subtly reinforces the meaning and importance of this crucial episode. The director tells his story to the woman in a train station. He is standing on board the train in the open door; she is on the platform. Then, while the director is still giving his account, the train begins to move, and the woman has to walk, then run, alongside the train. Soon she jumps on board to hear the end of his story. At the climactic moment of this scene and to our surprise we then see the two embrace and kiss passionately. At first this may seem like a plot cliché familiar from dozens of other films: star and leading lady must begin a romance. But the real point is something different. The actress we see here plays several characters in the film, both in the present and in the past. In a brief episode later she will play another lover of the director. More importantly she will appear as his mother in a long flashback in which the director reminisces about his youth. The story of his mystical encounter with Apollo is a reminiscence as well but one presented in a radically different way. Other film directors might show us in a flashback to Delos what the director saw there, but Angelopoulos grants us only a verbal account. Just as the images had been denied the director on Delos, so the images of the story he tells are now denied us, the viewers. Visually and verbally Angelopoulos weaves together the layers of his complex narrative. The story of Apollo which we hear but do not see points to the elusiveness of memory, of the director's and, by extension, the

---

[5] The description of the director's experience with Apollo on Delos as given by Horton 1999: 189 does not conform to the text quoted above. Horton: 202 gives Angelopoulos's own verbal description of the moment from an interview about two years before filming *Ulysses' Gaze*; it, too, is different from what appears on the screen: "One day while he is visiting the sacred island of Delos, the birthplace of Apollo, from a crack in the ground a marble head of Apollo mysteriously rises from the ground and shatters into many pieces." Fragments of a monumental archaic marble statue of Apollo dating to ca. 600 BC can still be seen on Delos.

[6] Quoted from Horton 1999: 202 (immediately following on the words quoted in the preceding note).

viewer's gaze, and of the cinema itself. The images of the train gathering speed while the director is telling his story make for an increasingly blurred background.

The fact that Apollo's head is said to have shattered takes on added resonance some time later in *Ulysses' Gaze*. The film contains an unforgettable sequence in which a gigantic granite statue of Lenin, toppled and sawed into several pieces, has been loaded onto a barge that slowly floats down a river. We first see the severed head of the statue being put on the barge by a crane. His encounter with the head of Apollo inspires the filmmaker to embark on his search for the unknown film, a symbol of his own "lost innocence" and of the origins of cinema and all art. But will Apollo reveal the secret of the lost film?

In the last sequence of *Ulysses' Gaze* the director tracks down the lost reels in war-torn Sarajevo. An old film archivist has saved them from destruction. He, too, is a preserver of culture and civilization in the midst of war. Together with his daughter and some little children he will soon die a senseless death in a civil-war massacre. But shortly before, the archivist had managed to begin developing the reels of film and had shown some of the film to the director. "A captive gaze . . . set free at last," the archivist observes. We see both men looking at the film strip; overjoyed at the discovery of these images, they break into spontaneous laughter and embrace. We are meant to conclude from this brief scene that the film strip being developed contains images from ninety years ago. The last scene of the film, however, in which the director himself finally projects and looks at the lost film, admits of two different interpretations. "There are several ways of looking at this," Angelopoulos has said.[7]

Angelopoulos shows the director, now completely alone, looking at the screen. We only see the flicker of the projector's light on an empty screen and hear the projector noise on the soundtrack. The realistic understanding of this scene is that the director has watched the old film. This view Angelopoulos himself seems to adopt: "I did shoot the scenes he sees, but finally we decided not to show them because it was too concrete . . . It doesn't matter what is on the film; maybe it's just rushes that were never supposed to be shown."[8] But there is also a different possibility, borne out by a circumstance apparently unnoticed by critics. The sound from the

---

[7] Fainaru 2001a: 98 (1996 interview).

[8] Fainaru 2001a: 98. Angelopoulos's entire description of this scene here is worth reading. Cf. Horton 1999: 195: " 'A's' eyes fill with tears as he looks toward us and thus up at the screen where the lost film has just finished running." According to Angelopoulos the three reels of film shot by the Manaki brothers do exist, but the chemical process necessary to develop them is unknown.

projector is steady and going on for longer than a "tail," the blank film strip at the end of a reel, would make possible. Nor do we hear the loud flapping sound of the film strip turning once the tail has run through the projector. The steady sound of the projector extends even beyond the visual part of *Ulysses' Gaze*. When the image fades out and the end credits appear in white letters on black background, the projector's sound continues to be audible until everything fades away with the last frame of *Ulysses' Gaze*. From this second perspective Angelopoulos shows us, his audience, what the director sees or has seen of the long-lost film: nothing. That is to say, the silent film's images, which presumably had been real enough a little earlier, have now faded or vanished, and we are reminded of the director's earlier words: "Nothing. Blank negative pictures of the world." As he had said about his experience on Delos: "The sun dipped into the sea, as if abandoning the scene." Does Apollo, the god of arts and culture, here also abandon the scene, turning away from the willful destruction that mankind is inflicting on itself and removing from modern man's gaze the innocent art he protects? The irrevocable vanishing of the long-lost but until now miraculously preserved images parallels the vanishing of Apollo himself from modern civilization. That, in turn, symbolizes the vanishing of all civilization, which in this film threatens to sink into barbarism. But there is still hope, as the words from the *Odyssey* which the director quotes in the final scene reveal.[9] Even the scene of the massacre that preceded it is framed by a reference to the Apollonian. The youth orchestra of Sarajevo was playing amidst civil-war ruins and continuing carnage. Music, after all, is one of Apollo's most important domains and a general symbol of culture and civilization.

The final minutes in Angelopoulos's mournful work on the nature of history, art, and culture and on the part that the medium of film has come to play in all three rank among the cinema's most haunting moments of visual poetry. *Ulysses' Gaze* begins with an epigraph slightly adapted from Plato, which summarizes Angelopoulos's perspective on history and civilization and, by implication, on the Apollonian: "And the soul, if it is going to know itself, must itself gaze into the soul."[10] This alludes to the Delphic maxim "Know Thyself." It is then entirely appropriate that Angelopulos's philosophy of art and culture should be a philosophy of

---

9  Cf. Angelopoulos's own words on this important point as quoted by Horton 1999: 199. Létoublon and Eades 2003: note 21 quote the director's final soliloquy and list the references to the *Odyssey* which his words contain.

10  Plato, *Alcibiades I*, 133b. This was one of Plato's most influential works, although some modern scholars question his authorship.

cinema: "The world needs cinema now more than ever. It may be the last important form of *resistance* to the deteriorating world in which we live."[11]

Apollo is most readily seen on screen in videos of theatrical productions of Greek tragedy. A well-known example is the 1981 adaptation by director Peter Hall and poet-translator Tony Harrison of Aeschylus' *Oresteia* for the National Theatre of Great Britain. The stage of Hall's production is patterned on the layout of the ancient Greek theater. This production is remarkable for Harrison's attempt to find a modern linguistic equivalent to Aeschylus' grand poetry, for bringing out, simultaneously, the remoteness of Greek tragedy and its closeness to us, also for its stylish use of music (by Harrison Birtwhistle) and, not least, for its acting with masks. Harrison has described the purpose of his decision to use masks in the following words: "I was interested in exploring the world of masks and the language that was spoken in order to get a better idea of what the poetic nature of the language was."[12] In *The Eumenides*, the last play of the *Oresteia*, Apollo and Athena were commanding presences on the stage, as even the small video screen reveals. Phoebus Apollo, god of light and sun, wears a golden mask and is dressed in white and gold.[13]

The temple of Apollo at Delphi, the setting of the opening scene of Aeschylus' *Eumenides*, was to have been transposed to modern black Africa in a film that was never made. Poet and filmmaker Pier Paolo Pasolini, a Marxist and vigorous critic of Western society, intended to film a modern adaptation of the *Oresteia* in Africa as a comment on Western capitalism and colonialism. Pasolini had to abandon this project, but while scouting

[11] Quoted from Horton 2001: 86 (1992 interview). The quotation also appears in Horton 1999: 3 and 196.

[12] Quoted from McDonald 1992: 145. Tony Harrison 1988: 18–22 discusses his views on masks in greater detail. A reprint of Tony Harrison 1988 appears in Astley 1991: 429–454, with 442–448 on masks. Cf. also Hall 2000: 24–30 and 33–36 and especially the chapter on this production in Wiles 2007: 125–152.

[13] An example of a different stage appearance is Michael Powell and Emeric Pressburger's film *The Life and Death of Colonel Blimp* (1943). It contains a brief scene in which the protagonist attends a musical comedy called *Ulysses* in a London theater in 1902. The stage reveals Mt. Olympus, where the council of the gods is deciding on Odysseus' return to Ithaca, a scene modeled on Book One of Homer's *Odyssey*. The divine assembly consists of Zeus, Athena, Hera, Poseidon (absent in Homer), Hermes, Ares, Aphrodite, and Apollo. Apollo appears holding a lyre and wearing a radiate crown on his head. As in Homer, he does not take part in the deliberations. – A marble statue of a seated Apollo holding a lyre briefly appears in the lobby of a theater in pre-Revolution Paris during the climactic duel in George Sidney's swashbuckler *Scaramouche* (1952). This sword fight, the longest in film history, ends below the base of a neoclassical statue.

locations and doing other preproduction work on his *Oresteia* he made an hour-long film essay: *Notes for an African Oresteia* (1970).[14] Pasolini's equivalent for the Delphic temple of the god who as leader of the Muses was associated with arts and sciences is nothing but the modern sanctuary of knowledge, a university. Pasolini himself comments on this in voice-over. I quote from the English-language version of his film:

The temple of Apollo as I will depict it metaphorically in my film of the *African Oresteia* – I'll show it as a university, and, to be more precise, the University of Dar-es-Salaam which, seen [here] from a distance, displays unmistakable signs of resembling the typical Anglo-Saxon neo-capitalistic university. The external aspect, elegant and confident in design, the internal organization make it a typical university of the kind that is frequently seen in black Africa.

These universities, as I repeat, follow a progressive neo-capitalistic pattern, and they are the seat of the future local intelligentsia in the culture and learning of the young African nations.

The University of Dar-es-Salaam, a city whose name means "House of Peace," parallels ancient Delphi as a place where opposites may meet in harmony: black Africa with its emerging states and societies, white civilization with its ancient educational and cultural traditions. So the encounter between Europe and Africa for once need not be a clash of cultures but rather can provide the basis for new levels of social development, learning, and unification. Pasolini aspires to nothing less than a modern equivalent of Apollo's sanctuary at Delphi, which had fulfilled comparable functions for the ancient Greek city-states.

The two films of Greek tragedy that Pasolini did complete, *Oedipus Rex* (1967) and *Medea* (1969), magnificently realized his artistic vision of antiquity and represent his cinema of poetry. Except for a modern prologue and epilogue Pasolini filmed *Oedipus Rex* in Morocco in order to strip Sophocles' play down to a layer of prehistoric myth. The settings are primitive, but Pasolini presents them in sophisticated ways. Non-Western music and a desert landscape tell us that we are in a time of myth, not of history or reality. As Greek writer-director Michael Cacoyannis has observed: "Pasolini did not make Greek tragedy. He made very striking films about the myths on which tragedy is based."[15] In *Oedipus Rex* this is best seen in the sequence in which Oedipus visits Apollo's oracle. Unlike the real site, which is elevated both geographically (up in the mountains)

---

[14] On Pasolini and Aeschylus see especially Gallo 1995 and Bonanno 1995. Todini 1995: 257–259 reprints Pasolini's own text on this film ("Nota per l'ambientazione dell'Orestiade in Africa"). The subtitle of Todini's book on Pasolini is a free translation of Aeschylus, *Eumenides* 850.

[15] McDonald and Winkler 2001: 81.

**Fig. 2.** *Oedipus Rex*. The Delphic Oracle in the African desert in Pasolini's cinema of poetry. (Arco Film)

and aesthetically (through its architecture), Pasolini's Delphic oracle is a tiny spot on the outskirts of a village in a barren, if austerely beautiful, desert landscape (Fig. 2). A grotesque, callous, and cruel Pythia informs Oedipus of his fate. I quote her words from the subtitles of the film's English release version:

In your fate it is written: "You will kill your father and will make love with your mother." [*Here she laughs uproariously.*] You understand? It's written in your fate: "You will kill your father, make love with your mother." Thus says the God, and it will surely come to pass. Now go away. Don't infect people [*literally*: "these people"] with your presence.

The priestess's words, her strange dress and appearance, and the setting all emphasize the devastating power of the god over a helpless and barely comprehending human. The Pythia's prophecy condemns Oedipus as someone polluted even before he actually commits any wrong – a particularly annihilating aspect of the divine. In this way Pasolini demonstrates several important aspects of tragedy: the dark and violent side of the gods, our inability to understand the divine will that may at any moment ruin our lives, our impotence in the face of a higher power that need not justify itself, and the utter isolation and loneliness that result. At the end of this sequence Pasolini expresses the Sophoclean themes of light and darkness and of vision and blindness by intercutting shots of a bright and sunny sky with blurry shots of a lowering sky from Oedipus' point of view. Pasolini also gives Oedipus a gesture that foreshadows his eventual fate, a gesture touching to those who know the outcome of his story: several times, Oedipus places his hand or arm over his eyes. The rising curve of pity and fear, of *eleos* and *phobos*, that Aristotle postulated for the catharsis of tragedy in his *Poetics* commences here.[16] The sequence effectively illustrates Oedipus' bewilderment, his intellectual incomprehension, and his sense of abandonment. Through the bizarre figure of the Pythia and her behavior Apollo, the cause of all this, becomes an almost demonic power. Pasolini appears to hint at the proximity of what, after Nietzsche, we have come to call the Apollonian to its opposite, the Dionysian.

The influence of Pasolini's film on cinematic retellings of ancient stories is considerable. It may be seen prominently in Franco Rossi's *Eneide* ("Aeneid," 1971), a six-hour adaptation of Virgil's *Aeneid* for public television. At *Aeneid* 3.73–120, Aeneas tells Dido, queen of Carthage, about his visit to Delos where he received a prophecy from Apollo. Rossi includes this episode in a brief flashback as part of Aeneas' account of his wanderings after the fall of Troy. But Rossi's Delos looks rather like Pasolini's Delphi: a vast desert with rocky and treeless mountains in the background and African-looking people. The sanctuary of Apollo, from which the prophecy emanates, is by no means the grand temple mentioned by Virgil's Aeneas; rather, it is a large wind-blown and ragged tent in the middle of a sandy plain. As did Pasolini, Rossi takes pains to present an exotic pre-classical world, one from which the civilization of Rome and its greatest poet can later be born.[17]

A Nietzschean moment even stronger than that in Pasolini's *Oedipus Rex* occurs in Jules Dassin's *A Dream of Passion* (1978). The theater of the Apollonian sanctuary at Delphi plays a major part in this film, in which a modern revival of Euripides' *Medea* is taking place. Famous Greek actress Melina Mercouri plays Maya, a famous Greek actress rehearsing the title part. To gain greater understanding of what may have driven a mother to kill her own children, Maya becomes absorbed by the case of Brenda, an American officer's wife who is a modern equivalent of Medea. (The film was inspired by an actual case in Athens.) At one point Maya, alone, enters the abandoned house in which the crime had occurred, and writer-director Dassin fuses two temporal and psychological levels. As in a flashback we

---

[16] Aristotle, *Poetics* 1449b24–28. Cf. also Chapter 3.

[17] In his six-hour television film *Quo Vadis?* (1985) Rossi includes a scene in which a statue of Apollo is said to belong to an oracle established by Pedanius Secundus, the urban prefect who was murdered by one of his slaves in 61 AD – out of jealousy, as Nero explains. Rossi's source is the episode in Tacitus, *Annals* 14.42–45, which, however, does not incorporate Apollo.

hear Brenda's voice-over and see her commit the murders. But we also see Maya watching Brenda, even momentarily taking her place as child killer. In this way Dassin conveys to the viewer how utterly Maya, an independent and rational – one might say, Apollonian – woman, falls under the spell of Dionysian violence and ecstasy (in its literal sense). Maya's creative mind attempts to reach rational understanding but is subdued by the irrational that it encounters. A third dimension that Dassin fuses with the other two is the performance of the play itself. The cinematic technique to convey all this to the viewer is intercutting.

The importance of the Delphic oracle for Greek history is nowhere better seen than in the part it played in 480 BC, when the invasion of Greece by Xerxes, king of Persia, at the head of an immense army was imminent. Against all military odds the Greeks managed first to delay the Persians at Thermopylae and then to defeat them decisively. In the cinema the Battle of Thermopylae found its greatest homage with Rudolph Maté's *The 300 Spartans* (1962), a film that combines fact, mainly taken from Herodotus, with the invention that is unavoidable for a coherent retelling of the battle and what led up to it for large audiences unfamiliar with history.[18] For example, exteriors were filmed in Greece at authentic locations, although the geography of Thermopylae and its surroundings has changed so much since the fifth century BC that it no longer fits the historical situation. Similarly the Delphic oracles are quoted accurately, if in abbreviated and simplified forms. (Zeus is referred to by his Roman name for the sake of audiences more familiar with Roman than Greek gods, although Athena is not called Minerva.) In an assembly of representatives from various Greek city-states who are debating what to do about the approaching Persians, one delegate hostile to Athens quotes Apollo's first oracle to the Athenians: "Fly to the world's end, doomed ones, leave your homes, for fire and the headlong god of war shall bring you low." But Themistocles, the Athenian leader, counters this with a quotation from Apollo's second and more hopeful prophecy to Athens: "Then far-seeing Jove grants this to the prayers of Athene: Safe shall the wooden wall continue for thee and thy children." Themistocles explains what the wooden wall is: "Our new Athenian ships, manned by the bravest sailors in the world. There's our wooden wall. The wall far-seeing Jove declares shall keep us safe. The gods don't lie." In this way Themistocles manages to unite all Greece against the Persians. That he is here played by Sir Ralph Richardson, one of the

---

[18] I briefly discuss Zach Snyder's *300* (2007), also about the battle of Thermopylae, at the end of Chapter 4.

most commanding actors of the British stage and screen, only reinforces his authority and wiliness.

In a later scene King Leonidas, soon to be the famous hero of Thermopylae, learns of Apollo's prophecy concerning Sparta and himself:

> Dwellers in glorious Sparta, hear now the words of your fate:
> Either your famous city goes down in front of the Persians,
> Or, if your city is spared, the land of Sparta must mourn
> For the death of one of her kings.

I have arranged these words differently from those of the oracles quoted above to indicate their rhythmic nature, which, surprisingly in a mainstream Hollywood film, manages to imitate, if loosely, the hexametrical verse in which the Delphic utterances were conveyed. This is an indication of how closely the film wishes to adhere to its source.[19] As is to be expected, Leonidas is equal to the momentous prophecy: "It is either Sparta or a Spartan king. I accept the challenge." During the battle at Thermopylae he will defiantly reject Xerxes' offer, made by Hydarnes, leader of the Persian Immortals, of sparing the Spartans' lives if they surrender. He does so, in both Greek and English, with one of the pithiest sayings ever recorded in antiquity: "*Molôn labe.* Come and get them!"[20]

Variations on the theme of the Delphic oracle appear in various cinematic contexts. The earliest example is the one-minute film *The Oracle of Delphi* (1903) by Georges Méliès, a modern story. A thief, played by Méliès himself, breaks into a storehouse to steal a precious object, but "a bearded figure emerges from the darkness and frightens the thief into returning his ill-gotten loot."[21] Méliès pioneered an exuberant use of trick cinematography such as double and multiple exposure, usually to comic effect. Special effects and other forms of trickery well serve filmmakers to present the supernatural phenomena that are part and parcel of ancient myths. So it

---

[19] The three oracles quoted above appear at Herodotus, *The Histories* 7.140–141 and 220. Green 1996: 67–68 and 95 gives the complete versions in English.

[20] Leonidas' reply is reported by Plutarch, *Sayings of Spartans* 11 (*Moralia* 225c–d). According to Plutarch, Leonidas answered in writing to a written command from Xerxes ("Send [i.e. hand over] your weapons") and referred to these weapons, not, as in the film, to the Spartans.

[21] Quotation from Niver 1985: 232, with additional information on this film. Méliès made several films on classical subjects. On Apollonian aspects of his works see Bessy and Lo Duca 1961: 14 (drawing by Méliès of a classicizing musician or dancer or perhaps even a Muse, holding a lyre above her head), 36 (drawing and text by Méliès of a satiric scene from the battle of the Lapiths and centaurs, a myth that led to one of the most famous ancient representations of Apollo, his statue on the temple of Zeus at Olympia), and 198 (design by Méliès of a scene for *Faust* with ruins of Greco-Roman architecture, part of which somewhat resembles the ruins of Apollo's temple at Delphi).

is no surprise that science-fiction and fantasy films should have oracular moments.

*The Matrix* (1999), written and directed by Andy and Larry Wachowski, is an eclectic science-fiction thriller loaded with innumerable references to popular culture, Eastern and Western religion, and various philosophical systems. Its main characters bear symbolic names like Neo (anagram of One), Morpheus, and Trinity. Neo, discovering that the world he lives in is really an illusion ruled by computers, is chosen to be the one to save mankind. Neo is taken to a woman called the Oracle in order to receive enlightenment. "She's a guide, Neo. She can help you to find the path," Morpheus explains. He also informs Neo that the Oracle is "very old": "She's been with us since the beginning." Surprisingly to Neo and to the viewers, this oracle is located in an apartment building in a lower-class section of a modern metropolis. The Oracle is an elderly and motherly woman who lives in a humble but cozy apartment, and her kitchen figures prominently in this sequence. "Not quite what you expected, right?" the Oracle observes to Neo. The famous motto "Know Thyself," one of the inscriptions on Apollo's temple at Delphi, appears in Latin (*Temet Nosce*) on a sign on the kitchen wall, and the Oracle translates it for Neo. As in Oedipus' case, the Oracle reveals part of the future to Neo ("You're going to have to make a choice") and warns him of what lies ahead ("I hate giving good people bad news"). But there is an unexpected twist. The Oracle concludes that Neo is not the One. Is she wrong? Can an oracle err? The subject of foreknowledge and fate appeared in a rather playful way a little earlier in this sequence when the Oracle mentions to Neo a vase with flowers, which he promptly breaks: "Don't worry about the vase." – "What vase?" – "*That* vase." She then asks Neo an intriguing question which, however, is left unanswered: "Would you still have broken it if I hadn't said anything?" On the soundtrack the popular standard "I'm Beginning to See the Light" provides an ironic comment during part of this sequence. At its beginning, when Neo and Morpheus entered the building, a blind old man, most likely a beggar, could briefly be seen sitting in the hallway. He nodded his head when the other two passed him as if he had recognized them. He may be an allusion to Tiresias, the blind seer in *Oedipus the King* or to the Oedipus of Sophocles' *Oedipus at Colonus*. The moment is also a brief and apparently paradoxical reminder of the theme of blindness and knowledge that is prominent in Sophocles' Oedipus plays. The two sequels of *The Matrix* – *The Matrix Reloaded* (2001) and *Matrix Revolutions* (2003) – also feature the Oracle, but do so less prominently. Still, in the third film the Latin motto from the first warrants a close-up inserted for special emphasis, and the same song can briefly be heard again on the soundtrack.

The plot of Steven Spielberg's *Minority Report* (2002) takes up the theme of fate and destiny in a futuristic crime thriller.[22] Three "precogs" – people endowed with precognition floating in a tank reminiscent of an amniotic sac – warn a special Pre-Crime police unit that murders are about to be committed; the police can then prevent these crimes. Complications ensue when one of the policemen learns that he has been identified as someone who is going to commit the murder of a man he does not even know. The precogs' surroundings in the film have vaguely religious overtones that contain distant reminiscences of ancient oracles.

In a kind of "East Meets West" adventure, the titular hero of Gordon Hessler's *The Golden Voyage of Sinbad* (1974) seeks information in the temple of the Oracle of All Knowledge. At the price of her own exhaustion and even evaporation, the temple guardian-and-priestess, a kind of Pythia figure, conjures up a theriomorphic divinity which utters its prophecy in verse, if only as doggerel. In Sam Wanamaker's *Sinbad and the Eye of the Tiger* (1977), Sinbad and his fellow adventurers travel to Hyperborea at the far north of the earth, a mythic country associated with Apollo.[23] Here they enter a sacred shrine inside a pyramid. (The film combines Arabian, Greek, and Egyptian visual and narrative elements.) A pillar of light rays magically descending from above is said to be "thrown down from the crown of Apollo itself," just as Apollo had earlier been mentioned as the source of the aurora borealis.

On a level artistically lower but representative of an especially popular film genre of the 1950s and 1960s are the Italian Hercules films. An oracle scene occurs in Carlo Ludovico Bragaglia's *Gli amori di Ercole* (1960).[24] Early in this film Hercules visits a grotto in which an unspecified but elaborately dressed prophetess resides. She is photographed from a low angle, appearing in subdued light and surrounded by clouds of smoke mysteriously swirling behind her. Hercules, a bit tired of heroism, asks her about his future:

Oracle, you who see the truth in shifting sand, in the moving tides of the sea, in the flight of birds across the skies, you to whom the stars reveal their secret and the Fates disclose the mysteries we mortals see only in our admonishing dreams, tell me if the gods have been placated at last, if after endless trials I shall have peace.

[22] On this film, especially its Oedipal themes, see Bakewell 2008.

[23] Ahl 1982 has detailed documentation.

[24] The film's English-language version, from which my quotation below is taken, is variously entitled *Loves of Hercules*, *The Love of Hercules*, and *Hercules vs. the Hydra*.

Hercules' apostrophe is elevated and flowery in a manner befitting an epic hero, but it is far from accurate because the ways he enumerates are not those in which such a prophetess receives her knowledge of the future. Observing the flight of birds, for instance, is augury and has nothing to do with oracles. Neither do dreams or the Fates. Perhaps this is the reason why the Pythia, if that is who she is, is rather aloof and unrevealing in her reply, which she ends with the unhelpful observation: "The mist returns; all is obscured by a cloud of blackness." In the vagueness of her reply, however, she adheres to the nature of most oracular utterances known from antiquity. Hercules' plea – "You must help me to bear my destiny" – remains unheeded. Predictably, however, our brawny hero will rise to all challenges that the plot holds in store for him.[25]

In 1962 an American Hercules visits Delphi in a rather low-comic context, one that has nothing at all to do with Apollo. Instead, Delphi is mentioned merely as a readily available name, chosen for being familiar to audiences whose knowledge of antiquity is not the strongest. This film is Edward Bernds's *The Three Stooges Meet Hercules*, in which a time machine transports the eponymous fools to a highly fanciful ancient Greece. Much of the film's forced comedy works by way of deliberate anachronism. Muscleman Hercules has to appear in the arena, and accordingly the *Delphi Daily* carries the headline: "Hercules Agrees to Final Bout." A poster proclaims, in Barnum-and-Bailey fashion, that "Mighty Hercules Meets the Nine-Headed Hydra" in the "Arena of Delphi" and further informs us: "Admission 5 Drachmas."

Muscleman epics were a staple of Italian cinema in the 1950s and 1960s and featured not only Hercules but also a large assortment of other classical, biblical, and freely invented heroes. Neo-mythologism was at its peak. So the gods, too, could take on bizarre neo-mythological aspects. Riccardo Freda's *The Giants of Thessaly* (1961), which is based – very loosely – on the story of Jason and the Argonauts, attributes powers to Apollo that ancient Greeks and Romans will have been highly astonished at finding associated with him. On a mysterious island the evil sorceress Gaia, who is modeled on Homer's Circe, has turned Jason's men into sheep. Gaia appears as a beautiful young woman but is really an old hag. Her good sister explains

---

[25] Shortly after this film, another cinematic Hercules receives guidance from a rather eerie (and masked) Sibyl in Mario Bava's *Ercole al centro della terra* (1961), a film remarkable for telling its neo-mythologism in the style of a horror film. The film's English titles are *Hercules in the Haunted World*, *Hercules vs. the Vampires*, *The Vampires vs. Hercules*, *Hercules at the Center of the Earth*, and *With Hercules to the Center of the Earth*. The titular vampires refer to Underworld monsters and to the presence of Christopher Lee in the role of the villainous King Lykos. Lee is best known for playing Count Dracula in several films.

**Fig. 3.** *The Magus.* The archaic smile on the face of Apollo. (Twentieth Century-Fox)

to Jason and us that Gaia is "the terrifying daughter of the great sun god." She had asked her father for "dazzling beauty so that no man thereafter could resist" her. But Apollo imposed a condition on Gaia: at sunset she turns into a horrid witch, who has to renew her good looks by praying to him: "Father of witchcraft, almighty Apollo!" Bizarrely, Gaia has to seduce Jason. If she succeeds, her beauty will become "eternal, immortal"; if she fails, her magic powers will end. No drachmas for guessing which of these alternatives occurs in the film.

The oracular or enigmatic nature of Apollo appears to good if brief effect in Guy Green's *The Magus* (1968), with a screenplay by John Fowles, the author of the novel on which the film is based. The film's critical standing is deservedly low. Its plot is muddled, its protagonist is as confused and bewildered as the spectator, and the ending is as incomprehensible as it is pointless. Unintentionally, however, one particular image in the film illustrates its very nature. The magus of the title resides on a Greek island modeled on Spetses and plays a perverse kind of mind game with the young Englishman who falls under his spell. The villa of the magus has various pieces of classical, Renaissance, and modern art on display, which may or may not be genuine. (The props used for the film were, of course, all imitations.) At the end the young Englishman finds out that the villa is deserted; all the furniture and almost all art works have vanished. But left in a kind of shuttered shrine against one of the walls in the living room he finds the bronze bust of Apollo that the magus had previously revealed to him (Fig. 3). The head of Apollo is modeled on those of archaic Greek sculptures of young men (*kouroi*); it also resembles that of the life-size terracotta statue of Aplu, the Etruscan Apollo, from Veii, now in the Villa

Giulia in Rome.[26] All these statues, and those of young women (*korai*), are most famous for their mysterious smiles. The archaic smile, as scholars call it, is one of the most fascinating features of pre-classical Greek art, likely to strike viewers as equally enigmatic as the smile of the Mona Lisa.[27] The Greek *kouros* type was frequently associated with Apollo.[28] Early in the film the magus mentions this smile, if without further comment or explanation, and director Green shows us a close-up of Apollo's bust in the center of the wide screen. He then cuts to a similar close-up of the magus's smiling face, also placed center screen. But given the uninvolving quality of the film, the magus's smile is likely to strike viewers as a meaningless smirk. By contrast, the archaic smile of Apollo, which we see again at film's end, remains unforgettable for its very refusal to yield to any interpretation the viewer might come up with. As one scholar has noted: "The 'archaic smile' . . . is not so much an emotion as a symbol, for they [the statues] are beyond emotion in the ordinary sense of the word."[29] Even if he plays no more than a minor part in a rather pretentious film, the god of light can still move in mysterious ways.

APOLLO'S LAST FRONTIER

In cinema and television even a commercial product designed for easy consumption by mass audiences can manage to make some serious points about myth and religion. This is the case in Episode 33 of the American television series *Star Trek*; its title is "Who Mourns for Adonais?" (1967), directed by Marc Daniels.[30] Arriving on an unknown planet, the crew of the spaceship Enterprise encounters Apollo, the last survivor of the ancient gods. He identifies himself with a thunderous greeting: "Welcome to Mt. Olympus, Captain Kirk!" His first words reveal that he is a god of knowledge and foresight. The earthlings initially do not know what to make of him, but fortunately a young lady on their crew with a vaguely

---

[26] All these works date to the sixth century BC. Photographs of *kouroi* whose faces look very much like that in *The Magus* may be found in Stewart 1990: vol. 2, figs. 117, 120, 125, and 127 ("Rampin rider" from the Acropolis of Athens), 135, and 168–169 (Apollo).

[27] On the archaic smile, which has parallels in or may have been influenced by oriental, especially Egyptian, art, cf. the various interpretations and comments made by Carpenter 1962: 191, Ridgway 1977: 14, Boardman 1978: 66, and Stewart 1990: vol. 1, 110. On the statues at large see Richter 1968 and 1970a, both extensively illustrated.

[28] On this see especially Burkert 1985: 143 (on *kouros* and Apollo as representations of ideal Greek culture), followed by Stewart 1990: vol. 1, 110.

[29] The quotation is from Pollitt 1999: 9.

[30] Wenskus 2002: 132–133 discusses this episode and mentions (130) that the motto of the Starfleet Academy (*Ex astris scientia*) is patterned on that of NASA's Apollo missions (*Ex luna scientia*).

Greek name – she is called Carolyn Palamas – has the requisite training as an A and A Officer, whose specialty is "archaeology, anthropology, ancient civilizations," as one crew member puts it. (Such an officer appears only in this episode.) A line in the dialogue at this moment is disarming in its naiveté; it expresses the general twentieth-century (and future) ignorance of classical antiquity: "We're going to need help in all those areas!"

Such help Carolyn is ready to provide. The information she gives Kirk and the others is largely accurate and only slightly neo-mythological:

Apollo – eh, twin brother of Artemis, son of the god Zeus and Leto, a mortal. He was the god of light and purity. He was skilled in the bow and the lyre.

The goddess Leto has become mortal for script purposes because this change informs viewers unschooled in Greek mythology that ancient gods used to have sexual relations with humans and prepares them for the ensuing almost-romance between Apollo and Carolyn. Through this liaison Apollo intends to repopulate his solitary planet with a new race of worshipers. The episode thus addresses some of the main issues that are important in Greek mythology and the literature derived from it. A god cannot exist without worshipers; in return for his demands – "I want from you what is rightfully mine: your loyalty, your tribute, and your worship," says Apollo – he offers "life in paradise." Apollo sees himself as the literal and figurative father of these and future humans. As an infatuated Carolyn says later: "He wants to provide for us. He'll give us everything we ever wanted. And he can do it, too."

There is also a brief explanation of the origin of religion and mythology from an appropriately futuristic perspective. Its neo-mythological overtones anticipate part of Erich von Däniken's *Chariots of the Gods* hypothesis.[31] Nevertheless Captain Kirk's speculation to Dr. McCoy about Apollo is in keeping with more rigorous scholarly analysis:

*Kirk*: Apollo's no god. But – he *could* have been taken for one, though – once. Say, five thousand years ago, a highly sophisticated group of space travelers landed on Earth, around the Mediterranean.
*McCoy*: Yes, to the simple shepherds and tribesmen of early Greece creatures like that *would* have been gods.
*Kirk*: Especially if they had the power to alter their forms at will and command great energy. In fact, they couldn't have been taken for anything else.

---

[31] The German title of Däniken 1968 (in English: Däniken 1970; reprinted in 1999 without the question mark) translates as "Remembrances of the Future: Unsolved Riddles of the Past." A companion book to this pseudo-scientific bestseller (Däniken 1973; in English: Däniken 1974) duly followed, as did a film: Harald Reinl's *Erinnerungen an die Zukunft* (1970; English title: *Chariots of the Gods*, without the question mark). The film's English ads asked: "Was God an Astronaut?"

Apollo himself explains why belief in classical myth declined and why humans turned away from the gods. His words to Carolyn not only corroborate Kirk's speculation about the original intergalactic abode of the gods but also echo ancient perspectives on man's intellectual development from belief to reason, from *mythos* to *logos*.[32] Rather surprisingly, Apollo's mention of the overreaching and dangerous ingenuity of the human mind even parallels the theme of Sophocles' famous *polla ta deina* ode from *Antigone*:

*Apollo*:   We're immortal, we gods. But the Earth changed, your fathers changed. They turned away until we were only memories. God [sic] cannot survive as a memory. We need love, admiration, worship, as you need food.
*Carolyn*:   You really think you're a god?
*Apollo*:   In a real sense we *were* gods. We had the power of life and death. We could have struck out from Olympus and destroyed. We had no wish to destroy. So we came home again. It was an empty place without worshipers, but we had no strength to leave. So we waited, all of us, through the long years . . . Even for a god there's a point of no return . . . But I knew you would come, you striving, bickering, foolishly brave humans. I knew you would come to the stars one day.

When angry, this Apollo goes into neo-mythological Zeus mode. He does not shoot arrows like his classical model, but the "far-shooting" Apollo of the future hurls lightning bolts and even causes a storm[33] (Fig. 4). When he demonstrates some of these powers, Carolyn brings up another fundamental question inherent in myth and religion: "How can they worship you if you hurt them?"

These moments show that even as hokey a product of mass culture as this can exhibit a certain degree of sophistication. But there is more. A rather sinister side to the apparently benign figure of Apollo becomes explicit when he paints a picture of the paradise he envisions as the result of his union with Carolyn. He tells her:

You'll all be provided for, cared for, happy. There is an order of things in this universe. Your species has denied it. I come to restore it. And for you: because you have the sensitivity to understand, I offer you more than your wildest dreams have ever imagined. You'll become the mother of a new race of gods. You'll inspire the universe. All men will revere you almost as a god yourself.

---

[32] The scholarly *locus classicus* for this is Nestle 1941, on which see Most 1999.

[33] This Apollo's use of lightning bolts is, however, not simply an instance of Hollywood's carelessness with or ignorance of myth. Ancient gods could, as it were, "borrow" Zeus' lightning on occasion. Alcibiades put an image of Eros, the god of love, wielding a lightning bolt on his shield (Plutarch, *Alcibiades* 16); the Indo-Greek king Menander put Athena with her father's lightning bolt on the reverse of a silver tetradrachm minted around 160–130 BC. Illustration in Green 1990: 322 fig. 104.

**Fig. 4.** *Star Trek*: "Who mourns for Adonais?" Apollo hurling lightning. (Paramount)

Apollo's speech points to twentieth-century totalitarianism, in which an all-powerful individual, accorded quasi-divine status, receives unquestioning obedience from his subjects so that a new and perfect race of supermen may achieve their earthly paradise in a new order under his leadership. Perhaps it is not by accident that Apollo, when he refers to the happiness of future humans, raises his right arm to a horizontal level in front of his body in a hint at the Fascist salute, a gesture emphasized by a medium close-up shot. We hardly need Kirk later telling Carolyn about Apollo: "He thrives on love, worship, attention . . . Accept him, and you'll condemn all of us to slavery, nothing less than slavery." This realization is based on Apollo's earlier show of force and on his words to Kirk: "We shall not debate, mortal . . . what I ask for I insist upon."

The episode's conclusion, although melodramatic and with an Apollo reduced to tears, still manages to be emotionally involving even to viewers who are not Trekkies. Modern and secularized, *homo technologicus* refuses to believe in and worship a traditional god. "We've outgrown you," Kirk tells Apollo, "you asked for something we can no longer give." (This is despite Kirk's earlier token affirmation of religion: "Mankind has no need for gods. We find the One quite adequate.") Such a refusal leads to Apollo's extinction. Rather touchingly the source of his interplanetary power – in science-fiction terms, his "energy" and "technology," which he controls through a mysterious "organ" in his chest – turns out to be his temple, which the Enterprise destroys. Apollo now chooses death: "The time is past," he realizes, "there is no room for gods." The episode thus illustrates the conclusion of Joseph Campbell's once influential view of myth in today's scientific and technological world. Having quoted Friedrich Nietzsche ("Dead are all the gods"), Campbell goes on to say:

> It is not only that there is no hiding place for the gods from the searching telescope and microscope; there is no such society any more as the gods once supported . . . Isolated societies, dream-bounded within a mythologically charged horizon, no longer exist except as areas to be exploited. And within the progressive societies themselves, every last vestige of the ancient human heritage of ritual, morality, and art is in full decay.[34]

Campbell's perspective on myth, here projected into the future, prompts Kirk to a poignant résumé about the ancient Greeks, on which the episode ends: "They gave us so much. The Greek civilization, much of our culture and philosophy come from the worship of those beings, the way they began, the Golden Age . . ."

This ending justifies the episode's title, which derives from high culture and may at first strike viewers as pretentious. "Who Mourns for Adonais?" is a quotation from line 415 of Shelley's "Adonais: An Elegy on the Death of John Keats" (1821), which in turn is based on the ancient Greek poems by Theocritus and Bion on the death of the proverbially handsome youth Adonis (or Adonais).[35] The death of the young poet and the extinction of the god of poetry are instances of loss and causes for mourning. In Shelley's poem, the Muse mourns for Adonais. But in today's age of advanced technology and general historical and cultural amnesia, where is the Muse to mourn for Apollo?[36]

---

[34] Quoted from Joseph Campbell 1968: 387–388.

[35] Theocritus 15 (*Syrakosiai ê Adôniazousai*: "The Women of Syracuse, or The Women at the Festival of Adonis"); Bion 1 (*Epitaphios Adônidos*: "Lament for Adonis"). Texts and English translations of these poems are easily accessible in Edmonds 1938: 175–195 and 385–395. For Shelley see Knerr 1984.

[36] Here is a list of some non-classical Apollos. In science fiction the name Apollo appears because of the names from Greek mythology that have been given to most constellations and that are also prominent in space travel. The television series *Battlestar Galactica* (1978) and related TV films have a Captain Apollo, advanced to Commander Apollo in *Battlestar Galactica: The Second Coming* (1999). William Hanna and Joseph Barbera's animated *Jetsons: The Movie* (1990), an expansion of their 1960s television series, includes someone called Apollo Blue. But Ron Howard's *Apollo 13* (1995), a film about that ill-fated moon mission, makes no mention of Apollo at all. – Several characters called Apollo appear in film stories set in modern times. In the silent era, B. A. Rolfe's crime drama *Miss*

THE MUSE'S INSPIRATION

Films in which the Muses appear are few.[37] Best known today is the animated Disney feature *Hercules* (1997), a musical comedy-adventure directed by John Musker and Ron Clements. Before the credits the camera moves over dusty images of ancient ruins and art works to a close-up of an amphora on which we see a large painting of Hercules wrestling the Nemean lion and above on the vase's neck a small one showing five dark women. A male off-screen narrator meanwhile introduces us to ancient Greece and Hercules and portentously intones: "What is the measure of a true hero? Ah, that is what our story is – ." But a female voice interrupts him, and we see the women on the vase come to life. Although only five, they are none other than the Muses.[38] They immediately assert their authority:

*First Muse*: Will you listen to him? He's makin' the story sound like some Greek tragedy.
*Second Muse* [*to narrator*]: Lighten up, dude!
*Third Muse*: We'll take it from here, darling.
*Narrator* [*resigned*]: You go, girl.

*139* (1921) features a Professor Apollo Cawber, and in D. W. Griffith's religious melodrama *The White Rose* (1923), set in the American South, a character is nicknamed Apollo. Another Apollo appears in Sydney Morgan's *Shadow of Egypt* of 1924. "Johnny Apollo" is the protagonist's alias in Henry Hathaway's 1940 *film noir* of that name. Another Apollo is in Daniel Mann's *A Dream of Kings* (1969), based on a work by Greek-American author Harry Mark Petrakis and set among Chicago's Greek population. The black boxer Apollo Creed is the eponymous hero's formidable antagonist in four of the five *Rocky* films directed by John G. Avildsen (1976) and Sylvester Stallone (1979, 1982, 1985). – In the late 1990s Greek mythology made a popular comeback to television in the series *Hercules: The Legendary Journeys* and in some television or video films spun off it or the Disney film discussed in this chapter, such as *Hercules: Zero to Hero* (1999). Greek gods, including Apollo, play prominent roles in this Hercules' adventures. So do the Muses. In the animated Japanese *Arion* (1986), directed by Mamoru Hamasu and Yoshikazu Yasuhiko, Apollo is a "bad guy" who also wants to rule over the Titans. Earlier, *The Illiac Passion* (1967), directed by Gregory J. Markopoulos and loosely based on Aeschylus' *Prometheus Bound*, also features an Apollo, although its ancient model did not. Other curios with an Apollo are the silent *The Triumph of Venus* (1918), directed by Edwin Bower Hesser, and *The Affairs of Aphrodite* (1970), directed by Alain Patrick. – The 1980s television series *Magnum, P. I.* featured Doberman guard dogs named Apollo and Zeus. From among related names I only list Apollonia, the first wife of Michael Corleone in Francis Ford Coppola's *The Godfather* (1972) and Apollonius of Tyana in George Pal's *7 Faces of Dr. Lao* (1964), originally a first-century AD Greek philosopher and the subject of a fictionalized biography from the early third century.

[37] A curiosity is the opening sequence of Stuart Walker's (and, uncredited, Mitchell Leisen's) romantic comedy *Tonight Is Ours* (1933), set at a masked ball. A still with star Claudette Colbert in a harlequin suit standing before a wall painting of one of the Muses, with the name Euterpe on its pedestal, may be found in Chierichetti 1995: 49.

[38] The Muses' earliest screen appearance may well be in George Méliès's brief farce *Jupiter's Thunder* of 1903, in which their statues come alive. Carmine Gallone's epic *The Last Days of Pompeii* (1926) brings the Muses to life in a similar fashion, if within a different plot context: in "a clever insanity scene," "Glaucus stares at a fresco of Zeus and the dancing Muses, and the figures on the wall suddenly come alive!" Quoted from Solomon 2001: 82.

With snappy gospel songs, the chorus of these Muses now takes over and provides a commentary on the film's action. The narrator is never heard from again. (His voice is that of Charlton Heston, who in his time had played real and fictional ancient heroes.) But these Muses first have to introduce themselves to their audiences, who may not otherwise recognize them: "We're the Muses, goddesses of the arts and proclaimers of heroes . . ." Having left the frame inside which they had been painted, they introduce, to continuing gospel rhythms, the mythical prehistory of Hercules, beginning with Zeus' defeat of the Titans: "He hurled his thunderbolt, / locked those suckers in a vault . . . And that's the gospel truth!" This last becomes their regular refrain.

Despite their warning about Greek tragedy in the prologue, the film has the Muses return in good tragic fashion throughout the story being told. Singing and dancing at appropriate moments in the story, they provide musical interludes and comment on the action, just as the chorus on the classical Greek stage had done in its *stasima*, the odes it performed on the stage. The Muses provide the cue – or is it the inspiration? – to the film's gleefully irreverent Americanized and multicultural narrative about a Hercules who grows from "zero to hero." Lest energy flag, they may even exhort one another ("Tell it, girl!"). That the facts of Hercules' life and adventures preserved in classical mythology take a backseat to their fanciful retelling is unavoidable. Despite some excesses as with a satyr called Phil (for Philoctetes) who becomes Hercules' friend and helper alongside his winged horse Pegasus, the film is a witty rewriting of Greek myth as a satire of modern consumerism and celebrity cults. "Herc" becomes a sports superstar and, for example, the sponsor of "Grecian Express" credit cards. His romantic entanglements with Megara ("Meg"), a slinky and sultry redhead with a New York accent, and his defeat of his arch-enemy Hades lead to the inevitable happy ending on Mt. Olympus. Here the Muses sing their final song ("A star is born"). They are prompted by Hermes ("Hit it, ladies!"), but Apollo as sun god is briefly to be seen and heard, too. As had been the case with the exit song (*exodos*) of the chorus on the Greek stage, the purpose of the Motown Muses' final ode is to bring home to the viewers the lesson to be learned from the story they have been watching:

> Just remember, in the darkest hour
> within your heart's the power
> for makin' you
> a hero, too.
> So don't lose hope when you're forlorn . . .

Although there is nothing profound here, it is amusing to see modern American obsessions, especially those with teenage self-esteem and the turmoil caused by adolescent stirrings of love and sex, being projected onto a story of venerable antiquity that is, at the same time, being told with state-of-the-art animation technology. But not least because of the infectious rhymes and rhythms of our Muses we leave the theater happy and entertained. Small wonder that the film inspired an animated television series and a video sequel.[39]

Two years after this *Hercules*, Sharon Stone in the title role of Albert Brooks's Hollywood-insider comedy *The Muse* provides a different kind of story inspiration, this time to various film producers, writers, and directors. Among these are Rob Reiner, Martin Scorsese, and James Cameron, for whose successes she turns out to have been responsible. This thoroughly modern Muse is a material girl who expects lavish and expensive presents and treats: "The happier she is, the better Muse she is. Don't you want the best Muse you can get?" On the other hand, she causes considerable domestic upheaval in the life and marriage of the film's main character, a failing screenwriter. "Never get too close to a Muse," he is warned by a more experienced friend. And: "You don't want to piss off a Muse. If you get them angry, they can do the opposite of what they're supposed to do." As befits a sex symbol, Stone even has a moment of callipygian nudity. But at the end a plot twist reveals her to be not a real Muse but an impostor, an escapee from a mental institution with a multiple personality. However, yet another twist gives her the upper hand, at least for a while. And a particular comment about Hollywood as producer of illusions and caterer to the fantasies of people around the globe may even remind us of all the neo-mythologism that the dream factory regularly turns out: "This is Hollywood . . . . People here believe anything, don't they?"

### TERPSICHORE'S EPIPHANY

The most fascinating of all films featuring the Muses is Alexander Hall's musical comedy-romance *Down to Earth* (1947), in which an earlier Hollywood sex symbol, Rita Hayworth, plays Terpsichore. Although it suffers from a stereotypical plot, this film is of considerable interest for its presentation of Greek culture in modern society. The plot is about one

---

[39] Solomon 2001: 123–124 points to a number of the film's cinematic sources and outlines its titanic commercial success.

**Fig. 5.** *Down to Earth.* "Swinging the Muses" and the wrong Terpsichore. (Columbia)

Danny Miller, a young and struggling producer and writer-director, who is in rehearsals and then try-outs for his Broadway musical "Swinging the Muses." In this show two American aviators, whose plane has crashed into Mt. Parnassus, promptly encounter the Muses – a novel kind of the venerable *gradus ad Parnassum* of old. Bizarrely, the chief Muse, Terpsichore, then wants to marry both of them. But the real Terpsichore up in the heavens gets wind of this windy story. Outraged, she comes down to earth, takes over the lead in the show – as herself, of course, although she does not reveal her true identity and takes an American name – and proceeds to change the show from a brash musical to something authentic. (She is, after all, the expert.) The contrast between both versions of "Swinging the Muses" is instructive. Our first glimpse of how its producer intends it to be is the film's biggest production number, a brassy and swinging big-band song in the musical and verbal style popular in the 1940s (Fig. 5). Eight of the American Muses, holding little toy lyres as a visual reminder of the Apollonian art of poetry and song, begin by introducing themselves and the show's topic, then call upon their sister, who is arriving just in time:

> In section Two-Four-Six A-B
> at your public library
> books on Greek mythology
> are gettin', gettin' dusty on the shelves.
>    It's nigh on two thousand years
> since we started our careers.
> No one digs us, it appears,
> so we must, we must talk about ourselves.
>    We're the nine Muses, nine Muses,
> and we live on Mt. Parnassus;
> we're the goddesses who
> bring art and culture to you.
>    Terpsichore, Terpsichore,
> give with the news of the Muse!

These hip-swinging Muses are swinging hipsters, up on the latest jive. So is Terpsichore, who now takes over:

> Well, hello, Jack, what's new outside?
> I just got back from a chariot ride.
> I heard I've been elected to
> tell you what we Muses do.
> The jive is that from way back when
> our kiss could inspire many men
> to sing, to dance, to act, to paint;
> it's up to us if they is or ain't.
> For instance, take a chick like me;
> they call me Terpsichore.
> I'm the goddess of song and dance;
> I put the ants in the dancers' pants.
> The nine of us in our careers
> kissed three million guys in two thousand years.

Together, the Muses proceed to provide a catalogue of "the characters we kissed," a witty potpourri of artists from Renaissance Europe – e.g. Bellini – to popular America – e.g. Benny Goodman. (Swing-era singer Kay Starr dubbed the voice of the actress playing Terpsichore in this scene.) But the divine Terpsichore is outraged and tells her sisters about Miller's show and her own portrayal as "a modern, jiving sexpot."[40] This leads to a clever and funny dialogue scene among the heavenly Muses (Fig. 6):

*Terpsichore*: It's disgraceful!
*A Muse*: What's so disgraceful about that?
*A Muse*: We've been glorified in song and story for centuries.

[40] Kobal 1978: 165.

**Fig. 6.** *Down to Earth.* The heavenly Muses aghast at Terpsichore's news about the American Muses' song. (Columbia)

*A Muse*: Shakespeare, Walt Whitman, Robert Burns!

*Terpsichore*: But this barbarian isn't Shakespeare, Whitman, or Burns. Why, he's portraying us in a low and vulgar manner on the public stage. [*The Muses gasp.*] According to him, I'm nothing but a man-chasing trollop.

*The Muses*: Oh no!

*Terpsichore*: Oh yes! And as for the rest of you, he says you kissed over three million men. [*Another gasp.*] Imagine that!

*A Muse*: That's scandalous!

*A Muse*: We haven't kissed a man in over two thousand years.

*A Muse* [*demurely*]: Except Apollo – once.

*A Muse*: That could only come from America . . .

*A Muse*: Who does this savage think inspired Michelangelo, Da Vinci, Rembrandt?

*Terpsichore*: Do you know who *he's* telling the world we inspired? The man who invented the skinless weenie – a frankfurter!

*A Muse*: A frankfurter – how ghastly!

This is followed by Terpsichore's decision to take matters into her own divine hands. After all, as she says: "The theater is *my* province. It belongs to me. I'll show this Miller imbecile a thing or two."

In all this we have a case of neo-mythologism as seen through the lens of irreverent American popular culture. By contrast, the scene from "Swinging the Muses" as re-choreographed by the real Terpsichore and the general reaction to it are revealing in what they tell us about the supposedly proper attitude toward classical culture. Gone now is all the original exuberance. Jazzy rhythms have been replaced by virtually atonal music. A pretentious vocalese replaces most dialogue, and the sexy swing of the Muses has turned into artsy modern dance. The dark setting conveys a somber atmosphere; everything has become high-brow and is subjected to a dose of severe seriousness. The Glory That Was Greece is meant to awe the spectators, not to entertain them. But can we only appreciate ancient Greece if we adopt a reverential attitude? Such a perspective is unappealing to modern society and therefore cannot prevail. To put it in the terms of a contemporary hit, a show about the Muses "don't mean a thing if it ain't got that swing." As we observe on screen, audiences are falling asleep. Not only that, but the theater-goers are mainly older high-society types, whose cultural pretensions the film briefly satirizes. After a performance of the new show a few elderly upper-class art connoisseurs approach Terpsichore with fulsome if utterly clichéd words of praise: "My dear, magnificent, magnificent! Sheer poetry – poetry of movement. Why, every scene a painting!" One of the art experts is an old lady with a suitably starchy name ("I'm Mrs. Fenimore Hume"), president of the Pure Art Forum. But it is evident that this kind of show will never open on Broadway, and Terpsichore eventually relents in order to save it from being a flop.

As we might expect, the Muse of theater and dance makes sure that she takes center stage and appears particularly attractive in her own production. Her clothing, for instance, is both elegant and revealing[41] (Fig. 7). For this there are two chief reasons, one within the film's plot and one outside. Terpsichore is now her own choreographer, and the filmmakers have to show off their star. As a result, the ballet that we are to consider bad and unsuitable for commercial success is the film's greatest set piece, a veritable show stopper:

the Greek Ballet . . . is at once pretentious, overdecorated (as well as overpopulated), and stunning in its performance values . . . The ballet is meant to be a takeoff on the elaborate "exotic" ballets of Ted Shawn and Ruth St. Denis . . . It also satirizes the mythological themes then current in the works of modern concert choreographer

---

[41] It was too revealing for the censors, who duly objected to "chiffon so diaphanous that she seemed to be wearing nothing under it" (Dick 1993: 152).

**Fig. 7.** *Down to Earth.* Terpsichore in her own production of the Greek ballet. (Columbia)

Martha Graham . . . Although the Greek Ballet is pretentious and overdone, as it is narratively supposed to be, it also was one of the most enthusiastically admired sequences in *Down to Earth* as a film – by reviewers, some of whom *also* thought that it fulfilled its diegetic [i.e. narrative] purpose (to be *bad*) admirably.[42]

These reviewers will most likely have been upper-middle-class men, if perhaps not of quite the stuffy kind as those of the Pure Art Forum. They may have responded as well to what in this ballet appears as real modern art paying homage to classical antiquity. The film's opening credits will have alerted them to the significance of this sequence, announcing a "Greek Ballet" with music by famous expatriate Italian composer Mario

---

[42] McLean 2004: 133 and 137. Cf. Kobal 1978: 165: "the highbrow-vs.-lowbrow theme backfires: the Greek ballet . . . is by far the best musical number in" the film, "not at all the constipated culture of . . . movie excursions into the ballet, with an intriguing score by a serious composer." As the film's choreographer put it: "There was a problem: to do a [dance] number that would be Terpsichore's idea of a number, and it had to ruin the show; it's very difficult to do what's supposed to be a boring number and still not be boring. I must say we solved it very well, and Rita is so beautiful in it she's not to be believed . . . She worked like a Trojan throughout the picture." Quoted from Kobal 1978: 165. On the film's production see Kobal: 164–167. Cf. Ringgold 1991: 166: "the average filmgoer couldn't discern much difference between esthetically adroit ballet and the awkwardly awful kind."

**Fig. 8.** *Down to Earth.* Terpsichore and her producer discussing Greek myth backstage. (Columbia)

Castelnuovo-Tedesco. He was evidently engaged to provide art (Pure Art?) and class to the film. But he also wrote musical scores for over two hundred Hollywood films and became one of the most influential teachers of younger and more famous film composers. In retrospect Castelnuovo-Tedesco may well have been the ideal choice to connect what could be regarded as two incompatibles: lofty European culture and barbarian or imbecile American popular culture.

Ironically, however, what is supposed to be the accurate presentation of Greek culture in this ballet is just as inauthentic as the "wrong" one had been: wrong costumes, silly headdresses, stereotypical décor. On this subject, an earlier scene is telling. Danny Miller and Terpsichore, whom he knows only as Kitty, are rehearsing. They are seen on the set and near a gigantic – and, of course, inauthentic – prop representing, of all things, a tragic mask (Fig. 8). Terpsichore is reading from her script:

*Terpsichore*: "I'm Terpsichore, the daughter of – of – ." Look, Mr. Miller, it says here "Zeus," but it's all wrong. Terpsichore is *not* the daughter of Zeus. *My* father – I mean, *her* father – was Dionysus.

*Miller*: No, no, Zeus.

*Terpsichore*: That's the popular belief. But *I* happen to know the facts. It's Dionysus.

*Miller*: I didn't put this show together with thumbtacks. It so happens that I
  looked up this particular item in the encyclopedia.

*Terpsichore*: I hate to disillusion you. But the encyclopedia is wrong.

*Miller*: No, Kitty – you know more than the Encyclopedia Britannica?

*Terpsichore*: About things like this, yes.

*Miller*: Aha!

*Terpsichore*: And now that we're on the subject: you got a lot of things wrong –

*Miller*: For instance?

*Terpsichore*: For instance, you've got me drinking ambrosia. Ambrosia is food.
  Nectar is the drink. And your scenery – why, it doesn't bear the faintest
  resemblance to Mt. Parnassus. As for your costumes –

*Miller*: Look, Kitty, I haven't time to fiddle around. Do you mind?

As ancient authors and modern encyclopedias and handbooks on Greek
myth unequivocally tell us, the Muses are indeed the daughters of Zeus and
not of Dionysus. So the "real" Terpsichore is wrong, and the "barbarian"
Miller is right. On the other hand, he is wrong and she is right about
nectar and ambrosia.[43] She is also right about his set decorations, but
her own set design is just as wrong as his had been. But none of this is a
problem for the film, just as most audiences would have overlooked that the
credits misspelled composer Castelnuovo-Tedesco's name ("Castelnuova-
Tedesco") or not taken offense at – or even have noticed – the strange
costuming of the stage Muses in the original version of "Swinging the
Muses." There eight of the Muses had dark pink ribbons on their white
dresses while Terpsichore was distinguished from them by a dress entirely in
pink. Moreover all these Muses wore head decorations of dark pink grapes.
The pink color – the Homeric term *oinops* ("wine-dark") will immediately
come to any classical scholar's mind – and even more the grapes are obvious
hints at Dionysus. So why does Miller have the daughters of Zeus dressed
as if they were indeed daughters of Dionysus? The Muses in Terpsichore's
reworking of the show do not wear these grapes, but they also no longer
hold lyres. Why don't they? No explanation is ever provided. Nor does there
seem to be a problem for the film's director and screenwriters with having

---

[43] Lack of familiarity with classical myth can lead a modern scholar astray: "Here the slippage becomes
  close to vertiginous, for she is correct; she *has* to be correct (she *is* Terpsichore, she knows who her
  own father is, and ambrosia *is* food). But *Danny* has to be correct in the film" (McLean 2004: 137).
  The slippage becomes less slippery if we remember that both Terpsichore and Danny are voicing
  lines provided by the screenwriters, who could have consulted an encyclopedia or a handbook on
  myth.

one of the Muses admit that she once kissed Apollo. Apollo is mentioned for his close association with the Muses, his half-sisters in myth, but nowhere in the ancient sources does he ever kiss any of them.[44] The moment is the more remarkable in that, to Puritan America, a kiss of the sort implied here between Apollo and one of the Muses would come uncomfortably close to the violation of a sexual taboo. From this modern perspective, even if the Muses *were* the daughters of Dionysus, it would be equally inappropriate for them to kiss Apollo because they would still be half-sisters to him. (Apollo and Dionysus are both sons of Zeus.) But then, what kind of kiss might this have been, anyway? The only context for the Muses' kiss mentioned in *Down to Earth* is that of artistic inspiration, not eroticism or love. (This also makes it acceptable that "Madame Tetrazzini" – that is, famous opera singer Luisa Tetrazzini – is listed among the "three million guys" whom the earthly Terpsichore reports the Muses to have kissed.) So again Apollo is an unsuitable object of such a kiss, because as the god of music and poetry and as leader of the Muses he hardly depends on them for inspiration.

A minor point is the Muses' age or rather the chronology of their existence. Both the "wrong" Muses and the real Terpsichore refer to a period of "two thousand years." But two millennia back from the mid-twentieth century brings us only into the Roman, not the Greek, period of antiquity. So the Muses are considerably older, even by millennia. Presumably the real Terpsichore would know how old she is. The reason for the erroneous chronology is that it does not matter: the scriptwriters' "two thousand years" serves to take us back to a generic antiquity, and to all intents and purposes that is quite sufficient. Who needs pedantry or exactitude? Neo-mythologism prevails.

There is, however, yet another side to all this. *Down to Earth* is a loose sequel to director Hall's *Here Comes Mr. Jordan* (1941), a romantic comedy about reincarnation. To appeal to the widest possible audience and to avoid disturbing anybody's religious sensibilities, this film's view of the afterlife is entirely secularized. The titular figure serves as a kind of modern Charon who organizes the dead souls' passage to heaven. An airplane is their means of transportation. This set-up duly recurs in *Down to Earth* but now makes

---

[44] It is true, however, that Pindar, *Pythian Ode* 4.176–177, and Ovid, *Metamorphoses* 10.167, call Orpheus, son of the Muse Calliope, a son of Apollo, which would make him the product of incest. But both poets are more likely to mean the phrase in a figurative sense (Orpheus as godlike singer). Orpheus' father is commonly the Thracian river god Oeagrus (so Pindar, Fragm. 139.9, and Plato, *Symposium* 179d).

for a strange mixture of Greek antiquity and American modernity, as when we see Terpsichore appealing to Mr. Jordan at the beginning for permission to come to earth and at the end for being allowed a reunion with Danny Miller, with whom she has fallen in love. In a flash-forward Mr. Jordan grants her a glimpse of Danny and herself at the moment of his boarding the heavenly plane once his time has come. Love conquers all – even at the price of mixing characters and plot devices that had better remained separate. The power of Hollywood to induce willing suspension of disbelief in its paying customers seems limitless.

So we may conclude that the filmmakers combine Greek myth, neo-mythologism, and their remarkable conceptions of Greek art and architecture in a gleefully unconcerned manner, at the same time throwing in a hefty measure of "cinematic intertextuality," as it might be called. Only scholars are liable to tear their hair. But do they not also run the risk of being as stuffy as the members of the Pure Art Forum?

What is most telling is the film's dual view of classical antiquity. If Greek myth is to be appealing to modern mass audiences, it has to be updated. In the process it is distorted and cannot avoid becoming neo-mythological. The real past is too alien and remote. Disney's *Hercules* with its multicultural characters and their relentlessly Americanized names ("Herc," "Phil," "Meg") is a recent case in point.[45] There is a lesson in this for all those who want to keep antiquity alive today, for most people derive their usually neo-mythological knowledge from films and television. In our society at large, books on Greek mythology and classical culture are indeed gettin' dusty on the shelves, but the stories told in the popular visual media save the day for a chick like Terpsichore.

Rita Hayworth's popular honorific was "love goddess," and advertisements for *Down to Earth* made sure that potential audiences realized her appeal: "The Screen's Most Gloriously Gorgeous Goddess."[46] A contemporary article by Winthrop Sargeant in *Life* magazine was preceded by a full-page color illustration of Hayworth as Terpsichore. Sargeant, who is occasionally glib and frequently condescending to his subject, compares Hayworth to Aphrodite and comments on *Down to Earth*:

---

[45] Such abbreviations have a long history, however, and are not exclusively American (or low-brow). In George Bernard Shaw's *Androcles and the Lion* (1913), for example, Androcles becomes "Andy" (and even "Andy Wandy" in his baby talk during his first encounter with the lion); his nagging wife Megaera is "Meggy." In the Danish film to be discussed in the next section of this chapter, Polyhymnia is regularly called "Polly" and "Hymnia."

[46] Quoted from Ringgold 1991: 165. *Down to Earth* was Columbia Studios' most expensive film and a great box-office success. Critical opinions were mixed.

It is a ritual in which the great American love goddess re-enacts her perpetual legend . . . she is Aphrodite. The proper heading for the discussion of this phenomenon is, obviously, not esthetics but theology . . . Its [the legend's] supernatural or purely mythological character is attested by the fact that it has nothing whatever to do with real life. The goddess, endowed by a vast priesthood of make-up men, costumers, cameramen and hairdressers with a concentrated allure no real woman could approach, moves through the ritual as its center and goal . . . Despite the fact that sex is presented here as sugar-frosted dream of romance rather than a procreative reality, no doubt is left as to its all-pervading power.

After discussing Americans' readiness to embrace the cult of the love goddess in its various incarnations (Clara Bow, Jean Harlow, Lana Turner, Betty Grable, and others), Sargeant continues: "the supreme enactment of her religious rite takes place in the darkened temples of American moviedom."[47] The epiphany of the love goddess or of Terpsichore on our silver screens, the domain of the god of light, grants the ancient gods a new kind of immortality.

### DOWN TO EARTH AGAIN

Two films inspired by *Down to Earth* further illustrate the range of cinematic neo-mythologism. A positive example is Torben Anton Svendsen's musical-comedy-romance *Mød mig paa Cassiopeia* ("Meet Me on Cassiopeia"; 1951), a classic of Danish cinema.[48] This time Polyhymnia, "the Muse of music and song," comes down to earth to help a struggling composer with an operetta ("Fly With Me") currently in rehearsal. He is suffering from composer's block, not least because the star of his show is his estranged wife, with whom he is still in love but who is flirting with his friend, a dashing aviator and ladykiller. The composer sees statues of Zeus and some of the Muses in a museum. "It had happened before that classical beauty brought down inspiration," he says. He also meets his friend's Greek aunt, who works in the museum as ancient art curator. Near a statue of Polyhymnia the aunt helpfully tells him that the Muses are "the daughters of the guy over there, Zeus," informs him that this one "takes care of composers," and urges him to inform the statue about his address, which he does ("I wish she'd take care of me"). Polyhymnia herself, played by a radiant Bodil Kjer on the cusp of her distinguished career on the Danish stage and screen, duly appears and offers her help (Fig. 9). At the same time she hopes that the

---

[47] Sargeant 1947: 81 and 82.
[48] An affectionate tribute to it is Lars Christiansen's short film *Two for Cassiopeia, a Love Story* (2000), which reworks the earlier film's story line.

**Fig. 9.** *Mød mig paa Cassiopeia.* Polyhymnia come down to earth. (Nordisk Film)

two of them will fall in love: "Venus says that kissing is wonderful." This ravishing Muse in Grecian-type dress is quickly at home in the modern world. Her strong feeling for feminine elegance makes her realize that Mt. Olympus is seriously behind in ladies' fashion: "I've worn the same white dress for two thousand years." She readily takes up smoking, indeed uses cigarette smoke along with her divine breath as a means to inspire the composer and others.

Virginal Polyhymnia then falls for the aviator and even inspires *him* to compose. But Zeus is concerned about his daughter's dallying with a mortal, and when she ignores his authority he himself comes down to earth as well. He appears at a costume ball given by the Greek aunt where his Olympian garb is entirely apropos. But Zeus parties too hard. He temporarily loses his lightning bolt, the source of most of his divine powers, and lands in jail for drunk and disorderly conduct. "Oh, daddy, always in trouble on earth," comments Polyhymnia.

The film is one of the most light-hearted comedies about the ancient gods, but it becomes even more effective through its bitter-sweet overtones. Polyhymnia has long been lonely on Olympus. Her refuge is Cassiopeia, her favorite constellation. When the aviator temporarily forgets his romantic promise to fly there with her, she feels abandoned; she also sees the composer's wife as a rival for her lover's affection. Dedicated to help with the opening of the show, however, she sticks by her duty. A highlight of the film is "Between Heaven and Earth," a poignant song Polyhymnia sings to herself:

> A Muse on her own has a hard time in this world.
> She's not in her place between heaven and earth.
> I toil and I sweat, but it's all to no avail;
> good humor and a nice body – everything fails!
> I was really looking forward [to] when I got here,
> but it's not as if anyone cares.
> The life of a Muse, what is it worth?
> It's just a speck of dust between heaven and earth.
>
> A Muse is a conscientious little meteor,
> always at work between heaven and earth.
> She comes when called and does the best she can,
> sacrifices herself just to save a man.
> But what does she get out of doing her job?
> Only trouble and strife, and then she must go back up.
> She never gets any praise for the things that she does;
> she's just a speck of dust between heaven and earth.
>
> There are plenty of men in the world both big and small;
> they promise you all between heaven and earth.
> But the man who makes my heart beat, he's so fine;
> I know he's the one who will never be mine.
> Earth girls go to their bridal dance;
> there will never be a Muse who gets the same chance.
> No, Muses should stay at home far away in their world;
> their hearts are broken between heaven and earth.[49]

This inelegant because rather literal translation does no justice to the song's melancholic nature, reinforced by the darkness that surrounds Polyhymnia on the empty theater stage. This Muse sings the blues, if not in a literal sense. "Love is horrid; I've learned that much," Polyhymnia concludes. But she is too rash, for can a charming story about an irresistible Muse end unhappily? Of course not, and a final plot twist proves what the composer had told her earlier: "Nothing is impossible in love." Although forced by Zeus to return to him on Olympus, Polyhymnia secures his agreement to a

---

[49] My quotations from the film, with occasional minimal adjustments, are all taken from the subtitles of the DVD edition published by Nordisk Film in 2000. It reproduces the original program book with the Danish text of Polyhymnia's and other songs, together with the scenes' soundtracks.

happy ending. The aviator realizes that he is seriously in love with her and attempts to fly to Cassiopeia to meet her. But this cannot be, and Zeus' lightning bolt forces him to return to earth. When he leaves his plane, he meets a stewardess who bears an uncanny resemblance to his beloved. They walk off together. In addition, the composer's show is a hit, and he and his wife are reunited.

Some neo-mythological humor reinforces the playfulness of Svendsen's film. When her aviator becomes too ardent in his kisses and embraces, Polyhymnia rebuffs him: "No. This is no good. It would upset the whole of mythology." Similarly the Greek aunt finds out that the man she thought was only a mortal in Zeus' costume really is Zeus. She immediately embarks on a scholarly project to have Zeus tell her the real stories of Greek mythology. "As for my adventure with Leda, whom I visited as a swan – quite frankly, a disappointment," Zeus reveals to her. "I prefer sex without feathers." The aunt, who is taking it all down, is delighted: "Sex without – . This book will be a scientific sensation: *The Truth About Zeus*. I'll be locked up." No doubt, *this* book on Greek mythology, if it could ever exist, would not be getting dusty on the shelves at your public library.

If *Mød mig paa Cassiopeia* is an elegant soufflé of a film, the opposite is true for Robert Greenwald's *Xanadu* (1980). The charm of the earlier work is sadly lacking, and its Terpsichore, a bland blonde played by pop singer Olivia Newton-John, is no match for Rita Hayworth's. This time around the artistic achievement, if such it can be called, around which the plot revolves is the opening of a disco-music roller rink, the eponymous Xanadu. In Los Angeles a young graphic artist makes his living painting advertisements but aspires to higher things. In frustration he tears up one of his drawings and throws it out of the window. But the wind carries some of the scraps to a mural on which the nine Muses are painted. They now magically come to life during the film's first musical number. Its vapid lyrics are sung, strangely enough, by a male voice: "I'm alive . . . Suddenly I am here today; / seems like forever from today . . . Is this really me? I'm alive . . ." Since the film reflects the youth culture of southern California in the late 1970s, one of the Muses then approaches the young man on roller skates, kisses him, and vanishes. Naturally he immediately falls in love with this mystery girl and in due course finds her. The inevitable romance ensues. Eventually she discloses her true identity to him:

*Terpsichore*: I'm not as I appear to you. Have you ever heard the expression "kissed by a Muse"? I am – I'm a Muse . . . I come from Mt. Helicon. I'm a daughter of Zeus. I have eight sisters. My real name is Terp – [*she is interrupted by his kiss*]. Look up the word "Muse" in a dictionary . . . Read it.

*Sonny [reads from a dictionary that happens to be handy]*: "Muse": . . . "Any of the
    nine sister goddesses in Greek mythology presiding over song and poetry and
    the arts and sciences . . ."

When Terpsichore then turns on the television set, she appears in an old *film
noir* that is being broadcast. Her black-and-white self and other characters
also interact with her modern self. This is meant to illustrate to the viewers
of *Xanadu* the supernatural and eternal nature of the Muses. Terpsichore
continues her cultural lesson with a brief neo-mythological recapitulation
of a point already made in *Down to Earth*:

We've been painted by Michelangelo. Shakespeare's written sonnets about us.
Beethoven's played music for us. We're not supposed to feel emotion or show any
feelings. Muses are just supposed to inspire. I fell in love . . . It was a mistake. I
broke the rules . . . I'll love you forever.

To ensure a happy ending the plot has Sonny discover and magically enter
the Muses' mural. But he finds himself and his Muse in a supernatural
limbo, from which the off-screen voice of Zeus bids him return. (Film
lovers will note with chagrin that distinguished British actor Wilfrid Hyde-
White provides this voice.) But Zeus is rather befuddled about time; being
immortal, he forgets the difference between a moment and eternity and
thus mistakenly grants Terpsichore her wish to remain with her earthly
lover, if only as a mortal. A second voice, also off-screen but female this
time, interferes. This seems to be Zeus' wife Hera, who often in Greek
myth lords it up over her hen-pecked husband. Here she calls him "dear"
in a condescending tone and manipulates him into granting the Muse's
request as if she were her mother. She also turns out to be as clueless about
time as Zeus is.

   *Xanadu* inspired the Razzie Awards for Worst Achievement in film, and
its director won, if that is the word, the first such award in the Worst
Director category. (*O tempora, o Musae!*) The film also holds a special
place in cinematic history in that dancer Gene Kelly had his last role in
it. He plays a relic from the swing era who had been inspired by the same
Terpsichore in the 1940s and is still in love with her. In 1944 Kelly had
co-starred with Rita Hayworth in Charles Vidor's glossy musical romance
*Cover Girl*. In homage to *Cover Girl* the character he plays in *Xanadu* has
the same name as did his character in the earlier film. The German release
title of *Cover Girl – Es tanzt die Göttin* ("The Goddess is Dancing") –
brings us full circle to our original Hollywood Muse.

   In a variation of the plot device in which gods or heroes from classical
mythology come down to earth, statues of them may come to life. The

best-known example is William A. Seiter's comedy-fantasy *One Touch of Venus* (1948), based on a 1944 Broadway musical with a score by Kurt Weill. (Ava Gardner is this film's love goddess.) A comic variation on this plot device is Lowell Sherman's *The Night Life of the Gods* (1935), in which an eccentric inventor brings statues of the gods in the Metropolitan Museum of Art in New York to life with his magic ring. Among them is Apollo, but he takes a backseat to some of the other gods, especially Bacchus, who lends himself more readily to comedy. In Walter Lang's *There's No Business Like Show Business* (1954), one of the earliest CinemaScope extravaganzas, a song-and-dance number has statues of young women come to life and dance. They are mute and are never identified as the Muses, but their number is nine, they wear pseudo-ancient garb, and the scenery around them features some classical-looking columns and amphoras.

A Muse of a radically different color – red – appears in Terry M. West's slasher film *Blood for the Muse* (2001). An alienated young clerk in a video store becomes obsessed with Melpomene, the Muse of tragedy, whom he believes he must attract by the serial murder of call girls. This film was never released theatrically even though gore seems to be a necessary ingredient in certain areas of cinema today.

### THE RETURN OF APOLLO

The preceding sections of this chapter have examined different approaches to Apollo and the Muses on the screen. Despite their variety all of the examples have one thing in common: none faithfully adheres to the literary or artistic tradition that has come down to us from antiquity. This is because invention is necessary for adaptations of classical culture to modern society and its mass media. Even the lowest level to which cinematic representations of the Olympians may descend reveals something about the nature of such adaptations, if only unintentionally. A case in point is Arthur Allan Seidelman's *Hercules in New York* (1970) with bodybuilder Arnold Schwarzenegger, billed as "Arnold Strong," in the title role. Scenes set on Mt. Olympus, filmed in Central Park with modern traffic audible on the soundtrack, include several of the gods. One handsome young male, wreathed and briefly seen instructing a younger god, presumably Cupid, in the art of archery, erroneously turns out to be not Apollo but Hermes. Apollo has only a verbal cameo, as it were, when Hercules, newly landed on earth and getting acquainted with the modern world, engages in the following dialogue with a New York pretzel vendor unaware of who the hulky naïf beside him in a taxi cab really is:

*Vendor*: I used to know a Greek guy . . . His name was Apollo. I never found out
   what his second name was.
*Hercules*: I know Apollo.
*Vendor*: You do? Well, is this a small world? You know Apollo? Gee. I wonder
   where Apollo is now . . .
*Hercules*: He's back home.
*Vendor*: He went home, huh? Yeah, well, he was all the time talking about how
   homesick he was . . . Say, he was a real nice guy, Apollo.
*Hercules*: Conceded. They say there's nobody handsomer than Apollo.
*Vendor*: Handsome? Apollo? Oh, you must be kidding. *Handsome?* With the big
   black wart on the end of his nose? And the little beady crossed eyes? . . . I
   wonder if Apollo ever got married. You know he was all the time looking for
   a wife . . .
*Hercules*: Diana and Terpsichore are in love with him. I think Hebe is attracted,
   too.
*Vendor*: That just shows you how desperate some women could be . . .

Their talk at cross purposes is representative of the low level of verbal and
visual humor in this film. So is the carefree mixture of Greek and Roman
names, with Zeus being married not to Hera but to Juno, etc. Evidently,
where mythology in popular culture is concerned, anything goes. This
case, however, is particularly telling because Hercules does not even know
that according to Greek myth the goddess Hebe whom he associates with
Apollo has nothing at all to do with the god but is none other than
his – Hercules' (better: Heracles') – own Olympian wife. This distortion
is probably an instance of the filmmakers' sheer ignorance. But who in the
target audience cares? Viewers who care about Apollo could conceivably
find a small measure of consolation in the fact that the filmmakers at least
know about the classical Apollo's beauty.[50]
   Even as infantile a film as *Hercules in New York* tells alert viewers something about the nature of filmic approaches to classical myth and culture.
They come to be, in their own right, part of the endless matrix, as it
might be called, of modern retellings of classical myths which are the most
powerful archetypes of our popular stories. A cinematic reincarnation of a
mythical figure closely associated with Apollo explains this phenomenon
to us. The Trojan princess Cassandra has received the gift of prophecy
from Apollo, but she is fated to make only negative predictions that no one
will believe. Near the end of Giorgio Ferroni's *La guerra di Troia* (1962)

---

[50] A brief comparable moment appears in the second episode, season two, of the television soap opera
   *Rome* (2007), in which someone is being described in these terms: "He wasn't Apollo, by no means."

Cassandra addresses Aeneas, the film's hero, during the night of Troy's fall.[51] I quote her words from the English-language version:

Troy is living her last night. For millenniums to come, men will search in her ashes to find the vestiges of her noble walls . . . The horrors we have seen in these years [of the Trojan War] will always live in legend.

The very film in which she makes this prophecy about the survival of Troy proves her right, in regard both to the sensational discovery and excavation of its site by Heinrich Schliemann and to Troy's quasi-mythical presence in popular culture. The cinema and related visual media are today the most powerful means to preserve the memory of ancient legends and myths. In this, of course, the neo-mythological outweighs the accurate. *La guerra di Troia* is itself an example of such a legend in that it is a very loose adaptation of parts of Homer's *Iliad* and Virgil's *Aeneid*. And this film is only one of many that have reworked stories from classical mythology since the earliest days of the cinema. A sequel to Ferroni's film released the same year that Cassandra made her prophecy was appropriately called *La leggenda di Enea*.[52] The fact that it features footage from the earlier film when Aeneas reminisces about the fall of Troy cleverly illustrates the survival of ancient myths in a new medium since here a modern retelling, that of *La guerra di Troia*, itself becomes elevated to a quasi-mythical level when it is reprised in *La leggenda di Enea*. Aeneas is played by the same actor in both films. But this actor is none other than muscleman Steve Reeves, who impersonated a number of heroes from ancient myth, most famously Hercules. So did several other actors. Audiences immediately recognize the interchangeable type of hero they are watching in any one film and feel at home in his company. The same, if on a smaller scale, is true for Cassandra.[53]

---

[51] The film's English titles are *The Wooden Horse of Troy*, *The Trojan Horse*, and *The Trojan War*.

[52] The film's English titles are *The Avenger*, *The Last Glory of Troy*, and *War of the Trojans*. It was directed by Giorgio Rivalta.

[53] Cassandras appear in Marc Allegret's *The Loves of Three Queens* (or *The Face That Launched a Thousand Ships*, 1953), Mario Camerini's *Ulysses* (1954), Franco Rossi's television *Odissea* (1968), Michael Cacoyannis's *The Trojan Women* (1971, played by Geneviève Bujold), Enzo G. Castellari's modern farce *Hector the Mighty* (1975), Woody Allen's comedy *Mighty Aphrodite* (1995), Chuck Russell's *The Scorpion King* (2002), John Kent Harrison's *Helen of Troy* (2003), a television epic, and in the animated Hercules films and series mentioned earlier. Noteworthy television adaptations of Aeschylus had Cassandras played by Mariangela Melato in Luca Ronconi's *Orestea* (1975) and by Helen Mirren in Bill Hays's *The Serpent Son* (1979), a three-part BBC adaptation of the *Oresteia* written by Kenneth McLeish and Frederic Raphael. Apollo appears in both. The British version is particularly remarkable for its distinguished cast of actresses (also Claire Bloom, Siân Phillips, Diana Rigg, and Billie Whitelaw). The short-lived British television comedy series *Up Pompeii* (1971) featured an unfunny Roman Cassandra.

Ultimately these figures are all members of a large mythic-heroic family which well illustrates the principle of cinematic intertextuality.

Cassandra's observation about the survival of Troy in popular legend is borne out nowhere more spectacularly than in Wolfgang Petersen's *Troy* (2004). The words of Thetis to her son Achilles even echo those of Ferroni's Cassandra: "They will write stories about your victories for thousands of years." But Cassandra herself is missing from *Troy* since the aristocracy of Troy and the roster of the Greek heroes fighting in the Trojan War have been rigorously limited in number for the sake of a compact plot.[54] On a narrative level *Troy* extensively changes ancient literature, especially Homer's *Iliad*, in a particularly noteworthy example of neo-mythologism. Most of the Olympian gods, for instance, are conspicuous by their absence. Zeus rates only one verbal mention. By contrast Apollo is of major importance, and the verbal and visual references to him reveal the variety that we may find in today's retellings of ancient myth. As he was in the *Iliad*, Apollo is still the chief guardian of Troy.[55] The Trojans' elite guard of warriors are even called Apollonians. "He thinks the sun god will protect him," says Agamemnon of Priam, and Priam tells Hector: "Apollo watches over us." Hector, however, is rather skeptical: "And how many battalions does the sun god command?" he asks his father in return, echoing Josef Stalin's contemptuous question about the number of divisions commanded by the Pope.[56] Princess Briseis, here Apollo's chief priestess and a member of the Trojan royal family, is a much more important figure in the plot of *Troy* than she was in the *Iliad*. But despite all this, Petersen's Troy does not seem to have a temple of Apollo within its walls except for the sanctuary (*temenos*) adjacent to Priam's palace to which Briseis flees in the film's last sequence. Apollo's main temple is located on the beach. It seems to be that of Apollo Thymbraeus, which stood outside the walls of

---

[54] Winkler 2006d examines the film from various perspectives.

[55] In Marino Girolami's *Fury of Achilles* (or *Achilles*, 1962), a neo-mythological muscleman epic that demonstrates its makers' close familiarity with the *Iliad*, Apollo plays a significant part throughout this unusual film, although he remains off-screen (unlike Athena or Thetis). On first meeting Chryseis, the captive daughter of Apollo's priest Chryses, Agamemnon boasts to her: "I am the king of kings." Unimpressed, she counters: "And I am consecrated to Apollo, the god of kings." Apollo miraculously reveals a treasure to Chryses with which to ransom his child; Apollo's voice is heard on the soundtrack. He later causes a sudden storm that mysteriously kills many of the Greeks; this is the film's equivalent of the plague Apollo sends them in Book One of the *Iliad*. The omniscient narrator portentously intones: "Like darkest night, the mighty god descended and wreaked his fury [sic] on the Grecian fleet."

[56] Stalin's saying is quoted in several versions and with varying dates and addressees. The most famous is in Churchill 1948: 135: "'Oho!' said Stalin. 'The Pope! How many divisions has *he* got?'"

**Fig. 10.** *Troy.* Achilles and the statue of far-shooting Apollo before his temple outside the walls of Troy. (Warner Bros.)

Troy.[57] Since it is unprotected, it easily falls into the hands of Achilles and his Myrmidons upon their landing and is despoiled and desecrated. Its architecture features large stone statues, both standing and sitting, that are reminiscent of ancient Egyptian statuary, just as the city of Troy displays an eclectic mix of Minoan, Egyptian, ancient Near Eastern, and archaic Greek decoration, statuary, and architecture. In front of Apollo's temple we see a visual representation of Homer's "far-shooting Apollo," which reminds us of the god's first appearance in Western literature in the *Iliad.*[58] This is a golden statue of the god, who is sitting, knees raised, and bending his bow (Fig. 10). A comparable marble relief of Apollo as a crouching archer was part of the decoration of the throne of Zeus in Zeus' temple at Olympia; its sculptor, Phidias, evidently was thinking of the Homeric scene.[59]

In an astonishing twist on ancient myth and religion, this statue and, by implication, the god it represents suffer a fate which illustrates the neo-mythological extreme to which modern directors or screenwriters may go

[57] *Cypria*, Argument 11; Ibycus S 224 (Page); Euripides, *Rhesus* 224–226; Strabo, *Geography* 13.1.35, with reference to Homer, *Iliad* 10.430; Servius on Virgil, *Aeneid* 3.85.13–19. According to the anti-Homeric accounts in Dictys of Crete, *Journal of the Trojan War* 4.10–11, and Dares the Phrygian, *The Fall of Troy* 34, Paris killed Achilles in this temple. On Dictys and Dares cf. Chapter 5.

[58] At *Iliad* 1.43–52 Apollo shoots his arrows into the Greek camp from a sitting position. A red-figure Apulian vase of ca. 400–385 BC shows Apollo as a standing archer before his temple (*Lexicon Iconographicum Mythologiae Classicae* 2.1: 239 ["Apollon / Apollo" no. 428]); cf. an amphora from Cerveteri of ca. 530–520 BC (*Lexicon Iconographicum Mythologiae Classicae* 2.1: 333 ["Apollo / Aplu" no. 1]).

[59] The statue in *Troy* also resembles statues of kneeling archers, including Heracles, on the east and west pediments of the temple of Aphaea on the island of Aegina. For illustrations see Ridgway 1970: figs. 5–7; she describes the temple (13–17) and the statues (16).

in order to present a compelling story to audiences only loosely familiar with antiquity. "The sun god is the patron of Troy, our enemy," Achilles says to his soldiers once they have taken Apollo's temple, and he exhorts them to loot and plunder. Achilles is duly warned against this course of action: "Apollo sees everything. Perhaps it is not wise to offend him." But Achilles pays no heed. In this he resembles numerous figures from Greek myth and tragedy who come to a well-deserved bad end in punishment for their hubris. But Achilles goes further than merely uttering blasphemous words. He decapitates the statue of Apollo with a stroke of his sword. In Greek myth Achilles had taken and desecrated this temple and killed Troilus, son of Apollo and Hecuba, inside the sanctuary and was himself eventually killed there by Paris' arrow. (The deaths of Agamemnon and Achilles in a kind of sanctuary of Apollo near Priam's palace in *Troy* is a variant on this tradition.) The character from ancient literature whom Achilles here resembles most closely in his attitude toward Apollo is Mezentius, the Etruscan leader in the war against Aeneas and the surviving Trojans in the *Aeneid*. Virgil memorably introduces Mezentius with the phrase *contemptor divum*: "spurner of gods."[60] Petersen's Achilles is such a man. He later tells Briseis, his prisoner: "I think your god is afraid of me" and rhetorically asks her: "where *is* he?" This question about the presence or absence of a god or gods – or of God – despite people's professed beliefs and despite the predominance of religious artifacts and buildings in all civilizations is equally ancient and modern; here, in a commercial work of popular culture, it effectively points to the eternal problem of man's place before the divine. Hector will later comment to Priam and the Trojan elders about Achilles' sacrilege: "Apollo didn't strike the man down. The gods won't fight this war for us." So when an anxious friend wishes for Apollo's protection for Hector before his duel with Achilles, an encounter which audiences know Hector will not survive, his words ("Apollo guard you, my prince!") are a poignant reminder that in the world of *Troy* just as in the modern world humans are essentially on their own.

Except for Hector, the Trojans are misled by their understanding of the divine. The omen of an eagle holding a serpent in its talons is misinterpreted as a sign of victory sent by Apollo. Later the Trojans discover the wooden horse among a number of dead bodies lying on a beach now deserted by the enemy. They recognize the devastation caused by a plague and connect all this to the Greeks' sacrilegious treatment of Apollo. A Trojan priest,

---

[60] Virgil, *Aeneid* 7.648.

presumably the film's equivalent of Laocoon, explains: "They desecrated the temple of Apollo, and now Apollo has desecrated their flesh." He is, of course, wrong. The real reason for the plague is never given, for the fact that Apollo does cause a plague among the Greeks in Book One of the *Iliad* is inadequate as an explanation here. Neo-mythologism can be as mysterious or unresolved in its implications as authentic ancient myth and literature often were. *Troy* provides us with a worthwhile example of the value of the former to think again of the latter.

Remarkable as the retelling of Greek myth in *Troy* may appear to today's audiences, it has a precursor in an earlier film also based on Homer, Mario Camerini's *Ulysses* (1954). Like Petersen's Achilles, Camerini's Odysseus can be contemptuous of gods. In Polyphemus' cave he invokes the principle of *xenia* ("guest friendship, hospitality") which Zeus guards, but only for the purpose of manipulating the Cyclops. More importantly and in a manner both neo-mythological and parallel to Achilles' decapitating the statue of Apollo, this Odysseus topples a statue of Neptune during the conquest of Troy and later, when his ship is caught in a storm, pushes another one overboard. "There's no Neptune out there," Odysseus shouts to his frightened crew, thereby denying if not the very existence then at least the power of the god over the very element he rules. (The use of the sea god's Roman name may be explained by the film's Italian origin.) Somewhat inconsistent with this is Odysseus' belief in Athena, his protector. "Prepare the fires for a sacrifice to Athena," he tells his men at one point. Odysseus' hubris toward Poseidon explains the god's persecution of him. (Andrey Konchalovsky's television film *The Odyssey* will use the same set-up for its plot in 1997.) Still in Troy, Cassandra curses Odysseus and prophesies him exile and death at sea. The latter part of her prophecy, as we know from the outset, will not be fulfilled, but the film does not address the issue of false prophecies deriving from true inspiration.

Odysseus' contempt of Poseidon contrasts with the far more religious atmosphere on Ithaca. Penelope has a large wall painting of Athena in her chambers. Presumably it had been there before Odysseus left for the Trojan War and is consistent with his belief in the goddess. But Apollo is even more prominent in this cinematic island kingdom. The courtyard of Odysseus' palace has several large stone sculptures of lions atop fortifications which in their posture resemble the row of ten marble lions on Delos. In antiquity lions were associated with Apollo as sun god.[61] In general they symbolize

---

[61] Cahn 1950 presents a detailed argument for this view, based on Apollo's associations with eastern and oriental sun gods.

royalty and power.[62] They do so here, too, but in addition they may be intended to refer specifically to Odysseus who upon his return will fall among the suitors as a lion does on his prey. More important in Camerini's film than the lions, however, is the contest of the bow to determine which suitor Penelope will accept for her new husband. It takes place during games in honor of Apollo, and we see a large bronze statue of Apollo before which the suitors sacrifice before the games. The archer god is indeed an appropriate divinity to have such a contest held in his honor, and the film indirectly takes up the reference to Apollo made in the *Odyssey* by Antinous, chief among the suitors.[63] In the film Antinous first objects to the archery contest: "This is no part of Apollo's games." Later a suitor who has unsuccessfully attempted to string Odysseus' bow exclaims: "Apollo is offended. He's taken away our strength." Antinous sarcastically replies: "How can Apollo take away what you never had?" Next to Neptune-Poseidon, Apollo is the god most frequently mentioned in *Ulysses*. Since Camerini's film has been popular for decades, the prominence of Apollo in *Troy* may even derive in part from that in the earlier film. If so, we have a case of one neo-mythological story influencing another – an illustration of the mythical matrix with which the cinema preserves our ancient traditions.[64]

If verbal references to Apollo occur in various contexts, so do his statues. The Apollo Belvedere, a Roman copy of a Greek original now in the Vatican, is probably the most famous type of the god's statuary. It can be seen (complete) in Carmine Gallone's *The Affairs of Messalina* (1951), in which it imparts a serene and pastoral atmosphere to the garden of Lucullus, to which its current owner, Valerius Asiaticus, has retired from the corruption and intrigues at court prior to his suicide. (The scene is loosely based on Tacitus, *Annals* 11.1.) A slightly different version of the Belvedere Apollo can be glimpsed momentarily in the background of a traveling shot inside Nero's palace in *Mio figlio Nerone* (1956) but serves no

---

[62] Another row of stone lions patterned after those on Delos appears in Robert Rossen's *Alexander the Great* (1956) before the palace of Philip of Macedon. A large statue of Athena Promachos – i.e. the goddess in full warrior garb – stands nearby. All this statuary signals Philip's and then Alexander's military power and imperial ambition.

[63] *Odyssey* 21.265–268. Similarly in Rossi's *Odissea* Antinous comforts the other suitors who have failed to string Odysseus' bow with the reminder: "Tomorrow is the festival of Apollo the archer. Let's postpone the contest till tomorrow. He will grant us the necessary strength."

[64] And there is more, outside cinema. Just one example is the headline on the front page of the *Herald Express* of Tampa, Arizona, which ran an article about Elvis Presley on September 20, 1956; its headline proclaimed: "Prof Sees Apollo Resemblance." The academic in question was Henry Wood, art historian at Arizona State University; a photograph of Elvis's face is juxtaposed to one giving a back view of the head of Apollo on an ancient statue. The resemblance must have been purely in the professor's imagination.

purpose whatever.[65] The same is true for the paired statues of the Apollo Belvedere and the god's sister Diana that are briefly on view flanking Pontius Pilate's and the Romans' box in the circus in William Wyler's *Ben-Hur: A Tale of the Christ* (1959), perhaps the most famous of all ancient epic films. In the opening sequence of Blake Edwards's farce *The Return of the Pink Panther* (1975) an ingenious thief steals the world's largest if fictional diamond from an equally fictional Eastern museum. To impress on viewers the circumstance that the museum is indeed great enough to have such a treasure in its collection, the statue of Apollo appears in several shots. It is the only work of art in this museum that is given such prominence, thereby lending an aura of high culture to the museum and a measure of credibility to the film's plot. The Belvedere Apollo also conveys high-class culture in Michael Apted's *Amazing Grace* (2006), a historical drama about the abolition of the British slave trade, while a head of the god on display at Balmoral Castle in Stephen Frears's *The Queen*, released the same year, does the same for the British royals. In Claude Autant-Lara's version of *The Count of Monte Cristo* (1961) by Alexandre Dumas it decorates the hall of the aristocratic villain who had acquired his fame and fortune by an act of treachery on his military campaign in Greece. Such uses of Apollo as visual markers of respectability have a long history in the cinema. An early example is Louis Feuillade's crime serial *Judex* (1917), in which Apollo's bust decorates the office of an outwardly respectable but villainous banker and the living room of the aristocratic family whom the banker had ruined. Feuillade appears to have used the same prop twice. The Belvedere Apollo appears in a scene of drug-induced hallucination to the protagonist of Oliver Stone's *The Doors* (1991). A partially painted reproduction of it (black hair, bright-red cloak) is briefly to be seen in Jean-Luc Godard's *Contempt* (1963). Its gaudy appearance here comments on the phony nature of unabashedly commercial filmmaking, the opposite of Godard's own cinema.[66]

Thematically more important is the early appearance of Apollo in Frank Borzage's *I've Always Loved You* (1946), a romantic melodrama set in the world of classical music. After the credits, which feature musical instruments, the camera pans onto the film's first set, a kind of conservatory with

---

[65] The film, directed by Steno (i.e. Stefano Vanzina or Vanzini, prolific purveyor of commercial trivia to Italian screens), is a loud and unsubtle farce about Nero's and his mother Agrippina's court intrigues. Its English-language titles are *Nero's Weekend*, *Nero's Mistress*, and *O.K. Nero*. Take your pick, not that it matters.

[66] On *Contempt* cf. my remarks in the Introduction and Epilogue.

fluted columns and a Meander decoration below its ceiling. The hall is rather overstuffed with accurate copies of ancient statues, which the camera passes by as it – and we – enter. The first of these works is a bust of Apollo as god of music. The film's grand finale, a concert given in Carnegie Hall, brings home the classical point in a manner impossible to overlook. In long-shot we see a gigantic pair of Corinthian columns supporting a huge architrave that decorate the background of the stage. They are placed at a diagonal angle and dominate the entire composition on the screen. Rarely have the unstated claims of traditional culture, here represented by classical music, found such a strong, perhaps even oppressive, visual statement as in this largely unknown film. A similar point had been made more subtly in Clarence Brown's version of *Anna Karenina* (1935). The upper-class pretentiousness of Karenin's home is immediately apparent to attentive viewers. A full-size statue of the Venus de Milo stands near the door of their huge and empty foyer, busts of Hermes and Apollo are upstairs in the hallway. The presence of Venus ironically comments on the emotional sterility in the Karenins' marriage and hints at the passion of Anna, here played by Greta Garbo, that will lead to her tragedy.

The largest statue of Apollo, however, that has ever appeared on the screen – even if it was never really built to ancient specifications – is the titular one of Sergio Leone's spectacle *The Colossus of Rhodes* (1961), made at the height of epic European filmmaking. The statue of Helios, the sun god, was one of the seven wonders of the ancient world.[67] It measured about 30–35 meters in height and was destroyed by an earthquake.[68] The posture of Helios is unknown since we have no ancient descriptions and no physical remains of the statue; modern imagination has come up with any number of fanciful recreations. During and since the Renaissance the statue has often been assumed to have served as a lighthouse or beacon, with Helios holding up a torch in the manner of the American Statue of Liberty, for which the Colossus was the chief model.[69] A painting by Czech artist Frantisek (or

---

[67] Pindar, *Olympian Ode* 7.54–76, tells the myth that explains why Helios was associated with the island of Rhodes. Scholarly literature on the Colossus is extensive; see especially Vedder 1999–2000. See further Higgins 1988, Vedder 2003b, and Brodersen 2004. The last-mentioned has the texts of the ancient sources.

[68] Cf. Pliny the Elder, *Natural History* 34.41; Polybius, *The Histories* 5.88–89.

[69] Belief in the ancient Colossus' torch is based on the literal understanding of a phrase in its dedicatory inscription that refers to the torch of freedom; cf. the *Greek Anthology* 6.171. Langglotz 1975–1976 corroborates that the Colossus of Rhodes had held a torch in his right hand. – The Statue of Liberty was referred to as "The New Colossus" in Emma Lazarus's well-known poem by that name (1883); see Lazarus 2005: 58.

**Fig. 11.** *The Colossus of Rhodes.* The head of the titular statue, with Apollo's archaic smile.
(Metro-Goldwyn-Mayer)

Frank) Kupka from 1906 even has the Greek god give what in Fascist Italy
would come to be called the "Roman salute" (*saluto romano*), the raised-
right-arm salute.[70] The colossus is commonly assumed to have stood at
or, with legs apart, across the entrance to the harbor of Rhodes, although
this location and this posture are not documented in our sources.[71] Leone's
film follows this tradition but modifies the appearance and function of the
statue considerably. Its head is loosely modeled on Greek or Roman statues
or busts of Apollo, to whom the Greeks built a number of colossal statues.[72]
But film viewers familiar with the ancient iconography of Helios will miss
the radiate crown that ancient artists regularly gave Helios to symbolize the
rays of the sun[73] (Fig. 11). Nevertheless the statue's face exhibits the archaic
smile discussed above. So does the gigantic stone statue on view in Freda's
*The Giants of Thessaly*, a film mentioned earlier as well.

[70] The painting, under the title "Colossus of Rhodes (City)" and now in the National Gallery, Prague,
is reproduced in a small black-and-white image in Vachtová 1968: 298 (catalogue no. 42) and in a
cropped full-page color image in Romer and Romer 1995: Plate 7 (erroneously attributed to "M.
Kupka" and dated to 1922). – On the gesture see Winkler 2009.

[71] Hoepfner 2003: 53–64 follows the standard tradition of placing the statue at the harbor entrance
but correctly rejects (13–18) the popular Renaissance tradition that it straddled the harbor entrance
so that ships passed underneath and between its legs (as in Leone's film); the book provides detailed
information, analyses, and a large number of valuable illustrations on all important aspects of the
Colossus' history, construction, archaeology, and reconstructions. Cf. Vedder 2003a.

[72] Cf., e.g., the illustrations in Hoepfner 2003: 6 ills. 3 (drawing reconstructing size and placement of
an Apollo statue on Delos, one of the largest archaic statues ever built) and 4 (photograph of never
completed marble colossus of Apollo lying in a quarry on the island of Naxos), 9 ill. 11 (diagram of
remains of Apollo statue from Tralles), and 40 ill. 59 (drawing of Apollo's temple at Delphi with the
sculpture of the god driving his golden chariot on the top of a high pediment).

[73] The head of Helios need not have been radiate, however; cf. on this Higgins 1988: 130 and 131 fig.
65 (two Rhodian coins with a radiate and a non-radiate Helios).

Similar to several modern images or paintings, Leone's colossus also serves as a kind of lighthouse, for the god holds a large bowl in his hands and in front of his chest; in this bowl a fire burns day and night. The film's plot is a free-wheeling historical invention analogous to neo-mythologism. There is an evil ruler, a power-hungry courtier who engages in a conspiracy with the Phoenicians, a group of patriotic Rhodians engaged in overthrowing the tyrant, and a noble Athenian who is drawn into all these conflicts for the sake of romance.[74] When the colossus is being dedicated, a priest proclaims: "To you, Apollo, god of the sun, we consecrate this superb effigy." But then he goes on to speak of the king's glory more than of the god's. Is the statue not quite what it appears to be? So it turns out, for by means of an anachronistic mechanism the bowl containing the fire can tilt and pour down destruction on any ship that passes through the statue's legs. Even more spectacularly and equally anachronistically, the top of Apollo's head can open in such a way that, from far away, he appears to wear the sun god's radiate crown after all. But this opening is there for a more sinister purpose, for catapults placed on a platform inside the head hurl burning oil through it. The statue thus functions primarily as a war engine. Impressive as the colossus appears throughout the film – as when soldiers fight our Athenian hero on its shoulder and arm at a vertiginous height or when the colossus finally topples over during the earthquake – the most remarkable because most sinister-looking moments occur when we see the radiate head spewing fiery comets of doom. This is certainly not the kind of "far-shooting Apollo" that Homer and the ancients knew, but it is an effective piece of cinematic neo-mythologism, especially when seen the way it was intended, on a gigantic screen.

More recently Apollo appeared again on the cinema screen a short six months after the release of *Troy*, if again not in person. Oliver Stone's *Alexander* displays statuary of most of the Olympian gods, including Apollo, in a few scenes. These statues are made to look like gilded bronze or painted marble and serve mainly decorative purposes, for instance during the triumphant entrance of Philip of Macedon immediately before his assassination. A gilded statue of the god holding a lyre can be seen among several other Olympian gods in the palace of old King Ptolemy at Alexandria as he is dictating his memoirs of Alexander the Great to his scribe Kadmos. Here Apollo represents culture and civilization, one of his chief functions. Ptolemy wistfully remembers Alexander's dream of unifying and civilizing a barbaric world. At the beginning Ptolemy had observed about

---

[74] Garofalo 1999: 275–296 gives a detailed plot outline and critical assessment of the film.

him: "In his presence, by the light of Apollo, we were better than ourselves." (The phrase "by the light of Apollo" recurs some time later as a kind of mild oath.) The scribe's name is appropriate, for in myth Kadmos, founder of Thebes, had come from Phoenicia and was believed to have introduced the Phoenicians' art of writing to Greece. The historian Herodotus reports that he himself had seen "Kadmeian letters," i.e. inscriptions written in letters no longer in use, in the temple of Ismenian Apollo in Thebes and quotes some examples.[75]

As god of medicine Apollo is briefly and obliquely mentioned in the scene in which Alexander's friend and lover Hephaistion dies in Babylon: "I can't explain this – I swear by Apollo," exclaims the hapless physician before he is hauled off to be undeservedly executed for his incompetence.[76] The same is largely true of the numerous verbal references to the gods, chiefly Zeus, Dionysus, and Apollo. But Apollo plays a more important part in one early scene although he is not present or directly involved. Young Alexander tames Bucephalas by observing that the horse is afraid of his shadow. He calms him down by turning him around, at the same time explaining to him that shadows are insubstantial and harmless because they are only cast by Apollo's sun: "It's just a trick of Apollo's. He's the god of – [*points*] – sun. But I'll show you how to outwit him, you and me together." This is the first instance of heroism on Alexander's part, and the mention of Apollo, not reported in Plutarch's account of this famous moment, is an appropriate addition.[77] History is subject to being re-imagined just as much as myth.[78]

Historical figures, heroes and heroines of myth and legend, and gods and goddesses all come back from the past or down to earth and visit us on our screens. In our visual culture classical antiquity in general and Apollo and the Muses in particular are a continuing presence. Only churls unaware of the fluid character of myth will deplore this, even if neo-mythologism in

---

[75] Herodotus, *The Histories* 5.58–61.

[76] A rather cursory reference to Apollo as god of medicine can be heard in the television film *Empire* (2005), which purports to tell the story of Octavius, the future Emperor Augustus. (Resemblances to actual history are fleeting.) In a scene in which young Octavius, seriously wounded, is about to be bled, the following dialogue occurs: "Which god do you worship in this house?" – "Apollo." – "Pray to him." The only redeeming aspect of this scene is its probably unintentional hint at the fact that Augustus believed in having a special affinity to Apollo.

[77] Plutarch, *Alexander* 6. For just one example of the analogy of Alexander and Apollo cf. the close similarity in their portraits on the two coins reproduced by Fox 1973: Plates 1 and 2 (following page 288). Fox was historical advisor on Stone's film.

[78] Uli Edel's television film *Caesar* (or *Julius Caesar*, 2002) contains the following statement: "Alexander – descended from the mighty god Apollo." Apollo is said to have shown Alexander how to deal with the Gordian Knot, one of the most famous moments in Alexander's life.

the cinema is not always as sophisticated as we might wish it to be. But then, classical literature itself long ago revealed to us the true nature of myth. None other than Apollo's Muses, the very goddesses who inspired epic poets, tragedians, historians, and other writers, are reported by the archaic poet Hesiod to have confessed, without any apology whatever:

> We know to tell many lies resembling the truth,
> but we also know, when we want, to pronounce truths.[79]

[79] Hesiod, *Theogony* 27–28; my translation.

# CHAPTER 3

# The complexities of Oedipus

"The Greatest Love Story of All Time!" Anybody who comes across this tagline is likely to think of Antony and Cleopatra, Romeo and Juliet, Tristan and Isolde, or some other pair of famous lovers, but an anonymous hack writing ad copy for a film about Oedipus was thinking along different lines. The single greatest impulse for Oedipus' prominence in Western culture since antiquity came with Sophocles' play *Oedipus the King* (or *Oedipus Rex*). The story of Oedipus, if not primarily as a love story, has been a staple of cinema since 1908, when André Calmette directed an *Oedipe roi* in France. He was followed by Giuseppe de Liguoro in Italy with *Edipo re* (1909 or 1910). Two more versions appeared shortly afterwards: *Oedipus Rex* (1911) by Theo Frenkel, who also played the part of Oedipus, and *Oedipus Rex* (1912) by Theo Bouwmeester. *La légende d'Oedipe* by Gaston Roudès came in 1913. Since then, Oedipus has remained an enduring presence on screen.[1]

Filmic retellings of the Oedipus story and of related themes such as parricide, incest, and the power of fate are too numerous and varied to be dealt with in their entirety. Instead, I will attempt to demonstrate their wide range by adducing and commenting on instances that, taken together, reveal their versatility and adaptability. I omit such cases as the Italian mystery *Oedipus Orca* (1976) by Eriprando Visconti (nephew of Luchino), the Japanese *Oedipus no yaiba* (1986; roughly, "Oedipus' Sword") by Toichiro Narushima, the American *Exploding Oedipus* (2001) by Mark Lafia, a modern story, and the French *L'origine du monde* ("The Origin of the World," 2001; it has a Sphinx character) by Jérôme Enrico. Television

---

[1] The second surviving ancient play about the myth, Seneca's tragedy *Oedipus*, has been adapted, rather loosely, only once: in a one-hour version by Turkmen stage director Ovliakuli Khodzhakuli in his film debut (*Edip*, 2004; in Kyrgyz); the director plays Laius. – Halter 1998 gives an overview of Oedipus in theater history. More specific is Hall and Macintosh 1995: 1–29 and 215–242 (chapters entitled "Regicide, Restoration, and the 'English' Oedipus" and "Revolutionary Oedipuses"). In general cf. Robert 1915, Edmunds 1981, 1985, and 2006, and Edmunds and Dundes 1995. On the question of Oedipus' guilt and how it has been viewed in and since antiquity cf. Lurje 2004.

and video versions of Sophocles' Oedipus plays will also be omitted except in contexts that make a reference appropriate.[2]

The cinema has told the story of Oedipus in adaptations of Sophocles' play as period dramas set in antiquity but more frequently in updated versions. The former attest to Sophocles' status in the history of Western literature. The latter, often with changes in names, characters, or plot, focus on themes such as blindness and the inscrutability of fate that are integral to the original myth and to Sophocles' play. Their preponderance in the cinema is largely due to Sigmund Freud's revival of the Oedipus myth, which has ensured that Oedipus is here to stay. Major cinematic genres like the western or the mystery film, for instance, contain strong Oedipal overtones. I will turn to the preliterate world of Greek myth in film and to a few films about Freud himself in the first section of this chapter. As has aptly been observed, Freud was "the discoverer of sexual inhibition as a mainspring of human behaviour; a gentleman, therefore, to whom Hollywood has every reason to be grateful."[3] Hollywood is commonly called "the dream factory," and analysis of the unconscious and subconscious is fundamental to cinema, both for filmmakers and for viewers or critics.[4] In the words of director Fritz Lang:

---

[2] For the record, the following are worth mentioning: *Das Geheimnis des Ödipus* ("The Secret of Oedipus," 1974), an East German television film by Kurt Jung-Alsen; *Oedipus the King* and *Oedipus at Colonus*, parts 1 and 3 of *The Theban Plays* (1984), directed for the BBC by Don Taylor; and the video versions of two operas: Mark-Anthony Turnage's *Greek* (1990), directed by Peter Maniura and Jonathan Moore, and Igor Stravinsky's *Oedipus Rex* (1992), directed by Julie Taymor. On the stage and video versions of the last see McDonald 2001: 133–157 and 221–224 (notes; chapter "Stravinsky's *Oedipus Rex*: The King in a Trap"). The plot of Rainer Simon's *Der Fall Ö* (*The Case for Decision Ö*, 1991), a German television film, combines the filming of Sophocles' play with a modern story which comments on contemporary issues of war. Mario Martone's *A Place on Earth* (2000) incorporates the director's stage production of Sophocles' play. The American television series *Bewitched* and *CSI: NY* each included an episode called "Oedipus Hex" (1966 and 2006). In "Rebel with a Cause" (1999), an episode of the series *Hercules: The Legendary Journeys*, Hercules saves Oedipus from committing suicide and helps him overthrow King Creon, and Antigone becomes the rightful queen of Thebes. – The ending of Sophocles' play is staged, rather inauthentically (Oedipus does not wear a mask), before the Roman emperor Vespasian in Boris Sagal's six-hour television film *Masada* (1981), where it is being followed by a mime performance of political satire. An announcer addresses Vespasian with these words: "Caesar, you have witnessed the *Oedipus* of Sophocles, a banquet for the soul. Then, if the imperial palate is ready for the laxative, we will proceed to our afterpiece. A newly commissioned dumb show, as usual unfit for the delicate sensibilities of the Vestal Virgins." The bizarre food metaphor is not intended to be funny.

[3] Halliwell 1995: 237.

[4] Cf. writer-director Ingmar Bergman's words on this: "To me, when cinematography is at its best, it is very close to the state of dreaming. You know, in any other art you can't create a situation that is as close to dreaming. Think only of the time gap. You can make things as long as you want, exactly as in a dream. You can make things as short as you want, exactly as in a dream. As a director, a creator of the picture, you are like a dreamer . . . Twice I have written down a dream and filmed it just as I had dreamt it. One is in *Wild Strawberries* [1957] with the coffin. Without any translation, it's just as it was. The other picture is *The Naked Night* [or *Sawdust and Tinsel*, 1953] . . . Writing and filmmaking and the creation of pictures are extremely close to our dreams." Quoted from Stevens 2006: 644.

I always laughed when people came to me and explained what it was that I was trying to do in my pictures. And then I happened to think in the following way. My profession makes me like a psychoanalyst. Unconsciously when you write a story, you have to psychoanalyse the characters. Then I have to make myself clear why the characters act the way they do so that I can explain it to the actors. Maybe the critic is a psychoanalyst too. Perhaps he finds I do certain things of which I am not conscious.[5]

So Freud was present, as it were, at the very birth of cinema.[6] His perspective on the Oedipus myth as retold by Sophocles can be traced throughout film history. Sophocles' version of the Oedipus story or thematic variants of it as more or less explicitly Freudian reworkings appear in epic, tragic, and comic films. These are the categories under which I will examine them in subsequent sections.

### FROM MYTH TO FREUD

The most highly mythical film of Oedipus is Pier Paolo Pasolini's *Oedipus Rex* (1967), a personal work imbued with its writer-director's autobiography.[7] Pasolini, who himself translated Sophocles' text, combines an archetypal and timeless story with a modern comment on the human condition.[8] His Oedipus is both an archaic figure and an Everyman. The film's prologue is set in Italy in the 1920s, the time of Pasolini's own infancy. Laius and Jocasta are patterned on Pasolini's parents, especially in their clothing and the décor of their home: "The baby in the prologue is I, his father is my father, an infantry officer, and the mother, a schoolmistress, is my mother."[9] Pasolini also shows us his version of the origin of the Oedipus

---

[5] Quoted from Bartlett 1962: 13. Cf. the following words by King Vidor on his direction of actors: "A psychiatrist friend of mine once spent the day on the set and said, 'You're doing the same thing I am.'" Quoted from Stevens 2006: 48. The text as printed has a charming Freudian slip (doubtless not Vidor's): "psychiatrist friend of mind." See in particular Langer 1953: 411–415 on cinema and "the dream mode," Kracauer 1960: 163–166, Mast 1977: 27–28; also Tyler 1944.

[6] On this cf. Quévrain and Charconnet-Méliès 1984. On Méliès's film *The Oracle of Delphi* see Chapter 2.

[7] On this film see Schwartz 1992: 505–517. Schwartz's book is the most detailed biography of Pasolini. Another is Siciliano 1982. The screenplay, a kind of verbal-cinematic poem, is available in Italian in Pasolini 1991: 349–449 and in English in Pasolini 1971. The former volume also contains Pasolini's essay "Perchè quella di Edipo è una storia" at 313–324. Stephen Snyder 1980: 86–93 provides an introduction ("*Oedipus Rex*: Consciousness and History"). On the film's structure and meaning see Greene 1990: 151–159 and Viano 1993: 173–186 and 335 (notes). See further Brunetta 1984 and Todini 1985. Mackinnon 1986: 126–146 discusses *Oedipus Rex* under the heading of "meta-tragedy." Cf. also Gigante 1995, Rossi and Taddei 1992, Fusillo 1996, and Riemer 2002.

[8] Pasolini on his translation: "I did a special translation, which is very straightforward and faithful to the original." Quotation from Stack 1970: 126. Pasolini discusses his film in Stack 119–129.

[9] Quoted from Schwartz 1992: 509.

**Fig. 12.** *Oedipus Rex.* Oedipus (in white robe, ctr.) as king of an archaic-mythic Thebes. (Arco Film)

Complex when Laius, jealous of his son in whom he sees a rival for his wife's affections, pulls baby Oedipus by the ankles. Pasolini has said that his relationship with his father had been distant and problematic and that he was always closer to his mother.[10] The goal Pasolini pursued with his film shows his particular understanding of Greek myth and psychoanalysis:

> I had two objectives: first to make a kind of complete metaphoric – and therefore mythicized – autobiography; and second to confront both the problem of psychoanalysis and the problem of the myth. But instead of projecting the myth onto psychoanalysis, I re-projected psychoanalysis on the myth. This was the fundamental operation in *Oedipus.*[11]

With the exposure of Oedipus Pasolini moves from modern Italy into a pre-historic and primitive society, in which he sets Oedipus' life until Oedipus has blinded himself (Fig. 12). Non-Western music and a desert landscape tell us that we are now in a time of myth, not of history or reality. In his next film, *Teorema* (1968), Pasolini was to use a very similar desert to denote the irruption of the archaic, the irrational, and the supernatural into modern society.[12] In *Oedipus Rex* everything becomes highly stylized. Pasolini filmed the main part of his story in Morocco to achieve an imaginative recreation of the earliest stage of what was later to become classical civilization.

[10] For an example see Pasolini's statement as quoted by Schwartz 1992: 512.
[11] Quoted from Schwartz 1992: 506. Cf. Stack 1970: 126–127.
[12] On *Teorema* and its connections to *Oedipus Rex* see Schwartz 1992: 517–527.

**Fig. 13.** *Oedipus Rex.* Oedipus at the crossroads after killing Laius. (Arco Film)

A good illustration of the archaic and elemental in human nature and society is the scene of Oedipus at the Delphic Oracle discussed in Chapter 2. In keeping with this archaic-mythic perspective, Pasolini's Oedipus is not the tragic hero of Sophocles' play, one of the highest achievements of classical Greek culture, but rather "an impetuous, unthinking, and violent hunter-warrior, product of a preliterate society riddled with superstition, subject to forces beyond his understanding and control."[13] The long sequence at the crossroads, in which Oedipus in a fit of rage kills his father and all his father's attendants except one, best illustrates Pasolini's conception of Oedipus and the elemental nature of his environment and society (Fig. 13). Remarkably, however, Pasolini adheres to Sophocles' conception of the tragic hero, for anger and a short temper characterize the protagonists of Sophoclean drama, as Bernard Knox has argued in detail.[14]

In the film's epilogue Oedipus, now blind, playing a pipe, and still wearing his ancient clothes, wanders through a modern city (Bologna) in 1967, then returns to the meadow where we had seen him in the film's prologue as an infant at his mother's breast. In his end is his beginning. The film's ending is indebted to Sophocles' *Oedipus at Colonus*, a play about Oedipus' reconciliation with the gods just before his death. The film's autobiographical settings, which frame the main story, and the chronology from the 1920s to the 1960s prove that Pasolini saw himself in Oedipus. Essayist, novelist, dramatist, poet, and filmmaker, Pasolini was perhaps

[13] Schwartz 1992: 510.    [14] Knox 1964, especially 21–27, and Knox 1998: 26–28.

best suited to tackle the story of Oedipus, making it modern and at the same time uncovering its archaic roots. *Oedipus Rex* effectively illustrates Pasolini's concept of the cinema of poetry. Similar to Pasolini himself, Oedipus, too, becomes a poet:

> Once Oedipus has blinded himself, he re-enters society by sublimating all his faults. One of the forms of sublimation is poetry. He plays the pipe, which means, metaphorically, he is a poet.[15]

Despite its strange settings and other divergences from the canonical version of the Oedipus story, Pasolini's *Oedipus Rex* is the most profound rendition of the myth and also of Sophocles' play that the cinema has ever achieved.

In *Freud* (1962) John Huston provides an extended version of the discovery of the Oedipus Complex.[16] The film follows Freud in the early

---

[15] Pasolini as quoted in Stack 1970: 129.

[16] The specific moment in Sophocles' play that Freud most closely echoes is Jocasta's observation to Oedipus that men usually dream of sleeping with their mothers (*Oedipus the King* 981–982). Such a dream (*as* a dream) is unlikely to make it onto the screen, but a scene in Guy Madden's *Careful* (1992), a homage to Grimms' Fairy Tales and German Expressionist cinema, comes close. – Gay 1988: 100 and 112–113, Rycroft 1995 s. v. "Oedipus Complex," and Boothe 2002 give largely non-technical explanations of the Oedipus Complex. See further Mullahy 1948 and Politzer 1970. On Freud's own identification with Oedipus and of his daughter Anna with Antigone see, e.g., Gay 1998: 442 and cf. 154. Cf. also Caldwell 1974a, Chase 1979, Bremmer 1986b, Vernant 1988, Schlesier 1999, and Mikics 2005. On Freud and classical antiquity in general see Eisner 1987, Goldhill 2004: 281–296 ("Finding the Fatherland – Where Freud's Oedipus Comes From") and 297–307 ("The Mother of All Stories – The Greek Oedipus"), Armstrong 2005, especially 47–62 and 260–262 (notes) on Sophocles and Oedipus, Armstrong 2006, and Bowlby 2007. Caldwell 1974b collects the major earlier works and lists references to Oedipus (120–121) and Freud (132–134). Schmitz 2007: 195–204 gives a recent overview. Ancient interpretations of dreams, about which we have the *Oneirocritica*, a handbook by Artemidorus of Daldi, include aspects that today strike us as Freudian (its title may accurately be rendered as "The Interpretations of Dreams"); cf. Musatti 1976. For a psychiatrist's approach to Greek culture and literature see Simon 1978 and 1988: 253–265 (chapter "Psychoanalytic Theories and Tragic Drama," with discussion of the Oedipus Complex). The subject of film and psychoanalysis is far too extensive to be treated in any depth here. Among many other works see, e.g., the overview by Allen 1999; further Metz 1982a, Kaplan 1990b, especially 1–16; Stam, Burgoyne, and Flitterman-Lewis 1992: 123–183; Heath 1999, Gabbard and Gabbard 1999; Lebeau 2001, especially 61–72 and 124–125 on Huston's *Freud*; Beller 2002: 66–71 (on psychoanalysis as "proto-film theory"), and Lapsley 2006: 67–104 and 283–286 (notes; chapter "Psychoanalysis"). Allen 1995: 120–154 ("Cinema, Psychoanalysis, and the Film Spectator") and 165–168 (notes), presents a more skeptical view. Gabbard 2001, Sabbadini 2003, and Brandell 2004 collect essays on various kinds of film. Cf. also Cavell 2005b. On psychoanalysis and a particular film genre (horror) see, e.g., Creed 1993 and Schneider 2004. Cf. Wood 2003: 108–114 on Wes Craven's *Last House on the Left* (1972). As representative of a radical feminist approach to film and Oedipus cf. Mulvey 1989b and 1989d, the latter a reflection on *Riddles of the Sphinx* (1977), an Oedipus film written and directed by her and Peter Wollen. Important are also Mulvey 1989f and 1989a, her influential articles on spectatorship (cf. Freud's scopophilia). On feminism and psychoanalysis in the cinema cf., e.g., Penley 1989. Wood 1998b applies feminist and psychoanalytic perspectives, e.g. at 218–221 ("Oedipus Rears His Head Again") on Max Ophüls's *Letter from an Unknown Woman* (1948). A recent case study is Kreisel 2005. *Hideous Kinky*, a 1992 novel by Esther Freud, great-granddaughter of Sigmund, that addresses, among other themes, infant sexuality, was

stages of his training and career, focusing on his work on hysteria with Josef Breuer – their cases, published in *Studies on Hysteria* (1895), are freely adapted – and on his discovery of the importance of suppressed memory and infantile sexuality, culminating in his formulation of the seduction theory and the Oedipus Complex. In the film's final sequence Freud for the first time presents his theory to a hostile and uncomprehending audience in a tumultuous lecture hall:

It is in the Oedipus Complex, the child's fixation on the parent of the opposite sex, that infantile eroticism reaches its climax. Each human being is confronted with the task of overcoming this complex within himself. If he succeeds, he will be a whole individual; if he fails, he will become a neurotic and himself wander forever, blind and homeless.

The last words quoted parallel the fate of Oedipus at the end of his life. The film closes with a brief scene in which Freud visits the grave of his father, with whom he can now be reconciled. It is accompanied by the narrator's summation of what we have seen in the course of the film. He begins with an Apollonian maxim:

Know thyself. Two thousand years ago, these words were carved on the temple at Delphi: Know thyself. They're the beginning of wisdom. In them lies the single hope of victory over man's oldest enemy: his vanity. This knowledge is now within our grasp. Will we use it? Let us hope.[17]

The narrator is none other than director Huston, who earlier had even spoken as Freud in the first person singular. Huston's film is an honorable attempt to convey an appreciation of one of the twentieth century's most influential and controversial figures to wide audiences, although it necessarily condenses, simplifies, and fictionalizes its subject matter.[18] The film itself reflects what it shows us about the fate of its subject: partly for fear of controversy the studio cut *Freud* by twenty minutes and retitled its

---

filmed by Gillies MacKinnon in 1998. Paul Verhoeven's thriller *Basic Instinct* (1992) is one popular and influential (if trashy) example of how Freud's views on sexuality may reappear in modern mass culture; the sequel *Basic Instinct 2*, directed by Michael Caton-Jones, was released in 2006. In contrast to the last-mentioned, Nicolas Roeg's *Bad Timing* (1980) is one of the few films to treat psychoanalysis and sexuality in a less than superficial way, with apposite comments on Freudian and, by implication, cinematic scopophilia.

[17] Classical scholars may quibble that the maxim on the temple of Apollo at Delphi is far older than two thousand years, just as in an early sequence of the film Professor Charcot is made to refer to the wrong Greek word in his etymological explanation of the term "hysteria": "The word 'hysteria' is from the Greek word *hysteron*, meaning 'womb.'" The correct word is *hystera*. (*Hysteron* means "later.")

[18] On this side of the film cf. Gay 1995. For a psychoanalyst's view of the film see Holland 1994 and 2006: 69–94 and 184–185 (notes; chapter "Huston's *Freud* and My Huston").

sanitized version *Freud: The Secret Passion*. Rather than making the film
acceptable to the prudish sector of its potential audiences, this version only
succeeded in distorting Huston's vision.[19]

Huston had conceived of his Freud as a kind of detective of the mind and
of his film as "an intellectual suspense story."[20] Despite the cuts imposed
on it, the film still works well as just such a story, perhaps not least because
Huston had been the writer-director of one of the most famous detective
films of all time, *The Maltese Falcon* (1941). His perspective adds a layer of
popular culture, that of mystery fiction and film, to the historical figure
of Freud. Small wonder then that Freud was to become a full-fledged
detective in Herbert Ross's *The Seven-Per-Cent Solution* (1976), a film
based on Nicholas Mayer's bestselling novel. Freud and none other than
Sherlock Holmes, a fictional contemporary, are the sleuths who together
solve a mystery.[21] From here it is only a small step to turn Freud into a
mostly fictional character as well, in films as disparate as the Australian farce
*Young Einstein* (1988), directed by Greg Pead under the pseudonym Yahoo
Serious, and *The Empty Mirror* (1999), directed by Barry J. Hershey, in
which Freud psychoanalyzes Adolf Hitler. In his romantic comedy *Lovesick*
(1983) writer-director Marshall Brickman, long-time collaborator of Woody
Allen (to whom I will turn below), even conjures Freud up from the dead.
Several other films, some biographical like Huston's, some incorporating
him into their fictional plots, have Freud as a character.

The ghost of Freud, as it were, had previously influenced one of the most
accomplished film adaptations of Shakespeare, Laurence Olivier's *Hamlet*
(1948). At London's Old Vic in 1937 Tyrone Guthrie (on whom below)
had directed Olivier in a version of Hamlet that was heavily indebted to
Freud via Ernest Jones, whom Guthrie and Olivier consulted. Jones was
the author of a psychoanalytic paper, later expanded into a short book,
on Hamlet and Oedipus, which presents a Hamlet ruled by his Oedipus
Complex.[22] As a result Hamlet's relations with his mother Gertrude and
his step-father Claudius were presented differently from any way they had

---

[19] On the film's genesis, the problems encountered during filming, and the eventual cuts see the
director's autobiography: Huston 1980: 294–305. *Freud* was partly based on an uncredited screenplay
by Jean-Paul Sartre (Sartre 1984; in English, Sartre 1985). On this and Huston's film see Janet Walker
and Waldman 1990. See further Fisher 1999 and Janet Walker 1999. Benoît Jacquot's *Princess Marie*
(2004), a three-hour French television film, probably comes closest to doing justice to the figure of
Freud on screen. It is a fictionalized retelling of Freud's relations with Marie Bonaparte. German
actor Heinz Bennent plays Freud, his daughter Anne plays Anna Freud. The princess is played by
Cathérine Deneuve.

[20] Huston 1980: 303.     [21] On Huston's Freud as detective cf. Wollen 1999.

[22] Jones 1949, the most extended version of what he originally published in *The American Journal of
Psychology* in 1910 as "The Oedipus Complex as an Explanation of Hamlet's Mystery."

been before. Olivier paid tribute to Jones and confessed to his belief in the Oedipus Complex almost forty years after making his film.[23]

Huston's *Freud* was portrayed by Montgomery Clift, who had previously played a neurosurgeon-plus-psychiatrist in *Suddenly, Last Summer* (1959), an adaptation of Tennessee Williams's play directed by Joseph. L. Mankiewicz and written by Gore Vidal and Williams. Although unavoidably sanitized – the 1992 version directed by Richard Eyre for British television is considerably more explicit – Mankiewicz's film succeeds in creating a steamy Southern atmosphere for its tale about Sebastian Venable, a gay sexual predator who himself becomes prey and is killed in a bizarre manner, about his overprotective and would-be incestuous mother Violet, and about Violet's jealousy of Catharine, Sebastian's frustrated young wife. On several occasions Violet describes to the doctor her peculiar closeness to her son in revealing terms: "I know it sounds hopelessly vain to say, but we were a famous couple. People didn't speak of Sebastian and his mother or Mrs. Venable and her son; no, they said 'Sebastian and Violet,' 'Violet and Sebastian' . . ." And: "My son and I had a rare and wonderful love and trust between us, a sort of contract, a covenant between us . . . We needed no one but one another." The Gothic-horror scene of Sebastian's death, revealed by Catharine in a flashback, is patterned on another famous Greek myth. This myth is best known from tragedy, although not one by Sophocles. In Euripides' *Bacchae* the vengeful god Dionysus brings about the death by dismemberment (*sparagmos*) of his enemy Pentheus, the king of Thebes, at the hands of Dionysus' frenzied followers, the Maenads or Bacchants, the play's eponymous women. Sebastian Venable meets a similar fate with strongly Euripidean overtones: a *sparagmos* followed by omophagy, the eating of the victim's raw flesh that could be part of the Dionysian ritual. Such Dionysian violence took place when the Maenads had gone up into the mountains (*oreibasia*); in a comparable manner the boys and young men who turn on Sebastian drive him to a small hill outside their village. In the film it is hardly necessary for Catharine to tell the doctor or for Mankiewicz to show viewers that the setting of the scene is indeed classical. In Catharine's anguished words, it was "a ruin . . . broken stones . . . like the entrance to a ruined temple, some ancient ruined temple."[24]

---

[23] Olivier 1986: 77–83. On the 1937 production see Holden 1988: 115–119.

[24] Lines 1216–1300 of Euripides' *Bacchae*, when Cadmus brings his daughter Agave back to rationality, are the clearest analogy in ancient literature to a modern psychotherapy session. Cf. Deveraux 1970, Hubback 1990, and Parsons 1990. For the wider context see especially Dodds 1951 and Simon 1978. Siegel 2005 examines classical aspects of play and film.

Oedipal overtones appear in science-fiction film, too. A case in point is *The Matrix* (1999), discussed in Chapter 2. The third film in the series, *Matrix Revolutions* (2003), contains an episode in which Neo is blinded but still has a kind of deeper second sight. This parallels Oedipus' fate: while he can see, he is blind to the truth; when he is blind, he can see, figuratively speaking, because he has acquired insight and self-knowledge.

## EPIC

The earliest literary form of ancient myth is epic poetry, and our first literary source for the Oedipus myth is Homer's *Odyssey* with its brief account of the myth's essentials.[25] Greek epics on Theban myths, such as *Thebaid*, *Oidipodeia*, and *Epigonoi* among others, do not survive; in Roman literature Statius' *Thebaid* does. In the cinema epic treatments of ancient material focuses primarily on heroes who exhibit martial virtues (Achilles), physical prowess (Heracles, Jason), mental agility (Odysseus), or a combination of these qualities. By contrast the figure of Oedipus does not readily lend itself to such films. Nevertheless we may encounter Oedipus in rather unusual epic company on the screen. According to Italian director Pietro Francisci and his screenwriters in their influential neo-mythological epic *Hercules* (1958), none other than their titular hero was responsible for Jason and the Argonauts obtaining the Golden Fleece. In the 1959 sequel, *Hercules and the Queen of Lydia* or, more heroically, *Hercules Unchained*, Hercules takes part in the war of the Seven against Thebes.[26] As he is traveling to Thebes in the company of his wife Iole and Odysseus' son Telemachus, they take shelter in a cave at Colonus, in which they find old and blind Oedipus. Oedipus' curse of his sons in Hercules' presence sets the stage for the latter's involvement in the fratricidal conflict that ensues. Hercules, here incarnated by American muscleman Steve Reeves, rises to each heroic occasion in the course of the film. His brief encounter with Oedipus, an old friend, is no more than an amusing curiosity, and after this early scene we hear or see no more of Oedipus. Besides this film, there are, to my knowledge, only three other films that incorporate short parts of Sophocles' *Oedipus at Colonus*. (The 1985 video version of Lee Breuer's stage play *The Gospel at Colonus* is not, strictly speaking, a film.) Pasolini touched upon the play in the epilogue of *Oedipus Rex*. Jean Cocteau's poetic

---

[25] *Odyssey* 11.271–280.
[26] On Francisci's Hercules films see Elley 1984: 55 and Solomon 2001: 117–120.

*The Testament of Orpheus* (1959) contains a brief appearance of the sphinx and of a blind Oedipus led by Antigone. This film also has a few other thematically important reminiscences of the Oedipus story.[27] The third is Amy Greenfield's art-house film *Antigone: Rites of Passion* (1989), in whose opening sequence father and daughter are wandering outcasts.[28]

The theme of Oedipal conflict between father and son occurs with remarkable frequency in the cinema.[29] Such conflict is a prominent feature in American society and literature. Towering father figures, especially self-made men or empire builders, overshadow and intimidate their sons who begin to resent or hate them. Father–son antagonism inevitably ensues. John Steinbeck's novel *East of Eden*, filmed by Elia Kazan in 1955, and Tennessee Williams's drama *Cat on a Hot Tin Roof*, filmed by Richard Brooks in 1958, are representative instances. Less profound variations may appear elsewhere, too, as in special-effects blockbuster films geared to reaching the widest possible audiences. Ang Lee's *The Hulk* (2003), derived from the Incredible Hulk comics and television series, and Gore Verbinski's *Pirates of the Caribbean: The Curse of the Black Pearl* (2003), a film based on a ride at Disneyland, are examples. The latter features a young man's ignorance of his late father's true identity and a curse from the gods. But a quintessentially American epic genre that is closely related to Greek myth and literature and also exhibits tragic overtones is the western. Since it is not often associated with classical culture, I point out some of the connections here. I have previously addressed this topic in greater detail, so I list only a few pertinent examples.[30]

Echoes of Greek myth by way of intrafamilial and Oedipal conflicts appear in King Vidor's *Duel in the Sun* (1946) and Howard Hawks's *Red*

---

[27] Cocteau never turned his chief work about Oedipus, *The Infernal Machine* (1931), into a film. *Oedipe Roi* is a short play based on his work for Stravinsky's oratorio *Oedipus Rex*. Cocteau also wrote an *Antigone*.

[28] In Jack Smight's *No Way to Treat a Lady* (1968), a psychological thriller about an upper-class and well-educated serial killer with a kind of reverse Oedipus Complex – feeling overshadowed by his late mother, he strangles middle-aged women – a large bronze statue by German sculptor Gerhard Marcks of Antigone leading her blind father elicits the killer's comment "I like its strength."

[29] It may do so even where least expected or for only a moment. A case in point is an early scene in Nick Nostro's *Spartacus and the Ten Gladiators* (or *Day of Vengeance*, 1964), one of the Italian muscleman epics set in antiquity. Their evil owner forces the eponymous Ten, who include a father and his son, to fight each other to the death in the arena. When they come face to face, the father refuses to fight. "Kill me, my son," he says in order to avoid mutual slaughter. He need not have worried too much. A predictable plot twist saves them both.

[30] The following is based in part on Winkler 1985. On the western as an Oedipal film genre cf. Cawelti 1999: 136–161, especially 141–143. Despite its heading ("The Freudian Western"), the chapter on John Ford's *The Searchers* (1956) in LoBrutto 2005: 273–279 is mainly a plot summary and has virtually nothing to say about Freudianism.

*River* (1948). Anthony Mann's *Winchester 73* (1950) shows the hero's revenge on his brother who had killed their father; Mann's *The Man from Laramie* (1955) extends and deepens this kind of conflict.[31] Mann was well aware of the affinities between the western and Greek myth: "it [the western] releases the characters. They can be more primitive; they can be more Greek, like *Oedipus Rex* or *Antigone* . . . because you are dealing . . . in a sweeping legend."[32]

Borden Chase, one of the most distinguished western screenwriters, reverses his *Winchester 73* theme in his script for John Sturges's *Backlash* (1956) with the figure of a guilty father instead of a guilty son. More directly Oedipal and Freudian plots occur in Raoul Walsh's *Pursued* (1947), Mann's *The Furies* (1950), Joseph H. Lewis's *The Halliday Brand* (1956), and Phil Karlson's *Gunman's Walk* (1958). Robert Aldrich's *The Last Sunset* (1960) involves the erotic attraction and near-incest between a father and his daughter, neither of whom knows about their blood relationship – this was the most daring such film for its time. Edward Dmytryk's *Broken Lance* (1954) and John Sturges's *Last Train from Gun Hill* (1959) both focus on father–son conflicts. The fact that *Broken Lance* is a western remake of Joseph L. Mankiewicz's *House of Strangers* (1949), a modern drama, indicates the versatility and adaptability of the western as a means to comment on universal aspects of the human condition. Examples of sons feeling overshadowed by their fathers are a staple in westerns as well. *Red River* and *The Man from Laramie* are famous examples. In Sturges's *Gunfight at the O.K. Corral* (1957) and Henry Hathaway's *The Sons of Katie Elder* (1965) such sons were played by Dennis Hopper, a specialist in portraying neurotic youths. (Rumor has it that in the latter film Hopper had problems playing opposite the powerful personality of its older star, John Wayne.) More robust was Chuck Connors playing opposite Burl Ives – the patriarch in Brooks's *Cat on a Hot Tin Roof* – in William Wyler's saga *The Big Country* (1958). Both are tough and savage characters who at one point have the following Freudian exchange when the son, returned home, is told that his father wants to see him:

*Son*: You want me, pa?
*Father*: Before you was born, I did.

---

[31] Basinger 2007: 102 briefly refers to Greek tragedy in her discussion of this film. Kitses 2004: 157 calls it "a loose reworking of *Oedipus Rex*." His mention of "an Oedipal journey basic to the Western" (170) appears in his examination of Mann's films but is applicable to much of the genre. Janet Walker 2001a examines Oedipal themes in specific westerns.
[32] Quoted from Wicking and Pattison 1969: 41.

Although this has a funny ring to it, the film reverts to a tragic mode when the father's rough code of honor forces him to kill his treacherous son.

Screenwriter Philip Yordan has said about the westerns he wrote: "I have always wanted to re-create a tragic mythology, giving a large role to destiny, solitude, nobility" – a clear echo of Sophocles.[33] Such echoes may occur in the western intentionally or unintentionally. Two films directed by Arthur Penn are examples. *The Left-Handed Gun* (1958) is "a Western of uncommon psychological complexity – 'Oedipus in the West,' as its director put it."[34] In *Little Big Man* (1970), on the other hand, a blind Indian chief who is expecting imminent death includes the following words in his prayer: "Thank you for my vision, and the blindness in which I saw further" – a sentiment that could describe Sophocles' Oedipus. By contrast *Lone Star* (1996), written and directed by John Sayles, is an Oedipal western in a twentieth-century setting.[35] The first trilogy of George Lucas's *Star Wars* saga, among other things a kind of futuristic western epic, reaches its climax not only with an archetypal Oedipal conflict but also – and in good Aristotelian fashion – with a combined recognition (*anagnôrisis*) and change of fortune (*peripeteia*). At the end of *Return of the Jedi* (1980) young hero Luke Skywalker and his nemesis, Darth Vader, are revealed to be son and father after they have come close to killing each other in a duel.

Modern American perspectives on Oedipus can be retroactively applied when a film is set in antiquity. This is the case with *Alexander the Great* (1956), a historical epic written and directed by Robert Rossen. In his view Alexander, the young prince of Macedon, had a highly Oedipal relationship with his parents, especially his father, King Philip. Alexander's subsequent victories and his conquest of the Persian Empire derive largely from the psychological tensions within his family in his formative years. As Rossen said in an interview, his film was meant to reveal "the various guilts Alexander felt toward his father," emotions that even determined Alexander's pursuit of Darius, King of Persia: "The chase for Darius is tied up with his tremendous feeling that as long as a father figure is alive in royalty, he has to kill him."[36] Rossen's best-known film, the 1949 adaptation of Robert Penn Warren's novel *All the King's Men*, had also featured a young man overshadowed by a powerful father figure. In Oliver Stone's *Alexander* (2004), a film much indebted to Rossen's, the titular hero is still part of a highly dysfunctional family: a hostile and overbearing father, blind in one

---

[33] Quoted from Buscombe 1988: 397.    [34] Kitses 2004: 231.
[35] Cf. Bakewell 2002.    [36] Quoted from Casty 1969: 34.

eye, who is about to kill his son at one point, and an exotic and domineering mother who wears revealing dresses and whom Alexander once
kisses full on the mouth, if without incestual overtones. King Philip tells
the story of Oedipus to his pre-teen son in front of a large wall painting of
Oedipus blinding himself. This and other painted scenes from Greek myth
involving violent family or clan relations (Medea, Prometheus) are done
in the style of ancient black-figure vase paintings. An adult Alexander will
later have occasion to remember these pictures, which appear in flashback.
As a reviewer noted, somewhat glibly: "Given parentage of that calibre,
the boy . . . was going to conquer nation-states all the way from Athens to
India, engraving his name in history, or he was going to wind up running a
club called Oedipussy on the wrong end of Mykonos."[37] But even classical
scholars have pointed out Freudian aspects about the historical Alexander.
One of them observes:

perhaps inevitably, a Freudian element has crept into the study of Alexander's
personality during recent years. Critics now point out that his distaste for sex, the
rumours of his homosexual liaisons . . . coupled with his partiality for middle-aged
or elderly ladies and the systematic domination of his early years by that formidable
matriarch Olympias [Alexander's mother], all suggest the presence in his nature of
something approaching an Oedipus complex.[38]

An ancient ruler with an Oedipal fixation, the Roman emperor Commodus, had appeared on the screen four years before *Alexander* in Ridley
Scott's *Gladiator*. This Commodus was in turn patterned on the same
historical figure in Anthony Mann's *The Fall of the Roman Empire* (1964),
the last film on Roman history from the age of silver-screen epics and
the unacknowledged plot source of *Gladiator*. In Mann's film Commodus,
historically the son of Emperor Marcus Aurelius, turns out to be the son
of a gladiator instead. This unexpected twist is based on an ancient source
that preserves rumors about Commodus' parentage and his mother's marital infidelities.[39] When he finds out that he is illegitimate, Commodus,
dedicated to his dead mother's memory, kills his father. In Scott's film,
in which there is no such gladiator, Commodus has a love-hate relationship with Marcus Aurelius and throttles the feeble old man in a murderous
embrace when he finds out that Marcus has passed him over for the purple.
In both films Commodus does his utmost to destroy the noble legacy of

---

[37] Lane 2004: 126.
[38] Green 1974: 486–487. Green 518 note 40 lists some of this scholarship, from which he dissents (56).
Cf. also Green 40 on the relationship between Alexander and his mother.
[39] *Historia Augusta*: "Marcus Antoninus" 19.1–7.

Marcus Aurelius. Director Mann's comment on his version of Commodus equally fits Scott's Commodus:

> he tries to kill his father's image, because this image is greater than his own. This is the story underneath the Oedipus drama. I don't know of any great man who ever had a great son. This must have been a terrible thing for the son – to live with the image of his father, for although this is a love-image, it can also be a hate-image. This theme is recurrent, because it is a very strong one . . . it reaches to heights and depths beyond more mundane stories.[40]

It attests to the ubiquity of the Oedipus story that a reference to Sophocles' Oedipus can occur in an epic film even when we least expect it. Claude Berri's *Manon of the Spring* concludes the story begun in his *Jean de Fleurette* (both 1986); the films are pastoral epics (to coin a phrase) based on novelist and filmmaker Marcel Pagnol, who had made his own film version of *Manon des sources* in 1953. A spring whose waters are vital for the crops planted in a poor mountain village and for the people's survival suddenly dries up for no apparent reason; this is the second time it happens in about fifteen years. Viewers know that both instances are due to human interference. The village priest correctly suspects foul play, and in a Sunday sermon he draws a classical analogy to the current crisis. I quote his words from the subtitles of the film's English-language DVD edition:

> I once read a Greek tragedy about the city of Thebes that was struck by a calamitous plague. So I ask myself: "Is there a criminal among us?" It's not impossible since the biggest crimes often escape human justice. But God knows of them all!

The priest then exhorts the guilty party to come forward and repent: "Whatever your offense, try to make amends. Repent, and you shall be saved. And your spring will flow better than before." At the end an old and blind woman with the oracular name Delphine will reveal to a father that he has caused the death of his son whose true identity he had never known; she functions as a Tiresias figure who brings about recognition and reversal. In view of the importance of fate in the Oedipus myth, an aspect to which I will turn below, Berri's choice of Giuseppe Verdi's *La forza del destino* as main musical theme in his film is more than apt.

### TRAGEDY

As noted, films on classical themes exhibit a wide variety of approaches, from costume dramas in ancient surroundings or sets, sometimes even in a

---

[40] Quoted from Wicking and Pattison 1969: 42.

**Fig. 14.** *Oedipus Rex.* Guthrie's masked actors: Oedipus and the chorus. (Image)

theatrical environment, to stories told in contemporary garb. Philip Saville's *Oedipus the King* (1968) takes place in the ruins of an actual Greek theater.[41] *Edipo Alcalde* (*Oedipus Mayor*), written by Gabriel García Márquez and directed by Jorge Triana, is a 1996 updating set in modern Colombia. This film reflects the social and political instability of contemporary Latin America and is in part indebted to the magical realism of Central and South American literature. Highly intriguing because of its use of masks is Tyrone Guthrie's *Oedipus Rex* (1957), a film of his stage production with a textual adaptation of Sophocles by William Butler Yeats. The result is a hybrid of theater and film (Fig. 14). Its most subtle effect occurs in the scene when Oedipus and Jocasta begin to realize who he really is, for to viewers absorbed in the drama their masks seem to come alive. While the Corinthian messenger is explaining to Oedipus why the king and queen of Corinth are not Oedipus' parents, the truth is already dawning on Jocasta. Guthrie shows us Jocasta in medium close-up with a slow horizontal movement of her head. Immediately he cuts to a frontal close-up of Oedipus, the camera looking up at him. Oedipus lowers his head toward the messenger in front of him to ask, quietly, where the Corinthian had found him. The viewers' impression at this moment is that Oedipus has been struck a blow from above as if by fate or the gods. He is changing from the mighty and somewhat arrogant king of Thebes to a figure of woe. The two close-ups express the Aristotelian concepts of *anagnôrisis* and

[41] MacKinnon 1986: 66–72 and, more briefly, Solomon 2001: 261 comment on this film.

*peripeteia,* here occurring simultaneously for the greatest possible impact, as Aristotle said, to evoke pity and fear (*eleos* and *phobos*) in the spectator.[42] It is the viewer's psychological involvement, not the actors or the director, that makes the masks come alive at these moments.[43]

Different aspects of Oedipal themes involving incest, father-son conflicts, murder within the family, and the inevitability of fate occur in numerous films which are not tragedies in the strict literary sense but which take recourse to what we may call "the tragic."[44] I point to some examples here. *The Erasers* (1969), directed by Lucien Deroisy and René Micha, is based on Alain Robbe-Grillet's novel of the same name, which presented an updated version of Sophocles' play in the guise of a mystery written in the style of the French *nouveau roman.* (Robbe-Grillet later wrote and directed films himself.) Roman Polanski's *Chinatown* (1974) and James Gray's *Little Odessa* (1994) show different cinematic approaches to tragic family situations.[45] Alan Parker's *Angel Heart* (1987) is a supernatural mystery-detective thriller with Sophoclean overtones.[46] Ernest R. Dickerson's *Never Die Alone* (2004) is a "gangsta" *film noir* in which a black drug lord narrates his own story from the grave after being killed by his son, who did not know his father. By contrast Bernardo Bertolucci's *The Conformist* (1971) and *Last Tango in Paris* (1973), among others, are European art-house films important for their basis in psychoanalysis. Volker Schlöndorff's *Voyager* (1991) combines the incest motif with that of man's ignorance of his fate and the inevitability of his destiny.[47] The film is

---

[42] Aristotle, *The Poetics* 1452a12–b13. Cf. Chapter 2.

[43] Differently Solomon 2001: 260. I discuss Guthrie's film and the ancient technique of masked acting in connection with cinema in Winkler 2002b: 50–55. On the film see also MacKinnon 1986: 51–55.

[44] On this see, e.g., Mason 1985 and Most 2000.

[45] On *Chinatown* see especially McGinnis 1975, Belton 1991, Kimball 2002, and Gamel 2001.

[46] Rabel 2003 examines the two works in connection with the film's source, William Hjortsberg's novel *Falling Angel.* A surprising analogy to the behavior of Pasolini's Oedipus at the crossroads may be found early in Akira Kurosawa's *Yojimbo* (1961); it equally leads the titular hero to his destiny and makes the film's plot possible.

[47] Still largely a taboo subject, incest may yet occur on the screen. Here are some noteworthy examples (excluding films with sibling incest). Remarkably and uniquely, the mother–son incest in Louis Malle's *Murmur of the Heart* (1971) has no adverse effects at all. David O. Russell's cult favorite *Spanking the Monkey* (1994), also including mother–son incest, ranges from black comedy to drama. Bernardo Bertolucci's *Luna* (1979) features a highly charged erotic moment between mother and adolescent son but without actual intercourse. Bryan Forbes's crime thriller *Deadfall* (1968) includes father–daughter incest as a plot twist. The one in Bertrand Tavernier's *Beatrice* (1988) is set in a dark and violent tale about the Hundred Years' War. Antonia Bird's *Priest* (1994) contains a plotline of secret father–daughter incest and one of homosexuality and social hypocrisy; both are combined into a cathartic conclusion of great emotional power. In Thomas Vinterberg's *The Celebration* (1998) father–daughter incest has caused the daughter's suicide, which in turn becomes the dark family secret that is eventually revealed at the titular family reunion. The father–daughter incest

based on Swiss-German author Max Frisch's novel *Homo Faber* – "Man the Smith" (that is, the shaper of his fortune). The Latin title refers to a famous ancient and later commonplace and is here to be understood ironically: man is *not* in charge of his fortune. The aspect of fate and its necessity – *ananke* in classical thought, as in Aeschylus' vivid phrase "the yoke of necessity"[48] – is the most fascinating Oedipal theme in cinema, although it is obvious that most filmmakers were not consciously taking recourse to the archetypes of Greek tragedy. In Edgar G. Ulmer's cult film *Detour* (1946), one of the bleakest of American *films noirs*, the yoke of fate turns into a noose when the protagonist unwittingly strangles his partner in crime, a ruthless and domineering woman (shades of Aeschylus' Clytemnestra), with a telephone cord. This unintentional killing utterly changes – that is to say, ruins – his life.

The cinema of Alfred Hitchcock is particularly rich in Oedipal themes, from *Shadow of a Doubt* (1943) and *Spellbound* (1945, with a Freudian dream sequence designed by Salvador Dalí) to *Rope* (1948), *Rear Window* (1954, on scopophilia), *Vertigo* (1958), and *Frenzy* (1973).[49] Three of Hitchcock's films from his most creative period stand out; they deserve close attention.

The oracle that Oedipus receives is an illustration of fate's implacability and the apparently undeserved punishment and suffering that may be

in Tim Roth's *The War Zone* (1999) occurs in a working-class British family. In Jordan Walker-Pearlman's *The Visit* (2000) a daughter kills the father who had forced her into an incestuous relationship and then turned against their child. Rocker Jim Morrison's song "The End" contains lyrics expressing an Oedipal fantasy about parricide and maternal incest; the song occurs in Oliver Stone's *The Doors* (1991), a film about Morrison and his group. Christophe Honoré's *My Mother* (2004) is an adaptation of Georges Bataille's 1966 novel of the same name. Varieties of extreme mother-fixations occur in a number of well-known films; especially noteworthy are the neurotic gangster in Raoul Walsh's classic *White Heat* (1949) with its famous last sequence ("Look, Ma! Top of the World!") and John Frankenheimer's paranoid-conspiracy thriller *The Manchurian Candidate* (1962). The protagonist's fixation in Federico Fellini's semi-autobiographical *8½* (1963) is a mild case by comparison. Writer-director Preston Sturges succeeds in both satirizing and affirming the American male's mother fixation in his political and military comedy *Hail the Conquering Hero* (1944).

[48] Aeschylus, *Agamemnon* 218–219.

[49] *Rear Window* and Michael Powell's *Peeping Tom* (1960) are the best-known (and possibly the most profound) films on scopophilia as analogues to cinema. In the words of Pechter 1982: 109, films are "always, by their nature, potentially pornographic, because always, in their allowing us to see and not be seen, potentially voyeuristic." The dream sequence of *Spellbound*, directed by William Cameron Menzies, was to have been significantly longer and more complex than it appears in the finished film. It originally included a moment in which the film's heroine, the dreamer's psychoanalyst with whom he has fallen in love, turned into a Greek statue. James Bigwood, "A Nightmare Ordered By Telephone," an illustrated essay included in the 2002 Criterion Collection DVD issue of the film, contains detailed information on the origin, design, and filming of the dream sequence. Conrad 2000 is a representative recent example of scholarship that discusses psychological and psychoanalytical aspects of Hitchcock's films. For the far-reaching influence of Hitchcock's Oedipal cinema cf. Silbergeld 2004.

meted out to unsuspecting humans. This in turn reveals to us the precariousness of our existence. The most striking cinematic restatement of this aspect of Oedipus' story, although without any explicit reference to him, occurs in the first half of Hitchcock's *Psycho* (1960). In its most notorious scene Marion Crane, a young woman who is on the run after an impulsive theft of a large sum of money in order to be able to live with her lover, is brutally stabbed to death in the shower. This occurs shortly after she had come to understand that the crime she committed to break free from her stifling life was only the beginning of a worse kind of entrapment. In conversation with Norman Bates, an apparently nice if shy young man, she comes to realize her guilt and the futility of her act, accepts her responsibility, and decides to atone by returning the money. "People never run away from anything," Norman observes to Marion. "We're all in our private traps . . . and none of us can ever get out." This will soon prove to be only too true. (Norman's statements concisely summarize much of psychoanalysis.) Hitchcock intends us to feel relief, as Marion herself does, at her decision to return because by now we have come to like her, even to identify with her emotionally. The shower she takes is, at first, a symbolic act of Marion cleansing herself of her crime. The sudden brutal attack on her is as incredible to us as it is to herself – a tragic *peripeteia* without any apparent *anagnôrisis* or reason. So far Hitchcock has closely adhered to the Aristotelian unities of time, place, and action in this modern tragedy, for we have been with Marion at every moment of the film until her murder, even following her into the shower. The shift of the plot's focus onto Norman Bates occurs in the scene of their conversation in his parlor; here, too, another Oedipal aspect is introduced. Marion and the viewers learn about Norman's strongest emotional attachment: "A boy's best friend," he tells her, "is his mother." Later we find out just how close Norman and his mother really are. By the end the Oedipal nature of the film has become powerfully evident.[50]

*The Birds* (1963) is a complex tale of love and family relations in the guise of an apocalyptic thriller. The murderous attacks by large flocks of previously harmless birds both symbolize and comment on the protagonists' emotional turmoils and inner conflicts, which the threat to their survival posed by the birds externalizes and untangles. A widowed mother is so strongly opposed to any woman in whom her son gets seriously interested that viewers suspect a suppressed incestuous motive. But the

---

[50] The entanglements of fate, responsibility for one's actions, and related Oedipal aspects are addressed in the radically different but thematically closely related plot of Milan Kundera's novel *The Unbearable Lightness of Being* (1984), filmed by Philip Kaufman in 1988.

film turns out to have greater depth than Hitchcock could have achieved with a facile Oedipal subtext. To a large extent the true theme of *The Birds* is loneliness and abandonment. A conversation about the mother's way of treating her son's girlfriends, conducted by a former flame and the woman he is currently interested in, conveys the underlying issues to the viewer; the dialogue clearly rejects an audience's popular understanding of psychoanalysis:

*Annie*: Her attitude nearly drove me crazy . . .

*Melanie*: What had you done [to displease her]?

*Annie*: Nothing. I simply existed. So, what's the answer? Jealous woman, right? Clinging, possessive mother? Wrong! With all due respect to Oedipus, I don't think that was the case . . . Lydia liked me. That's the strange part. Now that I'm no longer a threat we're very good friends.

*Melanie*: And why did she object to you?

*Annie*: 'Cause she was afraid.

*Melanie*: Afraid you'd take Mitch?

*Annie*: Afraid I'd *give* Mitch . . . Afraid of any woman who would give Mitch the one thing Lydia can't give him – love.

*Melanie*: That adds up to a jealous, possessive woman.

*Annie*: No, I don't think so. You see, she's not afraid of losing Mitch. She's only afraid of being abandoned.

Their common danger later enables mother and son to conquer their unhealthy relation and allows the mother for the first time to accept her son's new girlfriend as a future daughter-in-law.[51]

*The Birds* contains a strong parallel to Sophocles' Oedipus. Just as there seems to be no reason why Oedipus receives his oracle, so there is no reason for the birds' attacks. Their behavior is incomprehensible to us and remains unexplained. Robin Wood, Hitchcock's most perceptive critic, points to the shower scene in *Psycho* as a precedent that is analogous in terms of plot. His observations quoted below are convincing, but we are justified to broaden their cultural context and also to think of the question of cause and effect in connection with the oracle given to Oedipus:

Consider the totally arbitrary and pointless nature of the shower murder in *Psycho* from the point of view of Marion and her development at that point. From her point of view – which is after all that from which we have been watching the film – the murder has no dramatic, symbolic, or thematic justification . . . Marion is saved [through her decision to return the money]. It is partly because the murder

---

[51] The chapter on *The Birds* in Wood 2002: 152–172 brings out the film's themes and qualities; see especially 160 on the conversation scene excerpted here. Paul Burton 2001 gives a classicist's perspective on the film. In *Pilgrimage* (1933) director John Ford had portrayed a mother even worse than the one in *The Birds*.

is – again, from her point of view – entirely arbitrary and unpredictable that its effect is so shattering. We are made to feel at that moment the precariousness, the utter unreasonableness, of life . . . the murder of Marion Crane is in no way and to no extent either provoked or deserved.

The last sentence quoted is wholly applicable to Oedipus and his oracle. The sudden reversal of Oedipus' fate is equal to what Wood calls the "disturbing sense of precariousness, of unpredictability" in Marion's death. We may compare the parallel nature of Greek tragedy and much of Greek thought.[52] Wood then turns to *The Birds* in even stronger Sophoclean terms, if without realizing that he is doing so:

And this seems to me the function of the birds: they are a concrete embodiment of the arbitrary and unpredictable, of whatever makes human life and human relationships precarious, a reminder of fragility and instability that cannot be ignored or evaded and, beyond that, of the possibility that life is meaningless and absurd.[53]

As Wood and others have noted, the birds' attack on Melanie in the attic is a close parallel to the shower attack on Marion not only thematically but also stylistically, especially in the rapid editing of both sequences. Again Wood's analysis brings out the underlying Sophoclean parallel:

The appeal [of the extreme violence that we watch] is not sadistic: there is too strong a sense of participation: we know it is *our* agony, *our* anguish that we are witnessing, for the birds are waiting for all of us.[54]

This points us back to the nature of Sophocles' Oedipus as an Everyman. In real life we are just as unlikely to kill our fathers and marry our mothers as we are to be killed in the shower by a psychopath or almost killed by a flock of birds. But we respond emotionally to the fate of these characters and see ourselves in them.

In Hitchcock's *Marnie* (1964) parallels to Sophocles' *Oedipus the King* may not be immediately apparent, but they become evident in the assessment reached by Wood in a re-evaluation of the film.[55] While he does not refer to Sophocles at all but only considers *Marnie* from cinematic and psychoanalytic perspectives, his conclusion applies equally to the ancient play and the modern film:

---

[52] Cf. Nussbaum 2001.
[53] The three quotations are from Wood 2002: 153–154.    [54] Wood 2002: 171.
[55] Wood 2002: 388–405. This chapter, entitled "You Freud, Me Hitchcock: *Marnie* Revisited," complements the earlier one at 173–197.

Freud claimed (correctly, in my opinion) that our entire basic character is formed during the first five years of our lives, the period to which we have least access via memory. It is a truly terrifying perception, which is perhaps why *Marnie* is Hitchcock's most deeply disturbing film. The child Marnie is of course somewhat more than five years old, but the trauma (with its oblivion) places her in much the same situation as the rest of us, the adult Marnie formed by events of which she has no clear or coherent memory. Marnie is on one level a "special case" (not all of us have beaten sailors' heads in with pokers), yet she can also be read as an extreme case of ourselves, living our lives ("A blind man battering blind men") with only the very vaguest notion of how we, as human beings, have been formed, vaguely aware that our behavior is ultimately determined (hard as we struggle toward full consciousness) by events, relationships, circumstances which we may never be able to drag out from the confusion of our early memories.[56]

Both Oedipus and Marnie experienced a trauma in early childhood or very shortly after birth – the age difference is insignificant – which remains unremembered or dormant until a third party provides the necessary information about the event. To both, obtaining this knowledge is emotionally devastating but also liberating: they now know who they really are. As Wood rightly says, Marnie is a unique case and a kind of Everywoman at the same time. Previously Wood had made this point more explicitly:

if Marnie is extreme, she represents an extreme of something relevant to us all: the grip of the past on the present. If few of us are Marnies, there is something of Marnie in all of us . . . anyone, given the circumstances, could be Marnie.[57]

Oedipus, too, is such an extreme case who nevertheless can represent all of mankind: anyone, given the circumstances, could be Oedipus. If this were not so, it is doubtful whether the power and appeal of Sophocles' play could have remained undiminished over almost two and a half millennia, with or without Freud. Wood's quotation from William Butler Yeats's poem "A Dialogue of Self and Soul" (1933) is therefore even more apposite than he realized: "a blind man battering blind men."

It is no surprise then that scholars should link Hitchcock himself to the myth of Oedipus. In a chapter entitled "A Visit to the Sphinx," Peter Conrad discusses a publicity photograph of Hitchcock and the Egyptian Sphinx and comments:

Hitchcock had a perfect right to position himself competitively beside the Sphinx. She represents the terrors of our condition, compounded in the puzzles she set men to solve . . . Freud, following Oedipus, set out to tame the Sphinx . . . As interpreted by Freud, the legend offered therapeutic hope: Oedipus is the analyst,

---

[56] Wood 2002: 405.   [57] Wood 2002: 182.

vanquishing the monstrous irrationality of illness. Hitchcock, however, identified with the incubus, not with the clever hero who outwitted her. His own riddles, concealed in his films, are harder to solve, and the answers offer no reprieve for traumatized human beings.

He does dare us to try our luck, like Oedipus . . . The films play hide-and-seek with us, scattering false clues . . . [Hitchcock] did the enciphering or encoding, making up the mysteries, and derived his own pleasure from baffling the brains of would-be interpreters.[58]

Conrad adduces a revealing moment in Hitchcock's *Rear Window*, which points to the parallel situations of a fictional character and its creator and, simultaneously, of a psychoanalyst and a patient. The heroine,

persuaded of the salesman's guilt [of murdering his wife], adopts the voice of the analyst or the critic, like Oedipus outfacing the Sphinx. "Tell me everything you saw," she says to [the hero], adding after a brief pause, "and what you think it means." She knows that there are layered secrets awaiting retrieval beneath the surface, as in the sealed tombs of that Egyptian valley . . . Hitchcock, whenever he felt in danger of being found out, said that critics dug too deep: disdaining profundity, the films – he claimed – were just entertainments. Thus, like the Sphinx, he guarded his secret for a while longer.[59]

Hitchcock's *Strangers on a Train* (1951), based on Patricia Highsmith's psychological thriller, deals with a variation on the parent–child relationship and its attendant neuroses. A pampered and affluent young man wants to arrange the murder of his father in order to have his mother all to himself. The version of the film shown in Britain, slightly longer than the American release, made it as obvious as was then possible that he is a homosexual. A related variation on this theme in *film noir* is that of a young wife and her lover conspiring to kill her considerably older and unloved husband, who may be a father figure to the younger man and will be succeeded by him. The two most famous examples are based on novels by James M. Cain. One is *The Postman Always Rings Twice*, filmed under this title by Tay Garnett in 1946 and Bob Rafelson in 1981 and as *Ossessione* by Luchino Visconti in 1942, the beginning of Italian neorealist cinema. The other is *Double Indemnity*, filmed in 1944 by Billy Wilder and the inspiration for Lawrence Kasdan's *Body Heat* (1981) and John Dahl's *The Last Seduction* (1994).

---

[58] Conrad 2000: 231–232 and 234.
[59] Conrad 2000: 232. One of the most famous images to convey the enigmatic nature of cinema is the 1931 photo montage by Clarence Sinclair Bull which put the face of Greta Garbo on the Egyptian Sphinx.

A structural analogy to Sophocles' play, the one tragedy which Aristotle praises most highly in his *Poetics* as a perfect drama, can be found in what many consider to be the greatest film of all time, Orson Welles's *Citizen Kane* (1941). In both works the central character's life and fate is being reconstructed in the course of the story. Oedipus himself and the reporter searching for the meaning of Charles Foster Kane's enigmatic last word "Rosebud" collect information. On the stage we have speeches; their visual equivalent in the film are flashbacks. As has been observed about Sophocles' play: "Because of this way of telling its story, the play is also about narrative."[60] The same is true for Welles's film. American screenwriter and film teacher Michael Tierno calls *Citizen Kane* "perfect by Aristotle's standards" and concludes: "*Citizen Kane* is a 'perfect' American tragedy, just as *Oedipus Rex* is a 'perfect' Greek one."[61]

A dramatic form closely related to tragedy is melodrama. One of the most famous filmmakers in this genre was Douglas Sirk (originally Hans Detlev Sierck). He directed high-class melodramas in the 1930s in Germany and in the 1950s in Hollywood. The latter films used to be dismissed as ultra-romantic women's pictures or "weepies," but there is more going on under their glossy surface than meets the eye. In *All That Heaven Allows* (1955) Sirk uses a stereotypical romance to make bitter comments on the complacency, hypocrisy, and emotional coldness of apparently good upper-middle-class society. In his own words: "America then was feeling safe and sure of herself, a society primly sheltering its comfortable achievements and institutions."[62]

In the fictional New England town of Stoningham, whose very name reveals the character of most of its inhabitants, an attractive lonely widow with a teenage son and daughter falls in love with a younger man who is her social inferior. The pressures of bourgeois prejudice that her fellow townspeople bring to bear on her almost make her give up her one remaining chance at happiness. Early in the film she prepares to go out with an older man who wants to marry her but in whom she sees no more than a friend and companion. For the occasion she is wearing a red dress. (Elegant color compositions play a major thematic part in this film.) The dress precipitates the following conversation among her and her children, here slightly abbreviated:

---

[60] Segal 2001: 61.
[61] Tierno 2002: 107–108. There is some hyperbole and flippancy in this handbook on screenwriting, but Tierno's approach to Aristotle and film is sound.
[62] Quoted from Halliday 1972: 98.

*Son*: Holy cats, mother!
*Mother*: Do you like it?
*Son*: I guess it's all right, but isn't it – cut kinda low?
*Daughter*: A typical Oedipus reaction.
*Mother*: A what?
*Daughter*: A son subconsciously resents his mother being attracted to other men.
  We call it an Oedipus Complex. Happens all the time.

This leaves the mother speechless. But the brief exchange foreshadows what is to come. When their mother has become serious about her new man, her children come to resent her out of selfish concern for their own status in society. What had at first appeared to be model children turn out to be no more than egotists. Here and in other films, most famously *Imitation of Life* (1958), Sirk used melodrama as a vehicle for social criticism and brought his own experiences into his perspectives of American society. In Germany Sirk had become well acquainted with political and racial prejudices and hypocrisy since his political views were on the left and his wife was Jewish. They emigrated from Germany because of the Nazis. It is telling that the first major scene of *All That Heaven Allows* in which darker tones surface should be an Oedipal one. In interviews conducted in 1970 Sirk, who had had years of theatrical experience in Germany as a young man and had staged *Oedipus Rex* during the 1928–1929 season, again and again refers to Aeschylus, Sophocles, and Euripides when discussing his work.[63] Feminist film scholar Laura Mulvey observes: "While the Western and the gangster film celebrate the ups and downs endured by men of action, the melodramas of Douglas Sirk, like the tragedies of Euripides, probing the pent-up emotion, bitterness and disillusion well known to women, act as a corrective."[64]

COMEDY

In recent years psychoanalysis in general and the Oedipus Complex in particular have come under increasing attack. Parody and satire, however, have accompanied Oedipus and Freud for much longer. In the cinema Woody Allen has delivered a large body of work centered on the persona of a neurotic urban intellectual, invariably played by himself.[65] His best-known film incorporating *Oedipus Rex* is *Mighty Aphrodite* (1995), a love story with a twist reminiscent of the entanglements of classical myth and drama. A

[63] See Halliday 1972: 84, 93–96, 119, and 132. Sirk had learned Latin and Greek in Germany.
[64] Mulvey 1989c: 39. Her article was first published in the journal *Movie* in 1977.
[65] Cf. Cohen 2004.

chorus and characters from Sophocles' play appear in pseudo-ancient garb but in an authentic setting, the ruins of the Greek theater at Taormina on Sicily. They summarize the story of Oedipus and his family and introduce his modern descendant (of sorts) and his erotic predicaments. The verbal humor in the opening choral ode derives from the rhetoric of the kind we associate with serious drama. The chorus speaks of Oedipus' "lust for expiation" and calls him a "lost victim of bewildered desire." Such high-flowing language is then undercut by bathetic punch lines ("Children are serious stuff") and anachronisms. The ancient Greeks even become time travelers and directly take part in the film's plot, as when the chorus leader suddenly appears in New York City as advisor to the protagonist. After all, comment on the action is the chorus's main function, as everybody knows. *Deconstructing Harry* (1997), Allen's satire of psychoanalysis and the literature industry, contains a brief reference to Sophocles when author Harry tells Cookie, a prostitute: "A great writer named Sophocles said that it was probably best not to be born at all."[66] Her reply: "Harry, it's a little too late for that." In *Hollywood Ending* (2002) Allen plays a down-on-his-luck film director who develops a case of hysterical blindness when he begins to shoot the big film that is meant to give him the chance to return to his earlier form and fame.[67] By contrast, Allen's *Match Point* (2005) is a dark tale about love and fate, patterned along the lines of ancient tragedy.

The Oedipal archetype of the mother who won't let her adult son grow up or become independent is a staple of Jewish humor and duly recurs in Allen's work. A case in point is the short film he contributed to the 1989 anthology *New York Stories*. An overbearing mother magically ascends to the sky, from which her gigantic face hovers above the city, haunts her son, and wreaks havoc on his life. The first gag in this film is its title, a pun on the best-known version of that of Sophocles' work: "Oedipus Wrecks."[68]

A variation on the same subject had been filmed a year earlier by popular German comic Loriot (i.e. Viktor von Bülow) in his feature-length *Ödipussi*. A meek and well-mannered middle-aged man, played by the writer-director, is hopelessly under the thumb of his domineering mother.

---

[66] Cf. Sophocles, *Oedipus at Colonus* 1224–1225.

[67] A review of the film by Steve Warren in the Boston area paper *Bay Windows* of May 2, 2002 (*ArtsPlus* section, 35), is entitled "Oedipus Di-Rex-tor."

[68] Independent film and video artists turn to Oedipus, too. Here is one example. The New York University library website gives the following summary of the 26-minute short *Oedipus Hex*: "A free, updated, tongue-in-cheek retelling of the Oedipus story, set in present day New York. The title role is played by Ed . . . , a neurotic young man who is portraying Oedipus the King in a version of the play written by his gay lover. Mayhem ensues as Ed's real father turns out to be his psychiatrist."

She runs his life and interferes in his first-ever attempt at meeting a woman – a psychotherapist, no less. Appropriately for the Oedipal theme, the mother utterly infantilizes her son. Her term of endearment for him is "Pussi."[69] The repressed son's only escape from the tight grip of his mother is a dream. Late one night he happens to overturn his mother's photo on his nightstand. He goes to sleep feeling guilty, only to meet his mother in a kitschy slow-motion dream sequence. Impulsively he pulls her hat down over her ears and eyes. This rebellious action shocks him into waking up. Devoted son that he is, he immediately calls her on the telephone to reassure himself that she is all right. But the dream provides Pussi with a – for him – daring inspiration for his real-life revolt against his mother at the end of the film. It is unobtrusively symbolic. Pussi and his would-be girlfriend are back-seat passengers in a car driven by the mother through a peaceful country setting. The situation perfectly summarizes everything: life appears to be calm; the mother drives the car, drives her son and his entire life, and drives him crazy to boot. What to do? Again impulsively Pussi reaches for his mother's hat and pulls it down. The car now veers off the road and loses its way in the fields. This is the end, but it is not a happy ending. Nor is it a solution to Pussi's Oedipal dilemma. Loriot's satire ends on a note of whimsy and regret.

Yes, Oedipus certainly wrecks. He does so again in Harold Ramis's *Analyze This* (1999), a comedy-satire on both psychoanalysis and the Mafia. The combination works surprisingly well, as it will no longer do three years later in the weak sequel *Analyze That*. Robert De Niro, a specialist in playing ice-cold tough guys, here is a ruthless Mafioso but he is rather dim, soft at heart, and in the throes of a midlife-and-Mafia crisis. When he consults a therapist, he hears for the first time about the Oedipus Complex while discussing the death of his father:

*Analyst*: Any feelings of guilt?

*Mafioso*: About what? I didn't kill him.

*Analyst*: I know that, but I'm just speculating, Paul, that maybe in some way you may have wanted him to die.

*Mafioso*: Why would I want my father to die?

*Analyst*: Well, you said that you were fighting. He slapped you around because you were rebelling against his authority. There may have been some unresolved Oedipal conflict.

---

[69] The name Oedipus lends itself to easy punning, as in Frank Tuttle's musical comedy *Roman Scandals* (1933): Eddie, a young American played by the film's star, singer-comedian Eddie Cantor, imagines himself back in the Roman Empire. He now needs a classical name and becomes "Eddipus." The independent American short *An Enigma* (2001), directed by Dennis Neal Vaughn, features a character called Ed Rex.

*Mafioso*:  English! English!
*Analyst*:  Oedipus was a Greek king who killed his father and married his mother.
*Mafioso*:  Pfff! Fuckin' Greeks.
*Analyst*:  It's an instinctual developmental *drive*. The young boy wants to *replace* his father so that he can totally possess his *mother*.
*Mafioso*:  What're you saying? That I wanted to fuck my mother?
*Analyst*:  N-no. It's a primal fantasy –
*Mafioso*:  Have you ever *seen* my mother? Are you out of your fuckin' *mind*?
*Analyst*:  It's Freud.
*Mafioso*:  Well, then Freud's a sick fuck, and you are, too, for bringin' it up.
*Analyst*:  It's –
*Mafioso*:  Yecch!


The information about Freud and Oedipus leaves a lasting impression on our criminal, who will later confess: "I can't even call my mother on the phone after that thing you told me."[70]

Two earlier films are noteworthy for a more sophisticated comic incorporation of Greek drama into their modern settings. Vincente Minnelli's classic musical *The Band Wagon* (1953) uses Sophocles to demonstrate the culture clash between the Old World and the New, replete with a send-up of European pretentiousness. A famous but egomaniacal British actor, producer, and director – played by a famous British actor, producer, and director – contrasts with down-to-earth American straightforwardness. The difference is personified in the two actors, Jack Buchanan and Fred Astaire. An American cliché has it that European culture is high-brow and boring; at least on the American stage it can be no match for the excitement stirred up by the brassy and jazzy Broadway show whose genesis is the film's story. (Cf. *Down to Earth*, discussed in Chapter 2.) The first moment in which the film makes fun of high European culture occurs when we see the billboard announcing a theater's current program, a production of *Oedipus Rex*. The name of the star, producer, director, and adaptor (!) of the play appears four times, three of them in progressively larger type, and virtually shout out his egomania (Fig. 15). Sophocles is nowhere mentioned. Then we hear the star complain that a spotlight had not been on him accurately enough: "Don't let's keep it a secret I'm in the show!"

---

[70] In Clive Donner's *What's New, Pussycat?* (1965), written by Woody Allen, a psychiatrist (played by Peter Sellers) is satirized for being as dim-witted as he is lecherous. Theodore J. Flicker's *The President's Analyst* (1967) is a sharp satire of conspiracy-theory films. The application of psychoanalysis to cinema on the part of film scholars and critics may lend itself to ridicule as well; a classic example are the comments by Warshow 2001a: 287, on Tyler 1947; cf. Tyler 1969. Tyler is also the author of well-known books on sex and homosexuality in cinema.

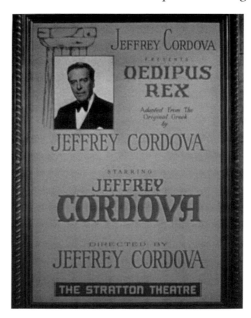

**Fig. 15.** *The Band Wagon.* The author of the play running on Broadway is conspicuous by his absence. (Metro-Goldwyn-Mayer)

*Never On Sunday* (1960) is one of the most famous films made in Greece, written and directed by expatriate American Jules Dassin, who also acts in it. Its heroine is Ilia, a ravishingly beautiful Piraeus prostitute with the proverbial heart of gold. Melina Mercouri, the future Mrs. Dassin, plays her as an incarnation of the carefree, life-affirming, and independent spirit of eternal Greece. Ilia loves Greek tragedy, but with a twist. She does not acknowledge the tragic circumstances of the fate of Medea or Oedipus and simply gives their stories a happy ending by having everybody survive or be reconciled. Ilia comments on *Oedipus Rex*: "One thing is very nice: always Oedipus is talking about his mother. I never saw such a good son who loves so much his mother." She then tells the plot in Greek and concludes (I quote from the English subtitles):

But let's forget all those cruel things. Poor Oedipus, he suffered, they hurt his eyes. But in the end he finds his family, and they all go to the sea shore.

One of Ilia's friends comments: "They *always* go to the sea shore." To Ilia the story of Oedipus may indeed be the greatest love story of all time.

Glossy color and widescreen comedies began to play with sexual innu-endo and risqué jokes (by contemporary standards) even more, usually involving psychoanalysis. Just one noteworthy example is George Cukor's *Something's Got to Give*, a comedy of remarriage filmed in 1962 but unfin-ished after a troubled production history and the death of its star, Marilyn Monroe. Steve Allen plays Dr. Herman Schlick, an anything-but-slick shrink with a to-be-expected German name and, to judge by surviv-ing footage, his own hang-ups when faced with a headstrong if neurotic woman. The good doctor did make it to the screen in Michael Gordon's *Move Over, Darling*, the studio's 1963 release of the same story but with a different cast. It includes the following line: "You know, I truly believe the most vital relationship a woman can establish is not between man and wife. It's the relationship between a woman and her analyst." Both Cukor's and Gordon's versions are remakes of Garson Kanin's *My Favorite Wife* (1940).

Luis Buñuel, cinema's great Surrealist and master of satire, contributed an utterly new Freudian complex to our modern *condition humaine*. In *The Discreet Charm of the Bourgeoisie* (1972) a ditzy young woman confesses that she did not have a happy childhood since she suffered from several complexes. The one she proceeds to identify is "le complexe d'Euclide": the Euclid Complex. This is a joke on the Electra Complex, the female equivalent, as it were, of the Oedipus Complex. The Electra Complex does not occur all that frequently in the cinema, but Nicholas Ray's *Rebel Without a Cause* (1955) and Alan Rudolph's *The Secret Lives of Dentists* (2002) provide examples.[71]

Very different from all these comedies is writer-director Mel Brooks's *History of the World, Part I* (1981). Its very title is a gag: there was never meant to be a second part. Sophistication does not interest Brooks. His film is an irreverent romp through various periods of history. In its longest seg-ment, "The Roman Empire," Brooks pokes fun at all and sundry clichés about antiquity and parodies the tradition of Hollywood spectacles. A famous character like Oedipus must not be missing from these shenani-gans. But Oedipus in Rome instead of Greece? No problem for Brooks,

---

[71] Ray's film, with its theme of insecure and alienated teenage children at sea in unstable family environments, is the more instructive of the two. Its protagonist is desperately looking for a bond with his weakling of a father; in a fit of rage directed chiefly against his mother, he knocks his father to the ground and begins to choke him, eliciting the mother's cry "You'll kill him! You want to kill your own *father*?" His Oedipal frustration is mirrored, if a bit schematically, in the film's second most important family, that of the young girl who will become the hero's love interest. She has problems with her father because she shows her love for him with so much affection that he rejects it. She does not, however, hate her mother, who is as meek and subdued vis-à-vis her husband as the hero's father is vis-à-vis his domineering wife.

**Fig. 16.** *History of the World, Part I.* Oedipus in Rome. (Universal)

because anything goes in his brand of comedy. His two protagonists, stand-up philosopher Comicus, played by Brooks himself, and hip black slave Josephus, encounter a blind beggar in the streets of Rome. We know that he is blind because we twice see him collide with obstacles in his path; we know that this is Oedipus because he wears a sign around his neck with a plea to passers-by: GIVE TO OEDIPUS (Fig. 16). But this Oedipus is a cool black dude in sunglasses. We might call him an ancient "hipster." The pay-off to the brief scene, which lasts no more than twelve seconds, is a raunchy verbal joke. Oedipus sees (!) Josephus approaching from behind and greets him with a "Hey, Josephus!" Josephus greets him back: "Hey, motherfucker!" The joke hinges on the fact that today this last word is ubiquitous in certain circles and has lost all of its literal meaning – but not here.[72] And is this blind but seeing Oedipus no more than a con artist? In *Mighty Aphrodite* Woody Allen includes a parallel moment when the blind prophet Tiresias says he saw that the protagonist's wife had a lover: "You had to be blind not to see it."

In Robert Zemeckis's comedy *Back to the Future* (1985) a time-traveling teenager meets his parents-to-be. They are still high-schoolers and are not even dating each other. Our hero now has to make sure that they begin a romance leading to marriage so that in due course he can be born and become who he is. Romantic complications ensue when his teenage mother, who cannot yet know or even understand his real identity, develops a crush on her future son. Amazed, he exclaims: "My mom has the hots for me!"

---

[72] A variation on this joke, if in a radically different (and not funny) context had appeared in Paul Humfress and Derek Jarman's *Sebastiane* (1976), a British film with Latin dialogue and English subtitles. The command "Age, Oedipus!" is rendered as "Come here, motherfucker!"

Jocasta a hot tomato? Sophocles could never have thought so, but in today's computer-driven age nothing is impossible. Jason Wishnow's *Oedipus* (2004) shows us just such a Jocasta – literally. Wishnow's film is a minimalist travesty of ancient epic films, as its tagline announces: THE STORY OF OEDIPUS, IN 8 MINUTES, PERFORMED BY VEGETABLES. Yes, you've read that correctly: Oedipus is a sad potato, Laius a mighty broccoli, Tiresias, the dour prophet of doom, a grim garlic, and Jocasta – but you already know. She and Oedipus even have a heavy-breathing sex scene. Small wonder that its young writer-director dedicated this "Mama's Boy Production" to his mother.

My examination of the story of Oedipus and related themes illustrates the pervasive presence of antiquity in the history of film in both adaptations and versions which on the surface have no connection to antiquity but often contain close thematic affinities. Chiefly this is due to the archetypal nature of classical myth, to the immense influence of Sophocles on Western literature, and to Freud, perhaps the single most effective modern figure to bridge the gap between the past and the present. So it seems appropriate to close with another Freudian Oedipus film, but one that was never made and that could never have been made despite Hollywood's propensity for titillation. As a young reporter in Vienna, future writer-director Billy Wilder had once attempted to interview Freud at his home – unsuccessfully, because Freud immediately showed him the door.[73] In his films Wilder repeatedly made fun of psychoanalysts, for instance in *The Emperor Waltz* (1948), *The Seven Year Itch* (1955), and *The Front Page* (1973).[74] Late in life Wilder told a German journalist the outline of a comedy he had thought about making. A son and his mother fall passionately in love. They decide to disregard all social prejudices and live together as husband and wife. After many happy years the mother reveals to her son a terrible truth: "I have to confess something. All these years I lied to you and cheated you, for I'm not really your mother." Hearing this, the young man collapses in tears and shoots himself dead.[75]

---

[73] Wilder recounts meeting Freud in Crowe 1999: 140–141 and in Chandler 2002: 37–38; cf. Karasek 2002: 47.

[74] Cf. Crowe 1999: 277 and Karasek 2002: 300. In Wilder's romantic comedy *Love in the Afternoon* (1957) a high-society lady repeatedly but mistakenly suspects her lapdog of misbehaving indoors and finally threatens it: "First thing tomorrow morning you're going to the analyst."

[75] I paraphrase the German text of Karasek 2002: 146.

CHAPTER 4

# *Patriotism and war:*
# *"Sweet and fitting it is to die*
# *for one's country"*

"War is the father of all things." This is the most familiar version of a famous saying by the Presocratic philosopher Heraclitus of Ephesus.[1] In Homer's *Iliad*, the first work of Western literature, Ares, the personification of war, is the most hateful of all gods even to his father Zeus.[2] As terrible as war always has been, it is often presented to be justifiable or necessary, especially as a supposed guarantor of peace: *si vis pacem, para bellum* ("if you want peace, prepare for war").[3] So many regard war for the sake of peace, war in defense of one's country, or preventive war outside one's own borders for the sake of homeland or national security as necessary, mainly those who can safely stay home. Most people who are against war can speak or act in its favor when duty calls and go as far as to demand or make what is euphemistically called the supreme sacrifice. Again and again one more war is to be waged to end all wars.[4] "Once more into the breach, dear friends, once more" – for king and country, home and family, freedom and our way of life, and all the values of civilization threatened by the enemy. Mission accomplished, we will lay down our arms, study war no more, and enjoy the fruits of lasting peace. In retrospect Cato the Elder appears to have put it most aptly: "War feeds itself."[5] Patriotic fervor may well be the most nourishing dish on war's menu.

---

[1] Heraclitus, Fragm. 53 Diels-Kranz. The fragment in its entirety reads: "War is the father of all, the king of all, and some he shows as gods, others as men; some he makes slaves, others free." It illustrates Heraclitus' idea of the endless conflict of opposites in a continuously changing world.

[2] Zeus says so himself at *Iliad* 5.890.

[3] Vegetius, *Epitome rei militaris* 3 (preface): "He who desires peace should prepare for war." Variations on this sentiment appear at Thucydides, *The Peloponnesian War* 1.124; Cato the Elder, *Monostichs* 91; Cicero, *Philippics* 7.6.19 and *On Duties* 1.23.80; Publilius Syrus, *Sentences* P 16; Livy, *From the Foundation of the City* 6.18.7; Cornelius Nepos, *Epaminondas* 5.4; Statius, *Thebaid* 7.554; Augustine, *City of God* 19.12; Curtius Rufus, *Histories of Alexander the Great* 7.30.

[4] Cf. the title of Vidal 2002.

[5] Quoted at Livy, *From the Foundation of the City* 34.9.12: *bellum se ipsum alet.*

## HOMER, HORACE, AND THE HEROIC TRADITION

"Sweet and fitting it is to die for one's country" – Horace's line is one of the most famous quotations from Roman literature.[6] It expresses a sentiment with which all who love their country will be predisposed to agree. Individual valor in battle – *virtus* to the Romans; in Greek, *andreia*, *aretê*, and related terms – constitutes the fundamental archaic concept of heroism. It was first and best described in the *Iliad*. The warrior's reward is "unperishing glory," the eternal remembrance of his heroic deeds in stories and in the epic songs which future generations will recite about him.[7] To attain such glory the hero proves himself to be "the best of the Achaians" (*aristos Achaiôn*). Accordingly the hero Peleus instructed his son Achilles, the greatest of the Greeks in the Trojan War, "to be always best in battle and pre-eminent beyond all others."[8] The words which the Lycian hero Sarpedon, a son of Zeus who fights on the side of the Trojans, speaks to Glaucus, his comrade-in-arms, spell out the heroic code in detail:

> Glaukos, why is it you and I are honoured before others
> with pride of place, the choice meats and the filled wine cups
> in Lykia, and all men look on us as if we were immortals,
> and we are appointed a great piece of land by the banks of Xanthos,
> good land, orchard and vineyard, and ploughland for the planting of wheat?
> Therefore it is our duty in the forefront of the Lykians
> to take our stand, and bear our part of the blazing of battle,
> so that a man of the close-armoured Lykians may say of us:
> "Indeed, these are no ignoble men who are lords of Lykia,
> these kings of ours, who feed upon the fat sheep appointed
> and drink the exquisite sweet wine, since indeed there is strength
> of valour in them, since they fight in the forefront of the Lykians."
> Man, supposing you and I, escaping this battle,
> would be able to live on forever, ageless, immortal,
> so neither would I myself go on fighting in the foremost
> nor would I urge you into the fighting where men win glory.
> But now, seeing that the spirits of death stand close about us
> in their thousands, no man can turn aside nor escape them,
> let us go on and win glory for ourselves, or yield it to others.[9]

---

[6] Horace, *Odes* 3.2.13: *dulce et decorum est pro patria mori*. The first six poems of Horace's third book of *Odes* are commonly called the Roman Odes; in them Horace addresses the young generation from the perspective of a teacher and, extolling traditional moral values, contrasts the virtues of the past with the incipient degeneracy of the present. As was commonly the case in ancient Greece and Rome, Horace considered education and instruction to be among the poet's important tasks; cf. *Epistles* 2.1.126–138 and *Art of Poetry* 391–407.

[7] *Iliad* 9.413: *kleos aphthiton*. On heroism and its implications see in detail Nagy 1999.

[8] *Iliad* 11.783. English quotations of the *Iliad* are taken from Lattimore 1951, here 255.

[9] *Iliad* 12.310–328; Lattimore 1951: 266–267.

Homeric heroes prove themselves as the best by an *aristeia*, either an extended killing spree, in which they slaughter large numbers of the enemy, or a duel, in which they defeat a famous enemy hero, or some combination of both.

The poet, however, presents the hero's undying glory as an ambiguous quality: "The Homeric hero is anxious for glory, and he faces the full horrors of death. But as there is no posthumous reward for the brave man in the other world, so the consolation of glory is a chilly one . . . The hero dies, not so much for his own glory, not even so much for his friends, as for the glory of song, which explains to a spellbound audience the greatness and fragility of the life of man." This song is the *Iliad* itself, and its central concern is "the meaning and the universality of human doom."[10] The poem's very beginning, the invocation of the Muse, which cites the anger of Achilles as the cause and starting point of the plot, makes this clear, in language both vivid and gruesome:

> Sing, goddess, the anger of Peleus' son Achilleus
> and its devastation, which put pains thousandfold upon the Achaians,
> hurled in their multitudes to the house of Hades strong souls
> of heroes, but gave their bodies to be the delicate feasting
> of dogs, of all birds, and the will of Zeus was accomplished . . . [11]

The anger of Achilles causes its greatest devastation not to the enemy but to the hero's own side. From the outset the poet emphasizes the dire nature of battle. For this reason the *Iliad* is not a glorification of war:

Warfare is accepted, like mortality, grief, and suffering, as an inevitable part of human life, arising partly from human weakness and partly from the will of the gods . . . it is not the poet's purpose to glorify war . . . Though they may glory in victory, the characters are not said to approve warfare itself . . . Homer sees warfare as a necessity in human affairs, and as a field on which to play out the unrelenting struggle for honor, even at the cost of one's life; but it is one of the evils the gods have decreed for mankind, not a glorious opportunity for heroism.[12]

The Horatian idea that the hero ought to take up arms to defend his country goes back to the *Iliad*. In Book Fifteen the Trojan attack comes close to turning the tide of the war, and Hector exhorts the Trojans and their allies:

---

[10] Griffin 1980: 102 and 69.    [11] *Iliad* 1.1–5; Lattimore 1951: 59.
[12] Edwards 1987: 154, 155, and 157. Cf. also Schein 1984: 84 and 163.

Fight on then by the ships together. He who among you
finds by spear thrown or spear thrust his death and destiny,
let him die. He has no dishonour when he dies defending
his country, for then his wife shall be saved and his children afterwards,
and his house and property shall not be damaged, if the Achaians
must go away with their ships to the beloved land of their fathers.[13]

A fragment by the seventh-century-BC Spartan poet Tyrtaeus, here quoted
in excerpts, derives from Homer and is the direct predecessor of Horace's
restatement:

> For it is fine to die in the front line,
>     a brave man fighting for his fatherland . . .
> So let us fight with spirit for our land,
>     die for our sons, and spare our lives no more.
> You young men, keep together, hold the line,
>     do not start panic or disgraceful rout.
> Keep grand and valiant spirits in your hearts,
>     be not in love with life – the fight's with men!
>     . . . But for the young man, still
>     in glorious prime, [death in battle] is all beautiful:
> alive, he draws men's eyes and women's hearts;
>     felled in the front line, he is lovely yet.
> Let every man then, feet set firm apart,
>     bite on his lip and stand against the foe.[14]

One more example of such poetry will suffice. In the fifth century
Simonides of Keos composed the following poem on the Spartan king
Leonidas, hero of Thermopylae:

> When men die [for their country,]
> fame is their fortune, fair their fate,
> their tomb an altar; in the place of wailing
> there is remembrance, and their dirge is praise.
> This winding-sheet is such
> as neither mould nor Time that conquers all
> can fade; this sepulchre
> of fine men has adopted as its sacristan

---

[13] *Iliad* 15.494–499; Lattimore 1951: 322.

[14] Tyrtaeus, Fragm. 10.1–2, 13–18, and 27–32 (West); quoted from West 1993: 24. There is evidence that three centuries later Tyrtaeus' poems were recited to Spartan armies (West, xii). On connections between Tyrtaeus' poem and the *Iliad* cf. Kullmann 1992a, especially 268 on the contrast between Tyrtaeus' and Homer's views of death in battle.

> Greece's good name. Witness Leonidas,
> the king of Sparta: he has left
> a monument of valour, and perennial fame.[15]

By Horace's time, however, the kind of personal heroism which the *Iliad* and later poetry present to us had ceased to be a decisive factor of victory. We find examples of it in Virgil's *Aeneid* and in the early books of the historian Livy, Roman authors contemporary with Horace. But the heroic struggles of Aeneas, his men, and their enemies and the greatest examples of *virtus* recounted in Livy are all set in the long-ago and quasi-mythical past. The heroism which Horace extols or seems to extol has become outdated.[16] Since the military reforms of Marius and Sulla and the campaigns of Pompey and Caesar, the nature of Roman warfare had significantly changed, despite some exceptions like those which Caesar describes in *The Gallic War* and *The Civil War*.[17] Now a commander's strategic planning and the sheer supremacy of his forces decide the outcome while individual soldiers function more like pawns on his chessboard than as well-springs of bravery at critical moments. At the battles of Pharsalus in 48 BC and at Philippi in 42 BC, for example, individual legionaries are small cogs in large military machines, whose most important tactical unit is the cohort, a body of 480–600 men.[18] Warfare in the late Roman republic and in the empire foreshadows modern mass warfare. When Horace wrote his poetry, Roman war had become largely anonymous.

To readers of Horace's Roman Odes who keep these circumstances in mind the patriotic sentiment of *dulce et decorum* thus becomes questionable (in the literal sense of the word). It should not necessarily be taken as a straightforward exhortation to lay down one's life for one's country in blind obedience to its call ("Right or wrong, my country!"). Nevertheless it has usually been taken as just such an absolute, perhaps even categorical, imperative to justify a martial course of action. Representative examples

---

[15] Simonides, Fragm. *P.M.G.* 531 Page; quoted from West 1993: 163. Simonides and Leonidas will be discussed further below. Funke 1997: 77–78 lists additional parallels from Greek and Roman literature; cf. 80–81.

[16] Syndikus 1973: 24–33 discusses this aspect of the ode in detail; see especially 26–27.

[17] Caesar's account of the heroism of the two centurions Pullo and Vorenus (*The Gallic War* 5.44) is a good example. A modern historian comments: "The two men . . . performed a spectacular feat . . . but Caesar does not say that he rewarded them or promoted them" (Southern 2006: 304). When a centurion's personal heroism did save the day, Caesar rewarded and promoted him (*The Civil War* 3.53).

[18] H. M. D. Parker 1993: 26–28 and 47–48 (on cohorts), Southern 2006: 194–199 (on battle and battle planning), and Webster 1979: 221–230 (on battle tactics) are examples of readily accessible work providing a first orientation on this subject. In general see Le Bohec 1993.

appear in two tragedies by French playwright Pierre Corneille.[19] Nathan Hale, an American spy who was hanged at age 21 by the British during the Revolutionary War, said under the gallows: "I only regret that I have but one life to lose for my country." His words derive from Joseph Addison's *Cato* (1713), a tragedy about Cato the Younger that was popular during and after the American Revolution. Shortly before his own death, Addison's Cato requests that the dead body of his son Marcus be brought to him:

> Full in my sight, that I may view at leisure
> The bloody corse, and count those glorious wounds.
> – How beautiful is death, when earned by virtue!
> Who would not be that youth? what pity is it
> That we can die but once to serve our country![20]

The twentieth century saw large-scale and increasingly technological and mechanized forms of war. These had their precursors in two major nineteenth-century wars, in which advanced technology and large supplies of *matériel* had become decisive but which still exhibited features of traditional warfare. Individual acts of heroism patterned on ancient and medieval codes of honor occurred in the Crimean War (1853–1856), made famous despite its slaughters in Alfred Lord Tennyson's poem "The Charge of the Light Brigade," and in the American Civil War (1861–1865), the first war to use, for instance, a primitive form of submarine.[21] The heroism

---

[19] *Le Cid* (1636), Act 4, Scene 5: *Mourir pour le pays n'est pas un triste sort; / C'est s'immortaliser par une belle mort* ("To die for one's country is not a sad fate; it is to become immortal by a beautiful death"); *Horace* (1640), Act 2, Scene 3: *Mourir pour le pays est un si digne sort, / qu'on briguerait en foule une si belle mort* ("To die for one's country is such a dignified fate that we should court in great numbers such a beautiful death"). In Alain Resnais's film *Mon oncle d'Amérique* (1980) the latter lines are quoted by a young boy as an illustration of rote learning; he then quotes what he has been taught about the supremacy of the white race.

[20] Joseph Addison, *Cato: A Tragedy* 4.4.78–82; quoted from Addison 2004: 84. Cf. the epigraph to Addison's "Freeholder, No. 5" of January 6, 1716, a quotation (in Latin) of Cicero, *On Duties* 1.57 ( . . . one's country, "for which no good man would hesitate to die if he could serve it" that way). S. J. Harrison 1993 adduces this passage from Cicero for an explanation of Horace's line. Cf. Cicero, *For Milo* 104; *For Balbus* 26; *For Sestius* 47; *On the Laws* 2.5; *Philippics* 14.31. Cf. Brutus' words in Shakespeare, *Julius Caesar* 3.2.46–48: "I have the same dagger for myself, when it shall please my country to need my death." Quoted from Shakespeare 1955: 80. – Addison's *Cato* was a favorite play of George Washington, who saw several productions of it. Hale was Washington's spy; Washington patterned himself on and was often compared to ancient Romans who stood ready to die for their freedom.

[21] Tennyson's poem inspired films in 1936 and 1968, both called *The Charge of the Light Brigade*. The former was unabashedly heroic; it was directed by Michael Curtiz, with the titular charge directed by B. Reeves Eason, who in 1924 had directed the chariot race for Fred Niblo's *Ben-Hur: A Tale of the Christ*. The latter, directed by Tony Richardson, was far more critical of military incompetence and irresponsibility. For examples of the influence of classical ideas about chivalry, heroism, and glorious death in the American Civil War see Richard F. Miller 2005 and Bundy 2005, a biography of Charles Russell Lowell, Jr., the brother of Robert Gould Shaw. The latter was the subject of Edward Zwick's film *Glory* (1989).

and valiant death of an individual soldier existed alongside the previously unimaginable killing potential of weapons of mass destruction. The futility of traditional chivalry became evident in the carnage resulting from cavalry attacks against machine-gun nests. Gallant defiance of death in the face of a technologically superior and hence unreachable or even faceless enemy had become anachronistic, a lesson usually learned by hindsight. Most of the heroes of these wars and the commanders who sent them to their deaths did not realize that their days were past. Still, patriotic heroism can commend death in battle. As late as 1949, for example, French surrealist and cubist writer Pierre Reverdy contributed the poem *Dulce et decorum est pro patria mori* to a volume commemorating Jean-Sébastien Galanis, who had died "for France" in 1940.

### CHIVALRY AND CLASSICAL CULTURE IN WORLD WAR I

The Great War was one of the most devastating reminders of the futility of personal bravery in the face of the enemy in the modern age. With around nine million dead, the war irrevocably brought about the end of a tradition, for heroism against industrial weaponry such as tanks, submarines, machine guns, poison gas, or flame throwers was almost always futile. Survival was rarely a result of gallantry. The unprecedented occurrences of shell shock among soldiers revealed more than anything else not only the war's inhumanity but also showed that mankind was on the brink of being conquered by its own ingenuity for devising new and ever more effective ways to kill.[22]

 This realization mainly came afterwards. During the war itself patriotic songs and poems took recourse to long-standing models, as in the sonnets of British poet Rupert Brooke. To most of the young recruits who left school to enlist, the war was "thoroughly romanticised by being linked with medieval chivalry and classical antiquity, and therefore directly back to their schooldays, where in classics and history they had absorbed the

---

[22] Cf. Kramer 2007, with additional references. – The moment in the World War I sequence in Charles Chaplin's *The Great Dictator* (1940) in which a shell dropped from a huge cannon takes on an independent "life" of its own brings home the point in a manner simultaneously funny and terrifying. The effectiveness of the scene lies in its humor stressing the absurdity of war and in its serious undertone showing the uncontrollable destructiveness of mechanization. By contrast, an Italian historical film made before World War I was unashamedly heroic and replete with the patriotic sentiments its title indicates; this was Enrico Guazzoni's *Pro patria mori* (1912), set in the Napoleonic wars. It had great popular success in France. Two years later Guazzoni followed it with another Napoleonic epic, *Scuola d'eroi* ("School of Heroes").

ideology that now sustained them."[23] What a modern cultural historian observed about Oxford University applies in general to upper-class British education of the early twentieth century: "Greats (the Literae Humaniores) were . . . a 'School of intrinsic merit' that stood 'alone as the best test of a man's ability'."[24] An example harking back to Homer's *Iliad* is the poem "Stand in the Trench, Achilles!" by Oxfordian Patrick Shaw-Stewart, who was killed in action in 1917:

> Was it so hard, Achilles,
>   So very hard to die?
> Thou knowest and I know not –
>   So much the happier I.
>
> I will go back this morning,
>   From Imbros over the sea;
> Stand in the trench, Achilles,
>   Flame-capped, and shout for me![25]

Poems which took their titles from Horace had become and remained popular as exhortation and justification. An example from the Boer War is James Rhoades's patriotic poem "Dulce et Decorum Est," which expresses the British officers' classical code of honor:

> We, nursed in high traditions,
>   And trained to nobler thought,
> Deem death to be less bitter
>   Than life too dearly bought.

The 1915 poem "Dulce et Decorum est pro Patria Mori" by Sydney Oswald, major in the King's Royal Rifle Corps, is a later example. Beginning with "They gave their lives for England," it commemorates the heroic deaths of men in one episode of the 1915 Gallipoli campaign.[26] As a modern historian recently observed: "Fuelled initially by Horatian ideals – *dulce et decorum est pro patria mori* – taught in all the grammar schools, *lycées*, and gymnasia of Europe and then driven by a stubbornness that in Britain was appropriately called bottom, the war of attrition decimated the old

---

[23] Richards 1988: 222. Cf. Fussell 1975: 27–28 and Larson 1999. See further Peter Parker 1987, Hynes 1990, Mosse 1990, and Todman 2005.

[24] Quoted from Deslandes 2005: 145. Deslandes quotes "Thoughts That Occur: 'The Schools'" of 1909.

[25] Quoted from Morris 1978: 335. The island of Imbros, situated near the Hellespont, is mentioned several times in the *Iliad*.

[26] The poem was published in Kyle 1916: 69–70. Another one with the same title, by Corporal Harold John Jarvis, appears in Kyle 1917: 73–76.

aristocracy and much of the intelligentsia of Europe . . . Because of its
staggering cost in talent and tradition, the war was bound to provoke . . . a
re-examination of the very foundations of civilization and society."[27]

Such re-examination occurred in the works of several young poets,
especially Siegfried Sassoon and Wilfred Owen, both of them heroes who
experienced the horrors of modern warfare. Owen was killed at age twenty-
five by machine-gun fire one week before Armistice Day; he had won the
Military Cross a month before his death. Owen was fully committed
to pacifism and voiced disillusionment with the traditional belief in the
Horatian sentiment. His best-known poem, drafted in 1917 and revised the
following year, is "Dulce et Decorum Est." Owen himself characterized
it as "a gas poem" that describes the death of one of his fellow soldiers
from poison gas. After giving the dying man's final moments in harrowing
detail, the poem's last stanza ends with an apostrophe to the reader:

> My friend, you would not tell with such high zest
> To children ardent for some desperate glory,
> The old Lie: Dulce et decorum est
> Pro patria mori.[28]

It has recently been observed that this and other poems by Owen "wage
war on the emotional paucity of their titles. 'Dulce et Decorum Est' simply
exposes its title to a flat contradiction in narrative: this is what dying for
your country is really like . . . The only way to stop the ruin of countless

---

[27] Eksteins 1998: 307.

[28] "Dulce et Decorum Est," 25–28; quoted along with the author's description from Owen 1983: 140.
The "friend" is Jessie Pope, the poem's original dedicatee and author of *Jessie Pope's War Poems*
(1915), *More War Poems* (1915), and *Simple Rhymes for Stirring Times* (1916). Pope had composed a
pro-war poem whose title was Horace's line. Contrast Elinor Jenkins's poem "Dulce and Decorum?"
(note the punctuation mark), in Jenkins 1921: 35. – Owen's poem "1914," 9–10, and the title of his
poem "Arms and the Boy" also refer to antiquity. The reference to the opening of Virgil's *Aeneid*
(*Arma virumque*; *Aeneid* 1.1) is via Siegfried Sassoon's poem "Arms and the Man" (Stallworthy
in Owen 1983: 154). Vandiver 1999 examines further classical parallels. In general see Fussell 1975
and Bergonzi 1996. Thematically comparable, if in the context of the American Civil War, is the
perspective expressed in a speech elaborately entitled "The Soldier's Faith: An Address Delivered on
Memorial Day, May 30, 1895, at a Meeting Called by the Graduating Class of Harvard University"
by Oliver Wendell Holmes, best accessible in Holmes 1995: 486–491. – In a number of contributions
to *The Classical Weekly* American classicists pointed out similarities of ancient warfare to the Great
War while it was being fought; see, for example, McCartney 1917–1918. Cf. also "The Classics and
Military Service," a recent collection of war reminiscences by classical scholars, in *The Classical
Bulletin*, especially Herbert 1998a and 1998b. A recent addition to such scholarship by a classicist
and Vietnam veteran is Tritle 2000. The tradition of Owen's view of Horace continues in, e.g., Tim
O'Brien 1975, a fictionalized account of the author's service as infantryman in Vietnam. Revealing
chapter headings are "Pro Patria," "Mori," "Centurion," and "Dulce et Decorum." Cf. Palaima
2000. Modern war correspondent Chris Hedges quotes the closing of Owen's "Dulce et Decorum
Est" as the epigraph for his meditations on war in Hedges 2002.

bodies is by stopping corruption at its verbal source, 'the old Lie', which is why the true poets must be truthful."[29]

But more than the poetry of these and others could do, one work in particular brought home to many people the overwhelming contrast, on the largest scale imaginable, between traditional *virtus* and the horrible reality of mass slaughter. This work is Erich Maria Remarque's best-selling 1929 novel *All Quiet on the Western Front*.[30] The book was filmed in the United States in 1930 by Lewis Milestone, a Russian emigrant.[31] Remarque had given his first-person novel an episodic flashback structure, written as the reminiscences of Paul Bäumer, its protagonist, except for the book's last paragraph, which reports Paul's death in a third-person statement. A film adaptation had to change this, and Milestone and his screenwriters adopted a linear third-person storyline. Unlike their German source, their film illustrates the legacy of Western civilization by focusing, paradigmatically and from the very beginning, on classical literature, prominently including Horace's *dulce et decorum*. By contrast Remarque had referred to Western culture in far more general terms and with only occasional mention of ancient literary or historical figures alongside more modern ones, giving a cross-section of higher education in the arts and sciences: "the whole gamut of culture from Plato to Goethe."[32]

The film proceeds in a more focused and dramatically more effective manner. Its first sequence is set in the classroom of a German *Gymnasium* (high school or grammar school) and captures the general euphoria of 1914. We witness a teacher exhorting his students toward patriotism while

[29] Kerr 1993: 296 and 97. Owen and Sassoon in turn became the inspiration for World War I fiction and films. Sassoon: R. C. Sherriff's play *Journey's End* (1929), filmed by James Whale in 1930 and a likely inspiration for *The Dawn Patrol* (a film discussed below) according to Kelly 1997: 74–75; Sassoon and Owen: Pat Barker's novel trilogy *Regeneration* (1991), *The Eye in the Door* (1994), and *The Ghost Road* (1995). The first of these was filmed under its original title by Gillies MacKinnon in 1997. The BBC television documentary *The Great War* (1964) featured a reading of Owen's poem in its episode on Passchendaele, "with the last line translated for the benefit of those whose Latin was not up to the magnitude of the Old Lie" (quoted from Todman 2005: 33). On Owen's poems, especially "Dulce et Decorum Est," in British education since the 1960s see Todman 166–172.

[30] Remarque 1929b; English translation: Remarque 1929a.

[31] For modern scholarship on this film, its production, and its reception in the US and abroad since its first release see Kelly 1998. On director Milestone, who had gone to school in Berlin, see Kelly 63–65. (The quotation in the title of his book is from Milestone.) See also Kelly 1997: 43–57 (chapter entitled "The Measure for All Anti-War Cinema: *All Quiet on the Western Front*"). The version restored by the Library of Congress supersedes all other editions; on the film and its restoration cf. Wills 1998. On World War I in film see also Isenberg 1981, Paris 2000, and Alan Burton 2002. Cf. further Winter 1995: 119–144 and 251–256 (notes; chapter called "Mythologies of War: Films, Popular Religion, and the Business of the Sacred").

[32] Remarque 1929a: 21. Remarque originally wrote "sämtliche Kulturkreise von Plato bis Goethe" (Remarque 1929b: 28), which literally translates as "all cultural circles from Plato to Goethe."

outside large numbers of volunteers are marching down the street to the sound of military music. In the course of his long speech, which lasts for over three and a half minutes of screen time, Professor Kantorek duly quotes Horace:

Now, my beloved friends . . . You are the life of the Fatherland, you boys . . . You are the gay heroes who will repulse the enemy when you are called upon to do so. It is not for me to suggest that any of you should stand up and offer to defend his country, but I wonder if such a thing is going through your heads. I know that in one of the schools the boys have risen up in the classroom and enlisted in a mass, and of course if such a thing should happen here, you would not blame me for a feeling of pride . . . Is the honor of wearing a uniform something from which we should run? . . . I know you've never desired the adulation of heroes – that has not been part of my teaching. We have sought to have made ourselves worthy, and let acclaim come when it would. But, to be foremost in battle is a virtue not to be despised. I believe it will be a quick war, that there will be few losses, but if losses there must be, then let us remember the Latin phrase which must have come to the lips of many a Roman when he stood in battle in a foreign land: *dulce et decorum est pro patria mori* – "sweet and fitting it is to die for the fatherland."

After haranguing some of the students individually, Kantorek ends: "Follow me! Enlist now!" And so they do, all of them.[33]

The conclusion of the teacher's speech contradicts some of his earlier statements (e.g., "It is with reluctance that I bring this subject up again") and the correct observation that it is not for him to call the young men to war. We are meant to realize that his own words condemn him as a liar and hypocrite, for it *has* been part of his teaching to instill unthinking acceptance of heroic values in the class. The words "to be foremost in battle" reinforce his old-fashioned values: they are a quotation from the *Iliad*.[34] So it becomes a poignant moment for the viewer when, during his translation of Horace's Latin, a close-up shows one of his students trembling with fear and anticipation of death; not long afterward he will

---

[33] The novel contains no such speech. Remarque merely has Paul report that the teacher kept haranguing his students during physical-education lessons ("in den Turnstunden"; Remarque 1929b: 16) until they volunteered to enlist. Kantorek was the chief target of attack in the novel, but the film transfers his function onto a formerly mild-mannered mailman, who in a chilling demonstration that clothes make the man turns into a sadistic drill sergeant. Detailed to the front, he proves himself a coward before the eyes of his former recruits.

[34] Cf. *Iliad* 6.206–209, Glaucus' summary of the heroic code: "my father / . . . sent me to Troy, and urged upon me repeated injunctions, / to be always among the bravest, and hold my head above others, / not shaming the generation of my fathers"; Lattimore 1951: 158. Cf. *Iliad* 11.783, quoted above.

be the class's first casualty. The film effectively questions the use of classical literature for militaristic and patriotic ends.

The classroom scene, for which there is no equivalent in Remarque's novel, is even more significant because the words of the teacher are questioned visually as well. Clearly visible on the screen behind Kantorek there is a large blackboard, on which we see three famous classical quotations, one from Greek, two from Roman literature. The Greek one is the beginning of Homer's *Odyssey*: "Tell me, Muse, of the man of many ways, who was driven . . ."[35] The line is here meant to indicate that the classics are the foundation of all secondary and higher education.[36] It also gives a concise definition of the classical epic hero who may have been most popular among the students. Odysseus' most famous epithet is *polytropos* ("of many turns," i.e. "wily"). This hero is a survivor who comes out of ten years of war unscathed and safely makes it through a dangerous decade-long return on which all of his comrades perish. After his return home to wife and child he has to fight yet another bloody battle, which he wins heroically. If we are surprised to see a quotation from the *Odyssey* rather than from the *Iliad* in a film dealing with war, we should keep in mind that the *Odyssey* was read more frequently than the *Iliad* in Greek courses in the *Gymnasium*.

The Latin quotations, however, have a more telling meaning for the film's subject and serve as ironic and critical comments on the teacher's words. Both are generally applicable beyond their original contexts and contain warnings or exhortations toward restraint and moderation and to foresight and responsible action. They are Ovid's *principiis obsta: sero medicina paratur* ("resist the beginnings: the remedy usually comes too late") and the anonymous *quidquid agis, prudenter agas et respice finem* ("whatever you do, do it with foresight and consider the result") from *The Deeds of the Romans*.[37] Both complement each other in their emphasis on beginning and end. Both were commonly encountered in Latin textbooks used in the *Gymnasium*. Although students were not generally aware that Ovid's line came from one of his erotic works, the *Remedies of Love* which was not read in schools, they encountered it as if it were an anonymous proverb, often shortened to *principiis obsta* and juxtaposed to *quidquid*

---

[35] *Odyssey* 1.1; the translation is from Lattimore 1965: 27.

[36] This is still the case in Mike Figgis's *The Browning Version* (1994), which updates its plot to the 1990s. The first five lines of the *Odyssey* appear on the blackboard in the classics master's classroom.

[37] Ovid, *Remedies of Love* 91; *Gesta Romanorum* 103 (page 431, lines 32–33 [Oesterley]). The latter text has a famous Greek equivalent in Solon's exhortation to King Croesus; see Herodotus, *Histories* 1.32.9, on which cf. the ancient scholion (commentary) on Dio Chrysostom, *Orations* 72.13. Cf. also Aesop, *Fables* 9 (Perry). The idea occurs elsewhere in ancient texts.

**Fig. 17.** *All Quiet on the Western Front.* The classical quotations on the blackboard: first version. (Universal)

*agis . . .* as examples of ancient wisdom. The implication is that this is a kind of advice which one would do well to heed. These two quotations point to the traditional wisdom of the ancients as the great exemplars of Western culture and education. To those viewers who recognize them, the classical texts reveal the teacher's utter lack of understanding and condemn his rashness, heedlessness, and hypocrisy. The implications are clear: instead of being enlightened by its educators to be able to make rational decisions based on understanding and forethought, the young generation is being manipulated and betrayed by the obtuse and the ignorant who are clamoring for war. Kantorek represents all educators; he is a stand-in for political and social authority figures.

Classical film philologists will notice that the scene described contains two versions of what appears on the blackboard. When the camera tracks into the classroom and pans left, then begins to retreat in a traveling shot to reveal the teacher, the desk, and the benches with some of the students, only two classical quotations are on the board: Ovid and Homer, the former above the latter (Fig. 17). After a cut the camera continues its traveling shot

**Fig. 18.** *All Quiet on the Western Front.* The classical quotations on the blackboard: second version. (Universal)

backward to reveal the whole room, and now there are three texts on the board. The original quotations have been moved left to make room for the third (Fig. 18). This indicates that the classroom scene was not filmed at one single time and that there may have been second thoughts about its classical background. The difference reveals that a change of camera position was necessary on the set; it occurs just before the moment when Kantorek begins the main part of his speech as quoted above.[38] Classical scholars will also notice that the three verse quotations are not arranged as lines of poetry and that the Greek spellings and accents are slightly off. The word *hos* ("who"), for instance, is omitted from the second appearance of the quotation from Homer. Such errors, however, do not detract from the importance of the texts; rather, they show that the quotations were significant enough, first, to be increased in number and, second, to be incorporated into the scene despite the filmmakers' lack of philological expertise.

---

[38] Mitchell 1985: 38 reports that there had been two camera takes during the filming of the classroom scene.

Viewers who understand the meaning of the classical lines on the board will be chilled to see what happens to them at the end of this scene – a foreboding of the students' eventual fate. There is a general uproar of euphoria and boyish enthusiasm for enlistment: "No more classes!" Some of the students cross out the two Latin texts from the board, and one writes "Nach Paris!" above them. The act of crossing out the Latin maxims symbolizes the students' turning away from classical wisdom under the very aegis of one who should know better. The teacher's unthinking obedience to the state ("Enlist now!") exemplifies his misappropriation of Horace's line and characterizes him as a petty-bourgeois civil servant who urges his charges toward death. The reality of war, as the film will show soon after, is utterly different from Kantorek's ossified and anachronistic idea of heroism and his thoughtless parroting of what he himself must have been taught in his own schooldays and on what he seems never to have reflected. Only the beginning of the *Odyssey* remains untouched. But this circumstance, too, carries its own importance. It is in ironic contrast to the eventual fate of the students: with the exception of one who ends up in a mental hospital none of the class will survive.

War in the early twentieth century is no longer an arena for glorious deeds. It looks much more like the battle scenes in *All Quiet on the Western Front*, which are so realistic and horrifying as to cure any attentive viewer of enthusiasm for war forever. Battle footage from *All Quiet on the Western Front* was included in several documentary films about World War I. Critic Sydney Carroll wrote about it in the London *Sunday Times* in June, 1930: "It brought the war back to me as nothing has ever done before since 1918."[39] Particularly wrenching is a long sequence in which French infantry attack the German trenches. Many of the French are mowed down by machine guns; those who have made it past the barrage of bullets and grenades then engage in close combat in the German trench. Bayonets and even spades are the main weapons in this claustrophobic slaughter. The ferocity of the killing to be witnessed on the screen – butchery rather than heroism – is the cinematic equivalent of the gruesome killings in the *Iliad*.[40] Such scenes negate all and any possibilities for mindless patriotism and stereotypical heroism, as does the whole film. Tyrtaeus' endorsement of death in battle ("felled in the front line, he is lovely yet") is no longer

---

[39] Quoted from Eksteins 2000: 18.

[40] The *Iliad* contains graphic descriptions of the inhumanity of battle, especially in its later books which describe the bloody and pitiless *aristeia* of Achilles. For a sample see *Iliad* 20.381–503, the beginning of Achilles' killing spree.

possible, if it ever had been true. It is no wonder that the National Socialists disrupted screenings of the film in Germany and shortly after taking power banned it.[41]

A later scene of *All Quiet on the Western Front* expresses the astonishing obtuseness of those who refused to see the true nature of the Great War even until the end. As was the case with the first scene set in the *Gymnasium*, Remarque's novel contains no equivalent of this one, either. After four years of war Paul has returned home after being wounded and visits his old school. Kantorek is again in the middle of the same kind of harangue we had heard him deliver earlier: "from the farms they have gone, from the schools, from the factories, gone bravely, nobly, ever forward, realizing that there is no other duty now but to serve the Fatherland." At first Kantorek greets Paul like a returning hero ("one of the iron youths who have made Germany invincible in the field . . . the kind of soldier every one of you should envy") and urges him to address his current class: "you must tell them what it means to serve your Fatherland . . . Don't you remember some deed of heroism, some touch of nobility . . . ?" But soon all present realize that they have little in common. There is only mutual incomprehension because the war has opened too wide a gulf between Paul and the others. A reference to Horace serves to bring out the extent of their irreconcilable differences:

> *Paul to Kantorek*: I've heard you in here, reciting that same old stuff: making more iron men, more young heroes – you still think it's beautiful and sweet to die for your country, don't you? [*Kantorek nods solemnly and emphatically.*] We used to think you knew. But the first bombardment taught us better. It's dirty and painful to die for your country. When it comes to "die for your country," it's better not to die at all. There are millions out there dying for their countries, and what good is it? . . . [*To the students:*] He tells you: "Go off and die!" Oh, but if you'll pardon me, it's easier to say "go off and die" than it is to do it.
>
> *A student*: Coward! [*General commotion.*]

Paul's denial of heroism on his and everyone else's part and his reluctance – or rather, inability – to describe the horrible reality of the trenches contrast with the teacher's stubbornness and stupidity, which are the same as before. In his ignorance Kantorek still sees the war as a *Helden-zone*, the propagandistic and patriotic German term for the "heroic zone" of the trenches and the battlefield. But as Paul tells him, there are "no lies"

---

[41] On the ban of *All Quiet on the Western Front* see Giesen 2003: 2–5.

**Fig. 19.** *All Quiet on the Western Front.* The erasure of education and civilization.
(Universal)

at the front, where sheer survival is the only issue. And again the visual quality of this scene reinforces the dialogue, showing us what fate classical wisdom is likely to undergo in times of war. We recognize the old classroom and its décor, all unchanged. When Paul begins to address the students, he and Kantorek appear on opposite sides of the screen, and the blackboard is visible in the background behind and between them. But now the classical quotations it had contained earlier have been erased. We only see a large cloud of white chalk although a little of the Latin words is still visible in the very place where we had seen them before (Fig. 19). This circumstance reveals that the point the filmmakers make with their blackboard is meant symbolically. While earlier two of the three classical sentiments had been crossed out but were still legible, here we are shown the virtually complete erasure of that classical education which generations of students had been receiving in school. War, we understand, wipes out not only foresight (*respice finem*) and wisdom (*principiis obsta, prudenter agas*) but also all possibility of *aretê* and *virtus* – as Paul restates to the youngsters in class and as we have already witnessed for most of the film's running time.

We also notice immediately that these students are considerably younger and even more impressionable than Paul and his classmates had been. This reveals the continuing indoctrination on the part of irresponsible authority figures and also indicates that the war will eventually claim the very young. As Paul says: "now they're sending babies, and they won't last a week." So it happened in 1918 and again in 1945. The last-ditch effort of the Nazis to postpone the unavoidable with the enlistment of old men and children was euphemistically and cynically called the "people's storm" (*Volkssturm*), the subject of Bernhard Wicki's powerful anti-war film *The Bridge* (1960). The erased blackboard in *All Quiet on the Western Front* is a visual masterstroke that makes clear what would be too long if put into words and contrary to the very nature of cinema, a medium which best works in images. The point is that Western civilization is running the danger of being obliterated by modern war, that we have reached the end of classical values and culture, and that an age of new technology, mass society, and mass killing is dawning.

The film's end returns us to the trenches. Paul is killed by a French sniper while reaching out for a solitary butterfly, a scene also not in Remarque.[42] The ending is particularly effective for its utter silence, with the exception of the vicious sound of the shot. But a viewer's familiarity with classical Greek can increase the emotional impact of this famous scene, gripping as it already is in its images of martial futility and mute accusation by the dead. One of the two Greek terms for "butterfly" is *psychê*, a word whose most common meaning is "soul." Paul's death thus takes on an emblematic meaning.[43] He is now an Everyman figure who represents the lost generation of World War I, trying to find or find again its soul in the devastating environment of modern war. But they are denied the return from the horrors of war to humanity or civilization. It is unlikely that director Milestone intended or was aware of the classical overtone of this scene, which he and German cinematographer Karl Freund invented and filmed after the production had closed down and the actors had been dismissed. (The hand on screen reaching for the butterfly is Milestone's.) But the additional meaning fits the film's other classical aspects.

[42] On the different versions of the ending and on the origin and filming of the one appearing in the final version see Kelly 1998: 90–94. Brownlow 1979: 214–219 quotes director Milestone on the film's production and on its ending.

[43] Cf. the allegorical painting by Dosso Dossi, "Jupiter, Mercury, and Virtue" (ca. 1523–1524), in which Jupiter is painting a picture of butterflies. The painting derives from the Latin dialogue *Virtus* ("Virtue") by Leon Battista Alberti, written in the 1430s but long attributed to the ancient Greek author Lucian, in which the goddess Virtue complains about her ill treatment at the hands of Fortuna (Fortune or Luck, but also Fate).

**Fig. 20.** *All Quiet on the Western Front.* The final image: the dead looking at the living. (Universal)

The final image on the screen is a montage of a war cemetery stretching endlessly into the distance, over which an image of Paul and his schoolmates is superimposed as they are walking away but turning their heads to look over their shoulders directly at us (Fig. 20). The moment is a silent accusation regarding the immense losses of World War I and a warning about the future. It also reminds us of Paul's words to the students in the film's second classroom scene: "You will know what I mean. Only, it's been a long while since we enlisted out of this classroom, so long I thought maybe the whole world had learned by this time." But the world never learns. The final scenes of John Ford's *The World Moves On* (1934) provides a good illustration. When World War I is over – we have watched battle scenes reminiscent, if not as harrowing, as those in *All Quiet on the Western Front* – a wounded British veteran comments: "between us all we've torn down everything that matters: faith, freedom, civilization." A victory parade shows us ranks of soldiers marching down the street, and images of a second and completely silent march are briefly superimposed at the top of the screen. Presumably these did not live to join the celebrations. (Ford, as often, is understating the point, leaving it to viewers to figure out the meaning of the ghostly parade.) In due course we watch documentary footage topical in the year of the film's release: Hitler and Mussolini among Nazi and Fascist soldiers; Japanese, Soviet, and even American displays of resurgent military might. The filmmakers cannot have known what was ahead, but we, watching this film now, know only too well. War feeds itself.

A film made in the Soviet Union about World War II, Mikhail Kalatozov's *The Cranes Are Flying* (1957), pays a brief homage to *All Quiet on the Western Front*. Almost immediately after we witness the poignant death of the young man whose story we have followed, we hear this official announcement, an echo of the one that closes Remarque's novel: "The Soviet Information Bureau reports no important changes on the fronts in the last twenty-four hours." *Im Osten nichts Neues*: All Quiet on the Eastern Front. "No important changes. That's good," someone comments with relief. This is the young man's father, who does not know what has happened. The deaths of Paul, his fellow schoolmates, and of Kalatozov's Boris illustrate a point made in a fragment from Euripides' lost tragedy *The Children of Temenus*: "War does not strike all. It likes to see brave young men fall but despises cowards. This is the very thing from which the commonwealth suffers."[44]

The thematic emphasis which Milestone and his screenwriters put on the classical background of their protagonists' education is remarkable in a film intended for popular audiences unfamiliar with these words and concepts. Their presence and the filmmakers' serious approach to the subject of war and heroism in modern times is a reminder that the cinema is an important link in the history of cultural and artistic expression, capable of making serious points to larger numbers of people than any other medium. In retrospect the school scenes are also an elegy to the lost culture and importance of antiquity in the modern world.[45] If the film were to be remade today, it would most likely not have a single reference to Greek or Roman literature. If it did, any Greek or Latin text and any quotation from Horace would be lost on most filmgoers. The 1979 remake, an inferior television film directed by Delbert Mann, contains no quotation of Horace. The teacher of its one school scene utters the expected platitudes – "You are our iron youth. Iron youth becomes iron heroes" – but his words are

---

[44] Euripides, Fragm. 728 Nauck; the prose translation is mine. The text continues: " . . . but it brings high glory to the fallen." Cf. also Sophocles, *Philoctetes* 436–437.

[45] In the spring of 1918 German classical scholar Richard Heinze gave a series of lectures on Roman culture and literature to German troops in Bucharest, which were published posthumously (Heinze 1933). The book's editor correctly characterizes Heinze's lectures, one of which is entitled "People and Army" ("Volk und Heer"), as "a monument of the high level of culture in our army" ("ein Denkmal für die Kulturhöhe unseres Heeres," 5). This seems to have been an exception.

far less chilling than those spoken in Milestone's film. And the blackboard shows only unidiomatic and misspelled German.

The traditional nobility to be encountered even in modern war is the subject of several significant films such as William Wellman's *Wings* (1927), the cinema's first aviation-combat film. In these and some other World War I films martial gallantry in a technological war is set among air-force pilots. World War I was the first war to make extensive use of airplanes, a circumstance which provided filmmakers with a new way to present spectacular air-combat sequences on the screen. Chivalry can still be preserved in the duels of individual flying aces, their "dogfights."[46] This is true for World War I films from the silent era to the 1970s, as in John Guillermin's *The Blue Max* (1966) or Roger Corman's *Von Richthofen and Brown* (1971). In such films Britain's Royal Flying Corps and the German *Luftwaffe* appear as the last holdouts of heroism in war.

The gallant pilots portrayed on the screen may be said to think and act in accordance with the words of the semi-legendary Roman general Camillus as reported by Plutarch:

War is indeed a grievous thing, and is waged with much injustice and violence; but even war has certain laws which good and brave men will respect, and we must not so hotly pursue victory as not to flee the favours of base and impious doers. The great general will wage war relying on his own native valour, not on the baseness of other men.[47]

Howard Hawks's *The Dawn Patrol* (1930) shows us the gallantry of aerial combat and the moral dilemma of a man who is himself no longer a combatant but whose responsibility it is to send the fliers under his command to face almost certain death again and again. The situation carries overtones of Greek tragedy in that the protagonist is faced with a quandary in which he necessarily becomes guilty, regardless of how he decides. As one critic has put it, "it is clear that being commander involves an almost debilitating responsibility for the lives of others . . . a consequence of a

---

[46] Both Wellman and Howard Hawks were World War I veterans. Wellman was a member of the Lafayette Flying Corps; he later directed *Legion of the Condemned* (1928) and *Lafayette Escadrille* (1958), both based on his own experiences. As he observed: "They gave me *Wings* because I was the only director who had been a flyer, in action. I was the only one who knew what the hell it was all about . . . the only director with experience at the front"; quoted from Brownlow 1968: 174. Hawks was a lieutenant in the Signal Corps (later, the Army Air Corps) and trained American pilots. *The Dawn Patrol* was remade by Edmund Goulding in 1938 under the same title and with all aerial footage from Hawks's film re-used; Hawks's film was retitled *The Flight Commander*, chiefly for television broadcasts. – A poem entitled "The Dawn Patrol" by Paul Bewsher, R.N.A.S., appears in Kyle 1917: 16–17.

[47] Plutarch, *Camillus* 10.3–4; quoted from Perrin 1914: 119. Camillus here reacts to an act of treason during the siege of Falerii, when a school teacher attempted to hand over his charges to him, thereby surrendering Falerii. The passage is quoted by McCartney 1917–1918: 144.

deplorable set of social circumstances wherein human activity is devoted primarily to killing."[48] Hawks's films often reveal an "instinctive stoicism, borne by many of the World War I generation though more evident in Hawks's work than in that of any other American director."[49]

The situation that a character has to decide and act in morally questionable circumstances, when what Aeschylus called "the yoke of necessity" is on his neck, is a theme familiar from classical tragedy.[50] *The Dawn Patrol* illustrates it without specific reference to antiquity but with recourse to a familiar pattern which may indeed be connected with ancient culture, as will become clear below. Hawks also gives the theme of heroic duty leading to death a twist typical of his body of work. This is the high degree of professionalism in the face of death that the men exhibit. Hawks presents a serious-minded and profound variant of the American cliché that "a man gotta do what a man gotta do." As he himself put it:

You create a character who has a problem and another man comes along and takes over his problem and in the finish he's spent himself and then another man has the problem and it keeps on going.[51]

Hawks expresses a similar point of view about his World War I film *The Road to Glory* (1936), which has a plot involving ground combat, and his aviation adventure film *Only Angels Have Wings* (1939; Hawks rightly disliked the title, imposed by the studio). In reply to the observation that the characters in such films do not complain about the dangerous circumstances in which they find themselves, he said:

You see, they know there's nothing to be gained by it . . . they accept commands, no matter what the command. That's what makes an Army function. But it's just a calm acceptance of a fact . . . Well, that's the only thing that keeps people going. They just have to say, "Joe [a pilot killed] wasn't good enough, and I'm better than Joe, so I'll go ahead and do it." And they find out they're not any better than Joe, but by then it's too late.[52]

---

[48] Poague 1982: 81. Poague, 102–109, examines Hawks's World War I film *The Road to Glory* from this perspective.

[49] McCarthy 1997: 223.

[50] Aeschylus, *Agamemnon* 218. (Cf. the brief mention in Chapter 3.) Regarding World War I we may compare the well-known refrain of Bartholomew Dowling's poem "The Revel," written in India and later turned into a popular song: "Hurrah for the next that dies!" It is sung in the remake of Hawks's film.

[51] Bogdanovich 1962: 51. Cf. McCarthy 1997: 216 on Hawks's aviation film *Ceiling Zero* (1936) as showing "the classical Hawksian grouping of professional men involved in a dangerous job that holds out the prospect of tragedy on a daily basis."

[52] Bogdanovich 1997: 377. On *The Road to Glory*, based on the French anti-war film *Wooden Crosses* (1932), directed by Raymond Bernard, and its connections to *The Dawn Patrol* see McCarthy 1997: 224–225.

The visual symbol in *The Dawn Patrol* which Hawks uses to draw his spectators emotionally close to the death of the fliers is a blackboard listing their names. When one of them dies, his name is silently erased from the board. The very understatement of the gesture tightens the moment's grip on the spectator's emotions. The pilots' "obligation to fly against death every dawn" leads to their apparent calm in the face of a certain fate, but the emotional undercurrents are nevertheless there.[53] In this and several later films Hawks demonstrates moving and accomplished examples of "grace under pressure," the quality associated primarily with the novels of his friend Ernest Hemingway.

The protagonists of most of Hawks's major films exhibit fatalism combined with a sense of professionalism. The German and British pilots in *The Dawn Patrol* consider themselves and each other more as professionals than as enemies; as a result, they do not hate each other. A quintessential example of this occurs in *The Dawn Patrol* when the British protagonist of the film gives a salute to the German flier who shoots him down. In Hawks's words: "It was man against man, but they had respect for the other person."[54]

On the ending of *Sergeant York* (1941), his film about the American World War I hero Alvin York, a pacifist who became a war hero by killing large numbers of Germans against his firm prior conviction, Hawks observed what may be a summary of the quandaries faced by men in war. The film was based on

a man who didn't believe in fighting . . . A man who actually was very religious was told to go out and do everything his religion said not to do, and he became a great hero doing just that. There was bound to be a good deal of confusion in his mind and actually I suppose it was a form of tragedy.[55]

*The Dawn Patrol* and *Sergeant York* show heroic characters and tragic situations whose roots go back to antiquity, but the films do not refer

---

[53] The quotation is from Mast 1982: 350.

[54] Bogdanovich 1997: 270. Cf. also Hawks's statement about *The Dawn Patrol* in McBride 1982: 27. Hawks concludes his remembrance of British RFC aviators at Bogdanovich 1997: 377 with the simple statement: "It isn't anything I've invented; it's just something I've seen that interests me, so I've used it." Cf. further Bogdanovich 269–270. Comparable perspectives on warfare occur in Hawks's *Today We Live* (1933), another of his World War I films, and in his World War II film *Air Force* (1943).

[55] Bogdanovich 1997: 319. Contrast, however, the comments by John Huston, one of the film's screenwriters, as quoted in McCarthy 1997: 307–308. On the film's genesis, production (including several inventions and changes of fact), and reception see McCarthy 300–318. The war sequence in *Sergeant York* is reminiscent of *All Quiet on the Western Front* both thematically (through their locale at the German front) and stylistically (the cinematographer of the earlier film also shot the battle sequence for Hawks's).

**Fig. 21.** *Grand Illusion.* Monsieur Pindare (l.) getting ready for work. (Réalisation d'art cinématographique-Criterion)

to classical culture. By contrast Jean Renoir's *Grand Illusion* (1937) does. Its original title (*La grande illusion*) is more accurately translated as "The Great Illusion" and derives from the 1910 book of this name by Norman Angell, who argued that the common economic interests of nations made war futile.[56]

In World War I Renoir had been an officer in the French cavalry and an air corps aviator. He had been wounded in the trenches in 1914. His film, set in the early stages of the war, illustrates the importance of cultural ideals in an environment of freedom lost, impending death, and the threat of the destruction of civilization in war. One scene in particular makes this point. The French prisoners of war, who are being kept in a German fortress, have tacked photographs of medieval and Renaissance art on the wall of their common room. More importantly the film shows us the tenacity of classical literature and education, here illustrated by the example of the Greek poet Pindar. One of the prisoners is obsessed with translating Pindar and has received the good-humored nickname "Monsieur Pindare" (Fig. 21).

[56] Angell 1910.

When he barges in on the others with his dictionaries to continue working on his translation, the following exchange takes place:

*Boeldieu*: Do you mind? Your dictionaries are going to be in my way.
*Demolder rather shyly*: I'm sorry, but it's such difficult work . . . Pindar has always been so badly translated.
*Boeldieu eyeing him through his monocle*: Really? I'm sorry to hear it. Rotten shame!
*Marechal coming over to talk to Demolder*: I never asked you before because basically I couldn't care less, but who is this chap of yours, Pindar?
*Demolder*: You can make fun of it if you like, but to me it's the most important thing in the whole world . . . No joking, I care about it more than about the war or even my own life . . . Pindar is the greatest of the Greek poets!
*Marechal*: The greatest Greek poet? Well, I never.[57]

This attempt to remember one's civilized and spiritually ennobling up-bringing is infused with some affectionate humor. Demolder is a teacher by profession, and his humanism contrasts strongly with Kantorek's callousness in *All Quiet on the Western Front*. The brief scene in *Grand Illusion* is also revealing in the choice of the poet who here stands in for the greatness of all antiquity. Pindar celebrated aristocratic values and virtues, standards of behavior not to be abandoned under any circumstances. But Pindar commemorates the achievements of the aristocrats, whose victories his odes immortalize, with frequent references to their mythical ancestors. Heroism, we may deduce, is best understood in retrospect. Contemporary reality may differ.

Renoir once characterized the war in the following terms: "In certain ways, that world war was still a war of formal people, of educated people – I would almost dare say, a gentlemen's war. That does not excuse it. Politeness, even chivalry, does not excuse massacre."[58] The film's two aristocratic antagonists, a German and a Frenchman, know that their day and the entire world of martial chivalry have already passed. In this, Renoir's film reflects the atmosphere of pre-World War II Europe, just as his film *The Rules of the Game* was to do in 1939. In *Grand Illusion* we observe the last

---

[57] Quoted from *Grand Illusion* 1968: 67. The preceding page of this translation of the film's screenplay identifies Demolder as "a professor of Greek," but the film itself does not contain this information. The translation is slightly sanitized and rather too British-sounding. Hamilton 2003: 36–44 is a postmodern interpretation of Pindar's presence in Renoir's film.

[58] "A Note from Jean Renoir," in *Grand Illusion* 1968: 8. In a promotion filmed upon his film's re-release Renoir said virtually the same: "May I say that, to a certain extent, the war of 1914 was almost a war of gentlemen." – In contrast to Renoir's nobility is the perspective on an earlier war in a later film. The Boer War in Bruce Beresford's *"Breaker" Morant* (1980) is ominously referred to as "a new kind of war . . . a war for a new century." In the words of the British: "This is a war . . . There are no rules here." And: "The gentlemen's war is over."

flowering of heroism and chivalry, which is here embodied primarily in the German aristocrat von Rauffenstein, a flying ace who holds the rank of *Rittmeister*. The term, originally referring to a cavalry captain, hints at his gallantry. (German *ritterlich* means "chivalrous.") An early scene in the film establishes his aristocratic nature both to his captive French enemies and to the spectators. Rauffenstein has just returned from a successful air mission, during which he shot down his twelfth French plane. He is now concerned with the well-being of the plane's survivors. He invites the captured French officers to his table, where they are treated with great generosity and courtesy. In antiquity hospitality was one of man's chief virtues and duties; its tradition here continues. Rauffenstein and his fellow German officers also honor their dead enemies. When an orderly brings in a wreath from the German flying corps for the French "shot down in flames," Rauffenstein and the others, risen from the table, toast their gallantry. Rauffenstein's words – "Möge die Erde unserem verstorbenen tapferen Feind leicht werden" ("May the earth be light to our deceased brave enemy") – contain a classical quotation. The phrase occurs in Greek in Euripides and in an epigram by Ammianus and in Latin in Martial, the best-known and immediate source.[59] As was the case with Ovid's line in *All Quiet on the Western Front*, Martial's also is generally taken out of context and is elevated into a serious and edifying sentiment. This circumstance reflects the general appropriation of classical culture on the part of well-educated modern people.

A second brief scene involving Pindar occurs a little after the one discussed. Von Rauffenstein and some of his soldiers are inspecting the quarters of their French prisoners, and one of the guards roughly snatches a large book from the table in order to examine it. This is Demolder's edition of Pindar, a battered old text with a commentary, to judge by its size. Demolder protests, calling out that it is a rare book. Rauffenstein now takes the book, looks at its spine, and softly murmurs "Pindar" to himself (Fig. 22). He recognizes the poet, and we are meant to deduce that he is familiar with his work. The tone of wistfulness in his voice is revealing, for it bridges millennia. At this moment two aristocrats meet, an aristocratic ancient poet and an aristocratic modern soldier. Rauffenstein returns the book to the table and, before leaving, says: "Poor old Pindar!" The words are meant for Demolder, a man of the people. But they point not only

---

[59] Euripides, *Alcestis* 462–463; Ammianus, *Anthologia Palatina* 11.226; Martial, *Epigrams* 9.29.11–12: *Sit tibi terra levis mollique tegaris harena. / Ne tua non possint eruere ossa canes* ("May the earth be light to you, and may you be covered by soft soil so that the dogs cannot dig up your bones"). An earlier variant in Roman literature without Martial's sarcastic conclusion is Tibullus, *Elegies* 2.4.49–50.

**Fig. 22.** *Grand Illusion.* Rauffenstein and the greatest Greek poet. (Réalisation d'art cinématographique-Criterion)

to the obvious class differences between Rauffenstein and Demolder but also to the fact that Pindar could keep company with aristocrats while Rauffenstein and his class now depend more and more on a society no longer aristocratic or chivalrous but thoroughly bourgeois, if not without its own values, sense of duty, and morals. The scene ends, however, with a moment of humor. Demolder has the last word concerning what he considers, understandably if wrongly, to be the Germans' general lack of culture as shown in their treatment of his Pindar: "They really are stupid."[60]

The same year that Renoir's film was released, a historical epic produced for and financed by the Italian government as part of its propaganda efforts on behalf of Italy's invasion of Ethiopia presented a radically different perspective. Carmine Gallone's *Scipione l'Africano* dealt with the heroism of Scipio Africanus the Elder and his eventual defeat of Hannibal at Zama in

---

[60] Dialogue quotations from *Grand Illusion* 1968: 69–70 except for the last one, which is omitted from translation. The English text also misidentifies the book in this scene as a dictionary and, accordingly, mistranslates Rauffenstein's comment. – Later Germans were not stupid about the humane message of Renoir's film. The Nazis confiscated the negative of *Grand Illusion* and took it to Berlin in 1940 after the fall of France.

202 BC.[61] The Scipio of this film is a precursor of Benito Mussolini, and the film's iconography is consciously modeled on contemporary Italy. Before his decisive victory Scipio exhorts his soldiers: "Legionaries, Fortune offers you the most beautiful of rewards: to die for your country. Legionaries: victory or death!"[62]

### SIMONIDES IN THE GREAT WAR AND IN VIETNAM

Epitaphs to the heroic dead have always been a feature of war. The best-known ancient one was composed by Simonides, a poet already mentioned, in commemoration of the three hundred Spartan warriors and their leader Leonidas. In 480 BC they had died at the battle of Thermopylae, defending Greece against an overwhelming Persian invading army under King Xerxes in a holding action which lasted three days and cost the Persians immense losses.[63] The heroic sacrifice of the Spartans and their allies took on legendary overtones almost immediately, not least because they were defeated and died as the result of an act of betrayal.[64] Thermopylae has often been compared to the siege and fall of the Alamo in 1836 because small bands of soldiers were holding out against overwhelming enemy forces.[65] While some historians have questioned the tactical value of both battles, the legends which have arisen around them are unambiguous in their emphasis on their decisive nature. The cinema has provided epic and largely fictionalized retellings of both events: Rudolf Maté's *The 300 Spartans* (1962), Zack Snyder's *300* (2007; on this below), and two films called *The Alamo*, one produced and directed by John Wayne in 1960, the other directed by John Lee Hancock in 2004.

Simonides' two-line epitaph for the stone monument erected on the spot where the Spartans fell is the most influential of all such inscriptions. With its brevity, which is a fitting testimonial to the Spartans' laconic wit,

---

[61] Literature on this film is extensive. I cite only Iaccio 2003b. The title of Iaccio 2003a indicates that Gallone's name has gone down in film history and cultural history because of this one film. It is available on DVD in an English-dubbed version as *The Defeat of Hannibal*. This version's running time is less than 85 minutes, omitting as much as 30 minutes of the original footage.

[62] Quoted, in my translation, from Brunetta 1993: 147 (where Zama is misidentified as Cannae).

[63] The chief ancient source on Thermopylae is Herodotus, *Histories* 7.175–177 and 201–233. See Green 1996, especially 124–129 and 134–143.

[64] On the legend see Green 1996: 139–140. The heroism of the Spartans makes even this modern scholar emotional: "Many of them were wounded; hardly a shield or helmet but bore witness to the fearful battering they had taken during the past forty-eight hours" (Green 141). The archaism "but" is revealing.

[65] Green 1996: 142 compares the "major setback" which the defeat of the Spartans and their allies had caused Greece with the evacuation of Dunkirk.

it perfectly captures the essence of heroic patriotism. It has been translated into numerous languages, beginning with Cicero's Latin version:

> *Dic, hospes, Spartae nos te hic vidisse iacentes,*
> *dum sanctis patriae legibus obsequimur.*[66]

> Tell them in Lacedaemon, passer-by,
> That here obedient to their word we lie.

> Stranger, tell the Spartans how we die:
> Obedient to their laws, here we lie.[67]

A comparably concise World War I epitaph was composed on the British soldiers who took, defended, and were killed in a trench on the Somme:

> The Devonshires held this trench.
> The Devonshires hold it still.[68]

A German inscription on the soldiers killed at Langemarck in Flanders in 1914 replaced "Sparta" by "Deutschland" but was otherwise identical to Friedrich Schiller's version. In "Common Form," however, a couplet composed in 1918 after his son John had been killed in the war, Rudyard Kipling echoed both Simonides – the dead themselves exhort the reader to tell about them – and Wilfred Owen's "old Lie":

> If any question why we died,
> Tell them, because our fathers lied.[69]

Simonides' influence extended beyond the Great War itself. *Tell England*, the 1922 novel by Ernest Raymond on the devastating Gallipoli campaign, which Raymond had witnessed as an army chaplain, is a case in

---

[66] Cicero, *Tusculan Disputations* 1.101. Simonides' original text (now *F.G.E.* XXII(b) Page) is preserved by Herodotus, *Histories* 7.228. The most famous modern version of Cicero's adaptation is the German one by Friedrich Schiller at lines 97–98 of his poem "Der Spaziergang": "Wanderer, kommst du nach Sparta, verkündige dorten, du habest / uns hier liegen gesehn, wie das Gesetz es befahl"; quoted from Schiller 1965: 228–234, at 231. It is the basis for the World War II story, set in a German *Gymnasium*, by Heinrich Böll, "Wanderer, kommst du nach Spa . . ." (1950); English translations in Böll 1956 and Böll 1986: 270–277 ("Stranger, Bear Word to the Spartans We . . ."). On Böll's story in the context of European literature and classical education after World War II see Theodore Ziolkowski 2000a: 549–551. On the influence of the battle of Thermopylae and of Simonides' epitaph on modern history and political ideology see Watt 1985 and Gelzer 1997.

[67] The translations are by Green 1996: 143 and Andrew Sinclair, the latter in Fussell 1975: 181.

[68] Quoted from Fussell 1975: 180. On Greek influences on Rudyard Kipling's popular "Epitaphs of the War" see Fussell 181.

[69] "Common Form" is one of Kipling's *Epitaphs of the War* (1914–1918), first published in *The Years Between* (1919). It is here quoted from Kipling 1941: 410.

point.[70] It became an immediate bestseller. Its hero was modeled on Rupert Brooke. The novel was filmed in 1931 by Anthony Asquith, the son of the British Prime Minister at the time of Gallipoli.[71] While its dustjacket described the novel as a "great romance of glorious youth," the film was considerably more serious in tone and comparable to *All Quiet on the Western Front*. (Director Asquith had lost a brother in the war.) Two schoolboy friends enlist in the army with great enthusiasm, but the reality shatters their illusions about heroism. Shortly after a reference to Simonides' epitaph and over a montage of machine-gun fire, bombings, and soldiers dead or being killed, one of the two screams three times: "This is what I'd like to tell England." His own gravestone in the British cemetery carries the inscription:

> Tell England, ye who pass this monument,
> We died for her, and here we rest content.

These words contrast with the negative view of war which parts of the film – and all of *All Quiet on the Western Front* – have shown us before. Both films refer to classical culture and ideals and emphasize the impressionability of schoolboys, although the film of *Tell England* omits several school scenes contained in the novel and is "a glorification of the public schoolboy and the class system."[72] A British film historian has summarized the overall nature of *Tell England* in the following terms: "war and indeed death, though messy and a trifle unpleasant, are a small price to pay for the preservation of the England of the fine, brave days before the war, the England which they, as public school boys, were produced and trained to defend."[73] Here again we return to Owen's "old Lie," the thoughtless and outdated acceptance of Horace's *dulce et decorum*.

A strong condemnation of meaningless heroism among the horrors of war came with Joseph Losey's *King and Country* (1964), which originally was to be called *Glory Hole* and was to open with the last scene of Milestone's film. Similar in theme to Stanley Kubrick's *Paths of Glory* (1957), *King and Country* deals with a court martial and execution; it was based on an actual case.[74] In a visual masterstroke the film's long opening sequence shows

---

[70] Raymond 1922.

[71] For information on this film see Kelly 1997: 75–78. A. P. Herbert, author of *The Secret Battle* (1919), a novel partly on the Gallipoli campaign, in which he had served, worked on the film's dialogue. A more recent film on the campaign is Australian Peter Weir's *Gallipoli* (1981), which is more in the spirit of Raymond's novel than Asquith's film of it (Richards 1988: 227–228).

[72] This and the preceding three quotations are from Kelly 1997: 75–76.  [73] Richards 1973: 154.

[74] On *King and Country* see Kelly 1997: 176–180, Caute 1994: 497–501, and, more briefly, Todman 2005: 35–36.

London's Wellington Arch and the monument to the Royal Artillery, the latter inscribed with the words "The Royal Fellowship of Death." These images are intercut with views of the desolation in the trenches and No Man's Land of Passchendaele in 1917 by means of historical photographs. The film was usually shown in black and white, but it was originally released sepia-tinted "to recall old photographs from that period."[75] In a dissolve, a photo of a uniformed skeleton lying in a trench reveals the figure of the man to be court-martialed.[76] After these images we hear, with a shudder of sad revulsion, the doomed man recite a poem by A. E. Housman:

> Here dead lie we because we did not choose
>   To live and shame the land from which we sprung.
> Life, to be sure, is nothing much to lose,
>   But young men think it is, and we were young.[77]

These lines remind us of Tyrtaeus and Simonides. Their author was one of the foremost classical scholars of his day. Although used anachronistically and probably not in accordance with Housman's intention, the poem foreshadows the eventual outcome of the young man's trial and the inhumanity of his execution. To director Losey

---

[75] Losey's words are taken from Ciment 1985: 248.

[76] Palmer and Riley 1993: 23–27 give a detailed description of the film's prologue, with illustrations. They misidentify, however, the figure of Victory at the top of the Wellington Arch as Peace, although the statue's classical iconography – winged, holding a crown or wreath of victory, and hovering above or driving a *quadriga* (four-horse chariot) – is unambiguous. (Cf. the sculpture on top of the Brandenburg Gate in Berlin.) The point of such monuments is the commemoration of martial heroism and victory, not of peace. The same error appears in Caute 1994: 497. – The photograph of the skeleton (from the Imperial War Museum) is best known from the cover of Taylor 1966, a paperback edition. Taylor's book first appeared in 1963, the year before Losey's film was released.

[77] The poem, quoted in a slightly different version in the film, was first drafted in 1895 and published for the first time in 1936 as number 35 in the posthumous collection *More Poems*. It is here quoted from Housman 1997: 137. Housman's poem inspired the title of Harold G. Moore and Galloway 1992, a book on the early Vietnam war, filmed by Randall Wallace as *We Were Soldiers* in 2002. On this film, in which a dying American says "I'm glad I can die for my country," cf. Denby 2002: 93: it "solemniz[es] sacrifice and death" but "never acknowledges that the Pentagon used such capable and intelligent men to lead us into a catastrophe without parallel in American history." – In his edition of the fifth book of Manilius Housman wittily changed Horace's line to *Dulce et decorum est pro patria mentiri* (". . . to lie for one's country") when he discussed the inadequacies and falsehoods which a German reviewer had perpetrated on an earlier volume of Housman's Manilius while extolling the virtues of German classical scholarship over Housman's. See Housman 1930: xxxvi, note. A comparable sentiment, this time in an ancient context that makes the Romans themselves the "bad guys," was voiced by American journalist and editor Charles Creighton Hazewell in 1858: "How, and under what circumstances Spartacus became a gladiator, is a point by no means clear. We cannot trust the Roman accounts, as it was a meritorious thing, in the opinion of a Roman, for a man to lie for his country, as well as to die for it." Quoted from Hazewell 1858: 291. The essay is virtually a hagiography of Spartacus.

*King and Country* is a story about hypocrisy, a story about people who are brought up to a certain way of life, who are given the means to extend their knowledge and to extend their understanding, but are not given the opportunity to use their minds in connection with it, and who finally have to face the fact that they have to be rebels . . . and outsiders in society for the rest of their lives, with all of the penalties this entails, or else they have to accept hypocrisy.[78]

The opening images of the Artillery Monument have already expressed this view, but his own experience of seeing the monument provided Losey with a key impulse to his film:

I took buses . . . and I used to ride by Hyde Park Corner every day and see this horrendous heroic monument which is such a joke in the light of what one knows about the war . . . I wanted to get some impression of what had been done. How the war was brought about is all in the [film's] title. The people were sold that war on the basis of king and country. And . . . now, there is still . . . the idiocy of this sentimental monument to people who just died the most miserable dog's deaths.[79]

The most devastating war of the twentieth century, however, was World War II. More films have been set in this than in any other war. The films often contained classical themes, especially of heroic death for one's country.[80] In particular, Thermopylae could be seen in Germany as an analogy to the battle of Stalingrad. When defeat was already unavoidable, Hermann Göring delivered a speech to the Germans that was transmitted by radio even to the embattled Sixth Army. The date was January 30, 1943, the tenth anniversary of the Nazis' seizure of power. Göring made one reference to German historical myth in the *Nibelungenlied*, the heroic medieval epic at whose end the Nibelungs all die in the burning hall of King

---

[78] Milne 1968: 126–128.

[79] Ciment 1985: 244; also in Kelly 1997: 178. For a recent expression of a comparable point of view cf. Barker 1994: 127: "He began to stroll towards the Achilles Monument. This was a frequent objective on his evening walks, for no particular reason except that its heroic grandeur both attracted and repelled him. It seemed to embody the same unreflecting admiration of courage that he found in 'The Charge of the Light Brigade', a poem that had meant a great deal to him as a boy, and still did, though what it meant had become considerably more complex. He stared up at the stupendous lunging figure, with its raised sword and shield, and thought, not for the first time, that he was looking at the representation of an ideal that no longer had validity." This novel is the second in Barker's trilogy mentioned above; it is set in 1918. The statue mentioned is a monumental sculpture in London's Hyde Park dedicated to the Duke of Wellington, conqueror of Napoleon.

[80] On the tendency to draw Homeric parallels to modern wars see the comments and examples in Winkler 2006a: 1–3. Steven Spielberg's *Saving Private Ryan* (1998), a film about D-Day and its aftermath, incidentally reveals a number of aspects of war which the *Iliad* had mentioned first. Despite the horrors it shows especially in its first half hour, the film on the whole glorifies war and heroism in its main plot far more than the *Iliad* had done and far more than its director and star would have the public believe.

Etzel the Hun. The story had been retold on the silent screen in Fritz Lang's two-part epic *Die Nibelungen* (1924), which the Nazis later appropriated for their own propaganda. In his speech Göring also mentioned Thermopylae, if more briefly.[81] He could count on all educated Germans to understand his references. A modern historian has summarized the reaction to Göring's speech at Stalingrad:

This speech was not well received in Stalingrad, where it was listened to on radios. The fact that it was Goering, of all people, who was delivering "our own funeral speech", heaped insult upon injury . . . Goering's voice was instantly recognized. "Turn it up!" somebody shouted. "Switch it off!" yelled others, cursing him . . . Some officers joked bitterly that the "suicide of the Jews" on the top of Masada might have been a more appropriate comparison than Thermopylae.[82]

German cinema dramatized the German soldiers' reaction in 1959 with Frank Wisbar's *Stalingrad: Dogs, Do You Want to Live Forever?* This was the first feature film on the catastrophe. The film incorporates documentary footage of World War II, but the sequence dealing with Göring's speech adduces only Thermopylae as a historical analogy. A narrator's voice introduces the occasion of his address, which is intercut with the reactions of German soldiers in a makeshift military hospital. On the radio, interrupted several times by static, Göring intones the Nazi ideology of heroism and doom over images of wounded and amputated soldiers. He slightly misquotes Schiller's version of Simonides' epitaph and then introduces a contemporary variant. I translate from the film's soundtrack, leaving the quotation in the original:

Should anybody once become weak, he should think of Stalingrad, where the fighting was done with the same heroic temper as it had been back then in Greece at the pass of Thermopylae, where Leonidas stood with his three hundred Spartans and did not yield . . . until the last man had fallen. That's why it's written there: *"Wanderer, kommst du nach Sparta, verkünde, du habest uns dort liegen gesehen, wie das Gesetz es befahl."* So we say today . . . German soldiers once again have proven what true heroism is. There they sealed their loyalty to the *Führer* with their deaths . . . And so it will be said in future: *"Wanderer, kommst du nach Deutschland, sage, du habest uns in Stalingrad liegen gesehen, wie das Gesetz es befahl."* [Literally: "Wanderer, when you come to Germany, say you have seen us lying at Stalingrad as the law commanded."] Yes, a soldier is meant to die. Should he happen to get out alive, he can only say: "I've just been lucky." Even a thousand years from now the name of Stalingrad will be uttered in reverence.

[81]  Cf. Rebenich 2002: 331 and 340 note 68.
[82]  Beevor 1998: 380 (and 472 for source references). The speech was published in the Nazi party's organ *Völkischer Beobachter* on January 31; a transcript of Göring's actual words, different in places, and introductory comments are in Krüger 1991: 170–187.

The screenwriters capture the cynicism of Nazi ideology, the emptiness of heroism, and the meaninglessness of death for one's country in an evil cause on the verge of being lost. The film's reference to antiquity is reinforced visually when the scene shifts to the street outside. In a long shot a few German soldiers are leaving the hospital. In the middle and foreground two neoclassical statues can be seen in the mud and rubble of the street. Both are of white marble and clearly visible in the otherwise dark shot. The one lying on its back in the foreground is a discus thrower, a variant of one of the most famous and most often reproduced works of ancient art, Myron's *Discobolus*. Russian gunfire now commences. One of the Germans is hit and collapses between the statues. Another one rushes up and drags the body away. A moment of unheroic death coupled with an act of common humanity says more about behavior in battle than any amount of empty rhetoric on the part of those who send others to their deaths but stay safely at home. The fate of the two marble statues and of the soldier indicates the descent of civilization into barbarism, for at this moment the composition of the shot visually balances the human body center left against the statue center right.

The film's prologue, which introduces the largely fictional and somewhat clichéd plot, had already prepared viewers for what was to come. It began with newsreel footage of German soldiers marching, goose-stepping, and on horseback and of Nazi salutes given to and by Adolf Hitler. Military music is playing on the soundtrack. A narrator comments on the attractiveness of military pomp: "Parades are splendid to watch. Accompanied by stirring music, polished boots strike the asphalt. Eyes sparkle. Everybody advances equally, step by step." A sudden cut then shows the result: frozen bodies of dead soldiers lying on snowy ground. The narrator's sentence continues: "And it only ends when snow and wind weave the shrouds to cover what had begun so radiantly and certain of victory. A dead soldier doesn't care who won or lost the war."

Later in 1943 the Nazis grandly celebrated the centenary of Friedrich Hölderlin, one of Germany's greatest poets and the elegist for classical Greek literature, philosophy, and art. Although he had written a number of patriotic poems, Hölderlin was anything but a simple-minded patriot or advocate of autocracy or dictatorship. After the defeat at Stalingrad Hölderlin became a kind of German *vates*, a prophetic and inspired poet who extolled the values of Western civilization now endangered by the barbaric East. The speaker of Hölderlin's 1799 poem "Der Tod fürs Vater-land" ("Death for One's Country") welcomes the approach of battle and the shedding of his "heart's blood" on the "sacrificial hill" of heroes for the survival of his country; he concludes that "not one too many" had fallen for the cause.[83] All this sounded just right for Nazi propaganda, but Hölderlin was not thinking of a Greater Germany but most likely had his own Swabia in mind. Ideology, however, need not be concerned with facts or details.

The propaganda of selling a war, this time the containment of godless communism, became important again with the American engagement in Vietnam. Several films dealt with the moral, social, and political problems raised by this war, either directly in films set in Vietnam or on the home front or indirectly, as in some western films.[84] But a thoroughly critical view of the war became possible only with temporal distance; while it was being fought, films were likely to contain positive or uplifting aspects, although such a cinematic apologia as John Wayne's *The Green Berets* (1968) remained an exception.

A Vietnam film with a classical analogy intended to comment on the American defeat was Ted Post's *Go Tell the Spartans* (1978), one of the earliest films critical of the war after its end. Its title quotes Simonides. But Thermopylae here means defeat. The film's emphasis on ancient history is intentional, for its source was a novel with a different title and only two passing mentions of Thermopylae.[85] The film is set in 1964 during the earliest stage of the war, when the Americans in Vietnam were officially only military "advisors," as they were called, not combatants. Major Asa Barker, the commander of a small American post, is beginning to have doubts about why the Americans are in this country. Army headquarters orders him to occupy Muc Wa, an outpost abandoned more than a decade ago when the French lost this part of their colonial empire. The arrogant and incompetent American general who instigates this occupation tells Barker: "You know what happened to the French in this country – they got the shit kicked out of them. But that's not going to happen to the U.S. Army, Asa." And: "Well, now, we wouldn't want to repeat the mistakes of the French, would we?" But that is exactly what the Americans are beginning

---

[83] The text of the poem is accessible in Hölderlin 1999: 216–217. Lines from this poem, including those quoted here, could be heard even before Stalingrad in Karl Ritter's film *Stukas* (1941); the setting is a conversation of two German officers on the Western front. Cf. Leiser 1974: 32–33 (in a chapter called "To Die for Germany").

[84] On Vietnam overtones in westerns see Winkler 1985: 534.

[85] Ford 1967: 65 ("There was an inscription of some kind [on a tombstone]. *Go, stranger, and tell the Spartans that we lie here in obedience to their laws* . . . The idea didn't thrill him as much as it had done in college. *What good is Greek history to an engineer?* he thought. *I should have stuck to Hemingway*") and 69 ("The inscription had nothing to do with Thermopylae, after all. It only said . . ."; here follow three French names).

**Fig. 23.** *Go Tell the Spartans.* Simonides' epitaph in Vietnam. (AVCO Embassy)

to do, and widespread incompetence combined with lack of understanding of the Vietnamese will eventually lead to their defeat. Barker, hardened by long experience, can only shake his head at the thoughtless patriotism of his recruits. A new corporal: "If I had to be a soldier, I wanted to be in the roughest, toughest outfit in the U.S. Army, sir." An idealistic lieutenant: "I feel that if my country is at war it's my duty to fight for it." When he is put in command of the occupation of Muc Wa, the lieutenant is elated ("We appreciate this opportunity to fight for our country, sir") and tells the Vietnamese under his command: "We will establish a fortress for liberty and justice." Their reaction is spontaneous derision.[86]

At Muc Wa the French had left a cemetery of their war dead with 302 graves. An inscription over its entrance gate gives a French version of Simonides' epitaph, which Corporal Courcey translates for the lieutenant (Fig. 23). He then comments: "I think it refers to the battle of Thermopylae,

---

[86] Herr 1977 is the classic account of the unheroic and inglorious side of the Vietnam war, incorporating extensive quotations from American soldiers about their experiences. Herr later wrote the narration for Francis Ford Coppola's *Apocalypse Now* and worked with Stanley Kubrick on *Full Metal Jacket.*

where the three hundred Spartans died trying to hold the pass – if you remember your Greek history, sir." The lieutenant later observes to Courcey about the French dead: "Brave men, corporal. They fought the battle and lost. But we *won't* lose. 'Cause we're Americans." Viewers know better. Those in the audience who remember their Greek history will already know how the film's plot must end and can draw an analogy to the entire Vietnam war.

The presence of the small, ragtag, and ill-prepared group of American soldiers and their Vietnamese allies at Muc Wa attracts the Viet Cong, and viewers begin to realize that the command to occupy it is misguided and ruinous. A large enemy force advances and attacks the beleaguered post, whose men are outnumbered. The lieutenant goes on a heroic but foolhardy rescue mission to save one of his men left behind on a patrol. This situation is as clichéd as his words to the sergeant who tries to hold him back: "Don't you see I *have* to go after him?" Audiences are familiar with such words and actions from countless adventure and war films. In more superficial films these missions usually succeed, but not here. The lieutenant finds his man dead and is himself killed when he attempts to return, becoming the first American casualty at Muc Wa. His burial in the French cemetery indicates that the fate of the Americans in Vietnam will be similar to that of the French.

Another huge Viet Cong force now prepares to attack, and headquarters orders Muc Wa to be evacuated. When Barker finds out that only the Americans can be taken out by helicopter but not the others, the corporal refuses to obey his order to save himself and stays with the abandoned Vietnamese; his example inspires Barker to remain, too. Anecdotes about similar behavior were told about Thermopylae as well.[87] The film also follows the story of Thermopylae with the retreat of most of the occupying forces before their final engagement with the enemy.[88] The group's night retreat from Muc Wa takes them past the French cemetery; shortly after, they are ambushed. We learn that, just like the Spartans, they have been betrayed. Barker is killed, and next morning the corporal, severely wounded himself, finds his corpse, stripped naked. This is another analogy to Thermopylae, for Xerxes had ordered Leonidas' corpse to be mutilated. Mutilation may well have taken place in such a situation in Vietnam, but it could not be shown on the screen. Courcey then stumbles back to the cemetery, where the film's final moments take place. A Viet Cong aims a rifle at him but is too exhausted to shoot, just as Courcey is too weak

---

[87] At Herodotus, *Histories* 7.221 and 229.     [88] Herodotus, *Histories* 7.219–220.

to defend himself. He can only say: "I'm going home, Charlie." He then stumbles off into the distance, and it is clear that he will soon collapse and die. None of those left behind at Muc Wa will go home. As a last sign of the Americans' complete failure in Vietnam and of the end of heroism we see the wooden board with the French version of Simonides' epitaph lying on the ground.

Heroism and patriotism cannot prevail in such a war. "Just don't be a hero," Barker had told Courcey after his refusal to leave Muc Wa. Even the group's experienced sergeant had suffered a nervous breakdown and committed suicide after the lieutenant's death. As Barker had said to Courcey during their last night, describing the military tour of duty in Vietnam: "This one's a sucker's tour, going nowhere, just round and round in circles." The film effectively plays on the viewer's knowledge of what followed after 1964: an ever-increasing buildup of military personnel and *matériel*. The ignorant general's confidence ("The only way we're gonna win this war is to get United States combat troops in here") is tragically misplaced. Military escalation will undermine the humanity even of the Americans, usually the "good guys" in fact, fiction, and film, and will lead to as infamous an atrocity as the massacre at My Lai. *Go Tell the Spartans* foreshadows this by showing the viewer the mistreatment of a prisoner of war in the American compound during the film's opening credits. The Gettysburg Address, which a G.I. recites in a haze of drugs during one scene, becomes a bitter and sardonic comment on the war and on the American way.

The film's visual style fully supports its dark theme. Everything appears bleak and flat, with washed-out colors which contrast with the lush visuals of Francis Ford Coppola's Vietnam war epic *Apocalypse Now* (1979), another film which examines the horrors of warfare and the price it exerts on the participants' humanity. The intentionally drab images of *Go Tell the Spartans* express its serious nature; the film looks almost like a documentary. Its director worked mainly in television and only occasionally in films and was not known as a visual stylist. But here lack of polish is an asset. With one exception the film dispenses entirely with anything that might distract from the story being told; there are no instances of visual dazzle, editing fireworks, or other cinematic gimmicks which might make the film more palatable to mass audiences and so increase its box-office appeal. Realism is sustained throughout the plot, the dialogue – as earthy in its vocabulary as it is sardonic and cynical in its humor – and the visuals. The exception is the musical theme that underscores the images of the French cemetery and the mention of the Spartans and makes them stand apart from the rest of the film. Many scenes have no musical accompaniment at all; in those which do we hear only a small number of the instruments usually associated with martial music, primarily drums sounding a march rhythm. But when we see the Spartans' epitaph and are told the story of Thermopylae, we hear a short trumpet fanfare, whose sound, unobtrusive to begin with, immediately recedes into a diminuendo. The effect is that of an echo, haunting and eerie. The music conjures up a feeling of nobility and sorrow for the fallen, both the Spartans and the French. But as the fanfare fades away we begin to realize that the Americans are doomed to meet their own Thermopylae. The musical theme recurs at the film's close over our final view of the cemetery. Now it expands its meaning, from "Go tell the Spartans" to "Go tell the Americans."

## HOMER, THUCYDIDES, AND HORACE IN WORLD WAR II

The most notorious and most barbaric side of World War II was the genocide of the European Jews. The seven-hour American television epic *Holocaust* (1978), directed by Marvin J. Chomsky, tells the fictional story of a Jewish family whose destruction exemplifies the fate of the Jews and of a German family which rises and eventually falls with Nazism. *Holocaust* was a popular and critical success in the United States; when shown on West German public television in early 1979, it generated a nationwide renewal of the debate over Germany's crimes in World War II, German anti-Semitism, and the Final Solution. A modern historian has assessed the film's power and its artistic limitations:

The purest product of commercial American television – its story simple, its characters mostly two-dimensional, its narrative structured for maximum impact – "Holocaust" . . . was execrated and abominated by European cineastes . . . , who accused it of turning German history into American soap opera . . . But these very limitations account for the show's impact. It ran for four consecutive nights on West German national [and public] television and was watched by an estimated twenty million viewers – well over half the adult population. It also happened to coincide with [a] trial, of former guards from the Majdanek death camp: a reminder to viewers that this was unfinished business. The public impact was enormous . . . Henceforward Germans would be among the best-informed Europeans on the subject of the *Shoah* and at the forefront of all efforts to maintain public awareness of their country's singular crime.[89]

Less than fifteen minutes into the film we meet the meek and baby-faced young German bourgeois who will turn into its chief villain as one of

---

[89] Quoted from Judt 2005: 811. The following discussion of *Holocaust* is taken from Winkler 2006b: 64–66.

the main architects of the Holocaust. He is an apolitical and non-violent law-school graduate, a husband and father of two little children. He is also unemployed and unable to care for his family. On the urging of his stronger-willed wife he joins the SS and swiftly rises to positions of power. When he is first wearing his black uniform at home and putting on its cap in front of a mirror, his wife and children are watching him. The mother has been holding her son in her arms, but when she puts him down, he runs off in fear and hides behind a door. The dialogue in this scene refers to one of the most famous and moving scenes in the *Iliad*, but with a twist:

*Husband* [*to son*]: Peter, how do you like your father? . . . Uniform's too much for him.
*Wife*: Erik [*sic*], you look heroic. [*The boy is peering out from behind the door.*] . . . Peter, it's only Daddy's uniform.
*Husband* [*diffident*]: I'm afraid my first day as a policeman is a dead loss. Like a scene from the *Iliad*: Hector goes to put on his shining helmet with the plume, and his little son moves away in terror, screaming, frightened at the aspect of his own father. Can't recall the rest; something about Hector asking Zeus to make the boy braver than he was.
*Wife*: I'll make you both brave.

In the *Iliad* the scene of Hector's farewell from his wife and terrified little child exemplifies the anguish of all warriors going off to battle, their uncertainty of survival and return, and their hope for a good outcome, often against all hope.[90] It is one of the most humane moments in classical literature, and every reader or listener is emotionally on Hector's and Andromache's side. Our knowledge that despite Hector's heroism Troy is doomed to a kind of ancient holocaust involves us even more closely. The brief moment in *Holocaust* chillingly turns the humanity of Homer into its opposite. The man whom we see leaving his family is anything but decent, patriotic, or heroic; he is about to turn himself into a soulless bureaucrat who coldly and rationally administers mass murder on an unprecedented scale and without any pangs of conscience. After the war he will kill himself with a poison capsule to avoid being tried for crimes against humanity. His descent into barbarism begins with *Kristallnacht* (i.e. "night of smashed glass"), when Erik organizes the country-wide violence against Jews and their property which signaled the onset of the Holocaust. There will be only one brief moment in this long film in which Erik exhibits something like an awareness of his enormous guilt. The fact that he has studied

[90] *Iliad* 6.390–502. The specific lines to which *Holocaust* refers are 399–400 (Hector's son in the arms of his nurse), 466–470 (the boy's terror at seeing Hector in his helmet with its moving horse-hair crest), 476–481 (Hector's prayer on behalf of his son).

law is a revealing irony, echoing the argument of Sophocles' *Antigone* that what is politically or ideologically right may supersede true right and law. Erik is not going out to defend his country, which will soon precipitate a world-wide war, and neither he nor his wife and children will be remembered the way Hector, Andromache, and their child will be. The scene is a chilling comment on the dehumanizing side of modern war, made the more devastating because of the virtually unlimited modern killing potential. Most of the television viewers will not have recognized the specific scene to which Erik refers, but they will have been familiar with Homer's name and may have concluded that Erik is rather well educated. (Presumably he read parts of the *Iliad* as a *Gymnasium* student.) So not even higher education can prevent a man's descent into the abyss.

*Holocaust* contains two other moments relevant to the present topic. Not long after the scene discussed we see a Jewish bookstore being vandalized during *Kristallnacht*. The most conspicuous feature of its display window is a large print of Raphael's painting "The School of Athens." Nazi thugs smash the window, throw out and burn the books, tear the print to shreds, and beat up the owner. The print serves the same function as did those of Renaissance art in *Grand Illusion*; its fate is a comment on the destruction of culture and civilization. Later a Jewish physician, one of the central characters of *Holocaust*, tries to console his wife with a quotation from Virgil when he is being deported: "Remember your Latin, Bertha: *amor vincit omnia* – 'love conquers all'." His daughter-in-law, who overhears him, will repeat the Latin words to her husband at Theresienstadt years later.[91]

Terrence Malick's epic *The Thin Red Line* (1998) deals with the American campaign at Guadalcanal. Lieutenant Colonel Tall, trained at West Point, is well educated in the classics, as an early moment in the film shows. Rose-colored sunlight is reflected from the clouds at dawn, and we see Tall on a walkie-talkie with Captain Staros, a Greek-American officer under his command, commenting: "*Eôs rhododaktylos* – 'rosy-fingered dawn.' You're Greek, aren't you, captain? Did you ever read Homer? We read Homer at the Point, in Greek." The words reveal Tall's feeling of superiority and foreshadow what becomes evident later: he is not to be trusted to be concerned about the welfare of his men but is out only for himself. Tall is an ambitious officer who has grown old without promotion to general. We have earlier seen him in conversation with a younger brigadier general, and a voice-over told us Tall's innermost thoughts: "Worked my ass off,

---

[91] Virgil, *Eclogues* 10.69: *omnia vincit amor*. The misquotation is common.

brown-nosed the generals, degraded myself – for them, and my family, my home." Tall is afraid of being passed over now that he has come within reach of general's rank. "The closer you are to Caesar, the greater the fear," he says to himself and to the film's viewers. He sees his last chance for advancement in a militarily insignificant but costly attack against a Japanese stronghold on a Pacific island. Echoing a similar scene from Kubrick's *Paths of Glory*, Tall orders his men to attack ("you charge right up that goddamn hill!") without understanding that his command means certain death for them. When Staros refuses to obey, Tall becomes almost hysterical in his insistence. His later words, although they are as eloquent as is appropriate for someone with his education despite his habitual cursing, summarize his character as ruthless, insecure, pompous, irresponsible in leadership, and incapable of assessing the situation he is faced with:

I'm convinced that the Japanese position can be broken right now. All we have to do is keep going, and we'll have this hill . . . by sundown . . . I've waited all my life for this. I've worked, slaved, eaten – oh – untold buckets of shit to have this opportunity. I don't intend to give it up now. You don't know what it feels like to be passed over.

Tall prevails, and his men take the Japanese stronghold at great cost. Tall then has a proclamation read to his battalion, in which he claims a great military success: "Our victory gives us the highest reasons of pride. It'll prove a milestone in the battle for Guadalcanal." His men and the viewers know better. Tall never receives his promotion, and his soldiers' sacrifices are in vain. His very name is a comment on his nature: he is tall only physically; his character is puny. He contrasts with the military aristocrats in *The Dawn Patrol* and *Grand Illusion*. The reference to Homer in *The Thin Red Line* tells us that we have come a long way from the one to Pindar in Renoir's film. Whereas classical literature had been meant to emphasize heroism and nobility of character in the earlier film, it reveals no more than shallow, even cynical, pretentiousness and egotism here.

The exquisite beauty of the scenery, the very opposite of such gritty films as *All Quiet on the Western Front* and *Go Tell the Spartans*, indicates that its director is attempting to present a war epic different from all others. But thematically Malick's film belongs in the tradition of military epics whose presentation of war is compromised by their emphasis on spectacle or heroics. Largely the same may be said about Franklin J. Schaffner's *Patton* (1970) although here we deal with a character more famous, more controversial, and more complex than most cinematic war heroes. Patton believed in reincarnation, a circumstance which enables the filmmakers to

**Fig. 24.** *Patton.* Patton and the ruins of Carthage, filmed at Volubilis in Morocco. The Arch of Caracalla is in the background. (Twentieth Century-Fox)

deal with other famous military leaders in history from antiquity to the recent past.[92] Visiting the classical ruins of the site where Carthage fell to the Romans in 146 BC, the film's Patton says matter-of-factly: "Two thousand years ago – I was here" (Fig. 24). He embodies the warrior general's spirit through the ages, just as the real Patton was an expert in military history. Several classical references in the film throw light on his character.[93]

Prior to the American invasion of Italy Patton is eager to convince his British allies that the best route is via Sicily. As the film presents it, Patton is successful, if only for the time being, for General Eisenhower, prompted by Field Marshal Montgomery, eventually turns down his plan. The Athenian invasion of Sicily set the precedent for Patton's plan: "I think

---

[92] On this see D'Este 1995: 320–328 (a chapter entitled "Past and Future Warrior Reincarnate"), with ancient examples at 322 and 323.

[93] The DVD edition of *Patton* contains an audio commentary by Charles M. Province, founder and president of the George S. Patton, Jr. Historical Society, who observes: "Patton understood that . . . every single act in history . . . is somehow related to some other act that occurs and then reflects upon some other act that occurs in the future . . . The main fascination for Patton in his search for the common elements of man's history and behavior was the significance and importance of military leadership . . . He knew about Greek phalanx, Roman legions, Napoleon's columns [etc.]. He knew everything . . . He could subjectively [sic] compare the heavy cavalry of Belisarius with a modern armored vehicle. He discovered a certain craftiness in the sixth-century tactics of Belisarius that he actually applied to the use of modern tanks in *his* time." Cf. D'Este 1995: 383 (on Patton and Caesar) and 708: "He referred frequently to the fact that his current battles were modern-day versions of the Romans'." On this last topic see the excerpt from Patton's November, 1918, lecture "Tank Tactics" in Blumenson 1972: 645. In his teens Patton had attended the Classical School for Boys in Pasadena, California; on its curriculum, and for excerpts from Patton's school compositions, which were on classical subjects, see Blumenson 36–42. Patton had chosen the Theban general Epaminondas as his ideal (D'Este 1995: 49, cf. Blumenson 1972: 40–42). Patton's best-known poem, "Through a Glass, Darkly," has a warrior's reincarnation through the ages for its subject. Semmes 1955: 212–214 prints its text.

it was Alcibiades in the Peloponnesian War, 415 BC – he said, 'If Syracusa [*sic*] falls, all Sicily falls, and then Italy.' He knew, you see, that Syracuse was the jugular of the island, and old Alcibiades always went for the throat. I propose to take Sicily in the same way."[94]

Patton wins over the British, gentlemen all, by appealing to their classical education. By contrast several scenes set in Berlin portray the High Command of the German army as an assembly of boorish ignoramuses. General Colonel Jodl, for instance, at one point does not even recognize the name Dulcinea, although Don Quixote has just been mentioned. According to the film the Germans lose World War II not least because of their ignorance of ancient and other military history. The one exception is an aide to Jodl, but he holds only a low rank and nobody heeds him. He has studied Patton and accurately predicts Patton's plan. Patton, he explains to Jodl, will invade Italy not via Sardinia but via Sicily because Sicily is the key to Italy, as it always has been. The key, he continues, to understanding Patton is the past, and Patton intends to land at Syracuse because the ancient Greeks had done so before: "Patton is a romantic warrior, who finds himself cast adrift into our time. Patton's secret is the past. He will endorse the attack on Sicily because the ancient Greeks did the same back then."[95]

German actors play the parts of German officers, and these words are heard on the soundtrack in German. Subtitles translate them for American audiences, not always accurately. The phrase "die alten Griechen" ("the ancient Greeks"), for instance, is rendered as "the Athenians." But the film omits to mention that the Athenians were successful in their invasion of

---

94  This is a loose summary of part of the speech made by Alcibiades to the Athenians, counseling them to launch their fateful Sicilian expedition. Cf. Thucydides, *The Peloponnesian War* 6.16–18. Cf. Essame 1974: 84. But in Hollywood not only Patton is up on his Thucydides during World War II. In Dan Curtis's epic 22.5-hour television saga *War and Remembrance* (1988) President Franklin D. Roosevelt says that he has "been reading Thucydides" about the invasion of Sicily; after the victory of El Alamein he observes: "I think we're going to rewrite Thucydides." – Two other classical overtones in *War and Remembrance* are worth mentioning, both Roman. When newly arrived Auschwitz prisoners are selected for the camp or for immediate death, a German officer silently gestures with his fist, his thumb extended either right or left. (The narrator's voice has told us what decision this implies.) A close-up of this fist, clad in black leather, with the thumb repeatedly pointing horizontally in both directions, is a strong reminder of similar Roman signals – thumbs up or down – familiar to modern filmgoers from the arena scenes in Hollywood's Roman films. And before the imminent fall of Berlin, the narrator refers to Hitler's former power with an allusion to Julius Caesar ("Adolf Hitler, the German war lord, who once bestrode Europe from the Atlantic to the Volga . . .") which echoes Cassius' well-known words to Brutus in Shakespeare: "he doth bestride the narrow world / Like a Colossus" (*Julius Caesar* 1.2.133–134).

95  In the film's original German: "Patton ist ein romantischer Krieger, der in unsere Zeit verschlagen wurde. Pattons Geheimnis ist die Vergangenheit. Er wird den Angriff auf Sizilien befürworten, weil die alten Griechen es damals auch so gemacht haben." A parallel to this is Patton's 1945 crossing of the Rhine where Caesar had crossed it, as his son was later to report; see Sobel 1997: 36.

Sicily only initially and that their expedition, on which they thoroughly overextended themselves, was a direct cause of the eventual destruction of their empire. The question then arises: is not the whole reference to Athenian history in *Patton* an instance of Hollywood falsifying fact – or better, of suppressing inconvenient facts – for the sake of plot? There have been and always will be instances of cavalier treatment of history in films, and *Patton* is open to such a charge, too, not only in regard to the suppression of the outcome of the Athenians' Sicilian expedition. We should, however, keep in mind that the historical Patton was fully aware of the Athenians' failure, for even as a schoolboy he had written that their general Nicias' procrastination on Sicily had "proved fatal" to the expedition.[96]

Patton's naming of Alcibiades should prompt us to ask another question: were the filmmakers, and particularly the screenwriters, not primarily interested in character rather than fact? We can attempt to answer this question if we consider the controversial nature of both Patton and Alcibiades. The following quotation gives us a good summary of Patton's character as the film shows him:

> Stronger motives still were his desire to hold the command and his hopes that it would be through him that Sicily . . . would be conquered – successes which would at the same time bring him personally . . . honour. For he was very much in the public eye . . . Although in a public capacity his conduct of the war was excellent, his way of life made him objectionable . . . as a person.

But this is not a modern historian's assessment of Patton but Thucydides' characterization of Alcibiades. The close fit of the words validates the filmmakers' references to the Peloponnesian War, which they give Patton and Jodl's aide. The analogy does not imply that Patton is Alcibiades reincarnate or that there are no differences between the two. The omissions from the text of Thucydides here quoted identify some of these differences, but they are minor in terms of characterizing the men in question. Thucydides speaks of "Sicily and Carthage" rather than only of Sicily and of "wealth and honour" rather than of honor alone and says that Alcibiades' personal conduct made him "objectionable to everyone as a person."[97] Not all of this applies to Patton. The objectionable sides of Patton were primarily his foul language, which he liberally used in public, his alienation of others by blunt and careless pronouncements, and the two notorious incidents,

---

[96] The quotation is from Blumenson 1972: 41. Cf. Essame 1974: 236 and D'Este 1995: 48.

[97] The text is from Thucydides 6.15.2–4, quoted in Warner 1954: 418–419. Warner's was the standard because most widely read English translation in the 1950s and 1960s.

one of them reproduced in the film, in which he slapped shell-shocked soldiers.[98] Patton's strategy regarding Sicily is a result of his rivalry with Montgomery and as such comparable to Alcibiades' rivalry with Nicias. If Patton as a youngster had condemned Nicias as ineffective and fatal, he must have seen greater value in Alcibiades. Patton and Alcibiades were energetic men of action. Even on a minor level they are similar. Thucydides refers to Alcibiades' "enthusiasm for horsebreeding," and the film later shows Patton riding a magnificent thoroughbred.[99] The historical Patton was an expert equestrian and had begun his army career in the cavalry. Thucydides is aware that great men are often claimed by other people in other places and at other times as their own. His Alcibiades says so himself:

> What I know is that people like this – all, in fact, whose brilliance in any direction has made them prominent – are unpopular in their lifetimes, especially with their equals and also with others with whom they come into contact; but with posterity you will find people claiming relationship with them, even where none exists, and you will find their countries boasting of them . . . as fellow-countrymen and doers of great deeds.[100]

While Patton, controversial as he was, did not betray and harm his country as Alcibiades came to do, he, too, lost favor with his superiors. The film makes Patton's fall from grace more poignant by connecting it closely to ancient history, this time Roman. The day after he has been reading Caesar Patton receives a reprimand for slapping a soldier: "I was re-reading Caesar's *Commentaries* last night. In battle Caesar wore a red robe to distinguish him from his men. I was struck by that fact . . ." This reference prepares the way for the film's final scene, in which Patton's affinity to triumphant Roman leaders makes it possible for the audience to leave the theater in a state of heightened emotional involvement with the protagonist. After Germany has surrendered, Eisenhower relieves Patton of his command of the Third Army. When Patton comes out of Eisenhower's office, a Roman bust is prominently on view in the corridor outside. A lonely Patton then leaves the city on a walk with his dog, revealing to us his thoughts in voice-over:

> For over a thousand years, Roman conquerors returning from the wars enjoyed the honor of a triumph, a tumultuous parade. In the procession came trumpeters and musicians and strange animals from the conquered territories, together with carts laden with treasure and captured ornaments. The conqueror rode in a triumphal

---

[98] Details at D'Este 1995: 533–535.   [99] Thucydides 6.15.3; Warner 1954: 418.
[100] Thucydides 6.16.5; Warner 1954: 419–420.

chariot, the day's prisoners walking in chains before him. Sometimes his children, robed in white, stood with him in the chariot, or rode the trace horses. A slave stood behind the conqueror, holding a golden crown and whispering in his ear a warning that all glory is fleeting.

The viewer leaves Patton on a deserted plain with a snow-capped mountain range on the horizon. For Patton there is no triumphal car and no tumultuous parade as others received it after victory. The film does not mention Patton's triumphal return to the United States in June, 1945, or the ticker tape parade he received in Boston.[101] This Patton ends in disgrace despite his achievements. But although he does not receive the glorious accolades from his country for which he has hoped, he is still heroic, as the majesty of nature surrounding him at the end tells us. Patton's unheroic death resulting from a car accident would not have fitted into the film's portrait and is therefore omitted. The voice-over soliloquy also tells us that Patton takes consolation in the past, for the Roman model will make it possible for him to live without the glory he believes he deserves. On several occasions the film had made it clear that Patton is much more a man of the past, perhaps even a man from classical antiquity reincarnated in modern times. While still near the site of Carthage, Patton remarks: "The world grew up . . . God, how I hate the twentieth century." As usual, Jodl's aide understands Patton best, calling him a dyed-in-the-wool general and a magnificent anachronism ("Mit Leib und Seele Feldherr – großartiger Anachronismus"). Later in the film Patton comments on the new technological warfare of the future: "Killing without heroics; nothing is glorified, nothing is reaffirmed; no heroes, no cowards, no troops, no generals, only those who are left alive and those who are left dead. I'm glad that I won't live to see it."[102]

One other feature of *Patton* is significant, concerning not its visuals or dialogue but its musical score. In *Go Tell the Spartans* the fanfare echoing into the distance comments on and emphasizes the film's theme. *Patton* also contains a fanfare, although one somewhat longer. Both express

---

[101] On Patton's return see D'Este 1995: 746–749.

[102] American writer-director Oliver Stone on *Patton*: "It glorified war, saying: 'Watch this man. This man, good or bad, is a heroic general in the Roman sense of the word. He adheres to the stricter standards of an older time of Julius Caesar,' and so forth." The quotation is from the 1997 documentary *The Making of "Patton"* (or: *"Patton": A Tribute to Franklin J. Schaffner*), directed by Michael M. Arick, which is included on the DVD edition of *Patton*. Stone used scenes from *Patton* in his film *Nixon* (1995); he argues that *Patton* influenced Nixon to expand the Vietnam war into Cambodia. For a similar perspective specifically on the prologue of *Patton* see Hoberman 2003: 269–270.

**Fig. 25.** *Patton.* The general in the film's opening scene. (Twentieth Century-Fox)

the ancient roots of modern war and are strikingly similar. The fanfare in *Go Tell the Spartans* is a direct homage to that in *Patton.* Composer Jerry Goldsmith wrote three musical themes to express different aspects of Patton's character. The fanfare "was supposed to be the archaic, his belief in reincarnation."[103] One of its numerous occurrences in *Patton* is at the ancient cemetery of Carthage, when Patton comments on the Greeks, Romans, and Carthaginians who once fought there. Later on, the film even contains an indirect reference to Thermopylae when Patton observes about the ruins on Malta: "In 1528 these forts were defended by four hundred Knights of Malta and eight hundred mercenaries against a force of forty thousand Turks."

The aspects of *Patton* here discussed are those most directly concerned with classical antiquity. But none of them contains the one image for which the film is most famous. This is its very opening, in which Patton, dressed in full regalia, appears before a huge American flag, salutes, and then addresses his troops[104] (Fig. 25). The speech is based on the one Patton gave to the Third Army in England on June 5, 1944. In the film Patton begins by referring to the Horatian *dulce et decorum*:

I want you to remember that no bastard ever won a war by dying for his country. He won it by making the other poor dumb bastard die for *his* country.

---

[103] Quoted from *The Making of "Patton".*

[104] The most detailed biography of Patton still opens with a discussion of this scene a quarter-century after the film was made (D'Este 1995: 1–2).

These words have no direct equivalent in their historical model.[105] We are therefore justified to conclude that the repudiation of Horace was purposely added by the screenwriters. It was, however, in keeping with Patton's beliefs. As one of his daughters said: "He was . . . fond of reminding us that 'any fool can die for his country because the band is playing and the flag is waving. It takes a real man to live for his country.'"[106]

Although perhaps not voiced in such pithy language before, Patton's words in the film are applicable at all times, and competent and responsible commanders plan and act accordingly.[107] I mention just one ancient example. During his siege of Jerusalem future emperor Titus forbade his soldiers to engage in personal heroics.[108] Horace, too, was aware that it is better to survive than to die for your country. The autobiographical parts of his poetry tell us so unequivocally.

### WHAT PRICE GLORY?

Any thoughtless repetition or uncritical appropriation of Horace's famous line neglects to examine its historical situation. Modern scholarship has shown that the sentiment has been consistently taken out of the context of Horace's own world view and been misunderstood and misinterpreted.[109] The verb "die" in place of the more readily expected "fight" is startling, too, because it emphasizes death rather than the survival on which both victory and a martial hero's reputation usually depend and which would be much more in the country's interest. Much earlier, Pindar had made the point that greatest glory is reserved for the man who valiantly defends his country, regardless of his survival or death.[110] Horace himself had famously

---

[105] The following passage comes closest: "Some men are cowards, yes, but they fight just the same, or get the hell shamed out of them watching men fight who are just as scared. . . . But the real man never lets fear of death overpower his honor, his sense of duty to his country, and his innate manhood." Quoted from D'Este 1995: 602. As D'Este 601–605 makes clear, Patton gave the same sort of speech, with minor variations, on several occasions.

[106] Sobel 1997: 9.

[107] A comparable statement, however, may be found among the Latin epigrams of John Owen (ca. 1564–1622), called "the English [really, Welsh] Martial." Epigram 1.48 is addressed *Ad Philopatrum* ("To Him Who Loves His Country") and reads: *Pro patria sit dulce mori licet atque decorum, / Vivere pro patria dulcius esse puto* ("It may be sweet and fitting to die for one's country, but I think to live for one's country is sweeter"). It also circulated in an English version by Thomas Harvey. Nineteenth-century students outdid Owen: *Dulce et decorum est pro patria mori, sed dulcius pro patria vivere, et dulcissimum pro patria bibere. Ergo, bibamus pro salute patriae* ("Sweet and fitting it is to die for one's country, but it is sweeter to live for one's country and sweetest to drink for [or: to] one's country. So let's drink to our country's health").

[108] Josephus, *The Jewish War* 5.316.

[109] Funke 1997: 84–88 gives a convincing interpretation, based on Horace's Epicureanism.

[110] Pindar, *Isthmian Ode* 7.26–30. Cf. Syndikus 1973: 28 on Horace's word choice.

*not* died for his country in battle but had saved himself by turning tail. As he describes it, in 42 BC the god Mercury had saved Horace, "shaking with fear," from the battle of Philippi in a "swift flight," with his shield "not well left behind." To throw away one's shield was antiquity's quintessential act of cowardice in war; ancient Greek even had a specific term for it: *rhipsaspia*. So Horace's own case reveals a complete lack of heroism.[111] A Spartan mother's exhortation to her son about to leave for battle provides us with a famous contrast: "Come back with your shield or on your shield."[112] Horace's biography throws a rather different light on his line, and readers of this ode would do well to remember it and not to imitate a jingoistic warmonger like the thoughtless Kantorek of *All Quiet on the Western Front*.[113]

In 1916 a German student in the *Unterprima* (Lower First) at his *Gymnasium* had noticed the discrepancy between Horace's biography and his much-quoted line. Future playwright and poet Bertolt Brecht wrote in a school essay on the standard topic of *dulce et decorum* that this could be regarded as nothing but "propaganda for a cause":

Only fools can go so far in their vanity to speak of an easy leap through the dark gate, and only as long as they believe themselves to be far away from their last hour. But if the skeleton man with his sickle approaches them, they hoist their shield on their backs and turn tail, just like the emperor's fat court jester at Philippi, who thought up this saying.[114]

The Great War was followed by one even worse, characterized by totalitarianism, various dictatorships, yet more destructive technology, and the

---

[111] Horace, *Odes* 2.7.9–14. The strong understatement "not well" carries the meaning of "dishonorably." Cf. *Odes* 3.4.25–28; cf. further *Odes* 2.7.1–2, *Satires* 1.7.18–19, and *Epistles* 2.2.46–48 (Horace's military service under Brutus) and *Satires* 1.6.48 (Horace the military tribune). Nisbet and Hubbard 1978: 113–114 list the classical parallels to Horace's *rhipsaspia* and emphasize the literary rather than autobiographical nature of *Odes* 2.7.10. Cf. further Nisbet and Hubbard 1978: 107–109. See also Hanson 2000: 63–65.

[112] Plutarch, *Sayings of Spartan Women*: "Women Unknown to Fame" 16 (= *Moralia* 241f). Aristotle in his *Aphorisms* (preserved by Stobaeus, *Florilegium* 7.31) attributes the saying to Gorgo, wife of King Leonidas, but it seems to have been a general Spartan maxim. With the brevity characteristic of Spartans, the Greek reported by Plutarch translates as "Either this or on this."

[113] Kantorek firmly belongs to the long tradition of misunderstanding Horace; cf. Funke 1997: 78–79 on Horace as school author. Funke 78 note 4 makes clear that Horace's ode is still a standard text in German school editions but rarely read today.

[114] Quoted, in my translation, from Witt 1966: 18 (in a brief section entitled "Horace 'Unmasked',," first published in 1949). The text introducing the excerpt from Brecht's essay notes that he frequently received failing grades for his unorthodox or anti-authoritarian views. For details about Brecht's writings while in school and about his wavering attitudes to World War II see Völker 1978: 8–10 and Hayman 1983: 17–18. Both biographers report that Brecht came close to being expelled for his Horace essay.

Holocaust. It has been said in post-World War II Germany that it is no longer possible to write poetry after Auschwitz and that to write or recite poetry is to be silent about the Holocaust.[115] Poetry here represents culture and civilization at large. The more important it is for us today to understand Horace's line correctly, aware of his biography and philosophy and of the history of Roman warfare. Perhaps we would do best to read Horace's ode and his other Roman Odes alongside Virgil's roughly contemporary *Aeneid*, a work which shows wary rather than unquestioning patriotism and deals with *virtus*, the horrors of war, and the high price which must be paid for victory and empire. With such a reading of Virgil and Horace we return to the *Iliad* as well.[116]

Achilles' last appearance in Homeric epic is especially important. In Book Eleven of the *Odyssey* Odysseus descends to the Underworld and converses with the shades of great heroes of the Trojan war: Agamemnon, Ajax, and Achilles. To console him for his untimely death, Odysseus tells Achilles about his glorious reputation and observes that even now Achilles holds a position of great authority among the dead. Achilles' reply, however, comes as a surprise to Odysseus and to us, Homer's audience:

> O shining Odysseus, never try to console me for dying.
> I would rather follow the plow as thrall to another
> Man, one with no land allotted him and not much to live on,
> Than be a king over all the perished dead . . . [117]

The mention of land allotment reveals that Achilles now repudiates the heroic code of the *Iliad*, in which "a great piece of land" was one of the most important indications of a hero's social status, as Sarpedon made clear to us in the passage quoted earlier. Achilles' words find a modern echo in one of the most haunting scenes of Stanley Kubrick's Vietnam film *Full Metal Jacket* (1987). Over a shot of an open mass grave of Vietnamese civilians the

---

[115] A well-known observation, voiced by German philosopher Theodor Adorno in his 1951 essay "Kulturkritik und Gesellschaft"; see its English translation ("Cultural Criticism and Society") in Adorno 1981: 17–34, at 34: "Cultural criticism finds itself faced with the final stage of the dialectic of culture and barbarism. To write poetry after Auschwitz is barbaric. And this corrodes even the knowledge of why it has become impossible to write poetry today."

[116] Modern Anglophone scholarship emphasizes this nuanced view of the *Aeneid* in contrast to older, mainly German, work which tended to regard the *Aeneid* as Augustan apologia. Representative examples of the American view are Putnam 1965, especially chapter 4 ("Tragic Victory"), and W. R. Johnson 1976. Interpretation has focused largely on Book Twelve of the *Aeneid* and on the poem's ending; for a recent overview, with extensive references to scholarship, see Horsfall 1995a. Schmidt 2001 gives a detailed summary. On the *Aeneid* and Homer see, e.g., Gransden 1984, with additional references.

[117] *Odyssey* 11.488–491; Lattimore 1965: 180.

film's protagonist and narrator summarizes the lesson of war: "The dead know only one thing: it is better to be alive."

The eponymous hero of Kubrick's *Barry Lyndon* (1975), who is really a rogue, undergoes his first experience of battle as a soldier in the British army during the Seven Years' War. Kubrick shows us a scene of pointless slaughter in a skirmish between the British and the French. Urged on by an ominously repetitive phrase played on fifes and drums, the British lines stoically march into the salvos of the French and receive the enemy's bullets without the slightest cover or defense. Afterwards the film's narrator draws the lesson from this carnage, which we learn along with Barry: "It is well to dream of glorious war in a snug armchair at home, but it is a very different thing to see it first-hand." This is a restatement of Lucretius' observation that one may find it sweet to watch the great battle lines lined up across the fields in a war when one is not exposed to danger oneself.[118] It also illustrates the proverbial Roman saying *galeatum sero duelli / paenitet,* which may be paraphrased thus: Once you've put on your helmet and are facing the enemy, it's too late to regret the war.[119]

In their different ways the films discussed in this chapter echo two other comments on war which we find in Roman literature. One is by Cicero: "uncertain is the end of war and its luck ambiguous."[120] The other is by Virgil: "there is no salvation in war."[121] A famous eighteenth-century English poem, which gave Kubrick the title for *Paths of Glory* and which Wisbar's Stalingrad film illustrates in its prologue, expresses a comparable point of view:

> The boast of heraldry, the pomp of power,
> And all that beauty, all that wealth e'er gave,
> Awaits alike th' inevitable hour:
> The paths of glory lead but to the grave.[122]

---

[118] Lucretius, *On the Nature of Things* 2.5–6: *suave etiam belli certamina magna tueri /per campos instructa tua sine parte pericli.*

[119] Juvenal, *Satires* 1.169–170. Roman soldiers did not put on their helmets until immediately before engaging the enemy. Cf. Hanson 2000: 60–62 for Greek parallels.

[120] Cicero, *Pro M. Marcello* 15: *incertus exitus et anceps fortuna belli* (sometimes changed to *incerti sunt exitus belli* – "uncertain are the results of war"), on Julius Caesar's preference for peace over war.

[121] Virgil, *Aeneid* 11.362: *nulla salus bello.*

[122] Thomas Gray, "Elegy Written in a Country Church-Yard" (1750; published 1751), 33–36. In the summer of 2006, the British rock group Kasabian ended their anti-war video "Empire" with Horace's Latin text, following a scene in which their lead singer is executed by the military. The Canadian rock band Protest the Hero uses Horace's line in a song called "Soft Targets Dig Softer Graves." The group 10000 Maniacs adapt most of Wilfred Owen's poem into their song "The Latin One," ending with "you would not tell me / not with such pride and such zest / the lies of history / dulce et decorum est / pro patria mori / some desperate glory / pro patria mori / as witness disturbs the story / pro patria mori / stand firm, boys, breathe the glory."

The entrance gate to the Memorial Amphitheater at Arlington National Cemetery bears out Gray's point, for Horace's line is carved into its marble. A particular moment in a film little known today gives us a variation on Gray from a different perspective. Two years before Milestone, John Ford had shown German euphoria for the Great War in an elaborate sequence in *Four Sons*. (A sign saying "Nach Paris" is twice visible on the screen.) By the time that the German defeat is inevitable, however, the atmosphere in the country has changed. A highly decorated colonel, whom we know as a martinet of the worst sort, is forced by his mutinous men to commit suicide shortly before the armistice. He opens a small box, takes out his medals, looks at them one last time, and pins them to his chest. Then he shoots himself. In his inevitable hour all the boast and pomp of his martial regalia have become meaningless – so much tin that is unable to save him from the lead of the bullet. We have never rooted for him during the film, but mainly through poetic understatement Ford makes his death poignant nevertheless.

So is it still sweet and fitting to die for your country? Or have the films that honestly and unflinchingly present a different view of death in battle succeeded in supplanting the empty heroism or patriotism of earlier days? Three films released in 2004 and 2007 and all set in various periods of Greek antiquity give us different answers. The first of these was Wolfgang Petersen's *Troy*, an epic loosely based on the *Iliad*. Its German-born director was quite explicit about modern parallels to the story of the Trojan War:

Look at the present! What the *Iliad* says about humans and wars is, simply, still true. Power-hungry Agamemnons who want to create a new world order – that is absolutely current.

Of course, we didn't start saying: Let's make a movie about American politics, but [we started] with Homer's epic. But while we were working on it we realized that the parallels to the things that were happening out there were obvious.

You develop such a story [for your film], and then almost the identical thing happens when you turn on the television. You can't help thinking that this Homer was a real genius, that he exactly understood us humans who apparently need wars again and again; also that someone like Agamemnon reappears again and again. Still, Homer was never interested in black-white, good-bad. Such a concept doesn't exist in reality. Only in the mind of George W. Bush . . . But this direct connection between Bush's power politics and that of Agamemnon in the *Iliad*, this desire to rule the world, to trample everything underfoot that gets in your way, that became evident only during filming. Only gradually did we realize how important Homer still is today.

Homer's story shows that projects driven by belief and fanaticism often end in disasters. You need only open the newspaper to notice that nothing has changed in this regard.[123]

The second ancient film of 2004 was *Alexander*, Oliver Stone's epic about Alexander the Great's conquest of the Persian Empire. It, too, will have brought to mind modern parallels, not least because of the prominence in this film of the city of Babylon, situated near modern Baghdad. Immediately before his decisive victory over King Darius at Gaugamela in 331 BC Alexander exhorts his troops:

But remember this: the greatest honor a man can ever achieve is to live with great courage and to die with his countrymen in battle for his home.

This is standard rhetoric before battle, but we may wonder how exactly Alexander is to be understood. It will be evident even to viewers unfamiliar with ancient history and the reasons for Alexander's campaigns that his army is *not* fighting a battle for its home. Rather, these words are spoken by the commander of an invasion force far away from home – "when he stood in a foreign land," as Kantorek had said about the Roman soldier in *All Quiet on the Western Front*. So the gigantic battle in *Alexander* that then follows can hardly be said to be waged for the Macedonian soldier's home, unless we understand a modern concept like national security that extends far beyond a country's borders to be part of Alexander's meaning. Even in the film's longest version writer-director Stone fails to present his protagonist in a clear and consistent rather than in an ambivalent or inconclusive manner. Was Alexander a military genius, an insecure youngster with an Oedipus Complex, a bloody conqueror, a political unifier and bringer of civilization, or a combination of some or all of these aspects? Stone leaves spectators wondering how he intends them to react to Alexander's grandiose if short-lived conquests. Many viewers will have assented to Alexander's patriotic speech; others are likely to have noticed its hollowness. Familiar and stale rhetoric is trotted out again for the never-changing purpose of political manipulation. This is the more surprising in view of Stone's far more serious film *Platoon* (1986), a highly critical examination of warfare in a foreign country based on his own experiences in Vietnam.

Zack Snyder's *300*, one of the biggest hits of 2007, tells the story of the Spartans' last stand at Thermopylae, but with a vengeance. A minimal plot, hardly any character motivation, and practically no outline of the

---

[123] I have translated these passages from Kniebe 2004, Arnold 2004, Zander 2004, and Wiethoff 2004 in the order cited.

historical or political background leave Snyder free to devote most of his film to loving depictions of slaughter, made horrendous if titillating by state-of-the-art computer technology. The film is morbidly fascinated with death in battle and appeals to those inexperienced in war and impressed by heroic-looking physiques pumped up to absurd levels. Its aesthetic is fascist. Its direct cinematic precursors are two of the most notorious films made in Nazi Germany, Leni Riefenstahl's *Triumph of the Will* (1935) and Veit Harlan's *Kolberg* (1945), the latter a lavish historical epic intended to shore up the German people's will to endure while the country's defeat and destruction were imminent. Closer to home, *300* is also in the tradition of popular views of Custer's Last Stand at the Little Bighorn, a defeat often regarded as a spiritual victory or as means to later military victory. "Your soldier has won his last battle," says General Sheridan to Custer's widow in Raoul Walsh's epic *They Died with Their Boots On* (1941), Custer's greatest apotheosis in the cinema.[124] Snyder makes sure that his viewers are aware of the Spartans' (and Athenians') victory over the Persians at Plataea in 479 BC, just as those who died at the Alamo are believed to have prepared the way for the American victory over Mexico. The last image of Leonidas lying dead on the battlefield among his men, arms stretched out in a Christ-like pose, could be regarded as a visual rendering of Tyrtaeus – "felled in the front line, he is lovely yet" – if the filmmakers could be believed to know of this Spartan poet and if the image were not excessively kitschy. *300* is a depressing because thoughtless and tasteless restatement of Horace, but as a sign of its time it is by no means negligible.[125] What Wilfred Owen, Kipling, Milestone, Renoir, Patton, and many others whom we have encountered above might have thought of *300* is easy to imagine.

The old lie is still with us, and it is still powerful. During the new American wars in Afghanistan and Iraq patriotism and death for one's country have been routinely and sometimes sincerely invoked on all sides of the political spectrum, if most opportunely by those who are in a position to send others out to die.[126] So it may be appropriate to turn to a different kind of cinema, that of politically engaged political documentary and

---

[124] On this film see Winkler 1996: 45–48.

[125] Cf. the following characterization of the film by Denby 2007: 89: "the movie is a porno-military curiosity – a muscle-magazine fantasy crossed with a video game and an army-recruiting film." Denby considers the film in connection with Antoine Fuqua's *Shooter* (2007) and concludes about both: "Made in a time of frustration, when Americans are fighting a war that they can neither win nor abandon, '300' and 'Shooter' feel like the products of a culture slowly and painfully going mad."

[126] Fick 2005 reports that he had been induced into military service by his studies of classical Greek history. Wright 2004: 276 describes an incident near Baghdad in which a dog feeds on a human corpse, the kind of archetypal horror of war first mentioned at the beginning of Homer's *Iliad* (1.4–5). *Plus ça change . . .*

satire. In *Fahrenheit 9/11* (2004) controversial filmmaker Michael Moore exposes and satirizes the corruption, greed, and cynicism of George W. Bush, Donald Rumsfeld, and Richard Cheney. Moore lets them condemn themselves in their own words, as when Secretary of Defense Rumsfeld speaks of the high degree of humanity with which the Americans are conducting the war in Iraq.[127] An American identified only by his initials unconsciously echoes the narrator of *Barry Lyndon* in a message to Moore that appears in Moore's companion volume to the film:

It's easy to profess patriotism and love of country from a stool at a local pub, fortified by a pint or two, when you aren't inconvenienced by sleeping in a sandy foxhole thousands of miles from family, friends, and everything familiar to you. It's easy to be patriotic when there's no chance CNN might startle you with the image of a series of flag-draped coffins being unloaded from the belly of a military transport plane because your president has ordered that those images not be publicly broadcast.

George W. Bush is perfectly willing to stand on the deck of the USS *Lincoln* and be filmed and photographed with living GIs for broadcast on the evening news, but he has no interest in broadcasting their images once they've died for our country.[128]

So it is a welcome change from the ordinary when a popular filmmaker presents both sides of the same story. In 2006 Clint Eastwood made *Flags of Our Fathers* and *Letters from Iwo Jima*, a pair of films that recreate the battle of Iwo Jima, one of the most horrible episodes of World War II. Patriotic death is a prominent feature on both sides. But Eastwood's films are not simple-minded.

In 1971 screenwriter and novelist Dalton Trumbo directed *Johnny Got His Gun*, a harrowing World War I film based on his 1939 novel of the same title. Trumbo ended his film with this somber reminder:

WAR DEAD SINCE 1914: OVER 80,000,000
MISSING OR MUTILATED: OVER 150,000,000
"DULCE ET DECORUM EST PRO PATRIA MORI"

What might the numbers be today?

---

[127] At a White House press conference excerpted in *Fahrenheit 9/11*, Rumsfeld said: "The targeting capabilities and the care that goes into targeting, is as impressive as anything anyone could see . . . the care that goes into it, the humanity that goes into it." His words are heard under images of explosions, shootings, and a little boy screaming while his head wound is being sewn up without anaesthetic. This text may also be found in Michael Moore 2004a: 76. This book contains the film's screenplay, source references, and public and critical reactions.

[128] Quoted from Michael Moore 2004b: 193–194; quotation at 194.

# CHAPTER 5

# Helen of Troy:
# Marriage and adultery
# according to Hollywood

The most beautiful among mortal women in ancient myth is Helen of Troy (originally, of Sparta). Famous in Western culture long before Eve, whose story depended for its familiarity on the spread of Christianity, Helen is the West's original *femme fatale*.[1] The most fascinating aspect of her story is her illicit love for Paris, the handsome son of King Priam of Troy. Aphrodite, the goddess of love, had promised Paris the most beautiful mortal woman in return for awarding Aphrodite the prize of supreme divine beauty. Unable to resist such a tempting bribe, Paris made his fateful judgment. He then traveled from Troy to Greece for his reward. Helen was the wife of Menelaus, king of Sparta, and mother of Hermione.[2] But she fell victim to the passion instilled in her by Aphrodite. As Virgil famously put it, if in a different context: "Love conquers all."[3] Helen, "crazed by the Trojan man," followed Paris to Troy.[4] Hence the Trojan War and the fall of Troy, antiquity's biggest myth.[5]

---

[1] Hughes 2005 surveys the variety of ancient and later views of Helen, who in some accounts took the initiative and herself seduced Paris. For more specialized studies of Helen in classical and later literature see Suzuki 1989, Gumpert 2001, and Bettini and Brillante 2002, all with extensive additional references.

[2] Homer, *Iliad* 3.174–175, mentions Helen's child. Some sources add a second child, a son called either Maraphius (Porphyry, *Homeric Questions* [at schol. D on *Iliad* 3.175]) or Nicostratus (Hesiod, *Catalogues of Women* 70 [= 175 Merkelbach–West]; Cinaethon, Fragm. 3 West; Apollodorus, *Library* 3.11.1 [= 3.133]). In a few obscure sources Helen is the mother of even more sons. For thorough introductions to the ancient literary and iconographic evidence concerning Helen and Menelaus see Ghali-Kahil 1955 and Kahil 1988 and 1997. On Helen's children see Ghali-Kahil 34–35.

[3] Virgil, *Eclogues* 10.69: *omnia vincit amor*. The expression had become proverbial in antiquity, as Macrobius, *Saturnalia* 5.16.7, attests.

[4] The quotation is from Alcaeus, Fragm. 283.3–4 Lobel–Page, in David A. Campbell 1990: 333.

[5] Cf. Edmunds 2002–2003. The diagram at Latacz 2006: 28–30 outlines the entire mythology relating to the Trojan War from its antecedents to its aftermath. On Helen in Homer see Ghali-Kahil 1955: vol. 1, 15–26. Roisman 2006 gives a recent assessment of her importance, with additional references. Cf. also Skutsch 1987.

Dangerous beauties for whose sake men rush to ruin themselves and others are naturals for popular storytelling in word and image. Especially gripping in tales of two lovers' irresistible passion for each other is the added complication of adultery, which makes one or both of them leave behind all sense of morality, shame, and responsible behavior. This kind of tale was admirably summarized in Samuel Johnson's comment about John Dryden's tragedy *All for Love, or the World Well Lost* (1678), which tells the story of Antony and Cleopatra. Its title and subtitle could equally characterize the love between Helen and Paris. In his *Life* of Dryden Johnson had written about the play:

it has one fault equal to many, though rather moral than critical, that, by admitting the romantick omnipotence of Love, he has recommended as laudable and worthy of imitation that conduct which, through all ages, the good have censured as vicious, and the bad despised as foolish.[6]

Hollywood has always taken care to affirm the omnipotence of love in its romantic films and to defuse the censure of the good people among viewers by recommending as laudable the conduct of the lovers, especially if these are played by popular stars. Hollywood can, of course, not avoid incurring the contempt of those whom Johnson called the bad and whom we may call the cynical, the realistic, or the hopelessly unromantic.

### GREEK MYTH AMERICANIZED

The love between Paris and Helen conquered the silver screen for the first time in 1908 with Luigi Maggi's epic *The Fall of Troy*.[7] In the era of sound, color, and widescreen, Hollywood twice told the story on a gigantic scale, in 1956 with Robert Wise's *Helen of Troy* and in 2004 with Wolfgang Petersen's *Troy*.[8] In anticipation of the latter the small screen produced

---

[6] Quoted from Samuel Johnson, "Dryden" 78, in Samuel Johnson 2006: 79–164; quotation at 96.

[7] Winkler 2006c is a list of films.

[8] Two other, if rather ill-fated, films should be mentioned as well. *The Private Life of Helen of Troy* (1927), directed by Alexander Korda in an attempt to expand his British production empire to Hollywood, survives only in short fragments and is excluded from discussion here. It is based on John Erskine's 1925 novel of the same name. For an impression of its visual splendor see Winkler 2006d: plate 11. *The Face That Launched a Thousand Ships* was intended as a star vehicle for screen siren Hedy Lamarr as Helen, but funds ran out during production. Usable footage (ca. 67 minutes) was released in 1953, then cut by more than half and incorporated into Lamarr's next project, *The Loves* (or *Love*) *of Three Queens*, in which she portrayed other famous figures from history, when funding for this film dried up, too. This film was released in 1955. The directors were Marc Allegret and Edgar G. Ulmer.

its own version with John Kent Harrison's *Helen of Troy* (2003).[9] These three films are of particular interest for the way in which they present to contemporary audiences the reason why their heroine did something that a decent American woman should never do: desert her husband and country and live in adultery with another man. On top of this, she causes a huge war. Can such a woman really be the heroine of a popular film, even have that film named after her? Where million-dollar epics are concerned, American studios and producers tread carefully in order not to offend the Puritan sensibilities of the predominantly middle-class audiences on whom they depend for their box office. For this reason someone who acts in as devastating a manner as Helen must remain acceptable to the majority of viewers. She must never appear to be driven merely by sexual desire. She need not be perfect, but she must not be all bad; instead, the story must leave some room for viewers to be able to feel for her. So a kind of balance has to be achieved. For example, a sinner or, in our case, an errant wife must realize that she did wrong, or she must pay a price in the end. Only in such ways is redemption possible for her. According to Hollywood's self-censorship, crime does not pay and sin must be punished or atoned for.[10] Poetic justice is important not only as a means to satisfy audiences' moral standards but also as the best strategy for writers and directors to have it both ways: to be able to thrill audiences with the titillating tale of a beautiful woman who is set on a course of bad behavior and to remain piously on the side of right and morality. This makes audience identification with someone famously infamous possible. Even better and commercially safer, though, if audiences can actually take her side, if they can be made to feel

[9] Wise's film had three credited screenwriters, among them classically trained scholar Hugh Gray. On the evolution of the script and Gray's contributions see the account in Eldridge 2006: 138–145. Petersen's script was written by David Benioff, whose second screenplay this was. Harrison's was by Ronni Kern, who had previously written the scripts for two comparable television films, the medieval *Guinevere* (1994), directed by Jud Taylor, and the biblical *Solomon and Sheba* (1995), directed by Robert M. Young.

[10] On the Hollywood Production Code and for discussions and illustrations of why it came about see Viera 1999 and Doherty 1999. Doherty 347–367 prints the Code and its Addenda and Amendments. Viera 219 is instructive on "compensating moral values," which are "good characters, the voice of morality, a lesson, regeneration of the transgressor, suffering, and punishment." A case in point of the Code's power and general American squeamishness about sexual morality is George Sidney's *The Three Musketeers* (1948), a lavish and glossy MGM production. In Alexandre Dumas's novel Constance Bonacieux, D'Artagnan's first love, was in a loveless marriage to D'Artagnan's landlord, a man more than twice her age; in the film she is the landlord's goddaughter: unmarried, virginal, and pure (and played by demurely pretty June Allyson). In Richard Lester's *The Three Musketeers* (1973), made in an age of considerably more relaxed standards, she can be a wife again when she falls for D'Artagnan (and can be played by sex symbol Raquel Welch). But then she had been Bonacieux's niece in Fred Niblo's silent version of 1921. The D'Artagnan of no film, however, is as much of a rake where the ladies are concerned as their original had been.

that she was not really bad but was justified in her course of action. Hence Hollywood's rewriting of this part of Helen's myth and the kind of white-washing that is the inevitable result. The marriage of Helen according to Hollywood is different from the way antiquity had seen it.

Classical texts do not tell us about the relationship, as we would call it today, of Helen and Menelaus before their marriage, but what they tell us about the manner in which this marriage came about gives us the necessary clues. Leda, the wife of the Spartan king Tyndareus, had become pregnant with Helen by Zeus.[11] When Helen was of marriageable age, numerous heroes from all over Greece sued for her hand.[12] Their chief reason was her beauty, but the fact that she had been raised as the daughter of a prominent king added to her attractiveness, for Helen's husband would eventually inherit Tyndareus' kingdom. Tyndareus had to avoid all discontent, strife, or possible bloodshed between and among rival suitors before and after the choice of Helen's bridegroom and defuse a situation that was potentially dangerous to himself. So, either on his own accord or on the advice of wily Odysseus, Tyndareus made the suitors swear an oath that they would abide by the choice once it had been made and that they would come to Helen's husband's aid if ever the need should arise.[13] There are two versions in our sources of what happened next. In the one Tyndareus himself chose Menelaus for Helen's husband.[14] No mention is made in this version that Helen protested or was unhappy with Tyndareus' choice. Apparently she had no problem accepting Menelaus. In the other version Tyndareus granted Helen freedom of choice, and she herself selected Menelaus from among the suitors. In the words of a popular Roman compendium of ancient mythology: "he [Tyndareus] left it to Helen's decision to place a crown [or a wreath] on the head of the one she wanted to marry."[15]

---

[11] On Helen's parentage (divine vs. mortal father) cf. Clader 1976. See also Skutsch 1987 and especially Edmunds 2007, with additional references.

[12] Hesiod, *Catalogues of Women* 68 (= 196–204 Merkelbach–West); Apollodorus, *Library* 3.10.8 (= 3.129–131); and Hyginus, *Fabulae* 81, list their names. Euripides, *Helen* 99, adds Achilles. Dio Chrysostom, *The Trojan Discourse* (= Oration 11) 46 and 48–50, adds that foreign suitors came as well, among them Paris. On the genealogy of Helen cf. Hyginus, *Fabulae* 77–80.

[13] On the oath, which Homer does not mention, cf. further Hesiod, *Catalogues of Women* 68.89–98 (= 204.76–85 Merkelbach–West; Tyndareus' idea); Euripides, *Iphigenia in Aulis* 51–65 (Tyndareus' idea again; cf. the quotation below); Isocrates, *Encomium of Helen* (= Oration 10) 39–41; and Thucydides, *The Peloponnesian War* 1.9.1 (the briefest possible mention). Stockert 1992: 185 lists the textual sources of the oath. On Euripides and the non-Homeric tradition of the myth of the Trojan War see Jouan 1966, especially 167–187 on the texts concerning Helen, Paris, and their elopement.

[14] So Apollodorus, *Library* 3.10.9 (= 3.132).

[15] Hyginus, *Fabulae* 78.2; my translation. Aristotle, *Rhetoric* 2.24.9 (1401b34), also says that Tyndareus had given Helen her choice. A bride freely choosing her groom is against custom.

In view of her later desertion of Menelaus the version in which Helen herself chose her husband-to-be is the more poignant and deserves closer attention. Why should Helen have chosen Menelaus? In characters from Bronze-Age mythology we cannot expect to find the level of psychological realism that we take for granted in the great fictional characters of nineteenth- and twentieth-century novels. So we may be tempted to discount small details in large myths. But the old myths were told again and again. Their protagonists acquired great psychological depth in the treatments of the Athenian dramatists of the fifth century BC, especially in the tragedies of Euripides. In one of his last plays, *Iphigenia in Aulis*, Agamemnon explains to the audience the reasons for the Greeks' expedition against Troy and specifically mentions how and why Helen came to choose Menelaus.[16] Agamemnon recounts the suitors' oath, then continues:

When they had sworn (for Tyndareus cleverly won them over to do this), he allowed his daughter to choose one of the suitors, him to whom the sweet breezes of Aphrodite were carrying her. She chose Menelaus . . . [17]

Helen's choice of Menelaus for her husband is now understandable: she had fallen in love with him. Even if she had not, as could have been the case in the other version, Menelaus would still have been her best choice, as our surviving texts make clear beyond any doubt. Long before Euripides the archaic poet Hesiod had mentioned that Menelaus was the richest of the suitors in all of Greece and was particularly eager to win her.[18] Sappho had called Menelaus "the best man" or "the man best of all."[19] Menelaus was also young and handsome, with attractive blond hair.[20] Even in this detail

---

[16] The play's textual problems and the question of the prologue's authenticity do not concern our subject. Even if Agamemnon's words are a later interpolation they still reflect at least a possible and, as placed into a famous work, a well-known and influential version of this part of the myth.

[17] Euripides, *Iphigenia in Aulis* 66–69; quoted from Kovacs 2002a: 173. Euripides additionally calls Tyndareus an "old man" (66) to emphasize his experience and wiliness. On Euripides' expression "sweet breezes" (*pnoai . . . philai*) cf. Stockert 1992: 189–190. Stockert sees a rather different force in the adjective but remarks that it places additional emphasis on the goddess's personal involvement in causing Helen's passion for Paris.

[18] Hesiod, *Catalogues of Women* 68.24–25, 52–54, and 99–100 (= 198.5–6, 204.41–42 and 89–91 Merkelbach–West; here the last-mentioned passage reads differently).

[19] Sappho, Fragm. 16.7–8 Voigt. Editors have emended Sappho's incompletely preserved text slightly differently as [*per ar*]*iston* and [*panar*]*iston*, but the meaning is not in doubt.

[20] On Menelaus' imposing appearance cf. Homer, *Iliad* 3.210 (testimony of the Trojan elder Antenor to Helen). "Blond" or "golden-haired" (*xanthos*) is a standard epithet of Menelaus in the *Iliad*, although several other heroes are blond, too. Even in the *Odyssey*, when he is significantly older, Menelaus is called "blond" no fewer than sixteen times. Cf. also Hesiod, *Catalogues of Women* 68.24 and 52 (= 198.5 and 204.41 Merkelbach–West), and Euripides, *Iphigenia in Aulis* 175 and *Orestes* 1452. Roman authors continue the tradition.

Menelaus was well suited to Helen, because she, too, was blond. Homer does not mention her hair color, but Sappho does: "blond Helen."[21] Unless she was in love with somebody else, which according to our sources was not the case, Helen need not have hesitated about her own or Tyndareus' choice of Menelaus. An ideal marriage seemed to be ahead for bride and groom, and for a number of years it was just that. To all intents and purposes theirs was a stable marriage, perhaps even a love match. Since there is no evidence to the contrary in surviving texts, we may assume that Helen was a faithful wife and a good mother. Only the sudden interference of Aphrodite which brought Paris to Sparta was to end the idyllic life of husband and wife, by now also parents. Had Paris not turned up, Helen and Menelaus might have lived happily ever after.

Ancient corroboration for such a view actually exists; our best authority is again Euripides. The ancients knew of a major variation of the myth concerning Helen's elopement, according to which it was not Helen but a deceptive phantom that went to Troy with Paris. Unknown to Menelaus, Agamemnon, and all the Greeks, the real Helen spent the years of the Trojan War in Egypt and was there reunited with Menelaus on his return after the destruction of Troy. The earliest mention of Helen's phantom of which we know occurs in Hesiod.[22] In the fifth century Herodotus, the father of history, reports and analyzes this story in some detail.[23] In this version Helen could remain a faithful if absent wife to Menelaus for ten years, and her fidelity and chastity are not in question. Herodotus specifically states that she had not been touched; Menelaus got back a Helen "who had not suffered anything bad."[24] The only guilt that could possibly be attached to the Helen who had been in Egypt is that of a brief misdeed earlier: according to one surviving text Helen had slept with Paris while still in Sparta.[25] Nothing, however, compels us to import that detail into this version of her story. If we wish to give her the benefit of the doubt,

---

[21] Sappho, Fragm. 23.5 Voigt. Sappho uses the same adjective for Helen as Homer does for Menelaus. – The different cover illustrations of John Erskine's novel *The Private Life of Helen of Troy* variously show a raven-haired Helen (e.g. the reprint editions Erskine 1925 and 1942) and a blond one (e.g. the reprints Erskine 1948 and 1956). Of the latter, the 1948 cover by Rudolph Belarski, known to connoisseurs as "that naughty nipple cover," is the most daring.

[22] Hesiod, Fragm. 358 Merkelbach–West. On the subject see especially Austin 1994: Part 2 ("The Revised Helen").

[23] Herodotus, *The Histories* 2.112–120. At 2.116 Herodotus deduces from *Iliad* 6.289–292, which he quotes, that Homer had known this version, too, but had excluded it because it did not fit his epic narrative of the Trojan War.

[24] Herodotus, *The Histories* 2.119; my translation.

[25] So in *Cypria*, Argument 2. Menelaus leaves Sparta for Crete on the tenth day of Paris' stay.

we can regard her as a pure wife. Her long wait for her husband may even remind us of that of Penelope, the quintessentially faithful wife in Greek myth, for Odysseus.

The Egyptian reunion of Helen and Menelaus after years of separation is the subject of Euripides' play *Helen*. (Euripides used the standard version for his plays *The Trojan Women* and *Orestes*.) The spouses, having just recognized each other, express their love:

*Menelaus*: O day of love-longing fulfilled, that has brought you to my arms.
   *Menelaus and Helen embrace.*
*Helen*: O Menelaus, man I love best, the time
   has been long delayed, but now my joy is come!
   My friends, with what gladness do I greet my husband
   and put my arms about him
   after all the days that have dawned.
*Menelaus*: And I, how glad I am to have you! There is much I would speak of,
   but for the moment I know not where to begin!
   My heart exults, the hair of my head
   stands on end, tears stream from my eyes!
   I throw my arms about you
   with pleasure <fresh>
   to receive you!
*Helen*: O husband!
   O sight I look on with my greatest joy! . . .
   My friends, my friends:
   no longer do I mourn or grieve for the past.
   I have my husband, for whose return from Troy I waited,
   waited so many years!
*Menelaus*: Yes, you have me, and I have you! It was hard to live through
   so many days, but now I recognize heaven's hand.
   My tears are those of joy: they have more in them
   of gratefulness than grief.[26]

But even the standard version, in which Helen *was* in Troy all through the war, contains a strong indication that husband and wife had originally been happy. Toward the end of the *Posthomerica*, an epic composed in the third century AD to bridge the chronological gap in the Trojan War narrative between the end of Homer's *Iliad* and the beginning of his *Odyssey*, Quintus of Smyrna includes a scene in which Menelaus and Helen are alone together at night after Troy has fallen. While the other Greeks were sleeping, reports Quintus,

---

[26] Euripides, *Helen* 623–637 and 648–655. The passages are quoted from Kovacs 2002b: 81, 83, and 85; textual layout slightly modified. On the play see further Holmberg 1995, with further references.

                                              in his quarters
Atreus' son [Menelaus] was conversing with his fair-tressed spouse.
Upon the eyes of those two sleep had not yet fallen;
The Kyprian goddess [Aphrodite] hovered over their hearts, to make them
Remember their former love bed and drive away all anguish.
Helen broke their silence with the following words:
"Don't start being angry, Menelaos, with me.
I did not leave your home and bed of my own accord,
But mighty Alexander [Paris] and the sons of Troy
Came and snatched me away while you were far from home.
I was constantly seeking to die a miserable death,
By means of the cruel noose or else by the lethal sword,
But people in the palace used soothing words to stop me,
In spite of the grief I felt for you and our dear daughter.
For her sake, for our wedded joy and for your own sake
I beg you to forget the terrible trouble I've caused you."
Menelaos in his wisdom made this answer:
"Stop thinking now about the suffering of our hearts.
Let that all be locked inside the black abode
Of oblivion. It's wrong to keep recalling evil deeds."
His words filled her with joy and freed her heart from fear,
Sensing as she did that her husband's bitter anger
Had ended. She threw her arms round him and from the eyes
Of both flowed tears of pleasant lamentation.
Joyfully then they lay down side by side
And their hearts recalled how they were joined in marriage.[27]

Helen also protests her innocence to Menelaus, if with much greater cal-
culation and rhetorical manipulation, in Euripides' *The Trojan Women*.[28]
The Helen of this play is clearly being insincere; the Helen of Quintus' epic
just as clearly means what she says. The important point to be deduced
from Quintus – the last line quoted above is especially revealing – and
from the reunion of husband and wife in Euripides' *Helen* as well as from
Agamemnon's words about Helen in *Iphigenia in Aulis* is that Helen and
Menelaus had lived together in marital harmony and love. So we may be
sure that they had been happy with each other until Aphrodite and Paris
destroyed their idyll.

    Hollywood's two silver-screen versions, however, introduce a major
change into the interactions of these characters by altogether eliminat-
ing the goddess Aphrodite. Since modern audiences do not believe in the

---

[27] Quintus of Smyrna, *Posthomerica* 14.149–174; quoted from James 2004: 223–224. On the various
    ancient texts that mention Agamemnon's presence at or absence from Sparta during Paris' visit cf.
    Stockert 1992: 194–195.
[28] Euripides, *The Trojan Women* 914–965.

ancient gods and today are barely familiar even with the names of most and since the gods are almost always a liability when actors impersonate them on the screen, pagan deities are liable to be omitted from films set in antiquity. Except when a film purposely incorporates them into its plot they tend to be limited to on-screen appearances as statues or to make their power or desires known through oracles, priests, or prophets. Well-known examples in which the Olympians play major parts are Don Chaffey's *Jason and the Argonauts* (1963) and Desmond Davis's *Clash of the Titans* (1981). These films, however, illustrate the dilemma filmmakers face when they have to present gods to their viewers. In director Petersen's words:

> Do you remember how Laurence Olivier as Zeus descended from the clouds in *Clash of the Titans*? At [seeing] this, the sixteen-year-old filmgoers today would giggle or yawn.
>  I think that, if we could consult with him up there, Homer would be the first today to advise: "Get rid of the gods." . . . the audience today can no longer deal with gods jumping out of the clouds and interfering.

As a result divine agency has to be replaced by human agency. As Petersen aptly said about audiences' expectations for *Troy*: "They want to see how Brad Pitt as Achilles takes his destiny in his own hand; they want Orlando Bloom [as Paris] to fight and then run away because he is a coward – and not because the gods command him to."[29] Greek writer-director Michael Cacoyannis, who made three films based on tragedies by Euripides, had expressed a view similar to Petersen's years earlier. When asked why he had eliminated the gods from his films, Cacoyannis replied: "To show them on the screen would be alienating to modern audiences, who should identify with the characters and be as moved as Euripides intended his audiences to be."[30] Notwithstanding the kinds of divine presence on screen as examined in Chapter 2, the gods have by and large lost their importance for popular adaptations of classical epic and tragedy. This is the inevitable, perhaps even logical, conclusion to a tradition of long standing, one that began with Homer. The famous "double motivation" in Homeric epic, which attributes causation to both divine and human levels simultaneously and which scholars often call "over-determination," is a noteworthy feature in the *Iliad*. Almost independently of each other, both a god and a hero are

---

[29] The quotations (in my translation) are taken from Arnold 2004 (the first and third passages) and Zander 2004 (the second passage). Zeus does not, however, descend from the clouds in *Clash of the Titans*.

[30] Quoted from McDonald and Winkler 2001: 79. Cacoyannis's films of Euripides are *Electra* (1962), *The Trojan Women* (1971), and *Iphigenia* (1977).

responsible for the latter's state of mind at a particular moment, or both equally want a specific course of action to take place.[31]

In the case of Hollywood's Helen and Paris, mortals indeed take charge of their destiny, and their decisions and behavior conform to the kind of psychological realism that audiences expect, even if it has to be forced onto a predetermined plot that used to work perfectly well in a different way. The subject of Petersen's *Troy* and Wise's *Helen of Troy* is the power of true love, the kind that has been regarded as ideal since the age of Romanticism. Although here it is dressed in ancient garb, it adheres to modern cinematic and narrative stereotypes. Consequently Aphrodite and everything supernatural has been radically excised from the romance of Paris and Helen in these two epics. Wise's film is the closest model for Petersen's, and both were produced by the same studio. Harrison's *Helen of Troy* is a partial exception, as we will see.

When a supernatural power is no longer available to cause Helen's passion for Paris, her love must be explained in a different way. Wise's and Petersen's films do so very cleverly. On the one hand they absolve Paris from the responsibility of coming to Sparta with evil intentions because he is not there to dishonor Menelaus, to violate the principle of hospitality, one of the most compelling social and ethical ancient codes of conduct, and to abduct his host's wife. Wise's Paris is a peaceful ambassador who wants to work toward a treaty between Troy and Greece while Petersen's is a member of just such an embassy led by his elder brother Hector. This had already been the case in *The Face That Launched a Thousand Ships*. Helen's irresistible beauty leads Paris astray. More importantly he is the noble rescuer of a damsel in distress rather than a callous seducer. Paris is the central male character and true hero of Wise's film while Petersen's Paris is one of three hero figures alongside Hector and Achilles. To make this change possible for Paris, however, the films need a new villain or villains. Conveniently Menelaus and his brother Agamemnon, the king of Mycenae and commander-in-chief of the Greek army before Troy, are available to play these parts. In both versions of *Helen of Troy* but especially in *Troy* Agamemnon has been turned into a power-hungry and ruthless politician. There exists, in fact, an ancient indication of this side of his character. According to Thucydides, the most analytic of Greek historians, Agamemnon was able to force the other Greek kings to wage war on Troy because he already possessed supreme political power.[32] In the films

---

[31] For a definition and discussions of examples see Edwards 1987: 135, 231, 263–264, and 318–319.

[32] Thucydides, *The Peloponnesian War* 1.9.

Agamemnon is less the leader of an alliance of noble kings coming to the assistance of one of their own or defending the honor of Greece than the chief of a horde of rapacious thugs lusting after the immense wealth of Troy and using Helen's elopement as a convenient pretext for a war of conquest and looting. Troy was "a tempting prize of war for the Greek nations," as the narrator of Wise's film puts it.[33]

The change in the films' presentation of Menelaus is pertinent to our topic. In all three he is overshadowed by his brother just as he had been in the ancient sources. For Wise and Petersen he had to be turned into a brutish husband, escape from whom becomes understandable and defensible if perhaps not wholly forgivable. Who in the second half of the twentieth century or early in the twenty-first could reproach a wife for running away from marital hell? As a result the cinematic marriage of Helen and Menelaus is already on the rocks before the appearance of Paris.[34] The husband is either pathetic or a monster, the wife is deeply unhappy, and the arriving adulterer becomes her savior from an unrelieved misery that without her rescuer would have lasted all her life. This change also conveys to audiences an important point about Helen's marital sexuality. Although no longer in the state of virginal purity that romantic stories have prized in their heroines since antiquity, she is unlikely to have had extensive sexual experience and, by implication, little if any joy in it.[35] Entrapped in a loveless marriage, she can be presented as a woman almost untouched

---

[33] This is not exclusively an American perspective on the Trojan War. The prologue to Cacoyannis's *The Trojan Women* informs viewers that with the fall of Troy "to the Greek ships passed the Trojan treasure – gold, gold in masses, armor, clothing, stripped from the dead. Troy's wealth was legend. For years the Greeks had looked toward the East and talked of the barbarian threat. When Helen, queen of Sparta, fled with Paris, deserting Menelaus for a Trojan's love, they were ready." Dio Chrysostom, *The Trojan Discourse* 64, states that the main reason why some of Helen's former suitors went to war over Helen was outrage at the dishonor to Greece while that of others was the expectation of great booty. Hector's words at *Iliad* 3.84–94 juxtapose Helen and Trojan treasures as the spoils of war in the context of the duel between Menelaus and Paris.

[34] An earlier hint at this marital situation occurred in an American novel by Rex Stout, serialized in 1916 in *All-Story* magazine (but not published as a book for eight decades), when Helen says: "Menelaus did not please me. He was merely my husband." The quotation is from Stout 1997: 19. Stout is best known as the creator of Nero Wolfe, private detective *extraordinaire*. But the mismatch of Helen and Menelaus goes further back. One of its most famous modern instances, this time as farce, was *La belle Hélène* (1864), the operetta by Henri Meilhac and Ludovic Halévy with music by Jacques Offenbach.

[35] So the beautiful (and blond) married female protagonist of Blake Edwards's marriage-and-adultery farce *10* (1979), who informs her smitten lover in one brief word that her chief interest in life is sex, cannot ever find true love. Her rueful lover realizes how superficial she is and returns to the older woman who really loves him. Women who relish their sexuality, whether married or not, are not quite the thing in mainstream Hollywood, as Richard Brooks's drama *Looking for Mr. Goodbar* had revealed two years before, to the shock or outrage of most viewers and to the detriment of its star's career.

despite her extraordinary beauty and allure. In modern parlance she is no more than Menelaus' "trophy wife." Since romance stories depend on their lovers' irresistible passion for each other, a Helen saddled with an unloved and unloving Menelaus is in a kind of second-best state: although married, she is innocent of all emotional attachments and ignorant of the power of love. The romantic ideal is still possible for her and Paris, for overwhelming passion hits both of them for the first time in their lives. So Paris' long-standing earlier relationship with the nymph Oenone in Greek myth is excluded from all three films as a matter of course.[36] Helen is his first, last, and greatest love, as he is hers.[37] The common happy ending of most romance stories comes with the lovers' wedding, the beginning of marital life which is excluded from such stories. As director John Ford once reported about *The Plough and the Stars* (1936), his film of Sean O'Casey's play:

After I'd finished the picture, [a] studio head said, "Why make a picture where a man and woman are married? The main thing about pictures is love or sex. Here you've got a man and woman married at the start – who's interested in that?" So after I left, he sent an assistant director out and they did a bunch of scenes where they *weren't* married. Completely ruined the damned thing – destroyed the whole story – which is about a man and his wife.[38]

Marriage is rarely the setting for tales of great love. But a marriage triangle, especially with a plot in which a wife takes a new lover, is of immediate interest since it shows the beginning of love. While husband and wife are not generally the subject of romance, spouse and adulterous lover are.

---

[36] So is Corythus, Paris' and Oenone's son. That Corythus as a handsome young man went to fight for the Trojans, that he fell in love with Helen, that she in turn was attracted to him, and that his own father had him executed for this is also unsuitable to filmic adaptations. Cf. Parthenius, *Erôtika pathêmata* (*Love Romances*) 34. Oenone made it onto the screen only once, in *The Face That Launched a Thousand Ships*.

[37] This also means that after the death of Paris, who in Greek myth does not survive as long as he tends to do in films, Helen's second Trojan lover-husband, Deiphobus, remains outside such a retelling. Stesichorus, Fragm. *P.M.G.* 223.5 Page, calls Helen "three times married," implying Menelaus, Paris, and Deiphobus; at Aeschylus, *Agamemnon* 62, she is "the woman . . . of many men" (i.e. husbands). Helen's children by Paris (variously, three or four sons and a daughter also called Helen) are excluded as well.

[38] Quoted from Bogdanovich 1978: 64–66. In Vincent Sherman's *Mr. Skeffington* (1944) the wife of the title character, an older man whom she does not love, is told by her psychiatrist: "That's where a husband comes in: when your romantic days are over." She is unfaithful, they divorce, but as we may expect in such a glossy Warner Brothers melodrama she eventually comes to appreciate his true worth. The happy and romantically secure marriage of Nick and Nora Charles in W. S. Van Dyke's *The Thin Man* (1934) and its sequels is not really a counter-example since the films are primarily sophisticated mysteries rather than romances.

One other circumstance is fundamental for the change in the Helen of all three films. She has no children. The most obvious reason is that audiences expect their romantic couples to be young and unmarried; when the latter state is not possible, they must at least be emotionally unattached to anyone else. Except in comedies children tend to be obstacles to new romances of their parents.[39] An unhappy wife and mother who has resigned herself to a life without love may yet try to find consolation and relief within her marriage by utterly devoting herself to her child or children, as is the case in highly melodramatic films ("weepies"). In this way she can distance herself emotionally from her husband and seek or find some measure of fulfillment or at least a quiet peace. The mother of a small child is unlikely to run off with a complete stranger. Most importantly, however, a mother in Helen's situation could not take her child or children along on as dangerous and uncertain a voyage as she undertakes with Paris but would have to desert them outright. This comes closer to constituting unforgivable behavior on her part than anything else she might do. In European and particularly in American culture mothers are sacred and venerable figures who only rarely leave their children willingly.[40] As the classic cases of Emma Bovary or Anna Karenina reveal, tragedy is likely to ensue if they do.[41] (The real-life case of Princess Diana is too well known to need discussion here.) By the same token examples of selfish, horrible, or downright evil mothers are extremely scarce in popular American culture; when they do appear, they stand out as scary exceptions that only prove the general rule.[42] For examples that a boorish husband justifies adultery but that motherhood still trumps passion we may turn to two silent films from 1929. Both starred Greta Garbo, who played *femmes fatales* several times (and who later became the screen's most famous Anna Karenina).[43] In Jacques Feyder's *The Kiss*,

---

[39] An example is Melville Shavelson's *Yours, Mine and Ours* (1968), a comedy of remarriage rather than marriage. (It was remade by Raja Gosnell in 2005.) Cavell 1985 studies this kind of film. The couples in the classic films he examines have no children.

[40] Hence the scandal that accompanied a real case. When actress Ingrid Bergman left her husband and small daughter and her new home country, America, to elope with Italian director Roberto Rossellini in 1949 and then became pregnant, she was reviled in the American press and even denounced on the floor of the US Senate.

[41] For overviews of the literary background, too extensive to be dealt with here, see, e.g., Tanner 1979, Overton 1996 and 2002, and Rippon 2002. All contain extensive further references.

[42] I mention only the mothers in Raoul Walsh's *White Heat* (1949), Joseph L. Mankiewicz's *Suddenly, Last Summer* (1959), Alfred Hitchcock's *Psycho* (1960), John Frankenheimer's *The Manchurian Candidate* (1962), Roger Corman's *Bloody Mama* (1970), and Robert Benton's *Kramer vs. Kramer* (1979) as examples. Contrast these with the apotheosis of the American mother, Ma Joad in John Ford's *The Grapes of Wrath* (1940).

[43] Garbo's character in Fred Niblo's *The Temptress* (1926) is another example, if only up to a point. At the beginning she is married to an older and unsuitable husband who moreover flirts with other

which is set in France, a flirtatious wife dallies with two men. Her husband surprises her in the arms of one of them and attacks her; she kills him, then confesses but is set free. A modern feminist scholar comments: "We comprehend, from the start, that [her] husband is an insensitive bore, and we root for her liberation." In John S. Robertson's *The Single Standard* – a title with an obvious wordplay – Garbo is a wife and mother who is about to fall again for a former lover from her wilder days but eventually rejects him: "One man must always be first in my life . . . and he is – my son." The same scholar observes about Robertson's heroine: "Though she eventually decides to stay with her family, it is fairly shocking that this wife and mother is ready to abandon them . . . we surmise that, had not motherhood intervened, adultery would have been fine."[44] The tie that binds strongest is that between mother and child.[45]

Over the decades Hollywood has firmly established the kind of marital setting in which screenwriters and directors are to show us their Helen. She must not be blamed for wanting to escape her wretched fate, Paris must turn into her one true love, and the films can have their cake and eat it, too, for they get away with telling a touching romance which results from an illicit affair but in which the lovers cannot live happily ever after. The adulterers are vindicated since love triumphs, the cuckolded but bad husband gets what he deserves, and the audience can thrill to a combination of beauty, heroic nobility, spectacle, and all-around sentimentality – a sure-fire recipe for success. But how exactly do the films manage to achieve this turn-around?

## WOLFGANG PETERSEN'S *TROY* AND ROBERT WISE'S *HELEN OF TROY*

*Troy*, the most recent instance, presents the simplest case. An opening text tells us that Menelaus is weary of war. We see him at home in Sparta hosting a banquet in honor of the Trojan ambassadors Hector and Paris. But if we believe that Menelaus is a positive character, a toast he immediately proposes tells us differently: "May the gods keep the wolves in the hills and

women and is morally corrupt. She meets a dashing and romantic stranger and immediately falls in love with him. Appropriately enough, her name is Elena. But the plot then turns in a different direction.

[44] The quotations are from Fischer 2003: 106 and 104. Fischer 102–109 describes the films' plotlines in detail and provides illustrations. In general cf. Staiger 1995.

[45] Exceptions may occur whenever a plot demands them. But as recently as 2007 a French film illustrates the power of mother love. The titular hero of Laurent Tirard's *Molière* has to renounce his love for a married woman, who stays in her unhappy marriage for her daughter's sake.

**Fig. 26.** *Troy.* Helen and Paris in Sparta. (Warner Bros.)

the women in our beds." These macho words are not quite what we expect to hear from a decent or happily married man. Their irony is obvious since we know what will soon happen. Tight close-ups on Helen and Paris, who have been exchanging meaningful glances, now follow. Their affair has already begun, as we are about to discover.[46] Alone in her bedroom, Helen and Paris kiss and undress (Fig. 26). Intercut into their love scene is a moment in which Menelaus kisses one of the dancing girls in the banquet hall. This makes it understandable to us what Helen, close to tears over the imminent departure of Paris, tells him about her past married life: "Before you came to Sparta, I was a ghost. I walked, and I ate, and I swam in the sea, but I was just a ghost." Once in Troy, she will elaborate: "Sparta was never my home. My parents sent me there when I was sixteen to marry Menelaus, but it was never my home." So much for her choosing him and choosing to be with him, as she does in the ancient myth. And so much for her being from Sparta, where Tyndareus had brought her up since her birth.

Petersen does not include Helen's elopement with Paris, as Wise and Harrison do. Instead, and largely from the perspective of an astonished Hector, we find Helen on board the Trojan ship returning home. The other films avoid such a narrative gap; they make the lovers' elopement the turning point of their plots. The plot construction in *Troy* makes it easier for us to accept and become emotionally engaged in another romance that will develop once the Trojan War has started and that will eclipse the first, the one between Achilles and Briseis. Briseis has been made over into a

---

[46] For more details on Petersen's Helen and her classical precursors see Cyrino 2006. On Helen and the film in general cf. further Cavallini 2005a: 53–79.

relative of the royal house of Troy rather than remaining the Lyrnessan princess from the myth. And of course she is virginal and not, as in the *Iliad*, the widow of a husband whom her new lover has slain. This new romance is both unexpected and predictable: unexpected since it is not the famous one audiences associate with the Trojan War, practically never included in films; predictable since it involves this film's biggest star, Brad Pitt, who cannot be left without his own love interest.[47]

When Menelaus finds out that Helen is no longer in Sparta, he viciously threatens one of the servant women in his household: "Where is she? I swear by the father of the gods I will gut you here if you don't tell me." Soon after, in Mycenae, he tells Agamemnon the reason for such a savage outburst: "I want her back so I can kill her with my own two hands. I won't rest till I've burned Troy to the ground." So much for his peaceable nature. By now everybody in the audience knows that Helen is well rid of him. When, in a surprising twist away from our mythical sources, Hector kills Menelaus, nobody in the audience feels sorry for him. Helen then passes the final verdict on her relationship with her husband: "He lived for fighting. And every day I was with him I wanted to walk into the sea and drown."

Roughly the same plot pattern, if with greater elaboration, appeared in Wise's version. Helen finds Paris, shipwrecked in a storm, on a beach close to Sparta. (Geography is not something filmmakers tend to be overly concerned with.) Since she is ravishingly beautiful and approaches him walking across the shallow water, he understandably mistakes her for Aphrodite, the foam-born goddess (Fig. 27). She, however, does not reveal her identity to him but pretends to be a slave. Next she saves him from a Spartan shore patrol that is looking for survivors of the Trojan ship which had been sighted. We learn that the most important Greek kings have assembled in Sparta to plan war against Troy. (In *The Face That Launched a Thousand Ships* Menelaus had been planning such a war as well.) We are given an idea about the oppressive environment in which Helen lives when she warns Paris: "Our soldiers have a habit of plunging a dagger into strangers." She hides him and urges him to return to Troy. But Paris falls immediately in love: "I'll offer to buy you from the queen . . . Don't you believe I could love a slave?" This in turn quickly makes him attractive to her when they meet shortly afterwards "under the magic of the moonlight," as Paris romantically puts it. She confesses: "My heart is yours, Paris, but

---

[47] The only Trojan-War epic in which Briseis plays a prominent part is Marino Girolami's *Fury of Achilles* (1962), an unusual muscleman epic in that it incorporates, if in a condensed or simplified manner, several scenes or moments from the *Iliad* that do not usually make it into Trojan War films.

**Fig. 27.** *Helen of Troy* (1956). Paris' first view of Helen. (Warner Bros.)

*I* can never be." Immediately they kiss. He still does not know who she is.

Once Paris is in Sparta and tries to work for peace between Troy and Greece, Menelaus quickly becomes suspicious that his beautiful wife already knows this handsome foreigner. In a crucial scene he confronts her in her private quarters to find out more. The scene is chiefly intended to demonstrate to viewers the unhappiness and emotional distance between husband and wife and to make the illicit love between wife and adulterer legitimate. Wise denies Menelaus even a shred of audience sympathy and makes viewers firmly root against him and for Helen and Paris. In the careful manner of its staging and in its dialogue it accomplishes this goal effectively if not at all subtly.

Menelaus barges in on a Helen in a pensive mood; she is with her handmaid Andraste and a deaf-mute older manservant.[48] Accompanied by ominous music on the soundtrack, Menelaus loudly bangs the bronze door when he enters and commands Helen: "Tell your servants to go." When she complies but the old man does not react, Menelaus yells at him: "Get out!" This is sufficient to reveal to us that he is rather a nasty sort and that he has never taken any interest in the people most closely associated with his wife, as her rebuke also tells us: "When will you learn? The man can neither speak nor hear." The only function of this servant's presence is to show Menelaus in a bad light from the beginning. The dialogue between him and Helen almost immediately turns into a shouting match. Wise shows us their emotional distance by keeping them apart from each other on the

---

[48] The maid's name is Adreste at Homer, *Odyssey* 4.123, and would have been more accurate in the film in this Ionic form or as Adraste.

**Fig. 28.** *Helen of Troy* (1956). The dysfunctional marriage of Helen and Menelaus. (Warner Bros.)

screen and by cutting back and forth between shots in which each appears alone. When Menelaus approaches Helen, her head turned away, it is only to threaten her about Paris: "I might do many things with this prince. I might send him home with his appearance altered." Walking away from him, Helen comments: "I imagined once I had married a king." Menelaus rushes after her and urgently asks: "Why did you marry him?" His next observation makes him sound like the stereotypical tyrant of melodrama: "When a king takes spoils, he robs no one. When he kills, he commits no murder. He fulfills justice." All viewers are meant to disagree with such a callous demonstration of autocratic *Realpolitik* and with Menelaus' warped sense of justice. "The way of a Spartan," Helen bitterly comments. Clearly she feels as little at home in Sparta as Petersen's Helen in hers. Her observation to Paris a bit later that she "hates cruelty" elicits his comment: "You're not a Spartan." She answers: "I am. The daughter of a king who chose a Spartan husband for me." Evidently she is not Spartan by birth.

The climax of the scene between Menelaus and Helen soon arrives. Helen keeps a guilty silence when Menelaus demands that she admit knowing Paris. Menelaus bursts out: "Silent as ever. No words for *me*, no words for your husband. I *am* your husband!" He roughly seizes her and pathetically pleads: "Say 'husband' to me." In a close shot he now pulls her to him, moving his hands to her neck (Fig. 28). For a brief moment we may think that he is about to caress her but quickly realize otherwise. In an even tighter close-up on both their faces Menelaus, repeating his last words, seems on the verge of strangling her. The story, of course, forbids this. So he utters a final threat against Paris, turns, and leaves. Despite his violent talk and behavior Menelaus has shown himself to be a pathetic weakling. Now he even has to strain to open and close the huge bronze door that he had banged shut when he entered. His defeat is complete. This marriage is dead. Wise drives home such a conclusion when he shows us Menelaus next, receiving the news of Helen's disappearance. He is participating in a kind of sauna-cum-orgy with Agamemnon and others. The room is drenched in lurid red light. The artificial nature of this lighting is obvious; so is the point it makes.

The quarrel between Helen and Menelaus clinches the way in which the film presents them as a married couple. Wise and his screenwriters now proceed to reinforce audiences' emotional attachment to Helen and Paris even more. When Helen has prepared Paris' escape from Sparta and meets him by the sea for their last farewell, they again talk about Troy, Sparta, and war. The appearance of an armed Spartan patrol forces them to hide in the bushes, and now comes what was to be expected: a tender love scene in which they kiss and embrace. Paris urges her: "Oh, Helen. Helen, you are a slave as long as Menelaus possesses you. Come away to freedom. Come to Troy with me." These words make evident to even the slowest viewer what is at stake, for Paris puts into thoroughly American terms why Helen should elope with him: her marriage is enslavement, her love will give her liberty. The operative word is "freedom," readily understandable to one and all. The script had prepared us for this theme when shortly before this meeting Helen had unexpectedly granted freedom to Andraste and, not entirely sensibly, had sent her away on her own. There was no dramatic reason for her doing so. Helen herself realizes this since she tells Andraste: "Freedom is made of quicksilver sometimes." In retrospect her kindness makes sense, for she herself deserves freedom even more. The fact that Helen sets her personal slave free also goes against the Homeric tradition because in the *Odyssey* Andraste (as Adreste) is Helen's maid a full twenty years later. The one mention of her name in the *Odyssey* is the source for her name in the film. The deviation from Homer occurs without any necessity; its only point is to prepare us for Helen's own change of fortune: from enslavement, as it were, to freedom. Viewers familiar with classical Greek may note a measure of irony here. The name of Helen's servant means "not running away" and is an adjective regularly used in Greek literature for slaves. (In its masculine form as a proper name, Adrastos is a speaking name of heroes who stand their ground in battle; four of them are mentioned in the *Iliad*.) In Wise's film, then, the slave obtains her freedom while remaining true to her name; her mistress will soon obtain hers by doing what a discontented slave might do: run away.

At this moment Helen still intends to remain in Sparta, but the screenplay makes sure that her own quicksilver moment rapidly arrives. Up on a coastal cliff the lovers are surprised by Spartan archers. Helen commands them to leave; their leader refuses. Paris takes advantage of the altercation between Helen and the officer, seizes her around the waist, and jumps into the sea with her. They escape unharmed. The manner of their flight absolves Helen from all responsibility, for it is not her but Paris who makes a decision for both of them. So far Helen has remained innocent; unlike Petersen's, she has not willingly left her husband, and she has no more than kissed Paris. Only later, having arrived in Troy, does she become responsible, although the film includes a brief scene in which Hecuba, queen of Troy and Paris' and Hector's mother, explicitly exempts Helen from guilt for the war and, by implication, for the eventual fall of the city. Hecuba calls her "a woman of self-determination, a queen, with more courage than I would have had to sail against the tides of heaven." King Priam officially proclaims her "a princess of Troy."[49] No bad woman could be so described or so honored in a work intended mainly for a middle-class audience. That director Wise had his American viewers firmly in mind with this kind of story becomes clear in his own words:

I think my aim in *Helen* . . . was to reflect the times and life of the period and to have a better understanding of the people. I wanted it to be modern in terms of the acting and delivery of the scenes. That's what I was after in my approach to it.[50]

The better understanding of this distant period has to come from the storyteller's necessity to make it modern not only in terms of acting but also in terms of character portrayal. Historical epics reflect the times and life of their own period far more than the past they ostensibly bring to life.

In the scenes discussed and at some other moments Wise and his writers take pains to exculpate Helen thoroughly. That this was their and their studio's intent becomes evident from "Interviewing Helen," one of three episodes of Warner Brothers' promotional television series *Behind the Cameras*, in which the studio advertised new films to millions of viewers before their release. Series host Gig Young meets Helen on the walls of Troy – ironically, right after the television network on which *Behind the Cameras* was aired had shown Michael Curtiz's *Casablanca* (1942), a famous melodrama in which a wife, married to an unloved older man, again meets her former lover who, at film's end, nobly puts the greater good of the war-torn world before their personal happiness. For viewers not overly familiar with the mythical past Young announces: "The time, by my wristwatch which

---

[49] Cf. Homer, *Iliad* 3.164, where Priam declares Helen's innocence.
[50] Quoted from Cary 1974: 65.

won't even be invented by another 2,900 years, is five in the morning. These are the battlements of the fabulous city of Troy, queen city of the ancient world . . . and at this moment center of the world's attention." When Helen appears, Young predictably characterizes "the run-away queen of Sparta" with Christopher Marlowe's immortal words: "The face that launched a thousand ships." Helen immediately asks: "Who says this of me?" Young's answer – "History" – elicits a passionate denial from her:

Then history lies. You think a woman and her love could be the cause of all this? . . . That is Greek talk to fool the Trojans. I am only the excuse for war, not the reason. My husband lusts not for his queen but for the treasures of Troy . . . This war has been his dream for years.

Helen's subsequent words do not exactly conform to the details of the film that viewers will encounter in theaters, but no matter. Over the footage of Paris jumping into the sea with her, Helen explains: "I fled with Paris to save my life . . . what I left behind in my husband's heart was hate, hate for all his ambitious friends to feed upon." Her life, however, is not in danger in Sparta.

The film's theatrical trailer shows us both sides of Helen, her responsibility for the Trojan War that anyone who has not yet seen *Helen of Troy* expects even if the film itself presents a very different Helen, and her absolution from guilt. Over the wooden horse entering the city, a headline exclaims: "Hers the *Sin* that inspired time's greatest treachery." The invention of the Wooden Horse, usually a triumph of ingenuity, here is the ultimate proof of sinister Greek slyness. But if the Greeks are bad, the Trojans must be good. "Beware the Greeks bearing gifts," Helen appropriately says in another clip from the film, almost quoting a famous expression from Virgil's *Aeneid*.[51] But does *Helen of Troy* really show us "All the Storied Wonders of Homer's Immortal 'ILIAD'," as another card in the trailer proclaims, or of Greek mythology and literature? Of course not. Instead it shows what the trailer's next card promises: "*All the Gloried Moments* of its Inspired Romance!" And this in "Olympian scope and vastness," as the announcer modestly proclaims. This is a story made new for modern audiences, for in Homer's immortal *Iliad* the romance of Paris and Helen had turned sour much earlier. Homer's Helen yearns for Menelaus, whom she calls a "better man" than Paris.[52]

---

[51] Virgil, *Aeneid* 2.49.
[52] Homer, *Iliad* 6.349–351. At *Iliad* 3.139–142, Helen weeps in her "sweet yearning" for Menelaus. Even more important is the bedroom scene between Helen and Paris at *Iliad* 3.383–447, on which see, e.g., Edwards 1987: 195–196. Edwards 195 speaks of "Helen's strength of mind and her contempt

But in Hollywood Menelaus cannot win. In *Helen of Troy* he cuts a pathetic figure; in *Troy* he is a hulking brute. Wise's Menelaus cannot defeat Paris in combat; Petersen's even gets himself killed. In neither film is Menelaus handsome, let alone blond. Both films had stacked the deck, as it were, against him from the start in such a radical and obvious way that viewers simply *must* regard his marriage to Helen as utterly unsuitable and as a sure recipe for misery. The actors cast in the part of Menelaus are far too old for the actresses who play Helen and can hardly represent a young and beautiful woman's love interest. Wise's spouses, Rossana Podestà (b. 1935) and Niall MacGinnis (b. 1913), are twenty-two years apart; Petersen's couple, Diane Kruger (b. 1976) and Brendan Gleeson (b. 1955), twenty-one. Both men are on the hefty side, their bulk reinforced by the unheroic and rather unattractive costumes they have to wear. All this contrasts with the slender beauty of their wives. No wonder that Helen is ready for a dashing young lover. She practically owes it to herself to elope. She owes this even more to her spectators and their expectations concerning romance. "I don't want a hero, my love. I want a man I can grow old with," Petersen's Helen tells Paris. That neither she nor Wise's Helen can spend a lifetime with the kind of Menelaus they are stuck with is self-evident. And so she remains a good woman.

Here a brief excursus to consider two ancient spectacles from the early 1950s is appropriate because they show us that Hollywood's justification for famous adulterous affairs tends to follow a predictable set-up. Henry King's *David and Bathsheba* (1951) is based on a sacred text from biblical antiquity.[53] King David lusts for the beautiful woman he has seen bathing in the nude and contrives her husband Uriah's death. David is suitably guilt-ridden afterwards; he repents and redeems himself. In this way viewers can stay on his side throughout, especially since he is played by Gregory Peck. Still, this David is not all bad even in his adultery because he and Bathsheba for the first time find an emotional bond that has been lacking from the lives of either, for both have loveless marriages. His first wife asks David shortly before he sees Bathsheba: "Does my presence displease the king?" "Of course not," he answers, but we know that this is only David's polite way of confirming her suspicion. A lonely David then learns that his pretty neighbor is just as lonely. "I first saw Uriah on our wedding day when my father brought me to his house," Bathsheba says. David only kisses her after he finds out about her situation: "I said nothing to you until you told

for Paris and for her own past folly." On Helen's (unchanged) view of Menelaus as expressed in retrospect several years later see Homer, *Odyssey* 4.259–264.
[53] 2 Samuel 11–12.

me that there is no love in your marriage. Yes, you told me that, and so did Uriah." David had previously made sure to find out what kind of man her husband was; Uriah turned out to be interested only in battle and glory, not love.[54] David then nobly sends Bathsheba away, but she confesses that she has been observing his loneliness and was hoping to end it. David, just as surprised at this as the audience, asks why she has not told him so when he made his desire known to her, and she replies: "Because first I had to know what was in your heart. If the law of Moses is to be broken, David, let us break it in full understanding of what we want from each other." Then she tells him that she will not be his lover but his wife, a proposition to which he agrees. We share their full understanding and agree, even at the price of Uriah's death. Love conquers all, as it must. "I need someone to share my heart," David says before another kiss at the scene's fade-out. So, Hollywood trusts, do we all.[55]

Three years later, ravishing redhead Susan Hayward, King's Bathsheba, appeared in Delmer Daves's Roman epic *Demetrius and the Gladiators* as one of the most scandalous adulteresses of history: Messalina, third wife of Emperor Claudius and a woman notorious for her nymphomania. Devastating portrayals of her in Tacitus and Juvenal have made sure that Messalina's name is still familiar.[56] As she was in history, this film's Messalina is unsuitably married to a much older husband. She finds romance with fictional gladiator Demetrius. But can such a wicked woman count on audience sympathy? Yes, because Demetrius is a Christian, and when no less a moral authority than St. Peter warns him about their sinful ways, Demetrius and Messalina end their dalliance. At the film's end, when Claudius becomes emperor, Messalina declares publicly that she will be a faithful wife from then on: "It's no secret from any of you that I've mocked my marriage vows, that I've openly disgraced my husband and myself. That . . . is ended. I am Caesar's wife, and I will act the part." This Messalina can be redeemed. She still loves Demetrius but nobly sacrifices her emotions for the greater good of the state. In history Claudius had Messalina executed for marrying one of her lovers in a public ceremony, but in this film the couple's marriage can be saved for a bitter-sweet ending. No moral conversion had occurred in Carmine Gallone's *The Affairs of Messalina*

---

[54] Cf. 2 Samuel 11.11. The biblical David meets Uriah after he has slept with Bathsheba and contrives the latter's death only when he hears that she is pregnant (2 Samuel 11.4–7).

[55] Bruce Beresford's *King David* (1985) still presents David in loveless marriage when he meets Bathsheba. Since this film covers David's entire life in the same running time that King's version devoted to his affair, Bathsheba is little more than a minor character.

[56] Tacitus, *Annals* 11.12 and 26–38; Juvenal, *Satires* 6.115–132. Messalina was about thirty-five years younger than Claudius; she married him when she was about fourteen.

(1951). Its Messalina met with a sticky end because she remained bad throughout – "EMPRESS OF LOVE IN AN ERA OF SIN!" and "HISTORY'S MOST WICKED WOMAN!" according to the film's English-language posters.

In Chapter 3 we encountered the contrast between Old-World sophistication and New-World simplicity. A film rather neglected today uses the same perspective and illustrates why the adulterous Helen of Greek myth does not work in "down home" American culture. In George Cukor's *Heller in Pink Tights* (1960), a comedy-melodrama set in the American west, a run-down troupe of traveling players arrives in a rough frontier town and begins rehearsals for *Beautiful Helen of Troy*, an adaptation of Jacques Offenbach's *operetta*. The star of the troupe plays Helen; the director is Paris (in a blond wig). Everybody wears tights and flamboyantly silly costumes. But the theater owner, a local bigwig, objects to the subject of their play. The scene is played mainly for humor. The dialogue, here quoted in excerpts, confirms our theme:

*Actor* [*Menelaus, in the most ridiculous costume of all*]:  A vile seducer outrages –
*Pierce* [*interrupts*]:  What's that? . . . What did he just say?
*Actress* [*Helen, quoting*]:  "A vile seducer."
*Pierce*:  That's what I *thought* he said. What kind of a show are you giving here, anyway?
*Director*:  This is a comic opera, Mr. Pierce. *La belle Hélène* – you know, the story of Helen of Troy?

Pierce needs a few explanations. But then he finds out that Helen, obviously attracted to Paris, is also married:

*Actress*:  But I'm not in love with my husband. But I am – how do you say – flighty? And besides, he's much older than I am . . .
*Pierce*:  Nope. It won't go in Cheyenne . . .
*Director*:  But this is a *classic*, Mr. Pierce!
*Pierce*:  What's so classy about her running around with you instead of her husband?
*Actress*:  But he's so much nicer, and he lets me do what I want.
*Pierce*:  Last month the mayor's wife started to run around with a young stud like him, and the mayor shot him stone dead. There wasn't a man in town that didn't shake his hand for doin' it, even the sheriff. No, sir . . . ; you can't get away with makin' fun of marriage in Cheyenne . . . If all you've got is this fiddle-faddle, you can pack up and keep goin'; I don't want you.

That is the end for *Beautiful Helen of Troy* in Wyoming. But Pierce the moralist then falls for the actress himself. And who could blame him since she is played by a blond Sophia Loren?

JOHN KENT HARRISON'S *HELEN OF TROY*

The third American screen perspective on the marriage of Helen and Menelaus presents a refreshing change from the two other trite versions. Harrison's *Helen of Troy* is unusual for incorporating Helen's childhood and for being distinctly if by no means radically feminist. We meet Helen as a teenage tomboy who is unaware of her budding sexuality. Her abduction by Theseus, the Judgment of Paris (before Helen's marriage), and her wedding to Menelaus are also included. The narrator assures us that he will tell us only the truth: "Let me tell you the real story. I know. I was there." But as always the story is treated with considerable neo-mythological freedom.[57] Supernatural aspects, put on screen by means of computer-generated images, preserve an aura of divine intervention that goes further than the mere invocation of gods and the display of their statuary in Wise's and Petersen's films. Paris, for example, sees an image of Helen in the golden apple that Aphrodite holds out to him; at the same moment, but far away, Helen sees Paris reflected in a pool of water. Both are smitten on the spot. From now on Helen only awaits the appearance of her unknown beau. This plot point determines her future and the way the film will present her marriage to Menelaus.

Helen's abduction from Sparta by Theseus, who reveals to her the identity of her true father Zeus, leads to a rescue mission on which her brother Pollux is killed. (His Greek name Polydeuces would have been a better choice than this Roman one.) Greek heroes including Odysseus, Agamemnon, Menelaus, and Achilles attend his funeral. Agamemnon and Menelaus had already met Helen on Agamemnon's wedding to her sister Clytemnestra, when Agamemnon had immediately begun lusting after Helen. At the end he receives his long-deserved come-uppance when Clytemnestra kills him in revenge for the sacrifice of their little daughter Iphigenia. Iphigenia's death is the climax of the film's first half and firmly establishes Agamemnon as arch villain of the Trojan War. But the character of Menelaus is conceived very differently. In true romantic fashion he falls in love with Helen at first sight but only worships her from afar. We realize that he is a decent sort, a "nice guy." And his age actually suits his future bride's: actor James Callis (b. 1971) is only four years older than Sienna Guillory (b. 1975), his

---

[57] The same observation concerning narrator and filmic story in a historical context applies to Oliver Stone's *Alexander* (2004), in which Alexander the Great's former general Ptolemy serves as narrator both on screen (he introduces the main story, told in flashback) and off screen (in voice-over). Ptolemy, who was there, knows what really happened (according to writer-director Stone's version).

**Fig. 29.** *Helen of Troy* (2003). Tyndareus blames Helen before the Greek kings. (Universal)

Helen. He is also good-looking and slim (if still not blond).[58] Most unusually, his is the voice that introduces the story before the opening credits. The chief function of narrators in epic films is to bridge the gap between characters and viewers, to make sure that temporal or cultural differences between past and present do not intrude too much on our enjoyment or understanding of the story we are watching. This is why most narrators speak to us from an omniscient or godlike perspective (and are males). If a narrator is also a character within his own story, we can be reassured that he is a "good guy." Once we come to realize that our narrator will play a major part in the story, we know implicitly that he will not be a villain. Harrison's Menelaus does not disappoint our expectation.

The Greek heroes, assembled in Sparta for Pollux' funeral, are all impressed by Helen's beauty. Tyndareus blames Helen for the death of his son and successor and angrily offers her to whoever may want her: "Is there any among you who will take this cursed woman? Is there any among you who wishes their home devastated, his country brought to ruin, his heart broken beyond repair?" (Fig. 29). These words are excessive, but they reinforce the traditional understanding of Helen that the film intends to change with its supposedly real story. At the same time we are meant to feel that Tyndareus is being unfair to Helen and to side with her, for the

---

[58] In retrospect one may think that Callis is miscast as Menelaus. Since he is much better-looking than the blandly handsome Paris of Matthew Marsden, the two actors might have switched parts for better effect. (So might Rossana Podestà and Brigitte Bardot, the Andraste of Wise's film.)

film can then show her to be no such ruinous woman after all. (The really destructive character is Agamemnon.) Only Menelaus takes pity on her in her public humiliation. He realizes that all the others except happily married Odysseus desire her for themselves. (In myth, however, Odysseus is among the suitors.) The Greeks now form a purely political alliance, choosing Agamemnon as their "high king."[59] "Can we agree to unite in time of war?" asks Agamemnon – not that any war is as yet on the horizon. To bring about the alliance Odysseus proposes the oath that binds them together and to cast lots for Helen. Menelaus immediately objects to her being used as a pawn in a political game and, to use a modern term, to be married off for reasons of state, not for love. But he agrees in order to ensure that among her suitors there is at least one – himself – who cares about her. To everybody's surprise and as if aided by supernatural powers – i.e. through a computerized special effect – Menelaus wins her hand.

Paris appears in Sparta on his peace mission on Menelaus' wedding day and recognizes his hitherto unknown love. So does she him. Their first meeting occurs during a scene that has no parallel in any other film. Before her wedding a nude Helen is forced to walk through a large hall filled with the Greek kings and their retinues and to display herself to everybody's eyes on a pedestal, her second public humiliation. None other than Agamemnon has cooked up the idea. The reaction on the part of most men (but not Menelaus) is predictable. In a concession to modern audience expectations and relaxed standards concerning nudity even on prime-time television, Harrison shows us Helen's walk on the screen. He films her first from behind in a medium close-up to full-length body shot as she enters the hall, then mainly in close-up head-and-shoulder profile during her walk, and finally in long-shot rear views while she steps up to the platform and stands immobile (Fig. 30). But why was this scene included? Audience titillation may be a partial reason, as are several moments of explicit on-screen violence throughout the film. But it is more likely that this is intended as a feminist moment, meant to point up male chauvinism by showing us a Helen exposed, both literally to lustful gazes and sexist comments and figuratively as victim of a ruthless power play.[60] Helen is

---

[59] This official-sounding title of Agamemnon's had previously occurred in Shanower 2001, the first installment of an ongoing series of highly cinematic graphic novels retelling the Trojan War myth. Numerous parallels to Shanower's version, detailed and surprisingly accurate if still free in some respects, recur in Harrison's and Petersen's films, whose screenwriters conceivably knew the first two volumes of Shanower's series.

[60] The "male gaze," as scholars like to call it, especially at females and their bodies, is a fundamental aspect of cinema, exemplified by this scene in *Helen of Troy*. Cf. Chapter 3 on scopophilia and the work by Laura Mulvey cited there. It is to be noted, however, that the filmmakers verbally pull their

**Fig. 30.** *Helen of Troy* (2003). Helen on display. (Universal)

not in love with Menelaus and does not know that he loves her, so she sees herself being condemned to the kind of marriage no modern audiences would want to wish on her or, for that matter, on themselves. On their wedding night and in their first scene together a shy Menelaus pays her a compliment, and she replies: "You're a generous man." She recognizes his nobility, but love this is not. That night Helen, still virginal, attempts to commit suicide, but Paris rescues her at the last moment. Her only escape from exposure and humiliation will be with him.

There is, however, more to the scene of Helen running a nude gauntlet. She knows in advance what awaits her, and this knowledge makes her defiant. "They can look all they want," she informs Clytemnestra, "but they'll never see me." Feminists among viewers may cheer this line, for it is intended to reveal her indomitable spirit in the face of male oppression. But the effect is limited, for even so defiant a Helen is condemned to remain an object of lecherous male gazes, both in the hall in Sparta and on the television screens in American living rooms. She has already been such an object in several earlier scenes and will continue to be one, for under her rather diaphanous gowns her physical charms are repeatedly on display. Her tomboyish curls and womanly curves move freely and frequently, more

punches far more than they do visually, for the only two audible comments in this scene are too tame to qualify as sexist heckling: "Truly magnificent" and "Breathtaking." Instead we get an obvious cop-out: a disembodied female voice chanting rather plaintively over Helen's walk, presumably meant to reveal her emotional state and to instill in us a measure of pity for her.

even than Diane Kruger's a year later on the big screen. Harrison grants his Helen two scenes of callipygian allure in motion, Petersen gives his only one static one. So the scene of Helen's nude walk is an exercise in hypocrisy: the filmmakers can titillate their viewers and tell them: *Look what an indomitable, even emancipated, mind we've given our Helen.* Simultaneously they engage in the stereotypical "objectification," as modern terminology has it, of a female character. In retrospect such a conclusion is unavoidable, for the film's pre-credit sequence – the one in which we first hear from Menelaus as our narrator – consists of a montage of important moments from the story and *begins* with a brief frontal view of Helen being undressed for her nude walk, for which we have no context as yet. In three other very brief shots the opening montage returns to this scene, if without showing her naked. But for a short moment it will soon show us Helen's nude backside from another scene in which she so appears. Wise's Helen insisted in her conversation with Gig Young, previously scripted by men, that she is not what most people believe her to be. Harrison's Helen, scripted by a feminist, cannot maintain anything of the sort. Could she actually speak for herself, she might well resent being subjected to such a double standard. Director Harrison, writer Kern, and actress Guillory apparently have no qualms about that. Nor, presumably, do most males in the audience.

No such custom as a nude prenuptial walk existed in antiquity, and Harrison and Kern do not pass it off as historically or mythically authentic. But later history records an at least partial analogy. In a pavilion especially built for this purpose on an island in the river Rhine, on May 7, 1770, fourteen-year-old Austrian princess Maria Antonia, en route from Vienna to Paris to marry the *dauphin* in an arranged marriage of state, was forced to strip naked and display herself before an assembly of French aristocrats who had come to inspect her. She broke out in tears but passed the test. Three years after Harrison's *Helen of Troy* Sofia Coppola's film *Marie Antoinette* contains a recreation of this historical episode. "All eyes will be fixed on you," her mother, Empress Maria Theresa, warned the bride in a letter detailing how the future *dauphine* was to conduct herself in her new environment.[61] In neither history nor film is this young woman able to preserve her invisibility while being fixed by everybody's eyes. Nor is Harrison's Helen. They can look at her all they want, and they *can* see her.

Helen's nude scene makes sense only in terms of plot purposes, for soon afterwards Helen will demonstrate her capability of taking her fate in her

---

[61] Quoted from Weber 2006: 19; source reference at Weber 300 notes 41 and 42. Weber 24–27 describes the episode in detail. Somewhat different is the short account in Fraser 2001: 60–61; her book was reprinted in 2006 as tie-in to the film.

own hands. As it was in Wise's film, Paris' life is in mortal danger, and Helen rescues him and accompanies him to the Trojan ship at anchor in the harbor of Sparta. Intending to stay, she tells Paris: "Go now! You're free." And: "You have my love . . . Now go! I beg you: please go!" They kiss in close-up, but she is still a faithful wife. However, when the ship with Paris on board has cast off, she suddenly changes her mind: "No," she tells herself. She jumps into the water and climbs on deck. This time the decision to run away is entirely hers. The scene of her nude walk now takes on added meaning because it has prepared us for her own agency in her elopement. Anyone, we believe, who can handle such an undignified spectacle as well as she did can take charge of her own life. In this, Helen differs greatly from the heroines of Wise and Petersen.

Arrived in Troy, Paris evokes Helen's treatment in Sparta before King Priam and the Trojan elders. To the objection of one of them that Helen "belongs to Sparta" Paris retorts:

Where she is treated worse than a Hittite whore? Forced to walk naked among Aegean kings who leer and spit obscenities. I did not *take* her. I saved her from a people who find no worth in women, place *no* value on beauty, and seek their only honor through glorious death in battle.

Paris then appeals to Priam's and the Trojans' sense of "kindness and compassion." Of course they keep her, and the plot can proceed as it must.

Even so Harrison's Helen is a less traditional character than the Helen of all other films. The very color of her hair gives us a clue. Rossana Podestà, a brunette, had to wear a gigantic if attractively braided blond wig. Diane Kruger, a real blonde, would turn out to be too bland to make much of an impression on anyone but a besotted Paris (much less to launch a thousand ships). Sienna Guillory's hair is fair but with a reddish tinge, shading over into what ancient Greeks described with the adjective *pyrrhos*. Yes, Harrison's Helen is a blonde, still the ideal to many American males, but there is no danger that she might be mistaken for a dumb one. "I gave myself up," Helen will say ten years later to Cassandra in Troy, in a reference to her futile attempt to save Paris and to end the war by offering herself to Agamemnon. "You gave yourself up, but you didn't surrender, did you?" answers Cassandra. "Did you?" No, this Helen does not surrender.

As in the *Iliad*, Menelaus and Paris duel over Helen and victory, but we are in for yet another surprise. Harrison's Menelaus, unlike Petersen's, is not out for revenge on Helen but only on Paris. "I'll have the Trojan's head on a spike," he had told Agamemnon on hearing of Helen's elopement. In their duel Menelaus succeeds in wounding Paris, but it turns out to have been an unfair fight, for Menelaus realizes that the sword blade with which he has wounded Paris had been poisoned, presumably by Agamemnon. Menelaus does not exploit this advantage; instead, he and Paris together catch their breath, sitting side by side in a manner comparable to that of two "buddies" in any American action film. "Do you honestly believe that you deserve her more than I do?" asks Menelaus. Paris replies: "Yes; yes, I do." Menelaus now confesses that he is ashamed of the way she had been treated in Sparta. They talk about Paris in Sparta, and in the process husband and adulterous lover almost bond with each other over their common love for Helen and their common problem with Agamemnon. Both agree that Agamemnon is not waging this war for Helen but only for Troy. "Then why are we trying to kill each other?" asks Paris, and Menelaus answers: "His amusement." Paris asks next: "Have you ever thought that someday you should defy him?" He is turning into a kind of psychological counselor to his arch rival and enemy. Such a moment could never have fit Wise's or Petersen's films.

Immediately after his greatest heroic exploit, killing Achilles, Paris is himself viciously killed by Agamemnon and dies in Helen's arms while having a last vision of Aphrodite. Amid general slaughter during the fall of Troy Agamemnon brutally kills Priam and rapes Helen in full view of Menelaus, who is helpless to prevent it. Agamemnon meets his own bloody end the very next day. With all the other heroes of the story dead except for Odysseus, who is not central to this version and has dropped out of the story, only Menelaus is left. His voice is again heard on the soundtrack to prepare us for his reunion with Helen and for the end of the film. "War is waged by nations, but it is human beings that pay the price," he begins. The survivors "are left with the memory of shame and misery and bloodshed. In these dark times the only thing we have left to hold on to is love, the one true gift of the gods. And it is through love that we hope and pray the gods will send us peace." These commonplaces accompany images of Helen wandering forlorn around Troy. She comes to the spot where Paris had died and touches the traces of his blood. A vision of Paris now appears to her, and they embrace. "Wherever you are, take me with you," she begs, but he cannot. "Will we ever meet again?" she asks, and he answers, sounding strangely like Jesus: "I've prepared your place." The vision fades on a gentle kiss. Now Menelaus appears behind her, sword in hand (and in close-up). Helen offers him the back of her neck as if she were no more than an animal to be slaughtered on a sacrificial altar. But of course Menelaus cannot kill her. "I do not thank you for my life," she says, and he understands. "I cannot love you," she continues. Menelaus resigns all claims to her, as his next words imply: "What will you do?" Her answer:

"I will follow." Anachronistically actress Guillory delivers it in the modern fashion that expresses uncertainty or tentativeness by inflecting the last word as if it were followed by a question mark. "I accept," Menelaus says simply. Then he turns and moves away. She follows, if after a last look at the place where Paris had died, and they walk off into the distance.[62]

In spite of the maudlin tone of this final scene the reunion of husband and wife is curiously moving. Harrison's version is far removed from those of Euripides or Quintus of Smyrna, but the mood of resignation on the part of both spouses fits the atmosphere evoked in Book Four of the *Odyssey*. Helen and Menelaus are back in Sparta. Ten years after the end of the war Odysseus' son Telemachus visits them in search of information about his father and receives their hospitality. An apparently joyful occasion is in progress at his arrival – a double wedding: of Hermione to Achilles' son and of Menelaus' son Megapenthes to a Spartan woman. Nevertheless, and despite the general splendor of his surroundings, Menelaus readily yields to reminiscences about the past, especially his own sufferings during eight years of return after the Trojan War and the death of his brother upon returning to Mycenae. Menelaus explicitly states that he takes no pleasure in being the lord of his wealth, that he would readily part with two thirds of his possessions if only those fallen in the war could be alive again, and that he regularly gives himself over to mourning and grief. He specifically mentions Odysseus as a cause for his sorrow.[63] When Helen appears, she is struck by Telemachus' similarity to his father; she, too, is immediately reminded of the war that had started, she says, over her "dog eyes."[64] All of them, including Nestor's son Pisistratus, Telemachus' travel companion, break into tears, thinking and speaking of Odysseus, the one hero who still has not overcome the aftermath of the war. Helen can only calm them by secretly pouring drops of a magic potion into their wine.[65]

It is unlikely that Harrison and Kern were thinking of Homer's *Odyssey* in connection with the ending of their film. Still they manage to capture the impact of a devastating war on a wife who was one of its causes (or pretexts) and the lingering impact of that war. Presumably their Helen

---

[62] A slight verbal echo of Homer, *Iliad* 3.255 ("the woman and the spoils shall follow the winner"), the herald's words before the duel of Menelaus and Paris, is probably unintentional. – Hedreen 1996 points out the variety of differences in ancient accounts and visual representations of this part of the myth.

[63] Homer, *Odyssey* 4.78–112.

[64] Homer, *Odyssey* 4.138–146. The adjective *kynôpis* (145) expresses Helen's strong sense of shame.

[65] Homer, *Odyssey* 4.184–186 and 219–233. Despite some liberties the fundamentally melancholic life of Helen and Menelaus as portrayed in the *Odyssey* is beautifully brought to life in the corresponding sequence of Franco Rossi's *Odissea* (1968).

and Menelaus will never be happy together, certainly not in any romantic sense of the word or in a way that a mass audience would wish for the titular heroine of an epic story. But despite some half-hearted grafting of feminism and contemporary psychology onto an ancient subject theirs is a better way to end a modern adaptation of antiquity's most famous myth than Wise, Petersen, and their screenwriters could think of. On its own neo-mythological terms and by its own route Harrison's film reaches a conclusion that conforms to the Homeric atmosphere.

### INNOCENT HELEN: PALINODES FROM STESICHORUS TO HOLLYWOOD

All three Hollywood adaptations of Helen's story either completely absolve her from responsibility for behavior that led to the most famous war in the history of Western civilization or present her in ways that make her involvement in the causes and conduct of this war understandable or forgivable. Two of them connect their twist on the myth with the answer to a question many viewers may have asked themselves: Why is someone who should be called Helen of Sparta better known as Helen of Troy? The films provide an easy-to-grasp explanation. David Benioff and Petersen's is the simplest:

*Paris* [*to Priam*]: Father, this is Helen.
*Priam*: Helen? Helen of Sparta?
*Paris*: Helen of Troy.

Kern and Harrison explain what amounts to a kind of name change rather melodramatically. Priam reaffirms Agamemnon's blame for everything and so justifies his fateful decision not to hand Helen back to the Greeks in a way that makes him appear rational, understanding, and benign. This Priam is a fatherly "nice guy":

*Priam* [*to Helen*]: We also agree that to sacrifice your honor or even your life will not appease his desire [for war] or make peace more likely. For these reasons we invite you to consider this city to be your home for as long as you shall live. Furthermore, should you choose to renounce any further affiliation with Sparta, you shall henceforth be known as Helen of Troy. Do you accept this offer?
*Helen*: I accept.

Wise and his writers, however, take the greatest care to justify Helen's name change. Priam naturally wishes to know not so much who she is as who she will be. Cassandra then comes up with the new name for Helen. I quote the relevant dialogue in abbreviated form:

*Priam*: By what name, my lady, shall we know you? . . .
*Helen*: I am Helen, queen of Sparta.
*Priam*: The wife of King Menelaus?
*Helen*: His wife no more. . . .
*Cassandra*: She will bring the disaster I have prophesied. Her name will be written in letters of fire. Helen. Helen of Troy.

But Helen must not be the cause of the inevitable fall of Troy, so a later scene absolves her of all responsibility. Helen secretly leaves Troy to give herself up to Menelaus and end the war, but Menelaus again proves to be as bad a husband as we already know. Paris nobly rescues Helen from the treacherous Greeks and takes her back to Troy. Priam now reaffirms her ties to the city and raises her status:

*Priam*: Helen, through you we have learned that they seek plunder, not justice . . . Cassandra, we have found there is great wisdom in you. What more can you tell us?
*Cassandra*: New storms shall ride the sky, but the guilt will be Athena's, not Helen's.
*Priam*: Thank you, Cassandra. [*To Helen*:] Such courage must not go unrewarded. Helen, you will be a princess of Troy.

Someone unexpected is responsible for Troy's fiery disaster. Athena, to the Trojans (and viewers) of this film a goddess of war, is conveniently on hand to be blamed for the catastrophe. Apparently not even the Greek kings are as evil as she is.

The process of whitewashing Helen has a venerable if today not very well-known history, which the ancients themselves started. The archaic choral poet Stesichorus used the term *palinode* ("recantation") to denote just such a thing. Stesichorus is himself the subject of myth-making because he was said to have lost his eyesight for disparaging Helen in a poem entitled *Helen* (or possibly in another composition, perhaps *The Fall of Troy*). It was Helen herself, now deified, who inflicted this punishment on the poet. Realizing the cause of his blindness, Stesichorus composed his *Palinode* and received his sight again. His poems survive only in fragments; our chief evidence for the *Palinode* is Plato's *Phaedrus*, in which Socrates says:

For those who have sinned in their telling of myths there is an ancient purification, known not to Homer but to Stesichorus: when he was blinded because of his slander of Helen he was not unaware of the reason like Homer [who was and remained blind], but being devoted to the Muses recognised the cause and immediately wrote,

> That story is not true, and you did not go on the well-benched ships and you did not reach the citadel of Troy;

and having composed all the Palinode, as it is called, he at once regained his sight.[66]

The story referred to as untrue is that of Helen's stay in Troy. In antiquity Stesichorus generally received the credit for starting the alternate account of her stay in Egypt.[67] Ancient authors already engaged in early neo-mythologism.[68]

Taking their cue from Stesichorus, three Greek orators presented the case for rather than against Helen as demonstrations of their rhetorical expertise. The first of them is Gorgias, the famous Athenian teacher of rhetoric in the late fifth century BC. In his *Encomium of Helen* he sets himself the task of acquitting Helen of responsibility for the Trojan War:

> <it is right to refute> those who rebuke Helen, a woman about whom the testimony of inspired poets has become univocal and unanimous as had the ill omen of her name, which has become a reminder of misfortunes. For my part, by introducing some reasoning into my speech, I wish to free the accused of blame and, having reproved her detractors as prevaricators and proved the truth, to free her from their ignorance . . . For either by will of Fate and decision of the gods and vote of Necessity did she do what she did, or by force reduced or by words seduced <or by love possessed>.[69]

Gorgias then refutes these four charges that have been brought against Helen; I quote only the essential passages:

> If . . . one must place blame on Fate and on a god, one must free Helen from disgrace.

---

[66] Plato, *Phaedrus* 243a; the translation is quoted from David A. Campbell 1991: 93. The lines quoted are now Fragm. *P.M.G.* 192 Page of Stesichorus' surviving work. The first line reappears at *Phaedrus* 244a. Cf. Isocrates, *Encomium on Helen* 64–65.

[67] As mentioned above, Hesiod was the first to refer to Helen's phantom and Herodotus deduced Homer's knowledge of this version. On Hesiod, Plato, Stesichorus, Euripides, and their contexts see Woodbury 1967.

[68] The neo-mythologism of Stesichorus is particularly noteworthy. Ancient testimony (*P.M.G.* 193 Page) mentions a second Palinode by Stesichorus, in which he may have blamed Hesiod for the story that Helen was the mother of Iphigenia by Theseus; cf. Bowra 1963. On Stesichorus' Helen see especially Austin 1994: 90–117. In general, and in connection with cinematic neo-mythologism, see Danek 2006, with additional references. See further Vöhler, Seidensticker, and Emmerich 2004, especially the editors' introduction ("Zum Begriff der Mythenkorrektur," 1–18), in which they distinguish among variation, correction, and criticism of myth.

[69] This and the following quotations are from Gorgias, *Encomium of Helen* 2, 6, 8, 14, 15, 19, and 21. The translations are taken from "Gorgias' Encomium of Helen," tr. George Kennedy, in Sprague 1972: 50–54.

But if she was raped by violence and illegally assaulted and unjustly insulted, it is clear that the raper, as the insulter, did the wronging, and the raped, as the insulted, did the suffering . . .

But if it was speech which persuaded her and deceived her heart, not even to this is it difficult to make an answer and to banish blame . . . The effect of speech upon the condition of the soul is comparable to the power of drugs over the nature of bodies.

. . . if it was love which did all these things, there will be no difficulty in escaping the charge of the sin which is alleged to have taken place . . . If, being a god, Love has the divine power of the gods, how could a lesser being reject and refuse it? But if it is a disease of human origin and a fault of the soul, it should not be blamed as a sin, but regarded as an affliction. For she came, as she did come, caught in the net of Fate, not by the plans of the mind, and by the constraints of love, not by the devices of art.

So far so good. Gorgias closes, however, by stating: "I wished to write a speech which would be a praise of Helen and a diversion to myself." He as much as admits that he is not being serious, that his oration is what Greek authors used to call a *paignion* ("playful trifle"). There is obviously nothing wrong with this approach, but it indicates that Gorgias practices what Sophists took pride in preaching *and* practicing: to make the weaker case appear the stronger, as the Sophist Protagoras had famously put it.[70] Gorgias' *Encomium* is a rhetorical exercise for its own sake and for the intellectual delight of his listeners, not a serious-minded rewriting of myth for the sake of elucidating a mythic-historical truth.

In his own *Encomium on Helen* Gorgias' student Isocrates, another influential Attic orator, specifically refers to an earlier work in Helen's defense; scholars identify it with Gorgias' encomium. Isocrates criticizes it for being more of a defense speech than a true encomium of the kind he is delivering. Noteworthy for our context is Isocrates' whitewashing of Paris, especially in connection with his famous judgment:

some . . . have before now reviled Alexander [= Paris]; but the folly of these accusers is easily discerned by all from the calumnies they have uttered. Are they not in a ridiculous state of mind if they think their own judgement is more competent than that which the gods chose as best. For surely they did not select any ordinary arbiter to decide a dispute about an issue that had got them into so fierce a quarrel, but obviously they were as anxious to select the most competent judge as they were concerned about the matter itself . . . only a mortal man of greatly superior intelligence could have received such honour as to become a judge of immortals.

---

[70] Protagoras' claim is attested at, e.g., Aristotle, *Rhetoric* 2.24.11 (1402a23), and Cicero, *Brutus* 8.30. A practical demonstration occurs in Aristophanes, *Clouds* 889–1104.

From this astonishing take on Paris follows Isocrates' conclusion about Paris' life with Helen:

> Would he not have been a fool if, knowing that the deities themselves were contending for the prize of beauty, he had himself scorned beauty, and had failed to regard as the greatest of gifts that for the possession of which he saw even those goddesses most earnestly striving?

Toward the end Isocrates mentions that Helen attained immortality and conferred on Menelaus the supreme gift a mortal can attain:

> she so amply recompensed Menelaus for the toils and perils which he had undergone because of her, that when all the race of the Pelopidae [descendents of Pelops, among them Agamemnon and Menelaus] had perished and were the victims of irremediable disasters, not only did she free him from these misfortunes but, having made him god instead of mortal, she established him as partner of her house and sharer of her throne forever.[71]

Even more astonishing may be what Dio Cocceianus, better known as Dio Chrysostom ("Goldmouth" on account of his oratorical skills), has to say about Helen in the first century AD. In his *Trojan Discourse* Dio reports what a venerable Egyptian priest told him about Helen and Menelaus: the complete opposite of what was commonly believed and told in Greece. The real story as preserved in Egyptian records is, according to this priest, beyond suspicion "since Menelaus had come to visit them [the Egyptians] and described everything just as it had occurred."[72] Dio follows Herodotus, who, as we saw, had also heard from Egyptian priests about Helen's stay in Egypt and specifically mentions that the Egyptians assured him that the source of their information was none other than Menelaus himself, for back then Menelaus had told *his* Egyptians what had really happened.[73] Herodotus concludes that this must be the correct account.[74] Here, as in Harrison's film, we get the truth straight from an impeccable eye-witness – or so we are told.

According to Dio's priest – or rather, according to Dio's rhetorical trickery – Tyndareus and his sons decided that they could lay the foundation for their eventual dominion over both Greece and Asia if Helen married

---

[71] Isocrates, *Encomium on Helen* 45–48 and 62; quoted from Van Hook 1945: 85–87 and 95. For proof of their immortality Isocrates refers to the tomb of Helen and Menelaus at Therapne outside Sparta, where they received cultic honors as gods; cf. Herodotus, *The Histories* 6.61, and Pausanias, *Description of Greece* 3.19.9. On Isocrates' work cf. Papillon 1996.

[72] Dio Chrysostom, *The Trojan Discourse* 38; quoted from Cohoon 1932: 475.

[73] Herodotus, *The Histories* 2.118.      [74] Herodotus, *The Histories* 2.120.

Paris after Clytemnestra had already married Agamemnon.[75] Dio reports via his Egyptian:

"Thus it was that Paris took Helen as his lawful wife after gaining the consent of her parents and brothers, and took her home with him amid great enthusiasm and rejoicing. And Priam, Hector, and all the others were delighted with the union and welcomed Helen with sacrifices and prayers.

"Then see," continued the priest, "how foolish the opposite story is. Can you imagine it possible for anyone to have become enamoured of a woman whom he had never seen, and then, that she could have let herself be persuaded to leave husband, fatherland, and all her relatives – and that, too, I believe, when she was the mother of a little daughter – and follow a man of another race? It is because this is so improbable that they [the Greeks] got up that cock-and-bull story about Aphrodite, which is still more preposterous . . .

"And how in the world after coming to Greece did he [Paris] become intimate with Helen, and talk to her, and finally persuade her to elope, without thinking of parents, country, husband, or daughter, or of her repute among the Greeks, nay, without fearing even her brothers, who were still living and had once before recovered her from Theseus and had not brooked her abduction? . . . It would have been impossible for her to go with Paris in any such way, but possible if she was given in marriage with the full consent of her kinsfolk."[76]

In the name of rationalism, common sense, and logic we are served a tale that is more radical than any neo-mythologism Hollywood could have dreamed up. The double mention of Helen's ties to Greece in Dio's passages quoted above is good rhetorical strategy: if you have to assert something important, drive it home by repetition. So the priest later summarizes the whole story of Helen and Paris and Tyndareus' wish to form an alliance by marriage with Troy yet again.[77] And again: "The reason was, in fact, that they [Tyndareus and his sons] had voluntarily given Helen in marriage since they preferred Paris to the other suitors on account of the greatness of his kingdom and his manly qualities, for he was no man's inferior in character."[78] Scholars who despair over the extent to which modern media distort the supposed truth of ancient myth or dismiss such versions as hopelessly inaccurate and therefore *infra dig* might do better to remember the ancients. They, not Hollywood writers or directors, take the cake of neo-mythologism. As we just saw, not only Helen but even Paris comes

---

[75] Dio Chrysostom, *The Trojan Discourse* 51.

[76] Dio Chrysostom, *The Trojan Discourse* 53–54, 58, and 60; quoted from Cohoon 1932: 487, 491, and 493. After his reference to the Judgment of Paris Dio has his priest discuss the "true" character of Priam, Hector, and other Trojans in support.

[77] Dio Chrysostom, *The Trojan Discourse* 68.

[78] Dio Chrysostom, *The Trojan Discourse* 73; quoted from Cohoon 1932: 503.

off better than anything screenwriters could begin to imagine. The vexed question *What is truth?* evidently does not apply to myth. But if we do attempt an answer, we are bound to say: *Truth in myth is anything that makes for an effective story from any given narrative point of view.*[79] So we find from antiquity to today various versions of the same story, even mutually exclusive ones. But which version of a myth is the "correct" one? For example, *was* Helen in Troy or not? Does it matter? Does not the existence of a dual tradition make for an altogether more fascinating tale about her?

Clever "corrections" of the traditional Trojan War myth on an even larger scale circulated in antiquity under the names of Dares the Phrygian (i.e. Trojan) and Dictys the Cretan, authors who – no surprise here – claimed to have been eye-witnesses of the war and were now finally telling the true story, if from opposite points of view.[80] To mention just two examples of Dares' neo-mythologism, Troy fell not because of Odysseus' invention of the wooden horse but because Aeneas betrayed his home city. And his Menelaus is not blond.[81] Dictys is of greater interest to us because his account is much longer than Dares'. Dictys, not unlike Benioff and Petersen, omits everything irrational or supernatural. The Greek heroes' oath occurs after and not before Helen's elopement.[82] Dictys' Helen, just arrived in Troy, informs King Priam that being married to Menelaus "did not suit her."[83] Still Dictys can claim, presumably with a straight face:

> As to what happened earlier at Troy [before the war], I have tried to make my report as accurate as possible, Ulysses being my source. The account that follows based as it is on my own observations, will meet, I hope, the highest critical standards . . . Everything I have written about the war between the Greeks and the barbarians, in which I took a very active part, is based on first-hand knowledge.[84]

Dictys and Dares do not, however, represent the extremes of ancient neo-mythologism. Lucian of Samosata, the satirical Sophist of the second century AD, briefly turned to the "true" story of the Trojan War in a dialogue called *The Dream, or The Cock*, in which he pokes fun at the Pythagorean concept of the transmigration of the soul. A talking rooster, who claims

---

[79] Cf. my comments in Winkler 2006a: 12–18.

[80] These two works now survive only in later Latin translations; that of Dares is considerably abridged and is not attested until the second century AD. The one by Dictys is generally dated to the first. For English versions of both, with additional background information, see R. M. Frazer 1966.

[81] Dares, *The Fall of Troy* 39–41 and 13.

[82] Dictys, *Journal of the Trojan War* 1.12; so also Dares, *The Fall of Troy* 11.

[83] Dictys, *Journal of the Trojan War* 1.10; quoted from R. M. Frazer 1966: 29.

[84] Dictys, *Journal of the Trojan War* 1.13 and 5.17; quoted from R. M. Frazer 1966: 30 and 118.

that his spirit descended from Apollo and entered any number of human and animal bodies – among the former Pythagoras himself and Pericles' mistress Aspasia – reveals to his astonished owner that at the time of the Trojan War he had been the Trojan hero Euphorbus and had killed Achilles' friend Patroclus but was in turn killed by Menelaus. Asked by his owner if everything had occurred as Homer tells it, the rooster contemptuously dismisses Homer as an ignoramus who during the war had been a camel in far-away Bactria (roughly, modern Afghanistan). As Euphorbus, of course, the rooster had known Helen. But Helen was not as beautiful as everyone believes; even worse, she was already an old woman. Lucian's palinodic animal, we realize, firmly has his tongue in his cheek, if such may be said about barnyard fowl.[85]

The works discussed here are not the only ancient ones that tamper with parts or details of the Trojan War narrative and its related myths in sometimes contradictory fashion.[86] But they suffice to show us that Hollywood's rewriting of classical myth is nothing radical or deplorable but rather something utterly traditional, if not necessarily meeting the highest critical standards. The films are modern palinodes. We can tell this even from the identical narrative stances of Stesichorus ("That story is not true" – he implies the claim *but mine is*), Dio Chrysostom ("Menelaus . . . described everything just as it had occurred" – i.e. differently from the common version; so already Herodotus), and Harrison (Menelaus saying "that is not the way it happened . . . I know. I was there"). Directors and screenwriters who turn to ancient myth might well be surprised by the extent of ancient "rewrites," to use a Hollywood term, if they knew of them. Conversely classical scholars who decry a film like *Troy* as un-Homeric ought to remember that in the first century AD Ptolemy Chennus wrote an epic in twenty-four books actually called the *Anti-Homer* (*Anthomêros*). Classical film philologists, however, who take a close look at both the ancient myths and the literary tradition based on them are not likely to be surprised by the carefree extent to which an epic film has changed a myth but rather by the very traditionalism with which all such changes occur.

Wise's Helen had already made this point, if unwittingly. Just before their escape from Sparta she had told Paris: "What is remembered is forever young." From this perspective the words of Paris to Helen in Petersen's *Troy* take on added resonance. He tells her: "We will be together again, in this world or the next. We will be together." And so they are, together again and

---

[85] Lucian, *The Dream, or The Cock* 16–17. Euphorbus appears in Books Sixteen and Seventeen of the *Iliad*, where he wounds but does not kill Patroclus and is killed by Menelaus.

[86] All the literary variations concerning Helen are dealt with in Ghali-Kahil 1955: vol. 1.

again in the world of film – a new world to the characters of the stories and a kind of "next" world that provides them with a continuing afterlife. For mythical figures the most powerful realm of survival today is the cinema. In the works of the ancient authors we encountered in this chapter Helen lost Paris but won back Menelaus. In Hollywood all three are remembered, but it is Helen and Paris rather than Helen and Menelaus who are forever young.

CHAPTER 6

# *Women in love*

*Cherchez la femme* – Alexandre Dumas may not have realized that *The Mohicans of Paris*, his serial novel that began to appear in 1854, was to provide the modern world with one of its most famous sayings. What Johann Wolfgang Goethe had earlier called *das Ewig-Weibliche* ("the eternal feminine") at the conclusion of his *Faust* has always been irresistible and fascinating to men.

Cinema, the prime medium to express men's dreams and fantasies, has featured an infinite variety of women since William Heise directed *The Kiss* for Thomas Edison's company in 1896. The title encompasses the scandalous film's entire "plot" of less than a minute. *The Kiss* provoked calls for instant censorship of the fledgling medium. But the allure of women has proven irrepressible. Georges Méliès made the first film based on an ancient love story in 1898 (*Pygmalion and Galatea*) and the first one to feature an ancient vamp in its title in 1899 (*Cleopatra*), thereby initiating the return of women from ancient literature, history, and myth. As the case of Helen of Troy demonstrates, there is no better medium to search for and find the eternal feminine of Greece and Rome than the cinema.

The depiction of ancient women in film warrants a far longer treatise than two chapters of one book can provide. The three examples I look at in this chapter reinforce what the preceding chapter on Helen of Troy has already indicated: classical film philology is extremely wide-ranging, not least where women are concerned. In the films examined here a woman from Greek literature has a contemporary American "relative," and one from ancient history reappears in two reconstructions of her world both made with great Hollywood splendor. Finally, a European retelling of a Greek myth invents for its central character a woman who had not even been part of the ancient story and who overshadows the heroine of the original. The sections of this chapter follow progressions from innocence to experience, from seduction to love, and from life to death. They show once again how versatile narrative cinema can be in its portrayals of antiquity and in its modernity.

### FROM INNOCENCE TO EXPERIENCE: CHLOE IN PLEASANTVILLE

Longus' novel *Daphnis and Chloe*, one of the most charming ancient love romances, is a "song of innocence and of experience," to appropriate a famous title by William Blake. In the novel innocence and experience work on two levels. One is within the story, which describes the protagonists' journey of erotic self-discovery from a state of naiveté to sexual knowledge and to marriage and future parenthood. The other and more fascinating level of innocence and experience is the basis of Longus' narrative strategy: an experienced author writes about inexperienced characters for experienced readers. While the novel's setting is the idyllic countryside, the author and his readers are urban sophisticates. Longus' narrative works mainly through the dramatic tension which arises from the difference between the story's protagonists and its readers and the simultaneous presence of innocence and experience on the two levels mentioned.[1] This tension is one of the reasons for the novel's lasting appeal and for its earlier reputation as a dirty book. It is also the one aspect that elevates it above the level of a predictable adventure romance. Nevertheless the characters in this kind of literature remain one-dimensional or, in E. M. Forster's well-known term, "flat."[2]

In "Forms of Time and the Chronotope in the Novel" literary scholar Mikhail Bakhtin devotes a long first section to "The Greek Romance."[3] The aspects of *chronos* ("time") and *topos* ("place, space"), closely related to what we today call the "space-time continuum," enable us to juxtapose Longus' novel, a work of ancient popular art, with a work of modern popular art which works in comparable ways. *Pleasantville* (1998), a film written and directed by Gary Ross, also shows us the journey from innocence

---

[1] Bowie 1996 surveys the audiences of the Greek novels in general. On Longus' readership and narrative strategy see Morgan 2003.

[2] Forster 1927: 67–78 (on "flat" and "round" characters) and 68–72 (on the narrative advantages of flat characters). See also Robert Louis Stevenson's 1882 essay "A Gossip on Romance," a defense of formula fiction as eloquent as it is convincing, now in Stevenson 1999: 51–64 and 186–188 (notes).

[3] Mikhail Bakhtin, "Forms of Time and the Chronotope in the Novel," in Bakhtin 1981: 84–258, especially 86–110 on Greek romance novels. Subsequent quotations from and references to the text are according to this translation. I have also consulted "Formen der Zeit und des Chronotopos im Roman" in Bachtin 1986: 7–209. Bakhtin wrote his long study in 1937–1938 (with "Concluding Remarks" added in 1973); it was first published in Russian in 1975. For classical perspectives on the text see Branham 1995 and 2002b. Branham 2000–2001 examines the temporal aspects of ancient novels.

to experience in matters of love and sexuality and touches directly on classical themes. Longus' novel has been filmed a few times more or less faithfully, but *Pleasantville* is a more interesting reworking of the ancient text.[4] Thematic connections between works that one would not expect to have anything in common can be more revealing than more or less straightforward adaptations.

In *Pleasantville* two modern teenagers, brother and sister, are supernaturally transported into a 1950s black-and-white television series called "Pleasantville," which is set entirely within this eponymous town. This Pleasantville might as well be named Perfectville because it represents the fulfillment of the American dream as suburban ideal: perfect weather, perfect town, perfect people, and no family, social, urban, or natural problems. Crime does not exist. The worst kind of crisis we see involves a treed cat. In an audio commentary writer-director Ross has described this Pleasantville as an "ultra-wholesome, ultra-perfect, homogenized world," a "sterile, perfect world," and a "sealed utopia." A title card appearing at the beginning of the film alerts us to the fairy-tale world with which we are about to become familiar: "Once Upon a Time . . ." Such descriptions remind us of what Bakhtin said about the Greek romance novels, including *Daphnis and Chloe*:

In this kind of time, nothing changes: the world remains as it was, the biographical life of the heroes does not change, their feelings do not change, people do not even age. This empty time leaves no traces anywhere, no indications of its passing.

And:

It goes without saying that in this type of time, an individual can be nothing other than completely *passive*, completely *unchanging* . . . to such an individual

---

[4] The best-known versions are *Daphnis and Chloe* (1931) by Orestis Laskos, who made a variant in 1969 as *Dafnis kai Khloi: Oi mikroi erastai* ("Daphnis and Chloe: The Young Lovers"), and *Young Aphrodites* (1963) by Nikos Koundouros, which is also indebted to the *Idylls* of Theocritus. On the third film see Renard 1969: 11 and Faulx 1969. A Spanish version appeared in 1976 as *La iniciación en el amor*, directed by Javier Aguirre. On these films see de España 1998: 414–418 and 427, 428, and 430 (filmography). De España 417 calls twelve-year-old Kleopatra Rota of *Young Aphrodites* "una *Lolita* helénica." An example of a modern analogy to Longus' Chloe is Marcel Pagnol's Manon in *Manon of the Spring*, filmed first by Pagnol himself in 1953 and again by Claude Berri in 1986. In the later version, which is more readily accessible, Emmanuelle Béart plays Manon. Here are some similarities to her classical predecessor: Manon is a goatherd; she dances and plays the harmonica, a modern equivalent to the rustic instruments played by Longus' country folk; she innocently bathes naked in a spring by a grotto. The evil character who watches her doing so and immediately falls in love with her but is eventually rejected partly redeems himself in death (overtones of Longus' Dorcon). When she marries, Manon in her bridal gown combines the purity of her natural beauty with the cultural refinement of society, a point which Longus emphasizes about Chloe (and to which I will turn below).

things can merely *happen*. He himself is deprived of any initiative. He is merely the physical subject of the action. And it follows that his actions will be by and large of an elementary-spatial sort . . . he *keeps on being the same person* and emerges . . . with his *identity* absolutely unchanged.[5]

Since in the black-and-white world of Pleasantville we are in the wholesome year 1958, there is, of course, no eroticism or sex. Teenagers go on dates to the soda fountain, hold hands, sit side by side in a car in Lovers' Lane looking at the surroundings, and that is all. But their idyllic existence is radically altered when our teenagers David and Jennifer arrive from the late 1990s. They are sexually experienced, Jennifer more so than David. In an early scene set in the present we learn that she had bought herself new underwear before a date she considered important. Longus' description of the sexual predator Lycaenion partly fits Jennifer: both are "imported . . . from town" and "young, pretty, and rather sophisticated."[6] In Pleasantville Jennifer introduces first her 1950s date and then, indirectly, several other youngsters to their erotic nature. Sexual knowledge spreads irresistibly among Pleasantville's teenagers and adults despite the futile attempts on the part of the town's mayor and several other good citizens, all middle-aged males in this patriarchal society. The transformation from innocence to experience appears on screen in a way as charming as it is clever. Ross takes full advantage of the visual nature of his medium and of modern computer technology to present his characters' gradual journey toward love and sexuality, greater self-knowledge, a deeper emotional and intellectual life, and an awareness of the world around them. More and more Ross infuses individual objects and people with color until at the completion of this process the originally black-and-white world of Pleasantville has become entirely polychrome. To his characters in the story as well as to his audiences in the theater Ross shows the radical changes which knowledge of any sort demands from all who embark on a quest for it.

   In the Book of Genesis God forbids Adam to eat the fruit of the tree of knowledge of good and evil; otherwise he has to die the same day.[7] But when Eve and Adam do eat the forbidden fruit, they do not die at all but acquire a new consciousness. Their first realization is not knowledge of good

---

[5] Bakhtin 1981: 91 and 105.

[6] *Daphnis and Chloe* 3.15.1. I quote Longus in the translation by Christopher Gill in Reardon 1989: 285–348; quotations at 324.

[7] Genesis 2.16–17. The reconstruction of the myth of the Fall of Man and the analysis of its likely original form by Sir James Frazer 1918: 45–77 is still worth reading. It is readily accessible, if in the abridged version from a 1923 one-volume edition but with original notes restored, in Dundes 1984: 72–97. A recent discussion is at Theodore Ziolkowski 2000b: 9–24 (chapter on "Adam: The Genesis of Consciousness").

and evil but awareness of their nakedness. Nudity here symbolizes their sexual awakening, from which all deeper knowledge derives. A parallel perspective occurs in Plato's *Symposium*, in which Socrates explains the true nature of Eros. Real love transcends the physical and ascends to the ultimate knowledge that "beauty is truth; truth, beauty," as John Keats put it in the best-known phrase of his "Ode on a Grecian Urn."[8] Knowledge of good and evil and the Platonic ideal are two sides of the same coin. In *Daphnis and Chloe* Longus is not quite this philosophical, but the concept that carnal knowledge leads to self-awareness and to a meaningful and happy life is the basis of his novel. Toward its end Chloe's natural beauty is supplemented by her elegant bridal dress – nature (*physis*) and culture (*technê*) are combined. Now she embodies true perfection, the ideal of both beauty and knowledge. As the narrator puts it:

Then you could learn what beauty is like, when it is properly presented. For when Chloe was dressed and had put her hair up and washed her face, she seemed so much more beautiful to everyone that even Daphnis scarcely recognized her.[9]

Knowledge of one's own nature leads to the development of other areas of knowledge: of one's surroundings and society, of arts and sciences, of civilization.

This latter aspect of knowledge is brought to the fore even more in Ross's film than in Longus' novel. The ignorant students of Pleasantville discover a great repository of culture in their library. We may be reminded of the library as Apollonian depository of civilization in Pasolini's *Notes for an African Oresteia*, mentioned in Chapter 2. Ross focuses on painting and literature as representative of all culture. The first painting shown to one of the main characters and simultaneously to its viewers is Masaccio's early fifteenth-century fresco of Adam and Eve's expulsion from the Garden of Eden. Regarding literature, three novels receive prominence of place: Mark Twain's *Adventures of Huckleberry Finn*, J. D. Salinger's *The Catcher in the Rye*, and D. H. Lawrence's *Lady Chatterley's Lover*. All three at some time have been banned or censored somewhere; this is the reason why Ross chose them, as he states in his commentary. For teenage readers identification with the protagonists of Twain's and Salinger's novels has often been an initiation into literature and the arts – that is to say, into knowledge and civilization at large. Their heroes' irreverence toward good society may be one of the reasons why the books are banned in some American middle and high schools even today. Lawrence's novel in particular was

---

[8] Socrates' exchange with Agathon and his subsequent speech are in Plato, *Symposium* 198a–212c.

[9] *Daphnis and Chloe* 4.32.1; quotation from Gill in Reardon 1989: 345.

considered as dangerous and notorious in the twentieth century as *Daphnis and Chloe* had been in the nineteenth. Here again Bakhtin helps us see both similarity and difference between *Daphnis and Chloe* and *Pleasantville*. After stating that "the homogenization of all that is heterogeneous in a Greek romance . . . is achieved only at the cost of the most extreme abstraction [and] schematization," he observes:

This most abstract of all chronotopes [the one in the Greek romance] is also the most static. In such a chronotope the world and the individual are finished items, absolutely immobile. In it there is no potential for evolution, for growth, for change. As a result of the action described in the novel, nothing in its world is destroyed, remade, changed or created anew. What we get is a mere affirmation of the identity between what had been at the beginning and what is at the end. Adventure-time [the time necessary for the development of the novel's plot] leaves no trace.[10]

The latter part of this quotation does not apply to the final state of things in Pleasantville, which has completely changed from its earlier idyllic existence. But even this difference is analogous to Longus' novel since the affirmation of the country life at the conclusion of *Daphnis and Chloe* occurs only because the dangers of the external world could be resisted successfully. In *Pleasantville* the people from the outside world, arrived from today's society, effect a radical change in the idyllic world, which turns out not to have been all that idyllic after all. The outside world, we may say, has conquered the idyllic one. But this conquest could take place only with the eventual cooperation of the inhabitants of the once-idyllic world. In Ross's words:

a lot [of *Pleasantville*] is about bringing knowledge into a sealed utopia, and is that good or bad? There *are* people who would like to return to a kind of unconscious Eden, the void of sex, before there was Eve, when there was only Adam and there was none of the attendant complications . . . it's about the getting of *all* knowledge . . . the consequences of knowledge, and the liberating nature of knowledge.

The incursion of knowledge – exemplified by sexuality, with which the process starts, just as in Longus' novel – destroys the paradisal state of innocence and ignorant perfection. This is the price necessary to be paid for evolution, growth, and change, for a meaningful life.

After these thematic connections between *Daphnis and Chloe* and *Pleasantville* I now turn to a specific scene in either work. These illustrate the simultaneous presence of innocence and experience from whose inherent

---

[10]  Bakhtin 1981: 110.

tension the narrative development of a love story may derive its greatest force and appeal. Both scenes are highly erotic, if in different ways. The one in *Pleasantville* is the most erotically charged in the entire film. But neither scene is in any way pornographic. Both are presented with great delicacy, with sympathy for and understanding of the characters involved, and with a touch of humor. In terms of plot or situation the two scenes have nothing at all in common. Nor do I wish to imply that writer-director Ross in any way imitated Longus. But both scenes effectively illustrate a specific moment of sexual awakening in analogous ways.

One of the most charming erotic vignettes in *Daphnis and Chloe* is the episode of the grasshopper or cicada which flies into Chloe's dress. This is a significant moment in Daphnis' and Chloe's journey toward their discovery of love. The narrator tells us that Daphnis "put his hands between her breasts and took out" the cicada.[11] He says nothing else about Daphnis' act, but experienced readers – that is to say, all readers – know that in order to do so Daphnis must touch her chest. Mentally readers automatically add this missing detail, the acme of eroticism in the little episode. What is omitted from verbal description is a turning point for Daphnis' awakening to love. This becomes evident from two authorial comments which prompt us to fill in the narrative gap. Before reading that Daphnis put his hand into Chloe's dress we have been informed that he did so by taking advantage of the situation (*prophaseôs labomenos*). This is by no means an indication of lechery on his part because he is still far too innocent. No, his act shows his tender desire to come to Chloe's rescue after the grasshopper has made her scream twice in surprise and fear. (Like Longus' readers Daphnis *is* amused by her reaction.) The authorial comment is a nudge to the reader. The disarming charm of the moment and Daphnis' equally disarming naiveté are expressed in the experienced author's gently ironic phrase "that obliging grasshopper" (*ton beltiston tettiga*). The moment is one of great intimacy and erotic vulnerability on the part of the two young lovers.

The corresponding moment in *Pleasantville*, also one of intimacy and vulnerability, occurs when Betty, the mother in the film's central television family, discovers her sexuality. Our two time-travelers have replaced her children. (We may deduce that conception in impossibly pure Pleasantville takes place asexually.) To her initial disbelief and surprise ("Your father would never do anything like that") the mother obtains the requisite information about sex from her experienced "daughter" Jennifer. Betty then takes a bath and discovers the erogenous nature of her body and her

---

[11] *Daphnis and Chloe* 1.26.3; this and the following quotation are from Gill in Reardon 1989: 300.

**Fig. 31.** *Pleasantville.* The discovery of the erotic nature of the body, here still in black and white, leads to knowledge and self-awareness. (New Line Cinema)

true self. But she becomes aware of her mind as well, for after she has gained self-knowledge she is no longer willing to remain a submissive housewife and fulfill her traditional and stereotypical 1950s role. She emancipates herself from husband and kitchen and even acts on her feelings for another man. While she is in the process of discovering her eroticism in the bathtub, she begins to see her surroundings in color (Fig. 31). Soon after, she leaves behind her black-and-white existence for good and turns into color herself. Ross has observed about this scene:

The sexual awakening is the first thing that occurs because it's the most primal, it's the most basic . . . If you look at this as kind of a growing up of the world that way, sort of that edenic allegory, this *is* the first impulse, and it's a primal thing and it's one that you can't deny . . . But there's higher levels of evolution than that; it's only the first . . . There are so many other things that are on a higher level of evolution and complexity than just that sexual impulse, yet I think if you're closed off to something that fundamental, it's very hard to be open to other things . . . it gives rise to a whole new world of nuance and beauty that's non-sexual . . .

Here Ross could easily have named Plato because his words are fully in the tradition of Platonic philosophy.

A later scene in the film also echoes the classical tradition with its *locus amoenus,* the "pleasant place" of a peaceful and ideal natural setting that is often the backdrop for scenes of love. A representative example from an ancient work of popular culture occurs in the anonymous *Aesop Romance* of the second century AD. Not all of its details, of course, recur in the film:

[Aesop] picked out a spot . . . that was green and peaceful, a wooded, shady place where all kinds of flowers bloomed amid the green grass and where a little stream wandered among the neighboring trees . . . The stream whispered and, as a gentle zephyr blew, the leaves of the trees around about were stirred and exhaled a sweet and soothing breath. There was much humming of cicadas from the branches, and the song of birds of many kinds and many haunts was to be heard. There the nightingale prolonged her plaintive song, and the branches of the olive murmured musically in a sympathetic refrain. On the slenderest branch of a pine-tree the stirring of the breeze mocked the blackbird's call. And mingling with it all in harmony, Echo, the imitator of voices, uttered her answering cries. The combined sound of all these was soothing to hear . . . [12]

In Pleasantville David takes Margaret, a girl who embodies a Chloe-like perfection of beauty and innocence, on a first date to Lovers' Lane. Ross himself makes clear that he is firmly in classical territory in this scene. The description in his audio commentary of the *locus amoenus* which we see on screen again sounds Platonic:

We took to calling the sequence the Athenian sequence because it did have a certain mind–body ideal, and that's the reason that the design of that gazebo in the background has certain Greek Revival elements in it, because I wanted that tableau across the lake to have almost an Elysian kind of quality to it in the same way that a lot of Greek Revival paintings of England in the eighteenth century would use a piece of Greek Revival architecture across a pond because they were all kind of in a romantic era drunk on that Athenian ideal.

Readers of Plato will remember a comparable *locus amoenus* as the setting of the *Phaedrus*, whose subject is the nature of love and beauty.[13] The work culminates in the discussion of the true nature of knowledge. Socrates and Phaedrus converse under a high plane tree with a spring at its roots. A nearby grotto is sacred to Pan, the river god Achelous, and the nymphs. Pan and the nymphs play major parts in *Daphnis and Chloe*. As in the novel and in the *Aesop Romance*, cicadas are present in Plato's dialogue, too. Ross cannot include any gods in his modern story, but he needs a supernatural figure for his time-traveling plot. This is the strange television repairman who makes it possible for David and Jennifer to appear in Pleasantville. This figure has quasi-divine powers and functions as a kind of *deus ex*

---

[12] *The Aesop Romance* 6; quoted from the translation by Lloyd W. Daly in William Hansen 1998: 111–162; quotation at 114. This translation first appeared in Daly 1961. *The Aesop Romance* is a fictional biography, comparable to that of Till Eulenspiegel in German literature.

[13] Plato, *Phaedrus* 229a–230c.

*machina* – indeed, at certain points, as a *deus in machina*. He is even comparable to Longus' Pan in some respects: ugly in appearance and easily angered, but also ready to help the youngsters out of danger and on their journey toward self-discovery. Ross also infuses his Lovers' Lane setting with almost supernatural beauty. When David and Margaret approach in their car, a gentle rain of pink petals descends on them and swirls around their still partly black-and-white environment. On the soundtrack the ballad "At Last," a well-known love song from a time of innocence and romance, provides an aural complement to the scene's visual magic.[14]

An observation by the narrator at the beginning of *Daphnis and Chloe* applies to this scene. In the novel's prologue the narrator tells us that he saw "a painting that told a story of love" and that this painting inspired in him "a yearning to depict the picture in words." His verbal account of the painting contains the following description (*ecphrasis*) of nature and an evaluation of its artistic quality:

> The grove itself was beautiful – thickly wooded, flowery, well watered; a single spring nourished everything, flowers and trees alike. But the picture was lovelier still, combining great artistic skill with an exciting, romantic subject.[15]

These words characterize, virtually without a change, the setting we see in the film (Fig. 32). In antiquity the *locus amoenus* originally took the form of an enclosed garden, a *paradeisos*.[16] The pastoral world of Daphnis

---

[14] The song, composed by Harry Warren and written by Mack Gordon, was introduced in the Glenn Miller film *Orchestra Wives* (1942), directed by Archie Mayo, and became a standard. Ross originally planned to have Sam Cooke sing "Cupid, draw back your bow" instead.

[15] *Daphnis and Chloe*, Prologue 1–2; quotations from Gill in Reardon 1989: 288–289.

[16] The tradition of the *locus amoenus* – the expression is Cicero's: *Letters to His Friends* 7.20.2, *On the Orator* 2.71.290 – in ancient and later literature is too extensive to be addressed here in detail. See especially Bremmer 2002: 109–127 and 178–184 (notes; Appendix entitled "The Birth of the Term 'Paradise'"). It begins with the garden of the Phaeacian king Alcinous in Homer (*Odyssey* 7.114–131). On the subject see especially Schönbeck 1964 and Elliger 1975: 258–263 and 443–444. Haß 1998 does not fulfill the promise of her subtitle but collects the literary evidence. Xenophon's park (*Anabasis* 5.3.7–11) was modeled on Persian gardens; cf. Xenophon, *Oeconomicus* 4.13–14. For the wider context see Moynihan 1979 and Hobhouse 2003, especially 8–13 ("Enclosed Paradise") and 54–59 ("Alexander and the Hellenic Legacy"). Cf. further the Greek and Roman tradition of idyllic, bucolic, and erotic poetry and, in Rome, that of the *laudes Italiae*. Cf. also Snell 1953: 281–309 and 322–323 (notes; chapter entitled "Arcadia: The Discovery of a Spiritual Landscape"). On the influence of classical literature on medieval culture see especially Curtius 1952: 183–202 (a chapter on ideal landscape), with discussions of Homer, Plato, Theocritus, and Virgil, among others, and with a section on the *locus amoenus* (190–200). Curtius 195–197 quotes and translates Petronius, *Satyricon* 131.8, and a fourth-century poem by Tiberianus (*Anthologia Latina* 1.2.809) as prime examples from Roman literature. For the Renaissance see the classic overview by Burckhardt 1995: 190–197 ("Discovery of the Beauty of Landscape") and more recently Jäger 1990: 87–99 and the textual excerpts at 272 (Lorenzo de' Medici on the paradise garden), 275–276 (Leonardo), 280 (Isabella d'Este), 282–283 (Ariosto), and 303–304 (Armina's garden in Tasso's *Gerusalemme liberata*). Cf. also Maureen Carroll 2003 and Hobhouse 2003, both with lavish illustrations.

**Fig. 32.** *Pleasantville.* The *locus amoenus* in Pleasantville. (New Line Cinema)

and Chloe is such a garden on a larger scale. While not walled in, the environment of the country folk is largely self-contained; they have little if any desire to look or travel outside. Pleasantville, too, is completely enclosed, if without any tangible borders. In a revealing scene set in the town's high school we learn that there is no outside and that it has never occurred to any of the students or their teacher to ask if there is any place beyond where they live. Jennifer brings up this subject but meets only with incomprehension.[17] Paradise and *locus amoenus* depend on literal or figurative separation from the real and far less perfect world.

Just as *Daphnis and Chloe* begins with a painting that encapsulates and exemplifies the story that follows, so the film begins with a series of clips from the *Pleasantville* TV series, a visual summary to introduce viewers to the nature of the place. The film then proceeds to emphasize painting and literature as sources for the people's discovery of their minds and bodies. A kiss represents the first stage of love in both works. In both the discovery of physical beauty depends on sight, as when Daphnis sees Chloe naked for the first time or when in *Pleasantville* a group of hitherto asexual adults observe a pretty girl in a tight sweater walking by.

In *Daphnis and Chloe* and in *Pleasantville* knowledge causes uncertainties, difficulties, even dangers, and it has unpleasant consequences.

---

[17] The film does not, however, treat this complete isolation of Pleasantville in its fictional universe with complete consistency. A visiting sports team from a neighboring town is defeated by the Pleasantville team – as it must be in such a perfect world – and Jennifer eventually leaves Pleasantville but not the 1950s to attend college elsewhere.

Dealing with these brings increased knowledge to those whose lives had previously been simple and easy. In "The Grand Inquisitor," a famous part of *The Brothers Karamazov*, Dostoyevsky had already expressed the contrast between "happy infants" and "sufferers who have taken upon themselves the curse of knowledge of good and evil."[18]

But greater knowledge may come to the outsiders, too. In the novel Chloe's kidnapper Lampis is eventually forgiven and allowed to be present at her wedding, and a full-scale war between the Methymneans and the Mytileneans is avoided with surprising effortlessness. The conciliatory ending of Shakespeare's *As You Like It* is an apposite example from the later pastoral tradition. At the end of the film David and Jennifer also react to the changes they have brought to Pleasantville but do so in different ways. Jennifer decides to stay in this world, simple and still backwards as it is despite its changes, whereas David returns to today. He had comforted Betty by applying make-up to her face to allow her to appear in black and white after she had turned into color; in this way she could save face in front of her husband and the town's mayor, both black-and-white reactionaries. In a reversal of this moment after his return David comforts his real mother, who is stuck in a hopeless love affair after the breakup of her family, by wiping off her make-up to allow her face to regain its natural beauty. This, too, is a moment reminiscent of *Daphnis and Chloe*: Chloe's face, when washed, reveals her innate beauty. David and Jennifer, Ross makes evident, have been both teachers and learners.

Are *Daphnis and Chloe* and *Pleasantville* instances of the *Bildungsroman*, the kind of nineteenth- and twentieth-century narrative that charts a character's or characters' progress toward knowledge, education, and self-reliance? In his study of the Greek romances Bakhtin gives a negative answer for Longus' novel – rightly so because the psychological realism of the modern novel is not to be expected from its ancient precursors. The same answer is appropriate for *Pleasantville*. The film deals with the process of learning and insight and touches on larger issues of knowledge and history such as McCarthyism and race relations, but all its characters, even those in the modern frame story, are intentionally left too schematic to be "round" in Forster's sense of the word. But with some appropriate changes one particular aspect of the *Bildungsroman* to which Bakhtin refers applies to the film. Bakhtin observes that in the novels of Stendhal, Balzac, and Flaubert

---

[18] Dostoyevsky 1958: 304.

the issue is primarily one of overturning and demolishing the world view and psychology of the idyll, which proved increasingly inadequate to the new capitalist world . . . the capitalist world is . . . not idealized, its inhumanity is laid bare, the destruction within it of all ethical systems . . . , the disintegration of all previous human relationships . . . , love, the family, friendship . . . – all of these are emphasized.[19]

In its frame story *Pleasantville* shows us a capitalist world whose social fabric is fraying. We could update Bakhtin's observations by replacing the term "capitalist world" with "technological world" to describe the life and society of today. In *Pleasantville* the supernatural power of the TV repairman makes it possible for David and Jennifer to return to the past – which, being on television, is itself a creation of modern technology. In today's visual media such technology creates a new variant on the idyllic chronotope which Bakhtin had found in the ancient novels. Now computer technology makes it possible for writer-director Ross to tell his story in the most effective way to large audiences. All the black-and-white images on the screen are really color images, for they were originally filmed in color and then digitally turned into black and white. Only in this way was it possible for Ross to show both colors and black-and-white side by side in individual frames and to make entire scenes appear convincing and realistic to technologically sophisticated viewers. From this perspective, then, we might be justified to call *Pleasantville* a kind of visual *Bildungsroman*: a highly technological world becomes the subject of a story about the journey from innocence to experience and knowledge and provides the means of telling this story. That it has numerous points of comparison with literary works almost two millennia old makes the phenomenon only the more remarkable.

Differences of time and space, of *chronos* and *topos*, between *Daphnis and Chloe* and *Pleasantville* and between an ancient literary medium and a modern medium of moving images remain. But the similarities in both stories and their narrative stances are too noticeable to be overlooked. So we may readily think of *Pleasantville* when we remember what the narrator of *Daphnis and Chloe* has to say about the purpose of his attempt to transpose the painting he describes at the beginning into a story. His work is meant to be

something for mankind to possess and enjoy. It will cure the sick, comfort the distressed, stir the memory of those who have loved, and educate those who

---

[19] Bakhtin 1981: 234–235.

haven't. For certainly no one has ever avoided Love, and no one will, as long as beauty exists, and eyes can see.[20]

### SEDUCTION BY LUXURY: CLEOPATRA AND HER ROYAL BARGE

During the reign of Cleopatra VII, the last queen of Egypt, the Roman Republic was on the verge of becoming a world power. The Romans themselves ascribed their rise in the western Mediterranean to their traditional virtues like frugality, hardihood, and tenacity. But in the wake of their political and military dealings with the eastern parts of the Mediterranean the Romans encountered a strange new world: civilizations far older than their own, divine rulers in absolute power, vast riches and luxury and, inseparable from these in Roman eyes, vice and depravity. The contrast between Rome and the East in historical fact and in the popular imagination ever since was greatest in regard to Egypt, the Hellenistic kingdom ruled by the successors of Alexander the Great. This contrast is the basis of what we now term Orientalism.[21] Its most famous representation is the description of the Battle of Actium among the decorations on the shield of Aeneas in Virgil's *Aeneid*. In that battle for supreme power Octavian, Julius Caesar's heir, defeated Cleopatra and Mark Antony in 31 BC and made Egypt a province of the Roman Empire. In the *Aeneid* the difference between the fully anthropomorphic Roman gods and the animal-headed Egyptian gods who participate in the battle is meant to point to the difference between both worlds.[22]

The contrast between East and West, here outlined in only the briefest terms, is focused most clearly on Rome's dealings with Cleopatra. One specific moment of her biography illustrates the public and private sides of her character especially well. This is her encounter with Mark Antony at Tarsus in Cilicia near the mouth of the river Cydnus in 41 BC. Cleopatra had sailed from Egypt to Tarsus in one of the most wondrous ships ever built. The summit meeting, to which she had been summoned by Antony to give a political account of herself but whose purpose she turned on its head by turning *his* head, reveals the fascination which Cleopatra has exerted over the historical and popular imagination since her own time.

Her royal barge is a symbol of her wealth and power as a queen, of her astuteness and wiliness as a politician, and of her irresistible seductiveness

---

[20] *Daphnis and Chloe*, Prologue 3–4; quotation from Gill in Reardon 1989: 289.
[21] Cf. especially Said 1978, a highly influential work.
[22] Virgil, *Aeneid* 8.630–728, especially 675–713.

as a woman. This tradition begins with the Greek biographer Plutarch (ca. 50–120 AD), who lived and wrote in a thoroughly Roman-dominated world. The chief goal of Plutarch's biographies was to present to his readers great men and occasionally women whose exemplary characters, as he observes, are revealed not only in their great deeds and accomplishments but often also in small gestures or sayings.[23] Details and anecdotes are Plutarch's chief means of bringing his subjects to life. This and his facility at dramatizing past events are among the principal reasons for the wide and enduring popularity of his writings. His description of Cleopatra's barge in his *Life* of Antony is a case in point. It prepares his readers for the unexpected reversal of the intended outcome of their meeting. The barge sets the stage for Cleopatra's utter bamboozling of Antony and makes her success in seducing him credible to all readers, then and now, but especially to Roman readers, in whose society women had never yet held as exalted a position as Cleopatra did. Not only that; the barge scene also shows that Antony's defeat by Cleopatra's cunning was all but unavoidable. For how could anyone, least of all a man with Antony's eye for the ladies, resist someone who appeared to him in the following manner:

she came sailing up the river Cydnus, in a barge with gilded stern and outspread sails of purple, while oars of silver beat time to the music of flutes and fifes and harps. She herself lay all along, under a canopy of cloth of gold, dressed as Venus in a picture, and beautiful young boys, like painted Cupids, stood on each side to fan her. Her maids were dressed like Sea Nymphs and Graces, some steering at the rudder, some working at the ropes. The perfumes diffused themselves from the vessel to the shore, which was covered with multitudes, part following the galley up the river on either bank, part running out of the city to see the sight.[24]

This vivid description was Shakespeare's model in *Antony and Cleopatra* for a famous passage intended to make Cleopatra's extraordinary character unforgettable. Shakespeare assigns Antony's friend Enobarbus the task to describe Cleopatra to the Romans Maecenas, Octavian's close

---

[23] Plutarch, *Life of Alexander* 1.

[24] Plutarch, *Life of Antony* 26. The quotation is from volume twelve in the Harvard Classics series (Plutarch 1909: 353). The volume's frontispiece is Alexander Cabanel's 1897 painting "Cleopatra Testing Poisons on Condemned Prisoners." Since the prisoners are not included in the reproduction, the effect of the image is to show Cleopatra as a languidly luxurious seductress. On the encounter of Antony and Cleopatra and on her vessel see the commentary by Pelling 1988: 186–189. – Antony's easy susceptibility to female charms is mentioned by Appian, *The Civil Wars* 5.8. Green 1990: 670 and 682 ascribes "philoprogenitive womanizing" to Antony and posthumous "mesmerizing fascination" to Cleopatra.

friend, and Agrippa, the architect of Cleopatra's eventual defeat at Actium. Until now both have only heard rumors about her. Shakespeare follows Plutarch more closely here than anywhere else in the play although he considerably heightens the erotic atmosphere of their meeting in view of the love tragedy to come. Taking his cue from Plutarch's report that Cleopatra appeared as the goddess of love accompanied by Cupids, Shakespeare outdoes his source by charging the whole atmosphere surrounding Cleopatra with such an air of eroticism that it extends even to nature itself:

> The barge she sat in, like a burnished throne,
> Burned on the water; the poop was beaten gold;
> Purple the sails, and so perfúmèd that
> The winds were love-sick with them; the oars were silver,
> Which to the tune of flutes kept stroke, and made
> The water which they beat to follow faster,
> As amorous of their strokes. For her own person,
> It beggared all description: she did lie
> In her pavilion, cloth-of-gold of tissue,
> O'erpicturing that Venus where we see
> The fancy outwork nature. On each side her
> Stood pretty dimpled boys, like smiling cupids,
> With divers-coloured fans, whose wind did seem
> To glow the delicate cheeks which they did cool,
> And what they undid did . . .
> Her gentlewomen, like the Néreïdes,
> So many mermaids, tended her i'th' eyes,
> And made their bends adornings. At the helm
> A seeming mermaid steers. The silken tackle
> Swell with the touches of those flower-soft hands
> That yarely frame the office. From the barge
> A strange invisible perfume hits the sense
> Of the adjacent wharfs. The city cast
> Her people out upon her, and . . .
> th'air, which, but for vacancy,
> Had gone to gaze on Cleopatra, too,
> And made a gap in nature.

Enobarbus' account prepares the way for the greatest encomium to Cleopatra ever written. Less than twenty lines later Enobarbus summarizes Cleopatra's fascination in the ringing words which have become the most famous passage from the play. Its beginning is now one of the most familiar quotations from the entire work:

Age cannot wither her, nor custom stale
Her infinite variety. Other women cloy
The appetites they feed, but she makes hungry
Where most she satisfies . . . [25]

The tributes to Cleopatra in Plutarch's and Shakespeare's descriptions of her arrival at Tarsus find their closest modern equivalent on the cinema screen. This decisive moment in history demands to be a prominent scene in any film about Cleopatra. Among cinematic reconstructions of her barge, two stand out: those in Cecil B. DeMille's *Cleopatra* of 1934 and in Joseph L. Mankiewicz's ill-fated *Cleopatra* of 1963.[26]

Cecil B. DeMille, whose name has become a byword for Hollywood epics of the 1930s, 1940s, and 1950s, was out to make "an epic with sex" about Cleopatra, as he put it without mincing words.[27] Since the silent era DeMille's trademark and the source of his commercial appeal had been a potent mixture of sex, sadism, and sanctimoniousness. With *Cleopatra* he succeeded only too well. DeMille made the barge scene the high point of his plot. At more than fifteen minutes this is the longest individual sequence and biggest set-piece in a 100-minute film. By comparison Caesar's triumphant entry into Rome and the Battle of Actium look downright puny. But there is a telling difference between DeMille's and Mankiewicz's approaches to the barge scene. Mankiewicz conveyed the sense of epic grandeur and sweeping spectacle to his viewers by going on location off the coast of Ibiza and showing us a real ship, then moving onto a soundstage to continue the sequence in which Cleopatra first wines and dines Antony and then seduces him. DeMille, on the other hand, did not have the luxury of a real ship; his barge was no more than a miniature, which we see only briefly. But he more than made up for this shortcoming with an extraordinary scene of the meeting of the two antagonists and soon-to-be lovers on board the ship. DeMille fully realized the goal he pursued with this sequence. As he described its purpose:

---

[25] Shakespeare, *Antony and Cleopatra* 2.2.201–224, 226–228, and 245–248. The text is quoted from Shakespeare 1995: 139–142 (accents added). On Shakespeare's sources for the play, especially Plutarch – via Sir Thomas North's 1579 translation from the French version by Jacques Amyot (1559) – see the editor's survey in Shakespeare 1995: 56–69.

[26] Americans have always been fascinated with antiquity, especially with what they conceive of being ancient luxury and ostentation. The first sea-going yacht built in America was Captain George Crowninshield's brigantine *Cleopatra's Barge*, launched in 1816. One of the bars in Caesars Palace in Las Vegas today has its own kind of Cleopatra's barge, with cocktail waitresses in skimpy fake-ancient miniskirts.

[27] Quoted from Higham 1973: 230.

Cleopatra is here putting on a show deliberately, with the intention of so astonishing the tough, hard soldier Antony that he will have to remain long enough for her to get in her deadly work. This entire barge sequence should be the most seductive, erotic, beautiful, rhythmic, sensuous series of scenes ever shown.[28]

DeMille filmed the indoor sequence on an immense set in lavish *art déco* style.[29] No ingenuity and no lavishness are spared to show us the luxury of Egypt and the seductiveness of its queen.[30] Even more to the point, there is no shortage of blatant sex. We see, for example, Cleopatra, her handmaid Charmian, and assorted dancers all sensuously dressed in tight-fitting and revealing clothes, a sexy lady riding on the back of a handsome bull and suggestively caressing its neck, a group of writhing sea nymphs, and a troupe of balletic leopard women engaged in make-believe cat fights and jumping through flaming hoops to the cracks of a male dancer's whip.[31] That this sequence was to be the high point of a never-before-seen Hollywood extravaganza had become evident during filming, as the account of an eye-witness attests. The description by a gossip columnist of her visit to the studio is worth quoting in some detail, even if her tone of breathless eagerness and her forced attempts at humor have dated rather badly:

[28] Quoted from Birchard 2004: 279.

[29] On *art déco* film sets and costumes see, e.g., Mandelbaum and Myers 1985 and Fischer 2003.

[30] This has been the case in all film portrayals of ancient vamps, not only Cleopatra. In lieu of a long excursus on this fascinating topic I limit myself to three revealing examples: Betty Blythe as the title character in J. Gordon Edwards's *The Queen of Sheba* (1921), Gina Lollobrigida in the same part in King Vidor's *Solomon and Sheba* (1959), and, perhaps most influentially, the aptly if pseudonymously named Theda Bara in the title part of Edwards's *Cleopatra* (1917). The studio publicized her name as being an anagram of "Arab death" to enhance the allure of her wily exoticism; her real name, however, told a rather different story for she was actually Theodosia Goodman, a nice Jewish girl from Cincinnati. Both of Edwards's epics are lost except for a few still photographs. (So is his *Salome* of 1918, again with Bara.) Concerning one part of her dress (if that is the word), Bara's may have been the most influential of all film Cleopatras. Her brassiere in the form of a metal snake curving around her curves may be the most ingenious piece of modern costume engineering ever invented for an ancient character, even if it lacks somewhat in support. A homage to it is worn by Rie Rasmussen in Brian de Palma's appropriately named contemporary thriller *Femme Fatale* (2002); an earlier variant winds itself around the chest of Julie Ege as slave girl Voluptua in the farcical British television series *Up Pompeii* (1971).

[31] DeMille even went so far as to suggest, in entirely good taste, of course, to those among his viewers who had the benefit of a classical education that the lady and the bull might be lovers: "when Antony tries to free himself from the spell being cast over him, I see a bull led before him, on the back of which lies a beautiful dancer, whose costume suggests, perhaps, the mate of the bull. Perhaps her headgear is horns, and her shoes are hoofs, like Edmund Dulac's EUROPA AND THE BULL." Quoted from Birchard 2004: 280. Mention of Dulac's painting elevates DeMille's outrageous idea to a level at which it becomes culturally acceptable.

C. B. De Mille is directing a super colossal spectacle . . . which is a sure-fire eye-popper-outer . . . The barge sequence is the *pièce de résistance* of the picture. It's the epitome of colossalness. It's the umpty-umph of all times. It's got everything. There's barbaric music more exciting to the senses than a shot in the arm – there's a nude girl dancing on the back of a black bull – there's a leopard dance with real leopards and real girls – there are dozens of half-clad slave girls and slave boys and burly Nubians – there're thousands of ostrich plumes waving exotically over the exquisite white body of Egypt's queen – there's a net drawn up from the sea from which beautiful maidens emerge, dripping with seaweed, with clams for the delectation of Antony. And last, but not least, there is Cleopatra, fascinating and beautiful witch of the Nile, luring Antony with the hottest lure of the season . . . when she puts her mind on a bit of luring – well – sex goes on a rampage. Poor old Antony can't take it.[32]

That all this exotic eroticism still delivers the goods today is due not only to DeMille but also in large measure to actress Claudette Colbert, whose Cleopatra comes closest of all in film history to conveying an idea of what Shakespeare may have had in mind about her infinite variety. Colbert was "that rarity for an historical epic, a star whose performance succeeds in matching, even outshining, a monumental production."[33] DeMille himself later observed: "In all her scenes . . . she was perfect. She was the imperious Queen. She was the vivacious, alluring woman. She was Egypt."[34]

Colbert's Cleopatra is a sex kitten, a cunning politician, a clever wit, a good sport, and a "buddy" who can match Antony goblet for goblet (Fig. 33). With her dark bangs and smoky voice this Cleopatra is nearly indistinguishable from an American high-society girl of the Roaring Twenties. The tradition of Hollywood's "sophisticated comedies" and DeMille's own experience of directing racy marriage and divorce farces during the Jazz Age helped considerably to lend coherence to the sequence. But Cleopatra is a passionate woman who finds out that she has been caught in the very trap which she had set for Antony to manipulate him with sex and seductiveness. She falls for him just as much as he falls for her. Claudette Colbert comes closest to an ideal Cleopatra for the twentieth century, surpassing the 1963 Cleopatra of Elizabeth Taylor in smarts and physical allure. Colbert looks ravishing in all her costumes, most of which she is barely wearing, while Taylor looks the more attractive the more she keeps herself covered.

The end of the barge scene brings the film's emotional and stylistic high point. Antony gets to bed Cleopatra but is unaware that not he but she is completely in charge, for with a slight nod of her head she signals her

---

[32] Elizabeth Wilson 1934: 21 and 69.   [33] Searles 1990: 44.   [34] DeMille 1959: 338.

**Fig. 33.** *Cleopatra* (1934). Cleopatra and Antony on her barge. (Paramount)

majordomo to have the barge sail away. Slow romantic music now rises
on the soundtrack. Experienced filmmaker that he is, DeMille rises to
the occasion that this moment affords him. When the lovers sink down
to consummate their passion, handmaids chastely draw veils before their
divan, and we are meant to realize that DeMille is a gentleman filmmaker
with good taste and a sense of discretion. But really the moment signals
the very opposite, driving home the point that Antony and Cleopatra
are beginning to make love. By piously hiding from view what he could
never show on the screen anyway, DeMille makes only too clear what is
happening. He ensures that we cannot miss the sexual climax that is now
about to take place by providing us with a visual one. DeMille moves his
camera along his vast stage and away from the lovers in an extended and
stately traveling shot that lasts for about a minute and twenty seconds.
But this traveling shot is unneccesary for the story and occurs solely for
the sake of the spectators. Its dramatic function is to reinforce the viewers'
sense of what is happening behind the curtains and to convey the film's
epic greatness to them, for the shot provides DeMille with an opportunity
to show off his gigantic set (Fig. 34).

**Fig. 34.** *Cleopatra* (1934). The immense studio set of Cleopatra's barge. (Paramount)

In this way DeMille cleverly transposes Plutarch's and Shakespeare's outdoor descriptions of Cleopatra's seductive luxuriousness indoors. He is not faithful to the letters of his literary sources, but he captures their spirit. He conveys a sense of the perfumed eroticism wafting in the air all around the barge when, inside, his camera shows us a veritable rain of presumably perfumed flower petals descending from the ceiling and a row of incense burners. In a visual masterstroke that takes the viewer by surprise the camera pulling back reveals two double rows of huge oar handles on either side of the screen. Their tips are decorated with gilded or silvered rams' heads. The measured movement of the oars, whose rowers remain largely invisible, increases the scene's aura of enchantment. The camera continues to move back along the entire set and then gradually rises to look down upon it, all the while showing us a symmetrical picture of the hall. The music and the rhythmic movement of the oars are parallel to the camera's movement. This elegant shot is the most accomplished transfer of outdoors to indoors. Concluding it, DeMille dissolves to the miniature of his barge moving into the nightly distance across a romantic-looking sea bathed in silvery moonlight.

As was customary for him, DeMille had extensive research done on ancient history and on Cleopatra's barge. The process by which he adapted Plutarch's account to his grandiose visual recreation of Cleopatra's seductive environment on board her vessel mixes fact with imagination. Our eye-witness to the filming quotes what she reports to have been DeMille's textual blueprint for the sequence on this "really gorgeous set." It combines an eclecticism of details taken from Plutarch and the eroticism taken from Shakespeare into a flight of free-wheeling fancy:

The royal galley was rowed by banks of silver-mounted oars, the great purple sails hanging idly in the still air of the evening. Around the helmsmen a number of beautiful slave-women were grouped in the guise of sea-nymphs and graces; and near them a company of musicians played a melody on their flutes, pipes and harps, for which the slow-moving oars seemed to beat time. Cleopatra herself, decked in the loose shimmering robes of the Goddess Venus, lay under an awning spangled with gold, while boys dressed as Cupids . . . stood on either side of her couch, fanning her with colored ostrich plumes of the Egyptian court. Before the royal canopy brazen censers . . . stood upon delicate pedestals, sending forth fragrant clouds of exquisitely prepared Egyptian incense.

Twelve triple couches, covered with embroideries and furnished with cushions, were set around the room, before each of which stood a table whereon rested golden dishes inlaid with precious stones, and drinking goblets of exquisite work-manship . . . Cleopatra caused the floor of the saloon to be strewn with roses to the depth of nearly two feet, the flowers being held in solid formation by nets which were tightly spread over them and fastened to the surrounding walls, the guests thus walking to their couches upon a perfumed mattress of blooms.[35]

The close-up that DeMille gives Cleopatra just before the tracking shot is the most beautiful and most affecting individual image in the entire film (Fig. 35). Claudette Colbert's face bears a serene and regal but also a smoldering expression; this Cleopatra is a beautiful, seductive, and sexually experienced woman. At the moment that we see her all woman and lover, however, she reveals herself all queen as well, because with her nod she effectively takes Antony prisoner.[36] The emotional intensity of the close-up prepares the way for the tracking shot during which everything – sound, image, and motion – is in perfect sync, completed by the dissolve to the moonlit barge and the scene's fade-out. Not only Antony, but we, too, have been thoroughly captivated by this charming and wily Cleopatra.

---

[35] Elizabeth Wilson 1934: 69.
[36] The moment is patterned on the scene in Shakespeare's play in which Sextus Pompey declines to take Octavian prisoner in a comparable situation (*Antony and Cleopatra* 2.7; after Plutarch, *Life of Antony* 32).

**Fig. 35.** *Cleopatra* (1934). Queen and seductress: the most ravishing single image in DeMille's film. (Paramount)

About thirty years later we see the most faithful and the greatest recon-struction of her barge in Mankiewicz's *Cleopatra*. That Plutarch was its acknowledged source becomes clear from the Movietonews featurette "The Fourth Star of *Cleopatra*," a promotional "documentary" that was shown in theaters before the release of the film in order to whet viewers' appetites for the epic to come. The short film takes us behind the scenes of the produc-tion of *Cleopatra* and presents us, in its narrator's words, with "the fabulous story behind a fabulous film about a fabulous woman – Cleopatra." After its three human stars Elizabeth Taylor (Cleopatra), Richard Burton (Mark Antony), and Rex Harrison (Julius Caesar), the titular fourth star is "the production itself," as the narrator tells us. We see drawings of the barge and witness its launch. Twentieth-Century Fox had built a sea-going vessel that was more than 250 feet long and cost $277,000.[37] The narrator has this to say about it:

[37] This information is from Beuselink 1988: 10. The size of Cleopatra's barge is quite accurately reproduced. The largest such vessel (in Greek, *thalamegos*: "cabin carrier") of which we know was 300 feet long; cf. Pelling 1988: 187–188. Bernstein 1994: 343–386 and 429–431 (notes) gives a detailed outline of the film's production history and the studio background. For older sources see especially Wanger and Hyams 1963 and Brodsky and Weiss 1963. Geist 1978: 302–345 is the chief scholarly source on this film.

Elizabeth Taylor had at her disposal a ship fit for a queen. Cleopatra's barge was designed to fit closely to this description by Plutarch: "She came sailing up the river Cydnus, in a barge with a gilded stern and outspread sails of purple, while oars of silver beat time to the music of flutes and fifes and harps. She herself lay under a canopy of cloth of gold, dressed as Venus."

The quotation from Plutarch is taken almost verbatim from the once popular Harvard Classics translation quoted above. In the early 1960s Plutarch's name was still so familiar to the American public that it could be mentioned without any information about who he was. In the promotional film the barge looks impressive even in its anachronistic modern surroundings, but its first appearance in the feature film is miraculous. The film suffered cruelly from major problems during production and post-production, and the studio eventually cut it by more than half of its intended length. As a result some of the release version is mediocre and occasionally ridiculous. But the film's greatness comes through in several scenes. For this, chief credit goes to writer-director Mankiewicz, one of the most intelligent and sophisticated filmmakers ever to work in Hollywood. His original conception of Antony and Cleopatra was meant to make for an epic film different from the standard kind:

> He had in mind more than a stereotypical epic with the traditional dashes of De Millian sex and violence. Mankiewicz understood Antony as a desperate follower in Caesar's capacious footsteps, but insecure in battle, politics and love and eventually destroyed by his fatal love for Cleopatra. As for the queen, the writer-director saw her as the first woman to rule in a man's world and in a man's way. With such ideas, Mankiewicz fired Elizabeth's imagination.[38]

The spectacular highlight of the first part of *Cleopatra* is her triumphal procession into the Roman Forum on a gigantic basalt sphinx drawn by slaves before Caesar, Antony, and the senate and people of Rome. Its equivalent in the second part is the barge scene. Mankiewicz succeeds exceptionally well in his adaptation of Plutarch's text to a visual medium, free as it is in several details. He manages to turn Cleopatra's arrival at Tarsus into a divine epiphany, as if a goddess were descending to earth and revealing herself in her glory to mortals. The scene's musical accompaniment prepares us for Cleopatra's quasi-Olympian arrival. To prepare his viewers for Cleopatra's "big, big scene," Mankiewicz invented a slightly titillating but also charming moment in which Cleopatra thinks of a way to meet Antony without appearing to yield to his summons and without leaving

---

[38] Quoted from Spoto 1995: 177. His penchant to adduce or quote classical literature (Catullus, for instance, appears at 192) is more pretentious than illuminating.

**Fig. 36.** *Cleopatra* (1963). Cleopatra and her bathtub toy. (Twentieth Century-Fox)

Egyptian soil.[39] The toy ship with which she plays in the bath in her palace at Alexandria is – of course – a small-scale model of her barge (Fig. 36). We will soon realize that it serves as a clever visual link from a private moment to a dramatic scene of overwhelming public display. Alex North composed one of the best scores ever written for a historical epic, surpassing even his earlier one for Stanley Kubrick's *Spartacus* (1960).[40] His music expresses both sides of Cleopatra's character. While we are still observing her in her bath, a gentle *pianissimo* rhythmically begins to insinuate itself into our ears, indicating the moment in which she conceives her idea of how to meet Antony. Under a dissolve on the screen it continues with a ravishing *crescendo* that prepares us for the effect which the first sight of her barge has on the people of Tarsus. For a moment we witness the surprised reactions of shepherds in the fields, women washing at the well, and several people falling on their knees or raising their hands as if to a divinity. The music even more than their behavior arouses our curiosity. The musical theme signifies the imperial power, wealth, and sensuousness of Cleopatra and the East. The same theme had accompanied Cleopatra's epiphany in the Roman Forum. There, to underscore her public appearance as a political figure, North had scored his theme primarily for brass, fifes, and drums; in the barge scene with its seductive and supernatural overtones the scoring is chiefly for strings, including a harp, and reeds. North here takes his cue

---

[39] The quotation is from Brodsky and Weiss 1963: 134. The authors were the studio's publicists for the film.

[40] Saada 1998 briefly discusses North's music for the film and concludes: "The score of *Cleopatra* is film music at its most subtly effective" (80).

**Fig. 37.** *Cleopatra* (1963). The real thing: Cleopatra's sea-going barge. (Twentieth Century-Fox)

directly from Plutarch: "the music of flutes and fifes and harps."[41] After the music has prepared us, Mankiewicz's cut to the actual appearance of the barge on the screen delivers the pay-off. Like the people of Tarsus we, too, are struck by wonder and amazement, particularly if we have the good fortune to see this scene as it was meant to be experienced: on a huge theater screen. Mankiewicz, with expert support from North, proves himself a consummate visual artist (Fig. 37).

The people's reaction, running up to see the barge or accompanying it along the shore, closely follows Plutarch. So do the shape and look of the barge and of Cleopatra's female attendants, although Mankiewicz is justified not to adhere slavishly to Plutarch in every detail. Despite fifty years of erotic titillation from Hollywood Cleopatra's beautiful young boys dressed as Cupids were probably too much for Puritan America to make it onto her modern barge. This barge proudly displays the purple sails which Plutarch mentions – now made of Dacron and flown in from California – but the oars are furnished with golden, not silver, blades. An eye-witness report about the day on which the scene was filmed states:

The barge is way out at sea, never so golden in the sun, never so sumptuously decorated and peopled. It is a thing of perfect beauty to mark the moment when she sails into Tarsus to meet Antony.[42]

---

[41] The film's other main theme, which describes Cleopatra the lover – i.e. the private Cleopatra – is one of the most gentle and haunting musical themes to be found in all of Hollywood's Roman epics. It is somewhat reminiscent of the love theme North had composed for *Spartacus*.

[42] Brodsky and Weiss 1963: 134.

We cannot smell the perfumes which "diffused themselves from the vessel to the shore," but the purple clouds which emanate from the barge fully convey the eroticism implied in Plutarch's words. His – and Shakespeare's – Cleopatra is dressed in Greek garb as the goddess of love and lies under a canopy; Mankiewicz's Cleopatra, standing up, wears an Egyptian dress of gold. This latter detail Mankiewicz takes from Shakespeare ("cloth-of-gold") who, in turn, had taken it from Plutarch. Cleopatra is at first separated from direct view by a diaphanous curtain which makes her canopy appear like a shrine. When her handmaids Iras and Charmian ritually draw the curtain aside, we witness the high point of Cleopatra's epiphany: the goddess revealing herself to the eyes of mortals, with a number of other handmaids prostrate on the steps before her. "Even Joe [Mankiewicz] seems pleased, and he is his toughest critic."[43]

The most notorious aspect of *Cleopatra* was not the film but the illicit and torrid romance of its stars, Taylor and Burton.[44] Their affair and the whole history of the making of *Cleopatra* carry some noteworthy parallels to ancient times. The struggle for power over the studio between Fox executives Spyros Skouras and Darryl F. Zanuck is *en miniature* a fight for supremacy. At Cleopatra's time Rome was fighting one with Antony and Octavian on opposing sides. (In the two pairs of antagonists those here named first both lost.) The result was a weakened Roman Empire, at least for a while, and an exhausted and almost bankrupt studio, at least for a while. But the Taylor–Burton affair exhibited specific parallels to the meeting of Cleopatra and Antony. Antony was known to be a ladies' man.[45] Cleopatra was, well, Cleopatra. Taylor and Burton both had a reputation as sexual predators, too. Taylor was the woman who had broken up the apparently happy home and marriage of Debbie Reynolds and Eddie Fisher and who in due course was to leave Fisher for Burton.[46] He was an inveterate seducer of beautiful women although like Antony he was a husband and father. Just as Antony had been disdainful of Cleopatra before meeting her on board her barge, so Burton was initially contemptuous of Taylor. Before flying down from England to meet her at Rome's Cinecittà studios for their first scene together, he said sarcastically: "I've got to don my breastplate

---

[43] Brodsky and Weiss 1963: 151.
[44] The following is indebted chiefly to Geist 1978: 302–345 and Kamp 1998. Cf. Heymann 1995: 234–260.
[45] Plutarch repeatedly refers to Antony's love life (*Life of Antony* 2, 4, 6, 9–10, and 24).
[46] Bernstein 1994: 376: "By the time she closed out on *Cleopatra*, she had been condemned by Vatican City officials, by letters to the [American] print media, and . . . by American politicians."

once more to play opposite Miss Tits."[47] Taylor was originally wary of Burton and determined not to become another one of his conquests. She had met him years earlier at a Hollywood party: "He flirted like mad with me, with everyone, with any girl who was even remotely pretty. I just thought, 'Ohhh, boy – I'm not gonna become a notch on *his* belt.'" These words are echoed in the film when Cleopatra declares, before agreeing to meet with Antony: "I do not intend to join that long list of queens who've quivered happily at being summoned by Lord Antony." But such determination was of no avail, as Taylor soon realized: "For the first scene, there was no dialogue – we had to just look at each other. And that was it – I was another notch." Walter Wanger, the film's producer, understood this well: "There comes a time during the making of a movie when the actors become the characters they play," he wrote in his diary after Taylor and Burton had filmed their first scene together. Mankiewicz, too, noticed the hidden passion early on and told Wanger: "Liz and Burton are not just *playing* Antony and Cleopatra." When the two ignored his shouts of "Cut!" during a love scene, Mankiewicz said: "I feel as if I'm intruding." Even the air of sensuality and eroticism which pervaded Cleopatra's barge had its modern parallel. In the words of actress Jean Marsh, who played Octavia, Antony's Roman wife: "the film was so extravagant, so louche, it affected everyone's lives. It was a hotbed of romance – Richard and Elizabeth weren't the only people who had an affair."[48]

As did his historical model, the film's Antony leaves Cleopatra and returns to Rome, where he marries Octavia for reasons of state. This, too, has a parallel in the Taylor–Burton romance. When Burton at one point told Taylor that their affair was over – he had been carrying on with a Copacabana dancer at the same time – she became hysterical and could not work the next day. In the film Cleopatra, informed that Antony has just married Octavia, stabs their bed and his clothes in a fit of uncontrollable rage. This scene, for which there is no ancient source, was filmed the same day Burton told the press that he would never leave his wife, Sybil Williams.

---

[47] Quoted from Geist 1978: 321; slightly differently also in Bragg 1988: 145. Burton had had the main part in Henry Koster's biblical epic *The Robe* (1953) and the title part in Robert Rossen's *Alexander the Great* (1956). According to Cottrell and Cashin 1972: 193, Burton was rumored to have been impressed with Taylor's body ("a miracle of construction") and chest ("apocalyptic") on first seeing her in 1952.

[48] Quotations (except for the one from the film) from Kamp 1998: 382–385. As Taylor remembered about her first scene with Burton on *Cleopatra* and, as she implies, about Burton's intention to seduce her: "If it had been a planned strategic campaign, Caesar couldn't have done it better. He was captivating. My heart went out to him." But this could work in both directions. Taylor's former husband Michael Wilding once described her as "a seething mass of feminine wiles." Both quotations are from Cottrell and Cashin 1972: 216 and 224.

A biographer of Burton reports on this scene: "The lines [of dialogue] were feeding the parts. When Elizabeth had to go mad – as Cleopatra – at the news that Antony had married the sister of Octavius, it was reported that she cried 'Sybil!' as she slashed the set to ribbons."[49] Taylor expended so much energy on acting the wrathful and jealous jilted woman that she hurt her hand, had to go to a hospital for X-rays, and was unable to return to work the following day. As *Time* magazine commented in an August, 1962, article on the Taylor–Burton affair: "If she loses him, she loses her reputation as a fatal beauty, an all-consuming man-eater, the Cleopatra of the twentieth century."[50] Sometimes history repeats itself even in a film studio, if not as tragedy or epic then as farce. A biographer of Taylor quotes the film's director and comments:

"She was the reverse of most other stars," said Mankiewicz. "For her, living life was a kind of acting." And the life she was now [i.e. during filming] living was astonishingly like that of Cleopatra. Acting . . . for Elizabeth . . . was a nonintellectual but complete involvement: no role was more seriously assumed than that of the queen of the Nile. From childhood, the cyclorama against which she had played out her life was the fantasy of her movie scripts, and none was more potent – or more enduring – than that of Cleopatra . . . Indeed, for the rest of her life, Elizabeth Taylor tended most often to apply the excessive blue eyelid makeup designed for *Cleopatra* . . . There was a modern version of that story [Cleopatra's] in the contours of her own life. Whether Elizabeth chose consciously to read it there does not matter: she lived, thenceforth, according to the pattern idealized in the account of the ultimate femme fatale.[51]

*Le scandale*, as Taylor, Burton, and others called it, made international celebrities of them both.[52] In retrospect it seems altogether fitting that circumstances of production should have forced director Mankiewicz to film the barge scene as the last major sequence of the film, when the scandal had become common knowledge. In this way the spectacle of a regal and seductive celebrity appearing on screen makes for a dual apotheosis, of Cleopatra and of her modern incarnation. Audiences were lured to the theaters less by the spectacular story of a notorious and sexy queen from the past than by the hot story of her modern counterpart. Sex and scandal always sell. The narrator of the promotional featurette could boast over shots of scantily clad dancing girls at a rehearsal: "These scenes from *Cleopatra* are renewing interest in ancient history all around the world." And in due course an American greeting card could proclaim: "Like

[49] Bragg 1988: 151.   [50] Quoted from Heymann 1995: 257.   [51] Spoto 1995: 196–197 and 203.
[52] Cf. Alexander Walker 1991: 237–245 (chapter "Le scandale") and 246–252 (chapter "L'amour fou").

Romeo and Juliet, like Antony and Cleopatra, like Liz and Dick – Love is forever."[53]

With *Cleopatra* Mankiewicz took pains to transcend the huge and stereotypical celluloid epics of the time by making what he termed "an intimate epic" – a film in which seriousness of theme takes precedence over spectacle and which integrates its characters into their monumental surroundings.[54] He succeeded more than might have been expected or thought possible. But not all cinematic Cleopatras are as alluring as Claudette Colbert's or Elizabeth Taylor's. Nor are the barge scenes in other films on as high a level of sophistication – and ostentation – as they are in these two films. William Castle's *Serpent of the Nile: The Loves of Cleopatra* (1953) is a case in point. Rhonda Fleming, its heroine, is sexy enough, but the film suffers from its budgetary restrictions although Castle partially makes up for these with his gaudy Technicolor images. A typical "B movie" produced at "barbarian" Harry Cohn's Columbia Pictures, the film reuses left-over sets from William Dieterle's *Salome*, the studio's would-be ancient spectacle made the same year as a vehicle for Rita Hayworth. Cleopatra's barge in *Serpent of the Nile* is no more than a stationary vessel seen in long shot at night. It is either a miniature or only a matte painting. Cleopatra's seduction of Antony is a small-scale rehash of DeMille's barge sequence, also filmed on a studio set. The observation by a Roman officer accompanying Antony on board – "This isn't a barge; it's a floating palace" – is intended to heighten viewers' anticipation of Cleopatra's first appearance, but the film lets them down. Castle's display of a troupe of exotic dancing girls and of some female dancers cracking whips is a faint echo of DeMille. Although it cannot claim true epic stature, Castle's film has one memorable moment when what at first appears as a golden statue of a young woman clad only in a bikini comes to life and begins a sensuous dance. The floor of the platform on which she had stood and to which she will return after her dance to assume her original pose is covered with gold coins – an effective if none-too-subtle lesson that sex and money go hand in hand. But a bizarre plot twist undermines the very purpose of the barge scene. Cleopatra of course succeeds in seducing Antony, but throughout the film she is really in love with his friend and companion, whom she summons back onto her barge later.

Like Rhonda Fleming, Chilean actress Leonor Varela in the 1999 television film *Cleopatra* is also alluring of face and body. But as written, filmed, and performed, her Cleopatra has neither elegance nor wit nor tragic depth.

---

[53] Quoted from Bragg 1988: 156.     [54] Quoted from Geist 1978: 338.

The barge scene is brief and perfunctory, not to say risible. This four-hour film, directed by Franc Roddam, is indebted to DeMille and even more to Mankiewicz. Its Cleopatra has a darker complexion than the earlier ones, presumably in deference to modern demands for multiculturalism. Repeating the Taylor–Burton model, Varela and her Antony, Greek-American Billy Zane, fell in love during filming and became engaged.[55] The general clumsiness of Roddam's handling of his epic material is most evident when Antony boards Cleopatra's barge by hoisting himself up on deck with his arms. At such a moment any sense of sophistication, elegance, and epic grandeur is lost.

Fortunately we have those other two incarnations of Cleopatra, which in their different ways manage to do justice to her. To Plutarch and Shakespeare Cleopatra seems to have been one of the most fascinating women in history. She still is to us, not least because the silver screen has given us memorable reincarnations of her.[56] But even second- or third-rate films cannot wither her, nor Hollywood custom stale her infinite variety.

### PRINCESS DEATH

Jean Cocteau's *Orphée* (1950) is a retelling of the myth of Orpheus and Eurydice in contemporary settings and illustrates how an imaginative poet can use the technological possibilities of cinema to deepen the modern appeal of an ancient myth.[57] The myth has come down to us in the versions

---

[55] Cf. Gary Allen Smith 2004: 54: "In the second half, Leonor Varela and Billy Zane seem to be playing Elizabeth Taylor and Richard Burton rather than Cleopatra and Antony. They are not up to the task." The couple later became unengaged.

[56] Four other film Cleopatras show their own kind of variety: Betty Kent in J. Stuart Blackton and Charles Kent's *Antony and Cleopatra* (1908); Vivien Leigh in Gabriel Pascal's *Caesar and Cleopatra* (1946), an elegant but stage-bound adaptation of George Bernard Shaw's play; Sophia Loren, playing a dual role in Mario Mattoli's otherwise dull mistaken-identity comedy *Two Nights with Cleopatra* (1953); and Amanda Barrie in Gerald Thomas's unsophisticated comedy *Carry On, Cleo* (1964). Other Cleopatras range from Japanese animation (Osamu Tezuka and Eiichi Yamamoto's *Cleopatra: Queen of Sex*, 1970) to pornography (Peter Perry's *The Notorious Cleopatra* [1970], promoted as "The Most ADULT Motion Picture ever made in HOLLYWOOD," and Rino di Silvestro's *The Erotic Dreams of Cleopatra* or *Cleopatra's Hot Nights* [1985]). A Cleopatra film is in production in Christopher Guest's *The Big Picture* (1989). For overviews, necessarily incomplete, of film Cleopatras see Elley 1984: 87–99 and Wyke 1997: 73–109 and 200–204 (notes). Characters named Cleopatra appear in numerous modern and futuristic film and television plots.

[57] That Cocteau is appreciated as a modern poet strongly indebted to antiquity is nicely illustrated by Kontaxopoulos 1999, a collection of essays on his life and work published in Greece. The Homeric epithet *polytropos* in the book's title ("Jean Cocteau, the Poet of Many Turns") is particularly well-suited to a creative artist of great versatility. The title of the editor's introduction (19–28) is a quotation of the beginning of Homer's *Odyssey* ("Tell me, Muse the man of many turns . . .").

of two of the greatest Roman poets, Virgil and Ovid.[58] Like them Cocteau gives us a moving meditation on love, life, death, and even love of death.[59] Through its contemporary setting the film adds a surface layer of modern history and culture to its source and incorporates references to occupied France in World War II, modern poetry, and the cult of the intellectual. But while it is rooted in its own time and culture, the film also demonstrates the timeless validity of the myth. Orphée, Cocteau's Orpheus, is a well-established and handsome young poet with a beloved wife, Eurydice. But his inspiration is waning, and he feels a need for poetic renewal. Orphée then encounters a beautiful but mysterious woman, the Princess, and her chauffeur Heurtebise.[60] Both are emissaries of the Underworld. In a major change to the original Cocteau gives Orphée a love that goes deeper than the one Orpheus has always been famous for. Orphée, already fascinated by another world which he believes to be a new source of inspiration, falls in love with the Princess, and she does with him. (She will later tell him: "I loved you even before our first meeting.") The Princess, not Eurydice, becomes the film's central female character. Cocteau makes this evident even visually. Eurydice appears in sensible everyday clothes like an upper-middle-class wife while the Princess is always elegantly dressed, predominantly in black, and looks more attractive than Eurydice.

To prevent Eurydice from becoming dramatically negligible, however, Cocteau has Heurtebise fall in love with her. The result of this love quadrangle is the stuff of tragedy: an impossible love twice over, for how can dead spirits, although anthropomorphic, fully conscious, and capable of emotion, be in love with the living? Out of jealousy the Princess will soon take it upon herself to kill Eurydice without being authorized to do so. Eurydice does not know that she has a rival in the Princess and is powerless against her. As a result we take pity on her, especially when Eurydice is close to despair because she senses but does not know for sure that her husband is attracted to the Princess. The interplay of knowledge and ignorance that features prominently in Greek tragedy – Sophocles' *Oedipus the King* is the

---

[58] Virgil, *Georgics* 4.453–527; Ovid, *Metamorphoses* 10.1–85 and 11.1–66.

[59] Cocteau summarizes the main themes of *Orphée* in Cocteau 1992: 158; a synopsis by him appears at 197–198. For an overview of the film's genesis and for reflections of Cocteau's own life and art see Steegmuller 1986: 478–484 and Williams 2006: 110–135 (chapter entitled "In the Zone: *Orphée*"). Cf. further Evans 1977, Tsakiridou 1997, and Schifano 2003. On homosexuality and masochism in Cocteau's aesthetics as it appears in his Orphic films see Greene 1988. Pucci 2005 surveys films about Orpheus and briefly discusses *Orphée*. On the wider cultural context cf. Strauss 1971.

[60] On the origin of Heurtebise, including Cocteau's poem "L'Ange Heurtebise" ("The Angel Heurtebise") and his earlier stage play *Orphée*, see Steegmuller 1986: 349–354; on the name's etymology and possible meanings cf. Williams 2006: 125 and 131.

most famous instance – is important in Cocteau's film as well. Orphée tells Heurtebise shortly after finding Eurydice dead that as a poet he had spoken and dreamed and sung about death and thought he knew death but really does not. Heurtebise now reveals to him the Princess's true nature.

For the sake of their love and to preserve Orphée's new inspiration as poet the Princess eventually transgresses the laws of the Underworld in full knowledge of the doom she will bring upon herself. The narrator explains: "The death of a poet requires a sacrifice to render him immortal." At the end of the film we observe the Princess and her helper Heurtebise being arrested and led away toward severe punishment. Now we give our pity to the Princess, who had dared defy the Underworld powers for the sake of love. "You are not allowed to be in love in this or the other world," the Princess had said to Heurtebise when she became aware of his love for Eurydice, but the words equally apply to herself, as Heurtebise reminds her. To save Orphée and to instill new poetic inspiration in him, the Princess eventually renounces him, makes it possible for him to escape the Underworld, and reunites him with Eurydice. Orphée and Eurydice will go on living but will remember nothing. "The actions of the Princess, which actuate the drama," said Cocteau, "are taken by her of her own accord and represent free will. A thing must be. It *is* . . . The entire mystery of free will resides in this, that it seems that the thing that is *need not be* . . . the Princess dares to substitute herself for destiny, to decide that a thing *may be*, instead of being."[61] The Princess is not a personification of Death in general, but every time she appears on earth she represents a specific individual's death. As Cocteau explained: "Death in my film is not Death represented symbolically by an elegant young woman, but the Death of Orphée. Each of us has our own which takes charge of us from the moment of birth."[62] This death appears as a woman because the French word for death (*la mort*) is feminine (after Latin *mors*). Thanatos, the Greek god of death in literature (e.g. in Euripides' *Alcestis*) and art (vase paintings) is always a male character since the word is masculine. (We have no representation of Death in surviving Roman art.) The sudden and unexplained appearance of the Princess's black car and her uniformed motorcade in the film's first sequence illustrates the ubiquity of death in our lives: *media vita in morte sumus*, in the words of a late-ancient or medieval Latin church song. Cocteau takes care that we do not miss

---

[61] Quoted from Cocteau 1954: 128–129. Fraignaut 1961 incorporates a number of quotations by Cocteau from the earlier book, with some differences in the translation.

[62] Cocteau 1992: 155. Cocteau also called her "one of the innumerable employees of Death" (Cocteau 1954: 127).

this important point. The Princess observes to Orphée that the shapes of death are countless. But she rejects the common view of death as a horrifying figure with scythe and shroud: "If I appeared to the living as they portray me, they would recognize me, and that wouldn't make our task easy."

Some time after making *Orphée* Cocteau wrote about death in terms that echo its portrayal in the film. The translator appropriately preserved the feminine pronoun for death in the following quotation:

I am amazed that so many people are troubled by her, since she is with us every second and should be accepted with resignation. How should one have such great fear of a person with whom one cohabits, who is closely mingled with our own substance? But there it is. One has grown used to making a fable out of her and to judging her from outside. Better to tell oneself that at birth one marries her and to make the best of her disposition, however deceitful it may be. For she knows how to make herself forgotten and to let us believe that she no longer inhabits the house. Each one of us houses his own death and reassures himself by what he invents about her – namely that she is an allegorical figure only appearing in the last act.

Expert at camouflage, when she seems to be furthest from us, she is our very joy of living. She is our youth. She is our growth. She is our loves.[63]

In one of the film's most haunting scenes the Princess, her face like a ghostly white mask, enters Orphée's and Eurydice's bedroom at night while they are asleep and gazes upon her beloved (Fig. 38). Cocteau here points to the identity of love and death, the latter generally associated with sleep. So love of death is in a way the strongest kind of love in human life. The film illustrates this by two kinds of reciprocal love, that of the dead Princess for living Orphée and that of Orphée for his death. Although the film is named after the most famous figure in the ancient myth, the Princess turns into its central because most profound character. She is the essence of love: the most beautiful, the most moving, the most complex, and the most immediately understandable synthesis of love and death, of *erôs* and *thanatos*.

These two Greek words may remind us of Freud. But with *Orphée* Cocteau is significantly more Greek than Freudian.[64] This is so not least

---

[63] Cocteau 1967: 84 (in a short essay entitled "On Death").

[64] Visual and verbal reminiscences of ancient culture are to be expected in a poetic retelling of a Greek myth, but Cocteau goes far beyond what might have been expected in providing even recherché allusions. The young poet Cégeste, the Princess's victim in the film's opening sequence, is named after Segesta, the Greek settlement in Sicily famous for its temple; the leader of the women at the café "Les Bacchantes" is called Aglaonice, a name not associated with the Orpheus myth. (Aglaonice was a Thessalian sorceress capable of drawing the moon down from the sky.) Orphée and Eurydice have

**Fig. 38.** *Orphée.* The Princess, her face like a death mask. (André Paulvé-Criterion)

because Cocteau himself embodies the philosophical concept of ideal love as outlined, for instance, in Plato's *Symposium*. Jean Marais, the handsome actor who plays Orphée, had been Cocteau's lover. Spiritually and physically Cocteau was the Socratic lover (*erastês*) to Marais, his beloved (*erômenos*). Marais was the reason why Cocteau returned to cinema after fifteen years.[65] His work with Cocteau made Marais a star. Through their love, one might say, they created two lasting masterpieces – three years before *Orphée* Marais had played the main part in Cocteau's equally haunting and poetic film *Beauty and the Beast* – and achieved a kind of Platonic immortality. A biographer of Cocteau gives a vivid assessment of Marais in the appropriate classical terms: "astonishingly handsome, 'an Antinoüs sprung from the people,' blond, with 'all the characteristics of those blue-eyed hyperboreans mentioned in Greek mythology,' . . . the Apollonian

several pieces of neoclassical decorations in their house, and the garden at its back is decorated with several life-size neoclassical statues. The title of Cocteau's film *The Testament of Orpheus* (on which below) alludes to ancient texts that were said to contain Orpheus' testament; for the texts, with comments, see Fragm. 245–248 in Kern 1922: 255–266. For a thorough overview and interpretation of Orpheus, Orphism, Orphic texts, and related aspects see Graf and Johnston 2007.

[65] Cocteau had directed *The Blood of a Poet* in 1930. The next film he directed was *Beauty and the Beast* in 1946, starring Marais.

Marais . . . of exceptional beauty."[66] Cocteau himself specifically connected *Orphée* with the Platonic ideas of the beautiful and the good:

The moral value that I seek, besides forging a bond between separate elements and making them gravitate towards one centre, endows the actors' eyes with a quality without which a film like *Orphée* would lose all its profound significance. The beauty of the soul, which the film camera records . . . , is more important for me than physical beauty. The beauty of François Périer [who played Heurtebise], although it's never mentioned in illustrated magazines, is in my eyes just as effective as that of Jean Marais, which the same magazines praise to the skies. They are equals in spiritual beauty.[67]

Cocteau's conception of death and the Underworld is more complex than it was in the Greek myth. Heurtebise is both an equivalent of Hermes, the Greek god who as *psychopompos* ("soul guide") led the spirits of the dead to the Underworld, and a newly conceived addition to the myth, for Heurtebise loves Eurydice more deeply than Orphée does. As Cocteau shows at the film's climax, the Princess wields no power in the Underworld, so she is not an equivalent of Persephone. And Cocteau's Underworld works like a modern bureaucracy. Three judges form a tribunal that is loosely patterned on Minos, Aeacus, and Rhadamanthys, the three Underworld judges in Greek myth. They wear dark business suits and sit behind an office table with files lying before them. A kind of clerk takes minutes and types out their paperwork. But even so Cocteau does not let us forget classical antiquity, for a large neoclassical vase can be seen in one of the otherwise sparely decorated Underworld rooms.

The most famous individual part of the ancient myth is Orpheus' descent to the Underworld. Orphée, guided by Heurtebise, descends from his house through what Cocteau called the Zone and defined as "the No Man's Land between life and death"[68] (Fig. 39). To separate the Zone visually from the upper world Cocteau made imaginative use of a film technology that now may look obvious. But the effects Cocteau wanted were not at all easy to achieve. For descent and ascent he used double exposure, rear projection, change from positive to negative images, slow motion, and running the film backward. Technical limitations were the very inspiration for Cocteau to visualize the supernatural and to create a work of haunting visual poetry. About the process of filming *Orphée* he observed: "We had to give up [some

---

[66] Steegmuller 1986: 434–435. The comparison of Marais with Antinous, the handsome young lover of Emperor Hadrian, is by German writer Ernst Jünger; that with the Hyperboreans, associated with Apollo in some of the god's ancient myths, is a translation from a 1950 book about Marais.
[67] Quoted from Cocteau 1954: 120.     [68] Quoted from Cocteau 1954: 127.

**Fig. 39.** *Orphée.* Heurtebise and Orphée in the Zone. (André Paulvé-Criterion)

of] our experiments . . . because they proved unusable . . . I'll add, however, that such failures were useful in that they excited our imagination and set it going, compelling it to solve the problem of trick effects without resorting to any tricks."[69] Of course Cocteau did use tricks; as he acknowledged, they were a source of his visual poetry: "It was a matter of using tricks in such a way that they resembled poetic form."[70]

The most thrilling part of Orphée's descent is the beginning. He and Heurtebise, later he and the Princess, start through the mirror in Orphée's and Eurydice's bedroom (Fig. 40). The mirror is the gateway to the nether realm, and the idea of using it for this purpose is a poetic masterstroke on Cocteau's part. He considered mirrors to be the doorways of death, as Heurtebise tells Orphée: "Mirrors are the gates through which Death comes and goes." This, Heurtebise continues, is "the secret of secrets." When the Princess for the first time visits the bedroom of Orphée and Eurydice while they are sleeping, we see her entering through the mirror (Fig. 41). The narrator later observes that she comes back every night, evidently in the same manner. But why the mirror? A mirror shows us what we look like at any given moment. Over the course of our lives it

---

[69] Quoted from Cocteau 1954: 102. Cocteau describes the complex technical side of filming, especially regarding passages through the Zone, in Cocteau 1954: 105–117.

[70] Quoted from Fraignaut 1961: 100; also, if slightly differently, in Cocteau 1954: 101.

**Fig. 40.** *Orphée*. Orphée, instructed by Heurtebise, approaches the mirror. (André Paulvé-Criterion)

**Fig. 41.** *Orphée*. The Princess's first visit through the mirror to the home of Orphée and Eurydice. (André Paulvé-Criterion)

reflects our aging process, if only momentarily. As Heurtebise explains to Orphée: "You look at yourself all your life in your mirror, and you'll see death at work." Heurtebise further observes that life is a long death. So Cocteau's observation that each one of us houses his own death applies most obviously to our mirrors. At the same time the mirror functions analogously to a still camera with its snapshots and portraits of our lives, but with the difference that we can preserve photographic images. Susan Sontag expressed this side of still photography in an essay called "In Plato's Cave":

All photographs are *memento mori*. To take a photograph is to participate in another person's (or thing's) mortality, vulnerability, mutability. Precisely by slicing out this moment and freezing it, all photographs testify to time's relentless melt.[71]

Photographs, films, and mirror images that appear in a film can be pre-served. They exist for as long as the film survives, well beyond the lifespan of the person who appears in such images. So the cinema, through its technical affinity to photography and its visual affinity to mirrors, becomes a preserver of human life, if only in mimetic images. We watch film actors long after they have died. This experience becomes poignant if we keep watching a favorite film over several years or even decades. We may start out being much younger than the actors, but suddenly we realize that we are older than they were when they played their parts. They never change, but we do. The figures on our screens then come to resemble the state of those described in John Keats's "Ode on a Grecian Urn": they shall remain – they cannot fade and will be forever young. They differ from Keats's young lovers and those coming to the sacrifice in that they move about and speak. They are not static like painted or sculpted figures, but their movements and sounds are limited to endless repetition. None of them can ever reach their endings on the screen, as we can and must do and as they have already done in real life. Photography and even more the cinema document the process of aging and dying but at the same time preserve a record of life beyond death, imparting a kind of immortality to us whose nature Greeks and Romans could have understood.

With its immortality the cinema reminds us of our mortality. It is, however, also a preserver of death itself, or rather of mankind's dying process, for it enables us to watch a number of different films in which the same actors have appeared over the years or over an entire lifetime.[72] Here

---

[71] Sontag 1977a: 15. This essay opens her book.

[72] This can be quite disconcerting to true cinema lovers who tend to return to their favorites again and again. They can follow the roads through life of stars from youth to old age – for example, John

the cinematic images, often called shadows and in this way analogous to the ancients' custom of referring to the dead as shades, record the inexorable approach of actors' deaths and remind us of our own. This applies even to a death figure like Cocteau's Princess. In *The Testament of Orpheus*, a loose sequel to *Orphée* made nine years later and beginning with the last scene of the earlier film, Cocteau himself plays an Orphic poet who dies, goes to the Underworld, and returns. In a scene reminiscent of the Underworld tribunal in *Orphée* he, too, encounters the Princess, who is played by the same actress. Heurtebise, again played by François Périer, also reappears; he and the Princess are now Underworld judges. With her black dress and appropriately severe hairstyle this dead and therefore deathless being closely resembles what she had looked like in the earlier film, but every viewer of *The Testament of Orpheus* who remembers *Orphée* will realize with a shock that now she is noticeably older (Fig. 42). Actress Maria Casarès, who died in 1996 at age 76, was about 28 and 38 when she appeared as the Princess. In *The Testament of Orpheus* the Princess seems to have survived the punishment to which she was being led at the end of *Orphée*.[73] Can her love have conquered even the Underworld powers just as Orpheus' love in the Greek myth had done? We cannot know for sure. It is the Princess, the

Wayne from 1928 to 1976 or Katharine Hepburn from 1932 to 1994. Even decades after he had been François Truffaut's Antoine Doinel from teenager (*The 400 Blows*, 1959) to adult (*Love on the Run*, 1979), viewers will always associate Jean-Pierre Léaud with his most famous character, who ages (up to a point) but remains deathless. And aficionados of both cinema and painting will remember that director Jean Renoir appeared in many photographs, documentaries, and interview films as an adult at various stages in his life, but he is also a young boy in some of his father's paintings, easily recognized by those who know him from his later years. These are just a few remarkable instances; readers will no doubt have thought of some other examples.

73 On this cf. Cocteau's words quoted in Fraignaut 1961: 104: "What is the punishment to which she exposes herself? This escapes me, and does not concern me . . . It was important (in my logic) that certain *données* [givens] be missing, opening up gaps into an inaccessible world." But Cocteau gives an explanation of sorts in the later film: the Princess's and Heurtebise's punishment is said to have been their appointment to condemn others, to be judges themselves. – The cinematic intertextuality, as we may call it, of the Princess and Orphée – or rather, of the actors portraying them – is worth contemplating beyond these two films by Cocteau. Another modern retelling of the Orpheus myth, Jacques Demy's film *Parking* (1985), in which Orpheus is a rock musician and the Underworld a modern parking garage, has Jean Marais in the part of Hades (or the Devil). About four years before *Orphée* Maria Casarès had played a ruthlessly vindictive woman in Robert Bresson's *Les dames du Bois de Boulogne* (1945), a contemporary adaptation of Denis Diderot's *Jacques le fataliste*. The femme fatale, appropriately named Hélène, feels rejected by her lover and uses a younger woman to exert her revenge on him. She comes close to driving the latter to her death on her wedding day, but her bridegroom's love for her prevails at the last moment. As Hélène, Casarès is simultaneously beautiful and erotic (Jacques is hopelessly in love with her), but she is also a bringer of doom. Casarès is dressed chiefly in black, although she does not look quite as severe as the Princess. The poetic dialogue in Bresson's film was written by Cocteau. As Susan Sontag has commented: "Maria Casarès' black-garbed demonic Hélène is, visually and emotionally, of a piece with her brilliant performance in Cocteau's *Orphée*." Quoted from Sontag 1966b: 193. Her essay had first appeared in *The Seventh Art* in 1964.

**Fig. 42.** *The Testament of Orpheus.* The aging Princess. (Canal + Image International)

dead but emotionally alive spirit of love and death, and not Orphée, the living human, whose love conquers all. Her last close-up in *Orphée* had shown her with tears in her eyes after renouncing her beloved, perhaps the film's most intense single image (Fig. 43). Orphée's love for her died in the forgetfulness she imposed on him to save him.

Cocteau's two films about Orpheus illustrate the dual nature of cinema as recorder of life and death and as a *memento mori*. Miraculously, however, the two films are anything but depressing reminders of our mortality. *Orphée* even has moments of humor. The modern retelling of the ancient myth yields a complex story of love overcoming the power of death and even existing within death. In the haunting but ultimately also comforting way in which *Orphée* affects us lies the greatness of Cocteau's art, worthy of Virgil's and Ovid's. Cocteau also echoes, if probably unconsciously, certain aspects of Orphism, the ancient mystery religion that believed in a judgment after death, in the soul's survival of death through reincarnation (*metempsychôsis*) and in the resulting lack of remembrance. Descent through a kind of Zone was a highlight in Orphism just as it is in *Orphée*. Surviving Orphic texts reveal through the voice of someone familiar with the Underworld what the soul will encounter on its journey, how it has to conduct itself, what it is to say, and what it will hear in reply.[74]

74 The texts are Fragm. 32 in Kern 1922: 104–109.

**Fig. 43.** *Orphée.* The last close-up on the Princess. (André Paulvé-Criterion)

*Orphée* shows that to re-imagine a myth's underlying themes is more likely to lead to a creative modern work than merely to adapt its plot elements. *Orphée* also demonstrates that the cinema is a medium uniquely suited to express the eternal closeness of life to death. As Cocteau observed:

Since my moral carriage is that of a man who limps with one foot in life and one in death, it was normal for me to arrive at a myth in which life and death confront each other . . . a film was the proper medium to express the incidents that occur on the frontier separating one world from another.[75]

*Orphée* proves Cocteau's point about being simultaneously connected to life and death. He was not only its creator but also its narrator.[76] A disembodied and omniscient entity who introduces us to and guides us through the story it tells comes close to resembling a deathless and quasi-divine being. But Cocteau also supplied the voice that transmits the mysterious poetic Underworld messages that fascinate Orphée and endanger Eurydice.[77] As such, Cocteau is an associate of death. Simultaneously, then, the poet who

---

[75] Fraignaut 1961: 100; slightly differently in Cocteau 1954: 101.

[76] On this aspect of the film see Fleishman 1992: 82–89.

[77] "The bird sings with its fingers" – this line comes from a letter written by Guillaume Apollinaire to Cocteau; cf. Steegmuller 1986: 482. Although we see another helper of the Princess, the young poet Cégeste who had been killed in the film's opening sequence, transmit the radio messages, the voice we hear on the soundtrack is Cocteau's.

creates the new version of the myth of Orpheus and Eurydice is the same person who announces and even takes a part in their impending death. Still, to Cocteau the cinema is a life-affirming art:

When I have manual work to do, I like to think that I take part in earthly things, and I put all my strength into it like a drowning man clinging to a wreck. This is why I took up film-making, where every minute is occupied by work which shields me from the void where I get lost.[78]

Not only is this a moving testimony to the importance of art in our lives, but it is also a clear justification of the important part that cinema can and perhaps should play in modern culture. In a classic essay on the nature of cinema André Bazin once traced the fundamental human impulse for artistic creation to our desire to conquer time and death: "death is but the victory of time." Taking the "mummy complex" of the ancient Egyptians as his starting point, Bazin noted that the mummies and the paintings, sculpture, and architecture that surrounded them were the Egyptians' way to extricate "bodily appearance . . . from the flow of time" and so to preserve it "in the hold of life." Mummies, their portraits, later portrait paintings and sculptures, and finally photographic images largely serve the same purpose, evinced by the "primordial function of statuary, namely, the preservation of life by a representation of life . . . the image helps us to remember the subject and to preserve him from a second spiritual death."[79] But photography has an advantage over previous forms of art: "All the arts are based on the presence of man, only photography derives an advantage from his absence."[80] Photography is in turn followed by the moving photographic images on film. The cinema is the greatest possible preserver of life in art and ultimately achieves "a larger concept, the creation of an ideal world in the likeness of the real."[81]

Cocteau's *Orphée* illustrates Bazin's points. The film reveals that our standard negative view of death might not be the best one. Cocteau's use of the hauntingly beautiful and uplifting "Dance of the Blessed Spirits" from Christoph Willibald Gluck's opera *Orpheus and Eurydice* on the soundtrack reinforces this side of the film. Its dual inspiration, the Orpheus myth for its plot and Cocteau's visual poetry for its style, makes *Orphée* one of the few films in which the figure of death is not only attractive in a way far removed from morbidity but also comprehensible as something or somebody we can

[78] Quoted from Cocteau 1954: 23.
[79] Bazin 1967b: 9–10. Bazin's mention of statuary implies other three- and two-dimensional arts of representation as well as other periods of art history since the Egyptians.
[80] Bazin 1967b: 13.    [81] Bazin 1967b: 10.

feel for.[82] *Orphée* may even help shield attentive and sensitive viewers from the void in their own lives. What Cocteau observed in the opening voice-over of *Orphée* takes on greater resonance in retrospect: "Where does our story take place, and at what time? It is the privilege of legends to be without age."

---

[82] The most haunting and profound other films about death (or Death) are Fritz Lang's *Destiny* (1921; its original title, *Der müde Tod*, translates as "Weary Death") and Ingmar Bergman's *The Seventh Seal* (1957). Closer in plot to *Orphée* are Mitchell Leisen's *Death Takes a Holiday* (1934), based on the 1924 play *La morte in vacanza* by Alberto Casella via its Broadway adaptation, and Marcel Carné's *Les visiteurs du soir* (1942). In both, emissaries from the other world (Death in the former and envoys of the Devil in the latter) visit the upper world and fall in love. The young mortal woman in Carné's film, part of the couple whose love extends beyond death, is played by Maria Déa, later Cocteau's Eurydice.

# Epilogue: "Bright shines the light"

Apollo was present at the birth of Western literature, for he set in motion the plot of Homer's *Iliad*. His sister Athena fulfills a comparable function in the *Odyssey*. In the *Iliad* she had aided and protected several of the Greek heroes, for instance advising Achilles to restrain his anger against Agamemnon. Throughout the *Odyssey* she is Odysseus' faithful guardian and engineers his return to Ithaca. As goddess of wisdom Athena is frequently associated with culture and civilization. The library at Pergamon, mentioned in Chapter 1, had a larger-than-life statue of her.[1] Athena's closeness to Apollo is most evident in *The Eumenides*, the concluding play of Aeschylus' *Oresteia*. The two gods work together toward Orestes' absolution from blood guilt for the murder of his mother.

The ending of Franco Rossi's *Odissea* ("The Odyssey," 1968) shows that in the cinema Athena can represent the ideal of culture and civilization just as much as Phoebus Apollo, the shining god of light. This six-hour production is among the greatest films ever made of a work of classical literature, and Rossi incorporates and presents Athena in unusually inspired ways.[2] Whenever she disguises herself as a mortal to remain unrecognized by the humans among whom she appears, actors play the people she impersonates. But when she and Zeus deliberate about the fate of Odysseus on Olympus, Rossi films ancient marble statuettes of these gods and adds their dialogue in voice-over. This is an elegant and economical way to avoid the pitfalls facing directors who have to present gods on screen. (Cf. the words of Wolfgang Petersen and Michael Cacoyannis quoted in Chapter 5.) Rossi in this way imparts a sense of inscrutability or mystery to the gods: we hear them speak, but nothing in their effigies moves. They remain remote from us humans even when we see them, even when they act in our interest.

---

[1] On this statue see Esther V. Hansen 1971: 272–273 and 355–356.

[2] This film, produced for Italian, German, and French public television, is the supreme adaptation of Homer to the screen. Winkler 2007c: 80–84 is a brief appreciation.

For his ending Rossi takes us again to Mount Olympus, but in a different way. Athena has watched over Odysseus' reunion with Penelope, and Rossi briefly shows us the same statue of the goddess we had seen earlier. It now serves as a transition to the narrator's concluding remarks about Olympus, expressed in stately and measured tones taken directly from the *Odyssey*. As representation of the abode of the immortal gods Rossi shows us some of the columns and stones of the Parthenon, Athena's temple on the Acropolis of her city, while the narrator describes an idealized Olympus. The final image in the film is a view through the space between two columns that dominate the screen on left and right as the camera recedes. At first we see this great classical site in the bright light of the sun, but the last shot rapidly fades to black. During these moments the omniscient narrator, who had accompanied us throughout the entire film, gently guides us toward closure while also imparting to us a sense of regret that we must now take our leave of the world of the Greek gods and of epic and myth. The narrator ends with a statement about the eternal presence of Greek light. On Mount Olympus, he tells us, "there is, they say, the always serene seat of the gods. It is not battered by winds, never drenched in rain; snow does not fall, but the air's expanse is always free of clouds. Bright shines the light."[3]

*Candida scorre la luce*: the original Italian is a literal translation of Homer's *leukê d' epidedromen aiglê*. The adjective *aiglêeis* ("shining, brilliant") appears in the Homeric epics only for Olympus. The most important quality of the abode of the immortals is light, a symbol of their divine essence.[4] Here it is associated with Athena. Apollo is not named or referred to, but the nature of the god of light is implied. The quotation expresses the Apollonian nature of cinema and the persistence of the cinema's vision beyond the end of a particular film. When the Roman poet Lucretius, imitating Homer, mentions the Olympian "light shining far and wide," he makes the importance of light for culture and civilization self-evident.[5]

One film that associates Athena with the Apollonian principles of light and civilization is completely under her aegis. Athena is the guiding spirit of

---

[3] Homer, *Odyssey* 6.42–45. The description occurs when Athena returns to Olympus after ensuring that Nausicaa, daughter of the king of the Phaeacians, to whose island Odysseus has just been driven by Poseidon's storm, will safely take Odysseus to her father's palace. The quotation from the film here given is my translation. The Italian translation of Homer which the narrator quotes is Onesti 1963: 158. Its cover advertised "the greatest story of adventures in the most modern translation." It was reprinted in 1968, the year Rossi's film was first broadcast. Spieker 1969 gives a detailed interpretation and appreciation of the Homeric passage.

[4] Cf. Spieker 1969: 149.  [5] Lucretius, *On the Nature of Things* 3.22: *large diffuso lumine.*

Chris Marker's *The Owl's Legacy* (or *The Legacy of the Owl*, 1989) a public-television film in thirteen parts of twenty-six minutes each.[6] In Greek myth and culture the owl is the bird of Athena as goddess of wisdom. Her standard Homeric epithet is *glaukôpis*, "owl-eyed" or "grey-eyed." Marker's film deals with all of Western (and some of Eastern) culture. Western civilization is Athena's legacy, a reflection of the persistence of ancient Greece in our world. Individual episodes deal with different arts and sciences, with philosophy and mythology, and with questions of life and death. Various philosophers, cultural critics, classical scholars, and two film directors, most of them accompanied by images of owls, appear in interviews to produce a "mosaic of different experiences and interpretations that are permitted on occasion to contradict each other."[7] In the episode on Greek mathematics, for example, French actress Arielle Dombasle "stars as a soft-focus muse who explains the mathematical principles discovered by Pythagoras." In homage to Plato the film features a number of symposia that complement the interviews and begin and end the whole work. A film scholar observes:

Many of the facets of ancient Greek thought and culture explored in the series . . . are the foundations of Marker's own approach to cinema and other audio-visual media as a perpetual dialogue with oneself and others, which seeks to generate reflective knowledge about the world.[8]

In "Let Us Praise Dziga Vertov," a prose poem composed in 1967, Marker refers to Vertov's concept of the cinema eye and exclaims: "O for a Muse of light . . ."[9] This Muse might as well be the goddess of wisdom and culture, who is close to the god of light and leader of the Muses.

If Athena is the patron goddess for Marker's film, Olympus and the Apollonian may be said to provide spiritual guidance in *These Encounters of Theirs* (2006) by writers and directors (and married couple) Jean-Marie Straub and Danièle Huillet. The following summary of their last work together points to some of the chief themes of their entire body of work and to the importance of antiquity for sophisticated and dedicated filmmakers. Their film is

---

[6] Lupton 2005: 170–176 gives titles and brief summaries of the episodes and a concise interpretation of the film. Detailed filmographic information, including the original French episode titles, appears in Alter 2006: 164.

[7] Lupton 2005: 171. The classicists include Marcel Detienne, Françoise Frontisi-Ducroux, Mark Griffith, David Halperin, François Lissarague, Oswyn Murray, Thomas G. Rosenmeyer, Renate Schleisser, Giulia Sissa, Deborah Steiner, Jean-Pierre Vernant, and John J. Winkler. The film directors are Theodoros Angelopoulos and Elia Kazan.

[8] Both of the preceding quotations are from Lupton 2005: 174.

[9] The poem's English version appears in Alter 2006: 135–136; quotation at 136.

a courageous confrontation with mortality . . . Placing five conversing pairs – people, gods, spirits, and a Huillet-like muse inspiring a Straub-like Hesiod – in Italian landscapes seemingly untouched for millennia, the directors describe a colossal arc from mythic prehistory to the present day and depict the wary mutual dependence of divine and human affairs. Filming at an Olympian remove from ordinary life, Straub and Huillet judge it severely and reach profound, disturbing conclusions: in an unwillingness to face death, modern mankind rejects the gods and despoils the divine realm of nature.[10]

Marker's and Straub and Huillet's films point to the continuing presence of the classical past in modern culture. Another film reveals the importance of this past for all of cinema. In 1995, the year of *Ulysses' Gaze*, Theodoros Angelopoulos made the fundamental connection between the ancient world and the cinema explicit by actually putting it on film. He contributed the final segment to *Lumière and Company*, a film anthology intended as homage to the cinema's founding fathers on the centenary of the medium's birth. Forty directors made films lasting about fifty-two seconds each, the length of the Lumière brothers' first works. The directors used the Lumières' original camera and shot in black and white. Their comments and additional video footage of each filming process accompany the individual segments. To celebrate the origin of cinema Angelopoulos took recourse to early classical literature. He filmed a particular moment in the *Odyssey*, that of Odysseus' awakening on the shore of Ithaca after his return. Odysseus wakes up on a rocky beach, looks around without realizing where he is, and then walks through the shallow water toward the camera and into a close-up of his face (Fig. 44). He gazes directly into the camera. Nothing else happens. In the style of silent cinema a text card at the beginning of Angelopoulos's mini-film had told us about Odysseus' state of mind at this moment: "I am lost! In which foreign country have I arrived?" As the card also informs us, these words are taken from the *Odyssey* itself.[11]

Odysseus' discovery of his homeland had been staged more freely as the ending of Jean-Luc Godard's film *Contempt* (1963), a loose adaptation of a novel by Alberto Moravia. A production team is in the process of filming

[10] Quoted from Brophy 2007. The film is based on Cesare Pavese's *Dialogues with Leucò* (1947), a philosophical work of dialogues between characters from ancient myth. (The titular lady is the sea goddess Leucothea.) At the beginning of *Works and Days* the archaic poet Hesiod described his spiritual awakening by the Muses. Straub and Huillet had made a film of Sophocles' *Antigone* after the German version by Friedrich Hölderlin in 1992.

[11] Homer, *Odyssey* 13.200. The text on the film's card, here given in my translation, is in French since *Lumière and Company* is, appropriately, a French production. The rocks on which Angelopoulos places his Odysseus are mentioned at 13.196.

**Fig. 44.** *Lumière and Company.* The Odysseus of Angelopoulos discovers the cinema.
(Fox Lorber)

the *Odyssey*. Replicas of statues of Apollo and Athena are briefly visible as props. The director is played by real-life director Fritz Lang, who was himself a master of epic cinema. Godard's Lang has his Odysseus walk to the edge of an elevated place from which he looks out across the sea (Fig. 45). This is the only moment in *Contempt* in which we watch a scene from the *Odyssey* being filmed. Evidently it was a crucial moment for Godard, intended to carry symbolic meaning. When asked "What scene are you shooting?" Lang replies: "Ulysses' first gaze when he sees his homeland again."[12]

The moment of Odysseus' first gaze is the last moment of his wanderings in the *Odyssey* and occurs half-way into the epic. At the end of *Ulysses' Gaze* Angelopoulos had the director within his own film quote T. S. Eliot: "In my end is my beginning."[13] Angelopoulos's contribution to *Lumière and Company* is that film's ending, but an ending that commemorates a new beginning. Before the final credits for *Lumière and Company* appear on screen, we see a sepia-tinted still image of the Lumières' camera on

[12] My translation is not as concise as the original French words ("Le premier regard d'Ulysse quand il revoirt sa patrie"), which echo the title of Claudio Monteverdi's opera *Il ritorno d'Ulisse in patria* (1640). They anticipate the French release title of Angelopoulos's film, *Le regard d'Ulysse*.
[13] This is a quotation from the last line of "East Coker," the second of Eliot's *Four Quartets* (1940). On *Ulysses' Gaze* see Chapter 2.

**Fig. 45.** *Contempt.* Filming the film within the film: director Fritz Lang (ctr.) filming Odysseus (with sword) looking out to sea. (Compagnia Cinematografica Champion-Canal + Image International)

the beach, like Odysseus heroically alone and gazing out to sea (Fig. 46). Angelopoulos's Odysseus lands on the shores of the new country of cinema, for the time of the image has come. Godard ends *Contempt* with a recreation of the same Homeric moment, thereby also pointing to what is to come after *his* film: the completion of the filming of Lang's *Odyssey.* Like the original *Odyssey,* this *Odyssey* film is a fiction. From Homer's *Odyssey* to Moravia's novel (in which no film of the *Odyssey* plays any part), to Godard's *Contempt* and Lang's film of the *Odyssey* – the interconnections of narrative in their two chief media, text and image, are compellingly evident in different but complementary ways. In ends are new beginnings.[14]

Having returned home, Homer's Odysseus is not lost. When he is looking over the island's geography he is looking at the place of a new beginning for himself and his family. Angelopoulos's Odysseus is not lost when he is gazing into the Lumières' camera. He has the future. Godard's Odysseus is looking out over the expanse of the Mediterranean as if from an Olympian height while being looked at by not one but two cameras, the one that purports to film him for Lang and the one that does film him for Godard and the viewers of *Contempt.* Homer's Odysseus will always have Athena. The cinema's Odysseus has Lang, Godard, Angelopoulos, Rossi,

---

[14] The two protagonists of Godard's *Les carabiniers* (1963) illustrate the importance of images, if from a different perspective. The brothers have names emblematic of Western culture: Ulysse and Michel-Ange. (Their women are called Venus and Cleopatra.) Poor farmers, they have been lured into joining a war in which everything is permitted them. A large number of picture postcards provide a kind of record of their exploits (and war crimes).

**Fig. 46.** *Lumière and Company.* An Odyssean moment for the Lumière brothers' film camera. (Fox Lorber)

and all the other directors who have told or will tell his story. The cinema itself, whose essence is light, has Apollo. Abel Gance, who had referred to Homer in his 1927 essay "The Time of the Image Has Come," said so in 1929:

For thirty years, the light of day has been our prisoner and we have been trying to make it repeat its most thrilling songs on our screens, during the night . . . We have married art and science, applying one to the other, to capture and fix the rhythms of light. That is cinema . . . We are living the first hour of the new dance of the muses around the new youth of Apollo, a dance of sounds and light around an incomparable hearth: our modern soul.[15]

A considerable number of the films discussed in this book have expressed or at least attempted to express our modern soul. An elegant restatement of Gance's view, if with a stronger assertion of the independence of film than Gance might have agreed to, came forty years later from French writer-director Robert Bresson:

[15] Gance 1929, quoted from the translation (in excerpts as "The Cinema of Tomorrow") by King 1984: 61–79, at 78. Cf. the similar passage about the Muses' dance around Sigalion in "The Time of the Image Has Come," quoted in my Introduction.

I've already said that other arts, or rather, other Muses, must not be mixed with the Muse of cinema. However, I believe they can be friends. I think the Muse of painting can be friends with cinema, but the Muse of literature can't really. Degas, the great painter, said a wonderful thing. He said the Muses never talk to each other, but sometimes they dance together. So the Muse of painting can dance with the Muse of cinema.[16]

Bresson here comes close to negating the affinity of film to literature, primarily in order to assert the difference between himself as cinematic *auteur* and literary authors. Bresson uttered the words quoted during the filming of *Mouchette* (1967), which is based on *Nouvelle histoire de Mouchette*, a 1937 novel by Georges Bernanos. But while upholding cinema's independence Bresson, filming a text, also acknowledges its connections to the other arts. In the same context he also speaks about the importance of music for his films. It is tempting to deduce that Bresson considers the Muse of cinema as the most important Muse today, the one closest to the god of cinema. If she is, film is the ultimate means of artistic expression.

Doubts, of course, may occur. Asked once if he found it more difficult with advancing age to express "some kind of truth" in his films, Angelopoulos replied:

Yes. More and more difficult. I think we must ask ourselves a question all the time, again and again. It's a question that I asked in *Ulysses' Gaze*: do I still see? Like the first time I put my eye to the camera, the first time I discovered the world through the camera lens, do I still have the innocence of the gaze that I first had?[17]

Nevertheless Angelopoulos may take comfort in the nature of cinema as the most powerful and lasting Apollonian art and in the persistence of its visions. So may we. Bright indeed shines Apollo's new light. As we remember, in the beginning society listened. Then society read. Now society views – more accurately: listens, reads, and views all at the same time. Godard and Angelopoulos show us how beginnings, middles, and ends meet and merge.

An observation by one of antiquity's most learned authors may serve as an answer to Angelopoulos's question "do I still see?" and as a kind of seal (*sphragis*) to this book. One of the compositions of Callimachus, the scholar-poet at the library of Alexandria whom we encountered in

---

[16] Bresson says these words in Theodor Kotulla's documentary *Zum Beispiel Bresson* (1967). They are here quoted according to the subtitles of this film on the Criterion Collection DVD of Bresson's film *Mouchette*, with slight changes of capitalization and punctuation.

[17] Quoted from Gray 2004, an interview conducted at the London Film Festival in November, 2004.

Chapter 1, is a *Hymn to Apollo*. What Callimachus observed about the god's appearances among humans holds true for Apollo's modern domain:

> Apollo's epiphanies are not for all;
> Magnificent to see the god
>     and graceless not to see him.[18]

---

[18] Callimachus, *Hymn to Apollo* 9–10; quoted from Lombardo and Rayor 1988: 7.

# Bibliography

Abel, Richard (ed.). 1988. *French Film Theory and Criticism: A History/Anthology 1907–1939*. Vol. 1: 1907–1929. Vol. 2: 1929–1939. Princeton University Press.

Abrams, M. H. 1953; rpt. 1977. *The Mirror and the Lamp: Romantic Theory and the Critical Tradition*. New York: Oxford University Press.

Addison, Joseph. 2004. *Cato: A Tragedy and Selected Essays*. Ed. Christine Dunn Henderson and Mark E. Yellin. Indianapolis: Liberty Fund.

Adorno, Theodor. 1981. *Prisms*. Tr. Samuel and Shierry Weber. Cambridge, MA: MIT Press.

Ahl, Frederick M. 1982. "Amber, Avallon, and Apollo's Singing Swan." *American Journal of Philology*, 103: 373–411.

2007. (tr.). *Virgil: Aeneid*. Oxford University Press.

and Hanna M. Roisman. 1996. *The Odyssey Re-Formed*. Ithaca: Cornell University Press.

Allen, Richard. 1995. *Projecting Illusion: Film Spectatorship and the Impression of Reality*. Cambridge University Press.

1999. "Psychoanalytic Film Theory." In Miller and Stam 1999: 123–145.

Almendros, Nestor. 1984; rpt. 1986. *A Man with a Camera*. Tr. Rachel Phillips Belash. New York: Farrar Straus Giroux.

Alter, Nora M. 2006. *Chris Marker*. Urbana: University of Illinois Press.

Alton, John. 1949; rpt. 1995. *Painting with Light*. Rpt. Berkeley: University of California Press.

Andrew, Dudley. 1984; rpt. 1996. *Film in the Aura of Art*. Princeton University Press.

1995. *Mists of Regret: Culture and Sensibility in Classic French Film*. Princeton University Press.

Angell, Sir Norman. 1910. *The Great Illusion: A Study of the Relation of Military Power in Nations to Their Economic and Social Advantage*. London: Heinemann.

Antonioni, Michelangelo. 1996. *The Architecture of Vision: Writings and Interviews on Cinema*. Ed. Carlo di Carlo and Giorgio Tinazzi; American ed. by Marga Cottino-Jones. New York: Marsilio.

Armstrong, Richard H. 2005. *A Compulsion for Antiquity: Freud and the Ancient World*. Ithaca: Cornell University Press.

2006. "Theory and Theatricality: Classical Drama and the Early Formation of Psychoanalysis." *Classical and Modern Literature*, 26 no. 1: 79–109.

Arnheim, Rudolf. 1957; rpt. 2006. *Film as Art.* Berkeley: University of California Press.

Arnold, Frank. 2004. "Wolfgang Petersen: Keine Welt in Schwarz und Weiss." *Kölner Stadtanzeiger* (May 14); http://www.ksta.de/artikel.jsp?id= 1084203219381.

Arrowsmith, William. 1969. "Film as Educator." *Journal of Aesthetic Education*, 3 no. 3: 75–83.

1995. *Antonioni: The Poet of Images.* Ed. Ted Perry. New York: Oxford University Press.

Asquith, Anthony. 1946. "The Tenth Muse Climbs Parnassus." *The Penguin Film Review*, 1 (August).

Astley, Neil (ed.). 1991. *Tony Harrison.* Newcastle upon Tyne: Bloodaxe Books.

Astruc, Alexandre. 1948. "Naissance d'une nouvelle avant-garde: la caméra-stylo." *L'écran français*, 144 (March 30).

1968. "The Birth of a New Avant-Garde: *La caméra-stylo.*" In Graham 1968: 17–23.

1992. *Du stylo à la caméra . . . et de la caméra au stylo: Écrits (1942–1984).* Paris: L'Archipel.

Austin, Norman. 1994. *Helen of Troy and Her Shameless Phantom.* Ithaca: Cornell University Press.

Bachtin, Michail M. 1986; rpt. 1989. *Formen der Zeit im Roman: Untersuchungen zur historischen Poetik.* Ed. Edward Kowalski and Michael Wegner; tr. Michael Dewey. Rpt. Frankfurt am Main: Fischer Taschenbuch Verlag.

Bakewell, Geoffrey W. 2002. "Oedipus Tex: *Lone Star*, Tragedy, and Postmodernism." *Classical and Modern Literature*, 22 no. 1: 35–48.

2008. "The One-Eyed Man Is King: Oedipal Vision in *Minority Report.*" *Arethusa*, 41: 95–112.

Bakhtin, M. M. 1981; rpt. 1996. *The Dialogic Imagination: Four Essays.* Ed. Michael Holquist; tr. Caryl Emerson and Michael Holquist. Austin: University of Texas Press.

Bann, Stephen, and John E. Bowlt (eds.). 1973. *Russian Formalism: A Collection of Articles and Texts in Translation.* New York: Barnes and Noble.

Baranski, Zygmunt G. (ed.). 1999a. *Pasolini Old and New: Surveys and Studies.* Dublin: Four Courts Press.

1999b. "The Texts of *Il vangelo secondo Matteo.*" In Baranski 1999a: 281–320.

Barck, Karlheinz, *et al.* (eds.). 2000. *Ästhetische Grundbegriffe: Historisches Wörterbuch in sieben Bänden.* Vol. 1: *Absenz-Darstellung.* Stuttgart: Metzler.

Barker, Pat. 1994. *The Eye in the Door.* New York: Dutton.

Barthes, Roland. 1968; rpt. 1988. *Writing Degree Zero.* Tr. Annette Lavers and Colin Smith. New York: Noonday Press.

1977; rpt. 1994. *Image, Music, Text.* Ed. and tr. Stephen Heath. New York: Hill and Wang.

1986; rpt. 1989. *The Rustle of Language*. Tr. Richard Howard. Berkeley: University of California Press.

Bartlett, Nicholas. 1962. "The Dark Struggle." *Film*, 32 (Summer): 11–13.

Basinger, Jeanine. 2007. *Anthony Mann*. 2nd ed. Middletown, CT: Wesleyan University Press.

Bazin, André. 1967a. "The Myth of Total Cinema." In Bazin 1967c: 17–22.

1967b. "The Ontology of the Photographic Image." In Bazin 1967c: 9–16.

1967c; rpt. 2005. *What Is Cinema?* Tr. Hugh Gray. Vol. 1. Berkeley: University of California Press.

and Charles Bitsch. 1958. "Entretien avec Orson Welles." *Cahiers du cinéma*, 84 (June): 1–13.

and Charles Bitsch. 2002. "Interview with Orson Welles (I)." In Estrin 2002: 35–47.

Beard, Mary, and John Henderson. 2000. *Classics: A Very Short Introduction*. Rev. ed. Oxford University Press.

Beevor, Anthony. 1998. *Stalingrad*. New York: Viking.

Behlmer, Rudy (ed.). 2001. *Henry Hathaway: A Directors Guild of America Oral History*. Lanham, MD: Scarecrow Press.

Beja, Morris. 1979. *Film and Literature: An Introduction*. New York: Longman.

Beller, Jonathan L. 2002. "Kino-I, Kino-World: Notes on the Cinematic Mode of Production." In Mirzoeff 2002: 60–85.

Belton, John. 1991. "Language, Oedipus, and *Chinatown*." *Modern Language Notes*, 106: 933–950.

Benedetti, Carla. 1999. *L'ombra lunga dell'autore: Indagine su una figura cancellata*. Milan: Feltrinelli.

2005. *The Empty Cage: Inquiry into the Mysterious Disappearance of the Author*. Tr. William J. Hartley. Ithaca: Cornell University Press.

Benediktson, D. Thomas. 2000. *Literature and the Visual Arts in Greece and Rome*. Norman: University of Oklahoma Press.

Berger, John. 1972; rpt. 1990. *Ways of Seeing*. London: BBC/Penguin.

Bergman, Ingmar. 1988; rpt. 1994. *The Magic Lantern: An Autobiography*. Tr. Joan Tate. New York: Penguin.

Bergmann, Bettina. 2006. "A Painted Garland: Weaving Words and Image in the House of the Epigrams in Pompeii." In Newby and Leader-Newby 2006: 60–101.

Bergonzi, Bernard. 1996. *Heroes' Twilight: A Study of the Literature of the Great War*. 3rd ed. Manchester: Carcanet.

Bergstrom, Janet (ed.). 1999. *Endless Night: Cinema and Psychoanalysis, Parallel Histories*. Berkeley: University of California Press.

Bernardi, Joanne. 2001. *Writing in Light: The Silent Scenario and the Japanese Pure Film Movement*. Detroit: Wayne State University Press.

Bernardini, Aldo, Vittorio Martinelli, and Matilde Tortora. 2005. *Enrico Guazzoni: regista pittore*. Doria (Cosenza): La Mongolfiera.

Bernstein, Matthew. 1994. *Walter Wanger, Hollywood Independent*. Berkeley: University of California Press.

Bertelli, Sergio. 1995. *I corsari del tempo: Gli errori e gli orrori dei film storici.* Florence: Ponte alle Grazie.

Bessy, Maurice, and Lo Duca. 1961. *Georges Méliès, mage: Édition du centenaire (1861–1961).* Paris: Pauvert.

Bettini, Maurizio, and Carlo Brillante. 2002. *Il mito di Elena: Immagini e racconti dalla Grecia a oggi.* Turin: Einaudi.

Beuselink, James. 1988. "Mankiewicz's Cleopatra." *Films in Review,* 39: 2–17.

Billard, Pierre. 1996. "An Interview with Michelangelo Antonioni." In Antonioni 1996: 141–147.

Birchard, Robert S. 2004. *Cecil B. DeMille's Hollywood.* Lexington: University Press of Kentucky.

Bloom, Harold. 1997. *The Anxiety of Influence: A Theory of Poetry.* 2nd ed. New York: Oxford University Press.

Blum, Rudolf. 1991. *Kallimachos: The Alexandrian Library and the Origins of Bibliography.* Tr. Hans H. Wellisch. Madison: University of Wisconsin Press.

Blumenson, Martin. 1972. *The Patton Papers 1885–1940.* Boston: Houghton Mifflin.

Boardman, John. 1978; corrected rpt. 1996. *Greek Sculpture: The Archaic Period: A Handbook.* New York: Oxford University Press.

Bogdanovich, Peter. 1961. *The Cinema of Orson Welles.* New York: Film Library of the Museum of Modern Art/Garden City: Doubleday.

    1962. "Interview with Howard Hawks." In Hillier and Wollen 1996: 50–67.

    1978. *John Ford.* 2nd ed. Berkeley: University of California Press.

    1997. *Who the Devil Made It: Conversations with Legendary Film Directors*; rpt. 1998. New York: Ballantine.

Böll, Heinrich. 1956. *Traveller, If You Come to Spa . . .* Tr. Mervyn Savill. London: Arco.

    1986. *The Stories of Heinrich Böll.* Tr. Leila Vennewitz. New York: Knopf.

Bonanno, Maria Grazia. 1995. "Pasolini e l'*Orestea*: Dal 'teatro di parola' al 'cinema di poesia'." In Todini 1995: 45–66.

Boothe, Brigitte. 2002. "Oedipus Complex." Tr. Harry Zohn. In Erwin 2002: 397–404.

Bordwell, David. 1985; rpt. 1997. *Narration in the Fiction Film.* London: Routledge.

    1989. "Historical Poetics of Cinema." In R. Barton Palmer 1989: 369–398.

    2005. *Figures Traced in Light: On Cinematic Staging.* Berkeley: University of California Press.

    2006. *The Way Hollywood Tells It: Story and Style in Modern Movies.* Berkeley: University of California Press.

    Kristin Thompson, and Janet Staiger. 1985; rpt. 1986. *The Classical Hollywood Cinema: Film Style and Mode of Production to 1960.* New York: Columbia University Press.

Boujut, Michel. 2002. "Five Days in the Life of Commander Welles." Tr. Alisa Hartz. In Estrin 2002: 173–176.

Bowie, Ewen. 1996. "The Ancient Readers of the Greek Novel." In Schmeling 1996: 87–106.

Bowlby, Rachel. 2007. *Freudian Mythologies: Greek Tragedy and Modern Identities.* New York: Oxford University Press.

Bowra, C. M. 1963. "The Two Palinodes of Stesichorus." *The Classical Review,* n.s. 13: 245–252.

Bragg, Melvin. 1988. *Richard Burton: A Life.* Boston: Little, Brown.

Brandell, Jerrold R. (ed.). 2004. *Celluloid Couches, Cinematic Clients: Psychoanalysis and Psychotherapy in the Movies.* Albany: State University of New York Press.

Branham, R. Bracht. 1995. "Inventing the Novel." In Mandelker 1995: 79–87 and 200.

    2000–2001. "Representing Time in Ancient Fiction." *Ancient Narrative,* 1: 1–31.

    2002a. (ed.). *Bakhtin and the Classics.* Evanston, IL: Northwestern University Press.

    2002b. "A Truer Story of the Novel?" In Branham 2002a: 161–186.

Branigan, Edward. 1984. *Point of View in the Cinema: A Theory of Narration and Subjectivity in Classical Film.* Berlin: Mouton.

    2006. *Projecting a Camera: Language-Games in Film Theory.* New York: Routledge.

Bremmer, Jan (ed.). 1986a; rpt. 1989. *Interpretations of Greek Mythology.* Totowa, NJ: Barnes and Noble.

    1986b. "Oedipus and the Greek Oedipus Complex." In Bremmer 1986a: 41–59.

    2002. *The Rise and Fall of the Afterlife.* London: Routledge.

Bresson, Robert. 1977. *Notes on Cinematography.* Tr. Jonathan Griffin. New York: Urizen Books.

Brilliant, Richard. 1984. *Visual Narratives: Storytelling in Etruscan and Roman Art.* Ithaca: Cornell University Press.

Brink, C. O. 1971. *Horace on Poetry.* Vol. 2: *The "Ars Poetica."* Cambridge University Press.

    1982. *Horace on Poetry.* Vol. 3: *Epistles Book II: The Letters to Augustus and Florus.* Cambridge University Press.

Brodersen, Kai. 2004. *Die Sieben Weltwunder: Legendäre Kunst- und Bauwerke der Antike.* 6th ed. Munich: Beck.

Brodsky, Jack, and Nathan Weiss. 1963. *The Cleopatra Papers: A Private Correspondence.* New York: Simon and Schuster.

Brophy, Richard. 2007. "*These Encounters of Theirs.*" *The New Yorker* (February 19 and 26): 49.

Browne, Nick. 1982. *The Rhetoric of Filmic Narration.* Ann Arbor: UMI Research Press.

Brownlow, Kevin. 1968. *The Parade's Gone By . . .* Berkeley: University of California Press.

    1979. *The War, the West, and the Wilderness.* New York: Knopf.

Brunetta, Gian Piero. 1984. "Itinerario di Pier Paolo Pasolini verso il mito di Edipo." *Rivista di Studi Italiani,* 2 no. 2: 92–98.

    1993. *Storia del cinema italiano.* 2nd ed. Vol. 2: *Il cinema del regime 1929–1945.* Rome: Editori Riuniti.

Bull, Malcolm. 2005. *The Mirror of the Gods: How Renaissance Artists Rediscovered the Pagan Gods*. New York: Oxford University Press.

Bulloch, A. W. 1985. "Hellenistic Poetry." In Easterling and Knox 1985: 541–621.

Bundy, Carol. 2005. *The Nature of Sacrifice: A Biography of Charles Russell Lowell, Jr., 1835–64*. New York: Farrar Straus Giroux.

Burckhardt, Jacob. 1995. *The Civilization of the Renaissance in Italy*. Tr. Samuel George Chatwynd Middlemore. 3rd ed. London: Phaidon.

Bureau, Patrick. 2006. "Andrei Tarkovsky: I Am For a Poetic Cinema." Tr. Susana Rossberg and John Gianvito. In Gianvito 2006: 3–5.

Burkert, Walter. 1985. *Greek Religion*. Tr. John Raffan. Cambridge, MA: Harvard University Press.

Burton, Alan. 2002. "Death or Glory? The Great War in British Film." In Monk and Sargeant 2002: 31–46.

Burton, Paul. 2001. "Avian Plague: Sophocles' *Oedipus Tyrannus* and Alfred Hitchcock's *The Birds*." *Mouseion*, 3 no. 1: 313–341.

Buscombe, Edward (ed.). 1988; rpt. 1996. *The BFI Companion to the Western*. London: Deutsch/British Film Institute.

Buxton, Richard (ed.). 1999. *From Myth to Reason? Studies in the Development of Greek Thought*. Oxford University Press.

Cahir, Linda Costanzo. 2006. *Literature into Film: Theory and Practical Approaches*. Jefferson, NC: McFarland.

Cahn, Herbert A. 1950. "Die Löwen des Apollon." *Museum Helveticum*, 7: 185–199.

Caldwell, Richard S. 1974a. "The Blindness of Oedipus." *International Review of Psycho-Analysis*, 1: 207–218.

    1974b. "Selected Bibliography on Psychoanalysis and Classical Studies." *Arethusa*, 7 no. 1: 115–134.

Campbell, David A. 1990; rpt. 2002. *Greek Lyric*. Vol. 1: *Sappho and Alcaeus*. Corrected ed. Cambridge, MA: Harvard University Press.

    1991; rpt. 2001. *Greek Lyric*. Vol. 3: *Stesichorus, Ibycus, Simonides, and Others*. Cambridge, MA: Harvard University Press.

Campbell, Joseph. 1968; several rpts. *The Hero with a Thousand Faces*. 2nd ed. Princeton University Press.

Cancik, Hubert, and Hubert Mohr. 2002. "Rezeptionsformen." *Der Neue Pauly*, 15.2: 759–770.

Canfora, Luciano. 1989; corrected rpt. 1991. *The Vanished Library*. Berkeley: University of California Press.

Cardullo, Bert (ed.). 2008. *Michelangelo Antonioni: Interviews*. Jackson: University Press of Mississippi.

Carnes, Mark C. (ed.). 1995. *Past Imperfect: History According to the Movies*. New York: Holt.

Carpenter, Rhys. 1962; rpt. 1978. *Greek Art: A Study of the Formal Evolution of Style*. Philadelphia: University of Pennsylvania Press.

Carr, David. 2006. "Moral Education at the Movies: On the Cinematic Treatment of Morally Significant Story and Narrative." *The Journal of Moral Education*, 35: 319–334.

Carroll, John M. 1980. *Toward a Structural Psychology of Cinema*. The Hague: Mouton.

Carroll, Maureen. 2003. *Earthly Paradises: Ancient Gardens in History and Archaeology*. Los Angeles: Getty Publications.

Carroll, Noël, and Jinhee Choi (eds.). 2006. *Philosophy of Film and Motion Pictures: An Anthology*. Oxford: Blackwell.

Carson, Anne. 2005. *Decreation: Poetry, Essays, Opera*. New York: Knopf.

Cary, John. 1974. *Spectacular! The Story of Epic Films*. Secaucus, NJ: Castle Books.

Casetti, Francesco. 1999. *Theories of Cinema: 1945–1995*. Tr. Francesca Chiostri, Elizabeth Gard Bartolini-Salimbeni, and Thomas Kelso. Austin: University of Texas Press.

Casty, Alan. 1969. *The Films of Robert Rossen*. New York: Museum of Modern Art.

Caughie, John (ed.). 1981. *Theories of Authorship: A Reader*. London: Routledge and Kegan Paul.

Caute, David. 1994. *Joseph Losey: A Revenge on Life*. London: Faber and Faber/New York: Oxford University Press.

Cavallini, Eleonora. 2005a. "A proposito di *Troy*." In Cavallini 2005b: 53–79.

   2005b. (ed.). *I Greci al cinema: Dal peplum 'd'autore' alla grafica computerizzata*. Bologna: d.u.press.

   2007. (ed.). *Omero mediatico: Aspetti della ricezione omerica nella civiltà contemporanea*. Bologna: d.u.press.

Cavell, Stanley. 1985. *Pursuits of Happiness: The Hollywood Comedy of Remarriage*. Cambridge, MA: Harvard University Press.

   2005a. *Cavell on Film*. Ed. William Rothman. Albany: State University of New York Press.

   2005b. "The Image of the Psychoanalyst in Film." In Cavell 2005a: 295–304.

   2005c. "Moral Reasoning: Teaching from the Core." In Cavell 2005a: 349–359.

Cawelti, John G. 1999. *The Six-Gun Mystique Sequel*. Bowling Green, OH: Bowling Green State University Press.

Ceplair, Larry, and Christopher Sharrett. 2006. "Defending *The Searchers*." *Cineaste*, 32 no. 1: 4.

Chandler, Charlotte. 2002. *Nobody's Perfect: Billy Wilder, A Personal Biography*. New York: Simon and Schuster.

Chase, Cynthia. 1979. "Oedipal Textuality: Reading Freud's Reading of *Oedipus*." *Diacritics*, 9 no. 4: 54–68.

Chatman, Seymour. 1978; rpt. 1989. *Story and Discourse: Narrative Structure in Fiction and Film*. Ithaca: Cornell University Press.

Chierichetti, David. 1995. *Mitchell Leisen, Hollywood Director*. Los Angeles: Photoventures Press.

Churchill, Winston S. 1948. *The Second World War*. Vol. 1: *The Gathering Storm*. Boston: Houghton Mifflin.

Ciment, Michel. 1985. *Conversations with Losey*. London: Methuen.

Clader, Linda Lee. 1976. *Helen: The Evolution from Divine to Heroic in Greek Epic Tradition*. Leiden: Brill.

Clair, René. 1930. "Les auteurs de film n'ont pas besoin de vous." *Pour Vous*, 85 (July 3): 3.

Clay, Diskin. 1982. "Georg Luck and a Decade of *AJP*." *American Journal of Philology*, 103: 1–3.

Clayton, Peter A., and Martin J. Price (eds.). 1988. *The Seven Wonders of the Ancient World*. London: Routledge.

Clifton, N. Roy. 1983. *The Figure in Film*. London: Associated University Presses.

Cobos, Juan, Miguel Rubio, and J. A. Pruneda. 1966. "A Trip to Don Quixoteland: Conversations with Orson Welles." *Cahiers du cinéma in English*, 5.

Cocteau, Jean. 1954; corrected rpt. 1972. *Cocteau on the Film: A Conversation Recorded by André Fraigneau*. Tr. Vera Traill. New York: Dover.

    1967; rpt. 1995. *The Difficulty of Being*. Tr. Elizabeth Sprigge. New York: Da Capo.

    1992; rpt. 1999. *The Art of Cinema*. Ed. André Bernard and Claude Gauteur, tr. Robin Buss. London: Boyars.

*Cocteau* (exhibition catalogue). 2003. Tr. Trista Selous. London: Holberton.

Cohen, Alain J.-J. 2004. "Woody Allen and Freud." In Brandell 2004: 127–145.

Cohoon, J. W. (tr.). 1932; several rpts. *Dio Chrysostom*. Vol. 1. London: Heinemann/ New York: Putnam.

Conrad, Peter. 2000. *The Hitchcock Murders*. London: Faber and Faber.

Conte, Gian Biagio. 1986. *The Rhetoric of Imitation: Genre and Poetic Memory in Virgil and Other Latin Poets*. Ed. Charles Segal. Ithaca: Cornell University Press.

Cooper, Stephen (ed.). 1994. *Perspectives on John Huston*. New York: Hall.

Corbier, Mireille. 2006. *Donner à voir, donner à lire: mémoire et communication dans la Rome ancienne*. Paris: CNRS Éditions.

Cottrell, John, and Fergus Cashin. 1972. *Richard Burton: Very Close Up*. Englewood Cliffs, NJ: Prentice-Hall.

Cowie, Peter. 1973. *The Cinema of Orson Welles*. Rev. ed.; rpt. 1989. New York: Da Capo.

Creed, Barbara. 1993. *The Monstrous-Feminine: Film, Feminism, Psychoanalysis*. London: Routledge.

Crowe, Cameron. 1999; rpt. 2001. *Conversations with Wilder*. New York: Knopf.

Culham, Phyllis, and Lowell Edmunds (eds.). 1989. *Classics: A Discipline and Profession in Crisis?* Lanham, MD: University Press of America.

Current, Richard Nelson, and Marcia Ewing Current. 1997. *Loie Fuller: Goddess of Light*. Boston: Northeastern University Press.

Curtius, Ernst Robert. 1952, rpt. 1990. *European Literature and the Latin Middle Ages*. Tr. Willard R. Trask. Princeton University Press.

Cyrino, Monica S. 2006. "Helen of *Troy*." In Winkler 2006d: 131–147.

Daly, Lloyd W. (tr.). 1961. *Aesop Without Morals*. New York: Yoseloff.

Danek, Georg. 1998. *Epos und Zitat: Studien zu den Quellen der Odyssee*. Vienna: Österreichische Akademie der Wissenschaften.

    2006. "The Story of Troy Through the Centuries." In Winkler 2006d: 68–84.

Däniken, Erich von. 1968; rpt. 1976. *Erinnerungen an die Zukunft: Ungelöste Rätsel der Vergangenheit.* Düsseldorf: Econ.

    1970, rpt. 1999. *Chariots of the Gods? Unsolved Mysteries of the Past.* Tr. Michael Heron. Rpt. New York: Berkley Books.

    1973. *Meine Welt in Bildern: Bildargumente für Theorien, Spekulationen und Erforschtes.* Düsseldorf: Econ.

    1974, rpt. 1975. *In Search of Ancient Gods: My Pictorial Evidence for the Impossible.* Tr. Michael Heron. New York: Bantam.

de Jong, Irene J. F., and J. P. Sullivan (eds.). 1994. *Modern Critical Theory and Classical Literature.* Leiden: Brill.

Dehon, Pierre-Jacques. 1994. "La conception antique de l'originalité et le cinéma américain contemporain." *Mosaic*, 27 no. 3: 1–18.

Deleuze, Gilles. 1986; rpt. 2005. *Cinema 1: The Movement Image.* Tr. Hugh Tomlinson and Barbara Habberjam. London: Continuum.

    1989; rpt. 2005. *Cinema 2: The Time Image.* Tr. Hugh Tomlinson and Robert Galeta. London: Continuum.

Delluc, Louis. 1921. "D'Oreste à Rio Jim." *Cinéa*, 31 (December 9): 14–15.

DeMille, Cecil B. 1959; rpt. 1985. *The Autobiography of Cecil B. DeMille.* Ed. Donald Hayne. New York: Garland.

Dêmopoulos, Michalis (ed.). 2003. *Sinemythologia: Oi ellênikoi mythoi ston pankosmio kinêmatografo.* Athens: Politistikê Olympiada.

Denby, David. 2002. "Good Guys." *The New Yorker* (March 11): 92–93.

    2007. "Men Gone Wild." *The New Yorker* (April 2): 88–89.

Depew, Mary, and Dirk Obbink (eds.). 2000. *Matrices of Genre: Authors, Canons, and Society.* Cambridge, MA: Harvard University Press.

Deslandes, Paul R. 2005. *Oxbridge Men: British Masculinity and the Undergraduate Experience, 1850–1920.* Bloomington: Indiana University Press.

D'Este, Carlo. 1995; rpt. 1996. *Patton: A Genius for War.* New York: Harper Collins.

Deveraux, George. 1970. "The Psychotherapy Scene in Euripides' *Bacchae.*" *Journal of Hellenic Studies*, 90: 35–48.

Dick, Bernard F. 1993. *The Merchant Prince of Poverty Row: Harry Cohn of Columbia Pictures.* Lexington: University Press of Kentucky.

Dmytryk, Edward. 1984. *On Screen Directing.* Boston: Focal Press.

Dodds, E. R. 1951; several rpts. *The Greeks and the Irrational.* Berkeley: University of California Press.

Doherty, Thomas. 1999. *Pre-Code Hollywood: Sex, Immorality, and Insurrection in American Cinema, 1930–1934.* New York: Columbia University Press.

Dostoyevsky, Fyodor M. 1958; several rpts. *The Brothers Karamazov.* Tr. David Magershack. Harmondsworth: Penguin.

Dummer, Jürgen, and Max Kunze (eds.). 1983. *Antikerezeption, Antikeverhältnis, Antikebegegnung in Vergangenheit und Gegenwart: Eine Aufsatzsammlung.* 3 vols. Stendal: Winckelmanngesellschaft.

Dundes, Alan (ed.). 1984. *Sacred Narrative: Readings in the Theory of Myth.* Berkeley: University of California Press.

Dunne, John Gregory. 1997; rpt. 1998. *Monster: Living Off the Big Screen*. New York: Vantage.

Durante, Marcello. 1960. "Ricerche sulla preistoria della lingua poetica greca: La terminologia relativa alla creazione poetica." *Atti della Accademia Nazionale dei Lincei*, 8th ser., 15: 231–249.

Durgnat, Raymond. 1967; rpt. 1971. *Films and Feelings*. Cambridge, MA: MIT Press.

Easterling, P. E., and B. M. W. Knox (eds.). 1985; rpt. 1992. *The Cambridge History of Classical Literature*. Vol. 1: *Greek Literature*. Cambridge University Press.

Edmonds, J. M. (ed.). 1938; several rpts. *The Greek Bucolic Poets*. Rev. ed. Cambridge, MA: Harvard University Press/London: Heinemann.

Edmunds, Lowell. 1981. *The Sphinx in the Oedipus Legend*. Königstein: Hain.

1985; rpt. 1996. *Oedipus: The Ancient Legend and Its Later Analogues*. Baltimore: Johns Hopkins University Press.

2002–2003. "The Abduction of the Beautiful Wife: The Basic Story of the Trojan War." *Studia Philologica Valentina*, 6 n.s. 3: 1–36.

2006. *Oedipus*. London: Routledge.

2007. "Helen's Divine Origins." *Electronic Antiquity*, 10 no. 2 (May). http://scholar.lib.vt.edu/ejournals/ElAnt/V10N2/Edmunds.pdf.

and Alan Dundes (eds.). 1995. *Oedipus: A Folklore Casebook*. 2nd ed. Madison: University of Wisconsin Press.

Edwards, Mark W. 1987; rpt. 1990. *Homer: Poet of the Iliad*. Baltimore: Johns Hopkins University Press.

Eigler, Ulrich (ed.). 2002. *Bewegte Antike: Antike Themen im modernen Film*. Stuttgart: Metzler.

Eisenstein, S. M. 1949; rpt. 1977. *Film Form: Essays in Film Theory*. Ed. and tr. Jay Leyda. San Diego: Harcourt Brace Jovanovich.

1988. *Selected Works*. Vol. 2: *Towards a Theory of Montage*. Ed. Michael Glenny and Richard Taylor; tr. Richard Taylor. London: British Film Institute.

2006. *The Eisenstein Collection*. Ed. Richard Taylor. London: Seagull Books.

Eisner, Robert. 1987. *The Road to Daulis: Psychoanalysis, Psychology, and Classical Mythology*. Syracuse University Press.

Eksteins, Modris. 1998. "Memory and the Great War." In Strachan 1998: 305–317.

2000. "*All Quiet on the Western Front*." In Ellwood 2000: 18–25.

Eldridge, David. 2006. *Hollywood's History Films*. London: Tauris.

Elley, Derek. 1984. *The Epic Film: Myth and History*. London: Routledge and Kegan Paul.

Elliger, Winfried. 1975. *Die Darstellung der Landschaft in der griechischen Dichtung*. Berlin: de Gruyter.

Ellwood, David W. (ed.). 2000. *The Movies as History: Visions of the Twentieth Century*. Stroud: Sutton/History Today.

Erhart, Walter, and Sigrid Nieberle (eds.). 2003. *Odysseen 2001: Fahrten-Passagen-Wanderungen*. Munich: Fink.

Erskine, John. 1925. *The Private Life of Helen of Troy*. New York: Grosset and Dunlap. Rpt. New York: Sun Dial Press, 1942; New York: Popular Library, 1948; New York: Graphic Press, 1956.

Erwin, Edward (ed.). 2002. *The Freud Encyclopedia: Theory, Therapy, and Culture*. New York: Routledge.

España, Rafael de. 1998. *El Peplum: La Antigüedad en el Cine*. N.p. [Barcelona]: Glénat.

Essame, H. 1974. *Patton: A Study in Command*. New York: Scribner.

Estrin, Mark W. (ed.). 2002. *Orson Welles: Interviews*. Jackson: University Press of Mississippi.

Evans, Arthur B. 1977. *Jean Cocteau and His Films of Orphic Identity*. London: Associated University Presses.

Fainaru, Dan. 2001a. "The Human Experience in One Gaze: *Ulysses' Gaze*." In Fainaru 2001b: 93–100.

    2001b. (ed.). *Theo Angelopoulos: Interviews*. Jackson: University Press of Mississippi.

Falkner, Thomas M., Nancy Felson, and David Konstan (eds.). 1999. *Contextualizing Classics: Ideology, Performance, Dialogue: Essays in Honor of John J. Peradotto*. Lanham, MD: Rowman and Littlefield.

Faulx, Jacques. 1969. "L'antiquité toute proche: 'Les Jeunes Aphrodites' de Nikos Koundouros." *Otia*, 17: 18–22.

Faure, Elie. 1922. *L'Arbre d'Eden*. Paris: Crès.

Fell, John L. 1986. *Film and the Narrative Tradition*. 2nd ed. Berkeley: University of California Press.

Fick, Nathaniel. 2005; rpt. 2006. *One Bullet Away: The Making of a Marine Officer*. New York: Mariner.

Finkelberg, Margalit. 1998. *The Birth of Literary Fiction in Ancient Greece*. Oxford: Clarendon Press.

Fischer, Lucy. 2003. *Designing Women: Cinema, Art Deco, and the Female Form*. New York: Columbia University Press.

Fisher, David James. 1999. "Sartre's Freud: Dimensions of Intersubjectivity in *The Freud Scenario*." In Bergstrom 1999: 126–152.

Fleishman, Avrom. 1992. *Narrated Films: Storytelling Situations in Cinema History*. Baltimore: Johns Hopkins University Press.

Ford, Andrew. 2002. *The Origins of Criticism: Literary Culture and Poetic Theory in Classical Greece*. Princeton University Press.

Ford, Daniel. 1967. *Incident at Muc Wa*. Garden City, NY: Doubleday.

Forster, E. M. 1927; rpt. n.d. (1985). *Aspects of the Novel*. San Diego: Harcourt Brace.

Fowler, H. W., and F. G. Fowler (trs.). 1905; rpt. 1949. *The Works of Lucian of Samosata*. Vol. 2. Oxford: Clarendon Press.

Fox, Robin Lane. 1973; rpt. 2004. *Alexander the Great*. London: Penguin.

Fraenkel, Eduard. 1950; corrected rpt. 1962, 1974. *Aeschylus: Agamemnon*. 3 vols. Oxford: Clarendon Press.

Fraigneau, André. 1961. *Cocteau*. Tr. Donald Lehmkuhl. London: Evergreen Books/New York: Grove.

Fraser, Antonia. 2001; rpt. 2006. *Marie Antoinette: The Journey*. New York: Anchor Books.

Fraser, P. M. 1972; rpt. 1984. *Ptolemaic Alexandria*. 3 vols. Oxford: Clarendon Press.

Frazer, R. M., Jr. (tr.). 1966; rpt. 1990. *The Trojan War: The Chronicles of Dictys of Crete and Dares the Phrygian*. Bloomington: Indiana University Press.

Frazer, Sir James G. 1918. *Folklore in the Old Testament: Studies in Comparative Religion, Legend and Law*. Vol. 1. London: Macmillan.

Funke, Hermann. 1997. "*Dulce et decorum.*" *Scripta Classica Israelica*, 16: 77–90.

Fusillo, Massimo. 1996. *La Grecia secondo Pasolini: Mito e cinema*. Florence: Scandicci/Nuova Italia.

Fussell, Paul. 1975; rpt. 2000. *The Great War and Modern Memory*. New York: Oxford University Press.

Gabbard, Glen O. (ed.). 2001. *Psychoanalysis and Film*. London: Karnac.

and Krin Gabbard. 1999. *Psychiatry and the Cinema*. 2nd ed. Washington: American Psychiatric Press.

Galan, Frantisek W. 1984. "Film as Poetry and Prose: Viktor Shklovsky's Contribution to Poetics of Cinema." *Essays in Poetics: The Journal of the British Neo-Formalist School*, 9: 95–104.

Galinsky, Karl. 1981a. "The First Interdisciplinary Field." *Humanities*, 2 no. 3: 1 and 3–4.

1981b. "The First Interdisciplinary Field." *ADFL* [Association of Departments of Foreign Languages] Bulletin, 13 no. 1 (September): 29–30.

Gallagher, Tag. 1984; rpt. 1986. *John Ford: The Man and His Films*. Los Angeles: University of California Press.

Gallo, Italo. 1995. "Pasolini traduttore di Eschilo." In Todini 1995: 33–43.

Gamel, Mary-Kay. 2001. "An American Tragedy: *Chinatown*." In Winkler 2001a: 148–171.

Gance, Abel. 1927. "Le temps de l'image est venu." *L'art cinématographique*, 2: 83–102.

1928. "Le sens moderne – comment on fait un film." *Conférencia*, 16: 197–209.

1929. "Autour du moi et du monde: le cinéma de demain." *Conférencia*, 23: 277–291.

Garofalo, Marcello. 1999; rpt. 2002. *Tutto il cinema di Sergio Leone*. Milan: Baldini and Castoldi.

Gay, Peter. 1988; rpt. 1998. *Freud: A Life for Our Time*. New York: Norton.

1995. "*Freud.*" In Carnes 1995: 170–173.

Geist, Kenneth L. 1978. *Pictures Will Talk: The Life and Films of Joseph L. Mankiewicz*. Corrected ed. New York: Da Capo.

Gelzer, Thomas. 1997. "Woher kommt Schillers Wanderer nach Sparta? Etappen der Geschichte eines berühmten Epigramms." In Knoepfler 1997: 409–428.

Genette, Gérard. 1997. *Palimpsests: Literature in the Second Degree.* Tr. Channa Newman and Claude Dubinsky. Lincoln, NE: University of Nebraska Press.

Georgakas, Dan. 2002–2003. "Greek Cinema for Beginners: A Thumbnail History." *Film Criticism*, 27 no. 2 (Winter): 2–8.

Gerstner, David A., and Janet Staiger (eds.). 2003. *Authorship and Film.* New York: Routledge.

Ghali-Kahil, Lilly B. 1955. *Les enlèvements et le retour d'Hélène dans les textes et les documents figurés.* 2 vols. Paris: de Bocccard.

Gianvito, John (ed.). 2006. *Andrei Tarkovsky: Interviews.* Jackson: University Press of Mississippi.

Giesen, Rolf. 2003. *Nazi Propaganda Films: A History and Filmography.* Jefferson, NC: McFarland.

Gigante, Marcello. 1995. "Edipo uomo qualunque?" In Todini 1995: 69–79.

Godard, Jean-Luc. 1958. "Bergmanorama." *Cahiers du cinéma*, 85 (July): 1–5.

Goethe, Johann Wolfgang von. 1902. *Goethes Werke.* Weimar Edition (1887–1919; 143 vols.). Section 4: *Goethes Briefe.* Vol. 26. Weimar: Böhlau. Rpt. Munich: Deutscher Taschenbuch Verlag, 1987 (vol. 119).

Gold, Barbara K. 2001. "From the New Editor." *American Journal of Philology*, 122: iii–iv.

Goldhill, Simon. 2004; rpt. 2005. *Love, Sex and Tragedy: How the Ancient World Shapes Our Lives.* University of Chicago Press.

Goldman, William. 1983; rpt. 1989. *Adventures in the Screen Trade: A Personal View of Hollywood and Screenwriting.* New York: Warner.

2000; rpt. 2001. *Which Lie Did I Tell? More Adventures in the Screen Trade.* New York: Vintage.

Graf, Fritz. 2009. *Apollo.* London: Routledge.

and Sarah Iles Johnston. 2007. *Ritual Texts for the Afterlife: Orpheus and the Bacchic Gold Tablets.* London: Routledge.

Graham, Peter (ed.). 1968. *The New Wave: Critical Landmarks.* Garden City, NY: Doubleday.

*Grand Illusion: A Film by Jean Renoir.* 1968. Tr. Marianne Alexandre and Andrew Sinclair. New York: Simon and Schuster.

Gransden, K. W. 1984. *Virgil's Iliad: An Essay on Epic Narrative.* Cambridge University Press.

Gray, Simon. 2004. Interview with Theodoros Angelopoulos. http://www.close-upfilm.com/features/Interviews/theoangelopoulos.htm.

Green, Peter. 1974; rpt. 1991. *Alexander of Macedon 356–323 B.C.: A Historical Biography.* Berkeley: University of California Press.

1990; corrected rpt. 1993. *Alexander to Actium: The Historical Evolution of the Hellenistic Age.* Berkeley: University of California Press.

1996; rpt. 1998. *The Greco-Persian Wars.* Berkeley: University of California Press.

Greene, Naomi. 1988. "Deadly Statues: Eros in the Films of Jean Cocteau." *The French Review*, 61 no. 6 (May): 890–898.

1990. *Pier Paolo Pasolini: Cinema as Heresy.* Princeton University Press.

Griffin, Jasper. 1980; rpt. 1988. *Homer on Life and Death.* Oxford: Clarendon Press.

Guidorizzi, Giulio, and Marxiano Melotti (eds.). 2005. *Orfeo e le sue metamorfosi: Mito, arte, poesia*. Rome: Carocci.

Gumpert, Matthew. 2001. *Grafting Helen: The Abduction of the Classical Past*. Madison: University of Wisconsin Press.

Gunning, Tom. 1991; rpt. 1994. *D. W. Griffith and the Origins of American Narrative Film: The Early Years at Biograph*. Urbana: University of Illinois Press.

Hadas, Moses. 1954; rpt. 1961. *Ancilla to Classical Reading*. New York: Columbia University Press.

Hadzsits, George Depue. 1920. "Media of Salvation." *The Classical Weekly*, 14 no. 9 (December 13): 70–71.

Hainsworth, J. B. 1991. *The Idea of Epic*. Berkeley: University of California Press.

Hall, Edith, and Fiona Macintosh (eds.). 1995. *Greek Tragedy and the British Theatre 1660–1914*. Oxford University Press.

Hall, Peter. 2000. *Exposed by the Mask: Form and Language in Drama*. New York: Theatre Communications Group.

Halliday, Jon. 1972. *Sirk on Sirk*. New York: Viking.

Halliwell, Leslie. 1995. *Halliwell's Filmgoer's and Video Viewer's Companion*. Ed. John Walker. 11th ed. New York: Harper.

Halter, Thomas. 1998. *König Oedipus: Von Sophokles zu Cocteau*. Stuttgart: Harrassowitz.

Hamilton, John T. 2003. *Soliciting Darkness: Pindar, Obscurity, and the Classical Tradition*. Cambridge, MA: Harvard University Press.

Hansen, Esther V. 1971. *The Attalids of Pergamon*. 2nd. ed. Ithaca: Cornell University Press.

Hansen, William (ed.). 1998. *Anthology of Ancient Greek Popular Literature*. Bloomington: Indiana University Press.

Hanson, Victor Davis. 2000. *The Western Way of War: Infantry Battle in Classical Greece*. 2nd ed. Berkeley: University of California Press.

   and John Heath. 2000. *Who Killed Homer? The Demise of Classical Education and the Recovery of Greek Wisdom*. New ed. Berkeley: University of California Press.

Harrington, John. 1973. *The Rhetoric of Film*. New York: Holt, Rinehart, and Winston.

Harrison, S. J. 1993. "*Dulce et decorum*: Horace Odes 3.2.13." *Rheinisches Museum für Philologie*, n.s. 136: 91–93.

Harrison, Tony. 1988. "Facing Up to the Muses." *Proceedings of the Classical Association* (Great Britain), 85: 7–29.

   1998. *Prometheus*. London: Faber and Faber.

   2007. *Collected Film Poetry*. London: Faber and Faber.

Haß, Petra. 1998. *Der locus amoenus in der antiken Literatur: Zu Theorie und Geschichte eines literarischen Motivs*. Bamberg: Wissenschaftlicher Verlag.

Hayman, Ronald. 1983. *Brecht: A Biography*. New York: Oxford University Press.

Hazewell, Creighton. 1858. "Spartacus." *The Atlantic Monthly*, 1 no. 3 (January): 288–300.

Heath, Stephen. 1999. "Cinema and Psychoanalysis: Parallel Histories." In Bergstrom 1999: 25–56.

Hedges, Chris. 2002; rpt. 2003. *War Is a Force That Gives Us Meaning.* New York: Anchor Books.

Hedreen, Guy. 1996. "Image, Text, and Story in the Recovery of Helen." *Classical Antiquity*, 15: 152–184.

Heinze, Richard. 1933; rpt. 1983. *Die augusteische Kultur.* 2nd ed. Ed. Alfred Körte. Darmstadt: Wissenschaftliche Buchgesellschaft.

Heinzle, Joachim, and Anneliese Waldschmidt (eds.). 1991. *Die Nibelungen: Ein deutscher Wahn, ein deutscher Alptraum: Studien und Dokumente zur Rezeption des Nibelungenstoffes im 19. und 20. Jahrhundert.* Frankfurt am Main: Suhrkamp.

Klaus Klein, and Ute Obhof (eds.). 2003. *Die Nibelungen: Sage, Epos, Mythos.* Wiesbaden: Reichert.

Henderson, Robert M. 1970; rpt. 1971. *D. W. Griffith: The Years at Biograph.* New York: Farrar Straus Giroux.

Hepworth, Cecil. 1900; rpt. 1970. *Animated Photography: The ABC of the Cinematograph.* 2nd ed. New York: Arno.

1948. "Those Were the Days: Reminiscences by a Pioneer of the Earliest Days of Cinematography." *The Penguin Film Review*, 6 (April).

Herbert, Kevin. 1998a. "Homer's Wingéd Words in the 873rd Bombardment Squadron, Sipan, 1945." *The Classical Bulletin*, 74: 35–46.

1998b. "Introduction: The Classics and Military Service." *The Classical Bulletin*, 74: 5–17.

Herr, Michael. *Dispatches.* 1977; rpt. 1991. New York: Vintage.

Heymann, C. David. 1995. *Liz: An Intimate Biography of Elizabeth Taylor.* New York: Birch Lane Press.

Hicks, Jeremy. 2007. *Dziga Vertov: Defining Documentary Film.* London: Tauris.

Higgins, Reynold. 1988. "The Colossus of Rhodes." In Clayton and Price 1988: 124–137 and 171–172.

Higham, Charles. 1970; rpt. 1986. *Hollywood Cameramen: Sources of Light.* New York: Garland.

1973; rpt. n.d. (1980). *Cecil B. DeMille.* New York: Da Capo.

Highet, Gilbert. 1949; several rpts. *The Classical Tradition: Greek and Roman Influences on Western Literature.* New York: Oxford University Press.

Hillier, Jim, and Peter Wollen (eds.). 1996. *Howard Hawks, American Artist.* London: British Film Institute.

Hoberman, J. 2003; rpt. 2005. *The Dream Life: Movies, Media and the Mythology of the Sixties.* New York: The Free Press.

Hobhouse, Penelope. 2003. *Gardens of Persia.* London: Cassell.

Hoepfner, Wolfram. 2003. *Der Koloß von Rhodos und die Bauten des Helios: Neue Forschungen zu einem der Sieben Weltwunder.* Mainz: von Zabern.

Hofmann, Heinz (ed.). 1999. *Antike Mythen in der europäischen Tradition.* Tübingen: Attempto.

Holden, Anthony. 1988. *Laurence Olivier.* New York: Atheneum.

Hölderlin, Friedrich. 1999. *Sämtliche Gedichte und Hyperion*. Ed. Jochen Schmidt. Frankfurt am Main: Insel.

Holland, Norman N. 1994. "How to See Huston's *Freud*." In Cooper 1994: 164–183.

2006. *Meeting Movies*. Madison, NJ: Fairleigh Dickinson University Press.

Holmberg, Ingrid E. 1995. "Euripides' *Helen*: Most Noble and Most Chaste." *American Journal of Philology*, 116: 19–42.

Holmes, Oliver Wendell. 1995. *The Collected Works of Justice Holmes: Complete Public Writings and Selected Judicial Opinions of Oliver Wendell Holmes*. Ed. Sheldon M. Novick. Vol. 3. University of Chicago Press.

Hopkinson, Neil (ed.). 1988; rpt. 2002. *A Hellenistic Anthology*. Cambridge University Press.

Horsfall, Nicholas. 1995a. "*Aeneid*." In Horsfall 1995b: 192–216.

1995b. (ed.). *A Companion to the Study of Virgil*. Leiden: Brill.

Horton, Andrew (ed.). 1997a. *The Last Modernist: The Films of Theo Angelopoulos*. Westport, CT: Greenwood Press.

1997b. "What Do Our Souls Seek? An Interview with Theo Angelopoulos." In Horton 1997a: 96–110.

1999. *The Films of Theo Angelopoulos: A Cinema of Contemplation*. New ed. Princeton University Press.

2001. "National Culture and Individual Vision." In Fainaru 2001b: 83–88.

Housman, A. E. (ed.). 1930. *M. Manili astronomicon liber quintus*. London: The Richards Press.

1997. *The Poems of A. E. Housman*. Ed. Archie Burnett. Oxford: Clarendon Press.

Hubback, Judith. 1990. "Tearing to Pieces: Pentheus, the *Bacchae* and Analytical Psychology." *Journal of Analytical Psychology*, 35: 3–18.

Hughes, Bettany. 2005; rpt. 2007. *Helen of Troy: Goddess, Princess, Whore*. New York: Vintage.

Huston, John. 1980; rpt. 1994. *An Open Book*. New York: Da Capo.

Hynes, Samuel. 1990; rpt. 1991. *A War Imagined: The First World War and English Culture*. New York: Atheneum.

Iaccio, Pasquale (ed.). 2003a. *Non solo Scipione: Il cinema di Carmine Gallone*. Naples: Liguori.

2003b. "*Scipione l'Africano: Un kolossal dell'epoca fascista*." In Iaccio 2003a: 51–86.

Innes, Doreen C. 1989. "Augustan Critics." In Kennedy 1989: 245–273.

Isenberg, Michael T. 1981. *War on Film: The American Cinema and World War I, 1914–1941*. Rutherford, NJ: Fairleigh Dickinson University Press.

Jäger, Michael. 1990. *Die Theorie des Schönen in der italienischen Renaissance*. Cologne: DuMont.

James, Alan (ed. and tr.). 2004. *Quintus of Smyrna: The Trojan Epic: Posthomerica*. Baltimore: Johns Hopkins University Press.

Jenkins, Elinor. 1921. *Poems by Elinor Jenkins, To Which Are Now Added Last Poems, and a Portrait*. London: Sidgwick and Jackson.

Johnson, Samuel. 2006. *The Lives of the Most Eminent English Poets; with Critical Observations on Their Works.* Ed. Roger Lonsdale. Vol. 2. Oxford: Clarendon Press.

Johnson, W. R. 1976; rpt. 1979. *Darkness Visible: A Study of Vergil's Aeneid.* Berkeley: University of California Press.

Jones, Ernest. 1910. "The Oedipus Complex as an Explanation of Hamlet's Mystery." *The American Journal of Psychology.*

   1949; rpt. 1976. *Hamlet and Oedipus.* New York: Norton.

Jouan, François. 1966. *Euripide et les légendes des chants cypriens: Des origins de la guerre de Troie à l'Iliade.* Paris: Les Belles Lettres.

Judt, Tony. 2005; rpt. 2006. *Postwar: A History of Europe Since 1945.* New York: Penguin.

Kael, Pauline. 1976. "Notes on the Nihilist Poetry of Sam Peckinpah." *The New Yorker* (January 12): 70–75.

   1980. *When the Lights Go Down.* New York: Holt, Rinehart, and Winston.

   1994. *For Keeps.* New York: Dutton.

Kaes, Anton (ed.). 1978. *Kino-Debatte: Texte zum Verhältnis von Literatur und Film 1909–1929.* Munich: Deutscher Taschenbuch Verlag/Tübingen: Niemeyer.

Kagan, Jeremy (ed.). 2006. *Directors Close Up: Interviews with Directors Nominated for Best Film by the Directors Guild of America.* 2nd ed. Lanham, MD: Scarecrow Press.

Kahil, Lilly. 1988. "Helene." *Lexicon Iconographicum Mythologiae Classicae,* 4, part 1, 498–563; part 2, 291–358.

   1997. "Menelaos." *Lexicon Iconographicum Mythologiae Classicae,* 8, part 1, 834–841; part 2, 562–565.

Kalat, David. 2001. *The Strange Case of Dr. Mabuse: A Study of the Twelve Films and Five Novels.* Jefferson, NC: McFarland.

Kamp, David. 1998. "When Liz Met Dick." *Vanity Fair* (April): 366–388 and 393–394.

Kaplan, E. Ann. 1990a. "Introduction: From Plato's Cave to Freud's Screen." In Kaplan 1990b: 1–23.

   1990b. (ed.). *Psychoanalysis and Cinema.* New York: Routledge.

Karasek, Hellmuth. 2002. *Billy Wilder: Eine Nahaufnahme.* 5th ed. Munich: Heyne.

Kawin, Bruce F. 1978; rpt. 2006. *Mindscreen: Bergman, Godard, and First-Person Film.* Normal, IL: Dalkey Archive Press.

Kazan, Elia. 2006. "On What Makes a Director." In Kagan 2006: 315–322.

Kelly, Andrew. 1997. *Cinema and the Great War.* London: Routledge.

   1998. *Filming All Quiet on the Western Front: "Brutal Cutting, Stupid Censors, Bigoted Politicos".* London: Tauris.

Kennedy, George A. (ed.). 1989. *The Cambridge History of Literary Criticism.* Vol. 1: *Classical Criticism.* Cambridge University Press.

Kermode, Frank. 1983, corrected ed. 1975. *The Classic: Literary Images of Permanence and Change.* Cambridge, MA: Harvard University Press.

Kern, Otto (ed.). 1922; rpt. 1963. *Orphicorum Fragmenta*. Berlin: Weidmann.

Kerr, Douglas. 1993. *Wilfred Owen's Voices: Language and Community*. Oxford: Clarendon Press.

Kimball, A. Samuel. 2002. "*Laius a tergo*, the Symbolic Order, the Production of the Future: *Chinatown*'s Primal Scene." *Literature and Psychology*, 48: 1–31.

King, Norman. 1984. *Abel Gance: A Politics of Spectacle*. London: British Film Institute.

Kipling, Rudyard. 1941. *The Burwash Edition of the Complete Works in Prose and Verse of Rudyard Kipling*. Vol. 26: *The Seven Seas/The Five Nations/The Years Between*. N.p. [New York]: Doubleday, Doran.

Kitses, Jim. 1969. *Horizons West: Anthony Mann, Budd Boetticher, Sam Peckinpah: Studies of Authorship within the Western*. London: Thames and Hudson/ British Film Institute.

2004. *Horizons West: Directing the Western from John Ford to Clint Eastwood*. London: British Film Institute.

Knerr, Anthony D. (ed.). 1984. *Shelley's Adonais: A Critical Edition*. New York: Columbia University Press.

Kniebe, Tobias. 2004. "Homer ist, wenn man trotzdem lacht: 'Troja'-Regisseur Wolfgang Petersen über die mythischen Wurzeln des Erzählens und den Achilles in uns allen." *Süddeutsche Zeitung* (May 11); http://www.sueddeutsche.de/kultur/artikel/607/31576/print.html.

Knoepfler, Denis (ed.). 1997. *Nomen Latinum: Mélanges de langue, de littérature et de civilisations latines offerts au professeur André Schneider*. Neuchâtel: Faculté de lettres/Geneva: Droz.

Knox, Bernard W. M. 1964; rpt. 1983. *The Heroic Temper: Studies in Sophoclean Tragedy*. Berkeley: University of California Press.

1998. *Oedipus at Thebes: Sophocles' Tragic Hero and His Time*. New ed. New Haven: Yale University Press.

Kobal, John. 1978; rpt. 1982. *Rita Hayworth: The Time, the Place and the Woman*. New York: Berkley Books.

Konstan, David. 1999. "*Arethusa* and the Politics of Criticism." In Falkner, Felson, and Konstan 1999: 335–346.

Kontaxopoulos, Giannis (ed.). 1999. *Zan Koktô: O polytropos poiêtês*. Athens: Exantas/Odos Panos.

Korenjak, Martin, and Karlheinz Töchterle (eds.). 2002. *Pontes II: Antike im Film*. Innsbruck: Studien Verlag.

Kovacs, David (ed. and tr.). 2002a. *Euripides: Bacchae, Iphigenia at Aulis, Rhesus*. Cambridge, MA: Harvard University Press.

2002b. (ed. and tr.). *Euripides: Helen, Phoenician Women, Orestes*. Cambridge, MA: Harvard University Press.

Kracauer, Siegfried. 1947; rpt. 1974. *From Caligari to Hitler: A Psychological History of the German Film*. Princeton University Press.

1960; rpt. 1997. *Theory of Film: The Redemption of Physical Reality*. Princeton University Press.

Kramer, Alan. 2007. *Dynamic of Destruction: Culture and Mass Killing in the First World War*. New York: Oxford University Press.

Kranz, Walther. 1961. "Sphragis: Ichform und Namernsiegel als Eingangs- und Schlußmotiv antiker Dichtung." *Rheinisches Museum für Philologie*, 104: 3–46 and 97–124.

1967. *Studien zur antiken Literatur und ihrem Fortwirken*. Ed. Ernst Vogt. Heidelberg: Winter.

Kreisel, Deanna K. 2005. "What Maxie Knew: The Gift and Oedipus in *What Maisie Knew* and *Rushmore*." *Mosaic*, 38 no. 2: 1–17.

Kristeller, Paul Oskar. 1951–1952. "The Modern System of the Arts: A Study in the History of Aesthetics." *Journal of the History of Ideas*, 12: 496–527 and 13: 17–46.

1983. "'Creativity' and 'Tradition'." *Journal of the History of Ideas*, 44: 105–113.

1990. *Renaissance Thought and the Arts*. Expanded ed. Princeton University Press.

Krüger, Peter. 1991. "Etzels Halle und Stalingrad: Die Rede Görings vom 30.1.1943." In Heinzle and Waldschmidt 1991: 151–190. Rpt. in Heinzle, Klein, and Obhof 2003: 375–403.

Kullmann, Wolfgang. 1992a. "Das Heldenideal der Ilias und die Zeit ihres Dichters." In Kulmann 1992b: 264–271.

1992b. *Homerische Motive: Beiträge zur Entstehung, Eigenart und Wirkung von Ilias und Odyssee*. Ed. Roland J. Müller. Stuttgart: Steiner.

Kunze, Max (ed.). 2003. *Die Sieben Weltwunder der Antike: Wege der Wiedergewinnung aus sechs Jahrhunderten*. Mainz: von Zabern.

Kyle, Galloway (ed.). 1916. *Soldier Poets: Songs of the Fighting Men*. London: Macdonald.

1917. (ed.). *More Songs by the Fighting Men*. London: Macdonald.

Labarthe, André. 1960. "Entretien avec Michelangelo Antonioni." *Cahiers du cinéma*, 112 (October): 1–10.

1996. "A Conversation with Michelangelo Antonioni." In Antonioni 1996: 133–140.

Lane, Anthony. 2004. "War-Torn." *The New Yorker* (December 6): 125–127.

Langer, Susanne K. 1953; several rpts. *Feeling and Form: A Theory of Art Developed from Philosophy in a New Key*. New York: Scribner.

Langglotz, Ernst. 1975–1976. "Eine Nachbildung des Helios von Rhodos." *Rendiconti della Pontifica Accademia di Roma di Archeologia*, 48: 141–150.

Lapsley, Robert. 2006. *Film Theory: An Introduction*. Manchester University Press.

Larson, Victoria Tietze. 1999. "Classics and the Acquisition and Validation of Power in Britain's 'Imperial Century' (1815–1914)." *International Journal of the Classical Tradition*, 6: 185–225.

Latacz, Joachim. 2006. "From Homer's Troy to Petersen's *Troy*." In Winkler 2006d: 27–42.

Lattimore, Richmond (tr.). 1951; several rpts. *The Iliad of Homer*. University of Chicago Press.

1965; several rpts. (tr.). *The Odyssey of Homer*. New York: Harper and Row.

Lazarus, Emma. 2005. *Selected Poems*. Ed. John Hollander. New York: The Library of America.

Lebeau, Vicky. 2001. *Psychoanalysis and Cinema: The Play of Shadows*. London: Wallflower.

Le Bohec, Yann. 1993; rpt. 2000. *The Imperial Roman Army*. London: Routledge.

Lee, Rensselaer W. 1967. *Ut pictura poesis: The Humanistic Theory of Painting*. 2nd ed. New York: Norton.

Leguèbe, Eric. 2001. "John Ford." Tr. Jenny Lefcourt. In Peary 2001: 70–74.

Lehman, Peter (ed.). 1990. *Close Viewings: An Anthology of New Film Criticism*. Tallahassee: Florida State University Press.

Leiser, Erwin. 1974; rpt. 1975. *Nazi Cinema*. Tr. Gertrud Mander and David Wilson. New York: Macmillan.

Leprohon, Pierre. 1972. *The Italian Cinema*. Tr. Roger Greaves and Oliver Stallybrass. London: Secker and Warburg/New York: Praeger.

Létoublon, Françoise, and Caroline Eades. 2003. "Apo tous arkhaious stous prosôpikous mythous: To prôto vlemma kai o arkhegonos logos ston Theodôro Angelopoulo." In Dêmopoulos 2003: 89–113.

Levinson, André. 1927. "Pour une poétique du film." *L'art cinématographique*, 4: 51–88.

Lieberg, Godo. 1982. *Poeta creator: Studien zu einer Figur der antiken Dichtung*. Amsterdam: Gieben.

Lindsay, Vachel. 1915; expanded ed. 1922; rpt. 2000. *The Art of the Moving Picture*. New York: Modern Library.

Littger, Stephan (ed.). 2006. *The Director's Cut: Picturing Hollywood in the 21st Century: Conversations with 21 Contemporary Filmmakers*. New York: Continuum.

LoBrutto, Vincent. 2005. *Becoming Film Literate: The Art and Craft of Motion Pictures*. Westport, CT: Praeger.

Lombardo, Stanley, and Diane Rayor (trs.). 1988. *Callimachus: Hymns, Epigrams, Select Fragments*. Baltimore: Johns Hopkins University Press.

Luck, Georg. 1987. "Diskin Clay, Editor of *AJP*, 1982–1987." *American Journal of Philology*, 108: v.

Luhr, William, and Peter Lehman. 1977. *Authorship and Narrative in the Cinema: Issues in Contemporary Aesthetics and Criticism*. New York: Putnam.

Lupton, Catherine. 2005. *Chris Marker: Memories of the Future*. London: Reaktion Books.

Lurje, Michael. 2004. *Die Suche nach der Schuld: Sophokles' Oedipus Rex, Aristoteles' Poetik und das Tragödienverständnis der Neuzeit*. Munich: Saur.

McBride, Joseph. 1982. *Hawks on Hawks*. Berkeley: University of California Press. 2001; rpt. 2003. *Searching For John Ford*. New York: St. Martin's.

MacCabe, Colin. 1999. *The Eloquence of the Vulgar: Language, Cinema and the Politics of Culture*. London: British Film Institute.

McCarthy, Todd. 1997; rpt. 2000. *Howard Hawks: The Grey Fox of Hollywood*. New York: Grove.

McCartney, Eugene S. 1917–1918. "The Ancients and the War." *The Classical Weekly*, 11: 142–144.

McDonald, Marianne. 1992. *Ancient Sun, Modern Light: Greek Drama on the Modern Stage*. New York: Columbia University Press.

    2001. *Sing Sorrow: Classics, History, and Heroines in Opera*. Westport, CT: Greenwood Press.

    and Martin M. Winkler. 2001. "Michael Cacoyannis and Irene Papas on Greek Tragedy." In Winkler 2001a: 72–89.

McGann, Jerome J. 1991. *The Textual Condition*. Princeton University Press.

McGinnis, Wayne D. 1975. "*Chinatown*: Roman Polanski's Contemporary Oedipus Story." *Literature/Film Quarterly*, 3: 249–251.

Mackinnon, Kenneth. 1986. *Greek Tragedy into Film*. Rutherford, NJ: Fairleigh Dickinson University Press.

McLean, Adrienne L. 2004. *Being Rita Hayworth: Labor, Identity, and Hollywood Stardom*. New Brunswick: Rutgers University Press.

McMurtry, Larry. 1987; rpt. 2001. *Film Flam: Essays on Hollywood*. New York: Simon and Schuster.

Magny, Claude-Edmonde. 1972. *The Age of the American Novel: The Film Aesthetic of Fiction Between the Two Wars*. Tr. Eleanor Hochman. New York: Ungar.

Malissard, Alain. 1974. *Étude filmique de la colonne Trajane: L'écriture de l'histoire et de l'épopée latines dans ses rapports avec le langage filmique*. Dissertation, Université de Tours.

    1982. "Une nouvelle approche de la Colonne Trajane." *Aufstieg und Niedergang der römischen Welt*, 2.12.1: 579–606.

Maltby, Richard. 2003. *Hollywood Cinema*. 2nd ed. Oxford: Blackwell.

Malthête-Méliès, Madeleine (ed.). 1984. *Méliès et la naissance du spectacle cinématographique*. Paris: Klincksieck.

Mandelbaum, Howard, and Eric Myers. 1985; rpt. 2000. *Screen Deco*. Santa Monica: Hennessey and Ingalls.

Mandelker, Amy (ed.). 1995. *Bakhtin in Contexts: Across the Disciplines*. Evanston, IL: Northwestern University Press.

Manvell, Roger. 1948. "The Poetry of the Film." *The Penguin Film Review*, 6 (April).

    1950. *Film*. New ed. Harmondsworth: Penguin.

Marie, Michel. 2003. *The French New Wave: An Artistic School*. Tr. Richard Neupert. Oxford: Blackwell.

Martindale, Charles. 1993. *Redeeming the Text: Latin Poetry and the Hermeneutics of Reception*. Cambridge University Press.

    2006. "Introduction: Thinking Through Reception." In Martindale and Thomas 2006: 1–13.

    and Richard F. Thomas (eds.). 2006. *Classics and the Uses of Reception*. Oxford: Blackwell.

Mason, H. A. 1985. *The Tragic Plane*. Oxford: Clarendon Press.

Mast, Gerald. 1977; rpt. 1983. *Film/Cinema/Movie: A Theory of Experience*. University of Chicago Press.

1982. *Howard Hawks, Storyteller*. New York: Oxford University Press.

Maurois, André. 1927. "La poésie du cinema." *L'art cinématographique*, 3: 1–37.

Melville, Ronald (tr.). 1997; rpt. 1999. *Lucretius: On the Nature of the Universe*. Oxford University Press.

Mench, Fred. 2001. "Film Sense in the *Aeneid*." In Winkler 2001a: 219–232.

Metz, Christian. 1974a; rpt. 1991. *Film Language: A Semiotics of the Cinema*. Tr. Michael Taylor. University of Chicago Press.

1974b. *Language and Cinema*. Tr. Donna Jean Umiker-Sebeok. The Hague: Mouton.

1982a. *The Imaginary Signifier: Psychoanalysis and the Cinema*. Tr. Celia Britton *et al*. Bloomington: Indiana University Press.

1982b. *Langage et cinéma*. New ed. Paris: Éditions Albatros.

1986. *Essais sur la signification au cinéma*. Vol. 2. 4th ed. Paris: Klincksieck.

1994. *Essais sur la signification au cinéma*. Vol. 1. 2nd ed. Paris: Klincksieck.

Michaels, Lloyd (ed.). 2000. *Ingmar Bergman's Persona*. Cambridge University Press.

Mikics, David. 2005. "Sophocles' *Oedipus Tyrannus* in Freud and Lacan." *Classical and Modern Literature*, 25 no. 2: 55–75.

Miller, Richard F. 2005. *Harvard's Civil War: A History of the Twentieth Massachusetts Volunteer Regiment*. Hanover, NH: University Press of New England.

Miller, Toby, and Robert Stam (eds.). 1999. *A Companion to Film Theory*. Oxford: Blackwell.

Milne, Tom. 1968. *Losey on Losey*. Garden City, NY: Doubleday.

Mirzoeff, Nicholas (ed.). 2002. *The Visual Culture Reader*. 2nd ed. London: Routledge.

Mitchell, George J. 1985. "Making *All Quiet on the Western Front*." *American Cinematographer*, 65 no. 9: 34–43.

Mittelstadt, Michael C. 1967. "Longus: Daphnis and Chloe and Roman Narrative Painting." *Latomus*, 26: 752–761.

Modonese, Piero Lauro (tr.). 1976. *Artemidoro di Daldi: Dell'interpretazione de' sogni*. Milan: Rizzoli.

Monaco, James. 1977. *The New Wave: Truffaut, Godard, Chabrol, Rohmer, Rivette*. New York: Oxford University Press.

2000. *How to Read a Film: The World of Movies, Media and Multimedia: Language, History, Theory*. New York: Oxford University Press.

Monk, Claire, and Amy Sargeant (eds.). 2002. *British Historical Cinema*. London: Routledge.

Moore, Harold G., and Joseph L. Galloway. 1992; rpt. 2004. *We Were Soldiers Once . . . and Young: Ia Drang – The Battle That Changed the War in Vietnam*. New York: Ballantine.

Moore, Michael. 2004a. *The Official* Fahrenheit 9/11 *Reader*. New York: Simon and Schuster.

2004b. *Will They Ever Trust Us Again? Letters from the War Zone*. New York: Simon and Schuster.

Morgan, John. 2003. "*Nymphs, Neighbours and Narrators*: A Narratological Approach to Longus." In Panayotakis, Zimmerman, and Keulen 2003: 171–189.

Morris, Jan (ed.). 1978. *The Oxford Book of Oxford*. Oxford University Press.

Mosse, George L. 1990; rpt. 1991. *Fallen Soldiers: Reshaping the Memory of the World Wars*. New York: Oxford University Press.

Most, Glenn W. 1999. "From Logos to Mythos." In Buxton 1999: 29–47.

2000. "Generating Genres: The Idea of the Tragic." In Depew and Obbink 2000: 15–35 and 247–248.

Moynihan, Elizabeth B. 1979; rpt. 1982. *Paradise as a Garden in Persia and Mughal India*. London: Scolar Press.

Mullahy, Patrick. 1948, rpt. 1955. *Oedipus: Myth and Complex: A Review of Psycho-analytic Theory*. New York: Grove Press.

Mulvey, Laura. 1989a. "Afterthoughts on 'Visual Pleasure and Narrative Cinema' Inspired by King Vidor's *Duel in the Sun* (1946)." In Mulvey 1989e: 29–38.

1989b. "Changes: Thoughts on Myth, Narrative and Historical Experience." In Mulvey 1989e: 159–176.

1989c. "Notes on Sirk and Melodrama." In Mulvey 1989e: 39–44.

1989d. "The Oedipus Myth: Beyond the Riddles of the Sphinx." In Mulvey 1989e: 177–201.

1989e. *Visual and Other Pleasures*. Bloomington: Indiana University Press.

1989f. "Visual Pleasure and Narrative Cinema." In Mulvey 1989e: 14–26.

Musatti, Cesare. 1976. "Introduction." In Modonese 1976: 7–23.

Nagy, Gregory. 1989. "Early Greek Views of Poets and Poetry." In Kennedy 1989: 1–77.

1999. *The Best of the Achaeans: Concepts of the Hero in Archaic Greek Poetry*. Rev. ed. Baltimore: Johns Hopkins University Press.

Narboni, Jean, and Tom Milne (eds.). 1972; rpt. 1986. *Godard on Godard*. Tr. Tom Milne. Rpt. New York: Da Capo.

Naremore, James. 1999. "Authorship." In Miller and Stam 1999: 9–24.

Nesselrath, Heinz-Günther (ed.). 1997. *Einleitung in die griechische Philologie*. Stuttgart: Teubner.

Nestle, Wilhelm. 1941; rpt. 1975. *Vom Mythos zum Logos: Die Selbstentfaltung des griechischen Denkens von Homer bis auf die Sophistik und Sokrates*. 2nd ed. Stuttgart: Kröner.

Neupert, Richard. 2002. *A History of the French New Wave Cinema*. Madison: University of Wisconsin Press.

Newby, Zarah, and Ruth Leader-Newby (eds.). 2006. *Art and Inscriptions in the Ancient World*. Cambridge University Press.

Newman, J. K. 2001a. "Ancient Poetics and Eisenstein's Films." In Winkler 2001a: 193–218.

Nichols, Bill (ed.). 1976. *Movies and Methods: An Anthology*. Berkeley: University of California Press.

Nietzsche, Friedrich. 1990. *Unmodern Observations*. Ed. William Arrowsmith. New Haven: Yale University Press.

Nilsson, Martin P. 1932; several rpts. *The Mycenaean Origin of Greek Mythology*. Berkeley: University of California Press.

Nisbet, R. G. M., and Margaret Hubbard. 1978; rpt. 1991. *A Commentary on Horace*: Odes, *Book II*. Oxford: Clarendon Press.

Niver, Kemp R. 1985. *Early Motion Pictures: The Paper Print Collection in the Library of Congress*. Ed. Bebe Bergsten. Washington: Library of Congress.

Nussbaum, Martha C. 2001. *The Fragility of Goodness: Luck and Ethics in Greek Tragedy and Philosophy*. 2nd ed. Cambridge University Press.

O'Brien, Geoffrey. 1993; rpt. 1995. *The Phantom Empire: Movies in the Mind of the 20th Century*. New York: Norton.

O'Brien, Tim. 1975; rpt. 1999. *If I Die in a Combat Zone, Box Me Up and Ship Me Home*. New York: Broadway Books.

Olivier, Laurence. 1986. *On Acting*. New York: Simon and Schuster.

Onesti, Rosa Calzecchi (tr.). 1963. *Omero: Odissea*. Turin: Einaudi.

Overton, Bill. 1996. *The Novel of Female Adultery: Love and Gender in Continental European Fiction, 1830–1900*. Basingstoke: Macmillan/New York: St. Martin's.

   2002. *Fictions of Female Adultery, 1684–1890: Theories and Circumtexts*. Basingstoke: Palgrave Macmillan.

Owen, Wilfred. 1983; rpt. 1984. *The Complete Poems and Fragments*. Ed. Jon Stallworthy. Vol. 1: *The Poems*. New York: Norton.

Pagnol, Marcel. 1930. "Le film parlant offre à l'écrivain des ressources nouvelles." *Le journal* (May 17).

   1933. "Cinématurgie de Paris." *Cahiers du film*, 1 (December 15): 3–8.

Palaima, Thomas G. 2000. "Courage and Prowess Afoot in Homer and the Vietnam of Tim O'Brien." *Classical and Modern Literature*, 20 no. 3: 1–22.

Palmer, James, and Michael Riley. 1993. *The Films of Joseph Losey*. Cambridge University Press.

Palmer, R. Barton (ed.). 1989. *The Cinematic Text: Methods and Approaches*. New York: AMS Press.

Panayotakis, Stelios, Maaike Zimmerman, and Wytse Keulen (eds.). 2003. *The Ancient Novel and Beyond*. Leiden: Brill.

Panofsky, Erwin. 1995. *Three Essays on Style*. Ed. Irving Lavin. Cambridge, MA: MIT Press.

Papillon, Terry. 1996. "Isocrates on Gorgias and Helen: The Unity of the Helen." *The Classical Journal*, 1: 377–391.

Paris, Michael (ed.). 2000. *The First World War and Popular Cinema: 1914 to the Present*. New Brunswick: Rutgers University Press.

Parker, H. M. D. 1993. *The Roman Legions*. Corrected rpt. New York: Barnes and Noble.

Parker, Peter. 1987. *The Old Lie: The Great War and the Public-School Ethos.* London: Constable.

Parsons, Michael. 1990. "Self-Knowledge Refused and Accepted: A Psychoanalytical Perspective on the *Bacchae* and the *Oedipus at Colonus.*" *Journal of Analytical Psychology,* 35: 19–40.

Pasolini, Pier Paolo. 1971. *Oedipus Rex: A Film.* Tr. John Mathews. London: Lorrimer.

   1988. *Heretical Empiricism.* Ed. Louise K. Barnett; tr. Ben Lawton and Louise K. Barnett. Bloomington: Indiana University Press.

   1991. *Il Vangelo secondo Matteo/Edipo re/Medea.* Milan: Garzanti/Gli elefanti.

Paul, Joanna. 2005. "Gladiator." *The Classical Review,* 55: 688–690.

Paulsen, Wolfgang (ed.). 1970. *Psychologie in der Literaturwissenschaft.* Heidelberg: Stiehm.

Pearcy, Lee T. 2005. *The Grammar of Our Civility: Classical Education in America.* Waco, TX: Baylor University Press.

Peary, Gerald (ed.). 2001. *John Ford: Interviews.* Jackson: University Press of Mississippi.

Pechter, William S. 1971. *Twenty-Four Times a Second: Films and Film-Makers.* New York: Harper and Row.

   1982. *Movies Plus One: Seven Years of Film Reviewing.* New York: Horizon Press.

Pelling, C. B. R. (ed.). 1988. *Plutarch: Life of Antony.* Cambridge University Press.

*Penguin Film Review, The.* 1977–1978. 2 vols. Rpt. Totowa, NJ: Rowman and Littlefield.

Penley, Constance. 1989. *The Future of an Illusion: Film, Feminism, and Psychoanalysis.* Minneapolis: University of Minnesota Press.

Perez, Gilberto. 1998. *The Material Ghost: Films and Their Medium.* Baltimore: Johns Hopkins University Press.

Perkins, V. F. 1972; rpt. 1993. *Film as Film: Understanding and Judging Movies.* New York: Da Capo.

Perrin, Bernadotte (tr.). 1914; several rpts. *Plutarch's Lives.* Vol. 2. London: Heinemann/New York: Macmillan.

Pfeiffer, Rudolf. 1961. *Philologia perennis.* Munich: Beck.

   1968; rpt. 1978. *History of Classical Scholarship: From the Beginnings to the End of the Hellenistic Age.* Oxford: Clarendon Press.

Phillips, Patrick. 2000. *Understanding Film Texts.* London: British Film Institute.

Plutarch. 1909; several rpts. *Plutarch's Lives.* New York: Collier.

Poague, Leland A. 1982. *Howard Hawks.* Boston: Twayne.

"Poetry and the Film: A Symposium" (1953). *Film Culture,* 29 (Summer, 1963): 55–63.

Politzer, Heinz. 1970. "Hatte Ödipus einen Ödipus-Komplex?" In Paulsen 1970: 115–139.

Pollitt, J. J. 1974; rpt. 1991. *The Ancient View of Greek Art: Criticism, History, and Terminology.* New Haven: Yale University Press.

1999. *Art and Experience in Classical Greece.* New ed. Cambridge University Press.

Powell, Anton, and Stephen Hodkinson (eds.). 2002. *Sparta Beyond the Mirage.* London: Classical Press of Wales/Duckworth.

Pucci, Giuseppe. 2005. "Orfeo e la decima Musa." In Guidorizzi and Melotti 2005: 168–178.

Pudovkin, Vsevolod. 2006. *Selected Essays.* Ed. Richard Taylor; tr. Richard Taylor and Evgeni Filippov. London: Seagull Books.

Putnam, Michael C. J. 1965; rpt. 1988. *The Poetry of the Aeneid.* Ithaca: Cornell University Press.

Quévrain, Anne-Marie, and Marie-George Charconnet-Méliès. 1984. "Méliès et Freud: Un avenir pour les marchands d'illusions?" In Malthête-Méliès 1984: 221–239.

Rabel, Robert J. 2003. "Murder at the Crossroads: *Oedipus Rex, Falling Angel,* and *Angel Heart.*" *Classical and Modern Literature,* 23 no. 1: 33–48.

Rafferty, Terrence. 2003. "Everybody Gets a Cut: DVDs Give Viewers Dozens of Choices – and That's the Problem." *The New York Times Magazine* (May 4): 58 and 60–61.

Raymond, Ernest. 1922; rpt. 1973. *Tell England: A Study in a Generation.* London: Cassell.

Reardon, B. P. (ed.). 1989; rpt. 2007. *Collected Ancient Greek Novels.* Berkeley: University of California Press.

Rebenich, Stefan. 2002. "From Thermopylae to Stalingrad: The Myth of Leonidas in German Historiography." In Powell and Hodkinson 2002: 323–349.

Remarque, Erich Maria. 1929a; several rpts. *All Quiet on the Western Front.* Tr. A. W. Wheen. New York: Grosset.

1929b; several rpts. *Im Westen nichts Neues.* Berlin: Propyläen-Verlag.

Renard, Jean. 1969. "Adaptations cinématographiques de thèmes antiques." *Otia,* 17: 3–17.

Richards, Jeffrey. 1973. *Visions of Yesterday.* London: Routledge and Kegan Paul.

1988. *Happiest Days: The Public Schools in English Fiction.* Manchester University Press.

Richardson, Robert. 1969; rpt. 1985. *Literature and Film.* New York: Garland.

Richter, Gisela M. A. 1968; rpt. 1988. *Korai: Archaic Greek Maidens: A Study of the Development of the Kore Type in Greek Sculpture.* New York: Hacker.

1970a. *Kouroi: Archaic Greek Youths: A Study of the Development of the Kouros Type in Greek Sculpture.* 3rd ed. London: Phaidon.

1970b. *Perspective in Greek and Roman Art.* London: Phaidon.

Ridgway, Brunilde Sismondo. 1970. *The Severe Style in Greek Sculpture.* Princeton University Press.

1977. *The Archaic Style in Greek Sculpture.* Princeton University Press.

Riemer, P. 2002. "Der sophokleische Ödipus im Spiegel von Pasolinis *Edipo re.*" In Eigler 2002: 80–87.

Ringgold, Gene. 1991. *The Complete Films of Rita Hayworth: The Legend and Career of a Love Goddess*. New York: Citadel Press.

Rippon, Maria R. 2002. *Judgment and Justification in the Nineteenth-Century Novel of Adultery*. Westport, CT: Greenwood Press.

Robert, Carl. 1915; rpt. 2003. *Oidipus: Geschichte eines poetischen Stoffes im griechischen Altertum*. 2 vols. Berlin: Weidmann.

Roberts, Graham. 2000. *The Man with the Movie Camera*. London: Tauris.

Rohmer, Eric. 1980; rpt. 2006. *Six Moral Tales*. Tr. Sabine d'Estrée. New York: Viking.

1989. *The Taste for Beauty*. Ed. Jean Narboni; tr. Carol Volk. Cambridge University Press.

Roisman, Hanna M. 2006. "Helen in the *Iliad*: *Causa Belli* and Victim of War: From Silent Weaver to Public Speaker." *American Journal of Philology*, 127: 1–36.

Rollet, Sylvie. 1995. "*Le regard d'Ulysse*: Un plaidoyer pour l'humanité du cinéma." *Positif*, 415 (September): 18–20.

Romer, John and Elizabeth. 1995; rpt. 2000. *The Seven Wonders of the World: A History of the Modern Imagination*. London: Seven Dials.

Rosenbaum, Jonathan (ed.). 1977. *Rivette: Texts and Interviews*. Tr. Amy Gateff and Tom Milne. London: British Film Institute.

Rosenberg, Bernard, and Harry Silverstein. 1970; rpt. 1976. *The Real Tinsel*. New York: Macmillan.

Rosenblum, Ralph, and Robert Karen. 1979; rpt. 1986. *When the Shooting Stops . . . the Cutting Begins: A Film Editor's Story*. New York: Da Capo.

Rosenmeyer, Patricia A. 1992; rpt. 2006. *The Poetics of Imitation: Anacreon and the Anacreontic Tradition*. Cambridge University Press.

Rossi, Flavia, and Nazareno Taddei. 1992. *Edipo re: Sofocle e Pasolini*. Rome: Edav.

Ruiz, Raúl. 1995. *Poetics of Cinema*. 3 vols. Tr. Brian Holmes. Paris: Dis voir.

Rumble, Patrick, and Bart Testa (eds.). 1994. *Pier Paolo Pasolini: Contemporary Perspectives*. University of Toronto Press.

Rycroft, Charles. 1995. *A Critical Dictionary of Psychoanalysis*. 2nd ed. London: Penguin.

Saada, Nicolas. 1998. "In the Mood." *Civilization*, 5 no. 1 (February–March): 76–81.

Sabbadini, Andrea (ed.). 2003. *The Couch and the Silver Screen: Psychoanalytic Reflections on European Cinema*. Hove: Brunner-Routledge.

Said, Edward. 1978; rpt. 1994. *Orientalism*. New York: Vintage.

Samuels, Charles Thomas. 1972; rpt. 1987. *Encountering Directors*. New York: Da Capo.

Sandys, Sir John Edwin. 1920; rpt. 1967. *A History of Classical Scholarship*. Vol. 1: *From the Sixth Century B.C. to the End of the Middle Ages*. 3rd ed. New York: Hafner.

Sargeant, Winthrop. 1947. "The Cult of the Love Goddess in America." *Life* (November 10): 81–82, 85–86, 89–90, 92, 94, and 96.

Sarris, Andrew. 1968; rpt. 1996. *The American Cinema: Directors and Directions 1929–1968*. New York: Da Capo.

    1975; rpt. 1976. *The John Ford Movie Mystery*. Bloomington: Indiana University Press.

    1977. "The Auteur Theory Revisited." *American Film*, 2 no. 9 (July–August): 49–53.

Sartre, Jean-Paul. 1984. *Le scénario Freud*. Ed. Jean-Bertrand Pontalis. Paris: Gallimard.

    1985; rpt. 1986. *The Freud Scenario*. Tr. Quintin Hoare. University of Chicago Press.

Schatz, Thomas. 1988; rpt. 1996. *The Genius of the System: Hollywood Filmmaking in the Studio Era*. New York: Holt.

Scheid, John, and Jesper Svenbro. 1996; rpt. 2001. *The Craft of Zeus: Myths of Weaving and Fabric*. Tr. Carol Volk. Cambridge, MA: Harvard University Press.

Schein, Seth L. 1984. *The Mortal Hero: An Introduction to Homer's Iliad*. Berkeley: University of California Press.

Schifano, Laurence. 2003. "Orphic Self-Portraits." In *Cocteau* 2003: 53–62.

Schiller, Friedrich. 1965; rpt. 1967. *Sämtliche Werke*. Ed. Gerhard Fricke and Herbert G. Göpfert. Vol. 1: *Gedichte/Dramen I*. 4th ed. Munich: Hanser.

Schlesier, Renate. 1999. "Auf den Spuren von Freuds Ödipus." In Hofmann 1999: 283–300.

Schmeling, Gareth (ed.). 1996. *The Novel in the Ancient World*. Leiden: Brill.

Schmidt, Ernst A. 2001. "The Meaning of Vergil's *Aeneid*: American and German Approaches." *The Classical World*, 94 (Winter): 145–171.

Schmitz, Thomas A. 2007. *Modern Literary Theory and Ancient Texts: An Introduction*. Oxford: Blackwell.

Schneider, Steven Jay (ed.). 2004. *Horror Film and Psychoanalysis: Freud's Worst Nightmare*. Cambridge University Press.

Schönbeck, Gerhard. 1964. *Der locus amoenus von Homer bis Horaz*. Cologne: Wasmund.

Schrader, Paul. 1972; rpt. 1988. *Transcendental Style in Film: Ozu, Bresson, Dreyer*. New York: Da Capo.

    2006. "Canon Fodder." *Film Comment*, 42 no. 5 (September–October): 33–49.

Schwartz, Barth David. 1992; rpt. 1995. *Pasolini Requiem*. New York: Vintage.

Scorsese, Martin, and Michael Henry Wilson. 1997. *A Personal Journey with Martin Scorsese Through American Movies*. New York: Miramax Books/Hyperion and British Film Institute.

Searles, Baird. 1990. *Epic! History on the Big Screen*. New York: Abrams.

Segal, Charles. 1985. "Literature and Interpretation: Conventions, History, and Universals." *Classical and Modern Literature*, 5 no. 2: 71–85.

    1986. *Interpreting Greek Tragedy: Myth, Poetry, Text*. Ithaca: Cornell University Press.

    1999. "Introduction: Retrospection on Classical Literary Criticism." In Falkner, Felson, and Konstan 1999: 1–15.

2001. *Oedipus Tyrannus: Tragic Heroism and the Limits of Knowledge.* 2nd ed. New York: Oxford University Press.

Semmes, Harry H. 1955. *Portrait of Patton.* New York: Appleton-Century-Crofts.

Seznec, Jean. 1953; rpt. 1995. *The Survival of the Pagan Gods: The Mythological Tradition and Its Place in Renaissance Humanism and Art.* Tr. Barbara F. Sessions. Princeton University Press.

Shakespeare, William. 1955; rpt. 1996. *Julius Caesar.* Ed. T. S. Dorsch. London: Routledge.

1995. *Antony and Cleopatra.* Ed. John Wilders. London: Routledge.

Shanower, Eric. 2001. *Age of Bronze.* Vol. 1: *A Thousand Ships.* Orange, CA: Image Comics.

Sharrett, Christopher. 2006. "Through a Door Darkly: A Reappraisal of John Ford's *The Searchers.*" *Cineaste,* 31 no. 4: 4–8.

Siciliano, Enzo. 1982. *Pasolini: A Biography.* Tr. John Shepley. New York: Random House.

Siegel, Janice. 2005. "Tennessee Williams' *Suddenly Last Summer* and Euripides' *Bacchae.*" *International Journal of the Classical Tradition,* 11: 538–570.

Silbergeld, Jerome. 2004. *Hitchcock with a Chinese Face: Cinematic Doubles, Oedipal Triangles, and China's Moral Voice.* Seattle: University of Washington Press.

Simon, Bennett. 1978; rpt. 1980. *Mind and Madness in Ancient Greece: The Classical Roots of Modern Psychiatry.* Ithaca: Cornell University Press.

1988. *Tragic Drama and the Family: Psychoanalytic Studies from Aeschylus to Beckett.* New Haven: Yale University Press.

Sitney, P. Adams (ed.). 1970; rpt. 2000. *Film Culture Reader.* New York: Cooper Square Press.

Skutsch, Otto. 1987. "Helen: Her Name and Nature." *Journal of Hellenic Studies,* 102: 188–193.

Smith, Alison. 1998. *Agnès Varda.* Manchester University Press.

Smith, Gary Allen. 2004. *Epic Films: Casts, Credits and Commentary on Over 350 Historical Spectacle Movies.* Jefferson, NC: McFarland.

Snell, Bruno. 1953; rpt. 1982. *The Discovery of the Mind: The Greek Origins of European Thought.* Tr. T. G. Rosenmeyer. New York: Harper.

Snyder, Jane McIntosh. 1981. "The Web of Song: Weaving Imagery in Homer and the Lyric Poets." *The Classical Journal,* 76 no. 3: 193–196.

Snyder, Stephen. 1980. *Pier Paolo Pasolini.* Boston: Twayne.

Sobel, Brian M. 1997. *The Fighting Pattons.* Westport, CT: Praeger.

Solomon, Jon (ed.). 1994. *Apollo: Origins and Influences.* Tucson: University of Arizona Press.

2001. *The Ancient World in the Cinema.* 2nd ed. New Haven: Yale University Press.

2006. "Viewing *Troy*: Authenticity, Criticism, Interpretation." In Winkler 2006d: 85–98.

Sontag, Susan. 1966a; rpt. 2001. *Against Interpretation and Other Essays*. New York: Picador.

—— 1966b. "Spiritual Style in the Films of Robert Bresson." In 1966a: 177–195.

—— 1967a. "Bergman's *Persona*." In Sontag 1967b: 123–145.

—— 1967b; rpt. 2002. *Styles of Radical Will*. New York: Farrar Straus Giroux.

—— 1977a. "In Plato's Cave." In Sontag 1977b: 3–24.

—— 1977b; rpt. 2001. *On Photography*. New York: Picador.

Sorlin, Pierre. 1980. *The Film in History: Restaging the Past*. Totowa: Barnes and Noble.

Southern, Pat. 2006. *The Roman Army: A Social and Institutional History*. Santa Barbara: ABC-Clio.

Spiegel, Alan. 1976. *Fiction and the Camera Eye: Visual Consciousness in Film and the Modern Novel*. Charlottesville: University Press of Virginia.

Spieker, Rainer. 1969. "Die Beschreibung des Olympos (Hom. Od. ʃ 41–47)." *Hermes*, 97: 136–161.

Spoto, Donald. 1995. *A Passion for Life: The Biography of Elizabeth Taylor*. New York: Harper Collins.

Spottiswoode, Raymond. 1935; rpt. 1973. *A Grammar of the Film: An Analysis of Film Technique*. Berkeley: University of California Press.

Sprague, Rosamond Kent (ed.). 1972; rpt. 2001. *The Older Sophists*. Indianapolis: Hackett.

Stack, Oswald. 1970. *Pasolini on Pasolini*. Bloomington: Indiana University Press.

Staiger, Janet. 1995. *Bad Women: Regulating Sexuality in Early American Cinema*. Minneapolis: University of Minnesota Press.

Stam, Robert, Robert Burgoyne, and Sandy Flitterman-Lewis. 1992. *New Vocabularies in Film Semiotics: Structuralism, Post-Structuralism and Beyond*. London: Routledge.

Stanford, W. B. 1954; rpt. 1968. *The Ulysses Theme: A Study of the Adaptability of a Traditional Hero*. Ann Arbor: University of Michigan Press.

Stansbury-O'Donnell, Mark. D. 1999. *Pictorial Narrative in Ancient Greek Art*. Cambridge University Press.

Steegmuller, Francis. 1986; rpt. 1992. *Cocteau: A Biography*. 2nd ed. Boston: Godine.

Steiner, Ann. 2007. *Reading Greek Vases*. Cambridge University Press.

Steiner, George (ed.). 1996. *Homer in English*. London: Penguin.

Stephenson, Ralph, and Guy Phelps. 1989. *The Cinema as Art*. 2nd ed. London: Penguin.

Stevens, George, Jr. 2006; rpt. 2007. *Conversations with the Great Moviemakers of Hollywood's Golden Age at the American Film Institute*. New York: Vintage.

Stevenson, Robert Louis. 1999. *R. L. Stevenson on Fiction: An Anthology of Literary and Critical Essays*. Ed. Glenda Norquay. Edinburgh University Press.

Stewart, Andrew. 1990. *Greek Sculpture: An Exploration*. 2 vols. New Haven: Yale University Press.

Stillinger, Jack. 1991. *Multiple Authorship and the Myth of Solitary Genius*. New York: Oxford University Press.

Stockert, Walter. 1992. *Euripides: Iphigenie in Aulis.* Vol. 2: *Detailkommentar.* Vienna: Verlag der österreichischen Akademie der Wissenschaften.

Stout, Rex. 1997. *The Great Legend.* New York: Carroll and Graf.

Strachan, Hew (ed.). 1998. *World War I: A History.* Oxford University Press.

Strauss, Walter A. 1971; rpt. 1997. *Descent and Return: The Orphic Theme in Modern Literature.* Cambridge, MA: Harvard University Press.

Sullivan, J. P. 1994. "Introduction: Critical Continuity and Contemporary Innovation." In de Jong and Sullivan 1994: 1–26.

Sütterlin, Axel. 1996. *Petronius Arbiter und Federico Fellini: Ein strukturanalytischer Vergleich.* Frankfurt am Main: Lang.

Suzuki, Mihoko. 1989; rpt. 1992. *Metamorphoses of Helen: Authority, Difference, and the Epic.* Ithaca: Cornell University Press.

Syndikus, Hans Peter. 1973; rpt. 1990. *Die Lyrik des Horaz: Eine Interpretation der Oden.* Vol. 2: *Drittes und viertes Buch.* Darmstadt: Wissenschaftliche Buchgesellschaft.

Tanner, Tony. 1979; rpt. 1981. *Adultery in the Novel: Contract and Transgression.* Baltimore: Johns Hopkins University Press.

Tarkovsky, Andrey. 1986; rpt. 2005. *Sculpting in Time: Reflections on the Cinema.* Tr. Kitty Hunter-Blair. Austin: University of Texas Press.

Taylor, A. J. P. 1963; rpt. 1966. *The First World War: An Illustrated History.* Harmondsworth: Penguin.

Thomas, Richard F. 1990. "Past and Future in Classical Philology." In Jan Ziolkowski 1990a: 66–74.

Thompson, Kristin. 1999. *Storytelling in the New Hollywood: Understanding Classical Narrative Technique.* Cambridge, MA: Harvard University Press.

"Thoughts That Occur: 'The Schools'." 1909. *'Varsity': A Social View of Oxford Life*: 501.

Tierno, Michael. 2002. *Aristotle's Poetics for Screenwriters: Storytelling Secrets from the Greatest Mind in Western Civilization.* New York: Hyperion.

Todini, Umberto. 1985. "Pasolini and the Afro-Greeks." Tr. Beverly Allen. *Stanford Italian Review*, 5: 219–222.

　　1995. (ed.). *Pasolini e l'antico: I doni della ragione.* Naples: Edizioni Scientifiche Italiane.

Todman, Dan. 2005. *The Great War: Myth and Memory.* London: Hambledon Continuum.

Tredell, Nicolas (ed.). 2002. *Cinemas of the Mind: A Critical History of Film Theory.* Duxford: Icon Books.

Tritle, Lawrence A. 2000. *From Melos to My Lai: War and Survival.* New York: Routledge.

Truffaut, François. 1954. "Une certaine tendance du cinéma français." *Cahiers du cinéma*, 31 (January): 15–29.

Tsakiridou, Cornelia A. (ed.). 1997. *Reviewing Orpheus: Essays on the Cinema and Art of Jean Cocteau.* Lewisburg, PA: Bucknell University Press.

Turovskaya, Maya. 1989. *Tarkovsky: Cinema as Poetry.* Ed. Ian Christie; tr. Natasha Ward. London: Faber and Faber.

Tyler, Parker. 1944; rpt. 1985. *The Hollywood Hallucination*. New York: Garland.

1947. *Chaplin: Last of the Clowns*. New York: Vanguard.

1969. *Sex Psyche Etcetera*. New York: Horizon Press.

Tynan, Kenneth. 1990; rpt. 1995. *Profiles*. Ed. Kathleen Tynan and Ernie Eban. New York: Random House.

Vachtová, Ludmila. 1968. *Frank Kupka: Pioneer of Abstract Art*. Tr. Zdenek Lederer. New York: McGraw-Hill.

Van Hook, Larue (ed. and tr.). 1945; rpt. 1998. *Isocrates*. Vol. 3. Cambridge, MA: Harvard University Press/London: Heinemann.

Vandiver, Elizabeth. 1999. " 'Millions of the Mouthless Dead': Charles Hamilton Sorley and Wilfred Owen in Homer's Hades." *International Journal of the Classical Tradition*, 5: 432–455.

Vedder, Ursula. 1999–2000. "Der Koloß von Rhodos: Mythos und Wirklichkeit eines Weltwunders." *Nürnberger Blätter zur Archäologie*, 16: 23–40.

2003a. "Der Koloß von Rhodos als Wächter über dem Hafeneingang." In Kunze 2003: 131–149.

2003b. "Weltwunder." *Der Neue Pauly*, 15.3: 1110–1117.

Vernant, Jean-Pierre. 1988. "Oedipus Without the Complex." In Vernant and Vidal-Nacquet 1988: 85–111.

and Pierre Vidal-Nacquet. 1988. *Myth and Tragedy in Ancient Greece*. Tr. Janet Lloyd. New York: Zone Books.

Vertov, Dziga. 1984. *Kino-Eye: The Writings of Dziga Vertov*. Ed. Annette Michelson; tr. Kevin O'Brien. Berkeley: University of California Press.

Viano, Maurizio. 1993. *A Certain Realism: Making Use of Pasolini's Film Theory and Practice*. Berkeley: University of California Press.

Vidal, Gore. 2002. *Perpetual War for Perpetual Peace: How We Got to Be So Hated*. New York: Thunder's Mouth Press.

Vidor, King. 1972. *On Film Making*. New York: McKay.

Viera, Mark A. 1999. *Sin in Soft Focus: Pre-Code Hollywood*. New York: Abrams.

Vogt, Ernst. 1997. "Griechische Philologie in der Neuzeit." In Nesselrath 1997: 117–132.

Völuer, Martin. 2002. "Die Melancholie am Ende des Jahrhunderts: Zum *Blick des Odysseus* von Theo Angelopoulos." In Korenjak and Töchterle 2002: 72–83.

Bernd Seidensticker, and Wolfgang Emmerich (eds.). 2004. *Mythenkorrekturen: Zu einer paradoxalen Form der Mythenrezeption*. Berlin: de Gruyter.

Völker, Klaus. 1978. *Brecht: A Biography*. tr. John Nowell. New York: Seabury Press.

Wagner, Walter. 1975. *You Must Remember This*. New York: Putnam.

2001. "One More Hurrah." In Peary 2001: 151–159.

Wagstaff, Christopher. 1999. "Reality into Poetry: Pasolini's Film Theory." In Baranski 1999a: 185–227.

Walker, Alexander. 1991; rpt. 2001. *Elizabeth: The Life of Elizabeth Taylor*. New York: Grove Press.

Walker, Janet. 1999. "Textual Trauma in *Kings Row* and *Freud*." In Bergstrom 1999: 171–187.

2001a. "Captive Images in the Traumatic Western: *The Searchers, Pursued, Once Upon the Time in the West*, and *Lone Star*." In Janet Walker 2001b: 219–251.

2001b. (ed.). *Westerns: Films Through History*. New York: Routledge.

and Diane Waldman. 1990. "John Huston's *Freud* and Textual Repression: A Psychoanalytic Feminist Reading." In Lehman 1990: 282–300.

Wanger, Walter, and Joe Hyams. 1963. *My Life With* Cleopatra. New York: Bantam.

Ward, David. 1994. "A Genial Analytic Mind: 'Film' and 'Cinema' in Pier Paolo Pasolini's Film Theory." In Rumble and Testa 1994: 127–151.

Warner, Rex (tr.). 1954; several rpts. *Thucydides: The Peloponnesian War*. Harmondsworth: Penguin.

Warshow, Robert. 2001a. "The Art of the Film." In Warshow 2001b: 285–287.

2001b. *The Immediate Experience: Movies, Comics, Theatre and Other Aspects of Popular Culture*. Enlarged ed. Cambridge, MA: Harvard University Press.

Watt, Roderick H. 1985. "'Wanderer, kommst du nach Sparta': History through Propaganda into Literary Commonplace." *Modern Language Review*, 80: 871–883.

Weber, Caroline. 2006; rpt. 2007. *Queen of Fashion: What Marie Antoinette Wore to the Revolution*. New York: Holt.

Webster, Graham. 1979; rpt. 1994. *The Roman Imperial Army of the First and Second Centuries A.D.* 2nd ed. New York: Barnes and Noble.

Wenskus, Otta. 2002. "*Star Trek*: Antike Mythen und moderne Energiewesen." In Korenjak and Töchterle 2002: 128–135.

West, M. L. 1993; rpt. 1994. *Greek Lyric Poetry*. Oxford University Press.

Wetzel, Michael. 2000. "Autor/Künstler." In Barck et al. 2000: 480–544.

Wexman, Virginia Wright (ed.). 2002. *Film and Authorship*. New Brunswick: Rutgers University Press.

White, John. 1956. *Perspective in Ancient Drawing and Painting*. London: Society for the Promotion of Hellenic Studies.

Wicking, Christopher, and Barrie Pattison. 1969. "Interviews with Anthony Mann." *Screen*, 10 no. 4: 32–54.

Wiethoff, Tobias. 2004. "Interview mit dem Regisseur Wolfgang Petersen: 'Ich gehe dahin, wo der Stoff ist'." *Westdeutsche Zeitung* (May 7); http://www.wz-newsline.de/seschat4/200/sro.php?redid=58942.

Wilamowitz-Moellendorff, U. von. 1982. *History of Classical Scholarship*. Ed. Hugh Lloyd-Jones; tr. Alan Harris. London: Duckworth/Baltimore: Johns Hopkins University Press.

Wiles, David. 2007. *Mask and Performance in Greek Tragedy: From Ancient Festival to Modern Experimentation*. Cambridge University Press.

Williams, James S. 2006. *Jean Cocteau*. Manchester University Press.

Wills, Garry. 1998. "War Refugee." *Civilization*, 5 no. 1 (February–March): 64–67.

Wilson, Elizabeth. 1934. "Intimate Moments With Cleopatra." *Silver Screen* (July): 20–21 and 69–70.

Wilson, George M. 1986. *Narration in Light: Studies in Cinematic Point of View*. Baltimore: Johns Hopkins University Press.

Winkler, Martin M. 1985. "Classical Mythology and the Western Film." *Comparative Literature Studies*, 22: 516–540.

1991a. (ed.). *Classics and Cinema*. London: Associated University Presses.

1991b. "Introduction." In Winkler 1991a: 9–13.

1996. "Homeric *kleos* and the Western Film." *Syllecta Classica*, 7: 43–54.

2000–2001. "The Cinematic Nature of the Opening Scene of Heliodoros' *Aithiopika*." *Ancient Narrative*, 1: 161–184.

2001a. (ed.). *Classical Myth and Culture in the Cinema*. New York: Oxford University Press.

2001b. "Introduction." In Winkler 2001a: 3–22.

2002a. "*Cleopatra* (1963)." *Amphora*, 1 no. 2: 13–14.

2002b. "The Face of Tragedy: From Theatrical Mask to Cinematic Close-Up." *Mouseion*, 3 no. 2: 43–70.

2003. "Quomodo stemma *Gladiatoris* pelliculae more philologico sit constituendum." *American Journal of Philology*, 124: 137–141.

2004a. "*Gladiator* and the Traditions of Historical Cinema." In Winkler 2004b: 16–30.

2004b. (ed.). *Gladiator: Film and History*. Oxford: Blackwell.

2006a. "Editor's Introduction." In Winkler 2006d: 1–19.

2006b. "The *Iliad* and the Cinema." In Winkler 2006d: 43–67.

2006c. "The Trojan War on the Screen: An Annotated Filmography." In Winkler 2006d: 202–215.

2006d. (ed.). *Troy: From Homer's Iliad to Hollywood Epic*. Oxford: Blackwell.

2007a. "'Culturally Significant and Not Just Simple Entertainment': History and the Marketing of *Spartacus*." In Winkler 2007d: 198–232.

2007b. "Greek Myth on the Screen." In Woodard 2007: 453–479.

2007c. "Leaves of Homeric Storytelling: Wolfgang Petersen's *Troy* and Franco Rossi's *Odissea*." In Cavallini 2007: 77–85.

2007d. (ed.). *Spartacus: Film and History*. Oxford: Blackwell.

2009. *The Roman Salute: Cinema, History, Ideology*. Columbus: Ohio State University Press.

Winter, Jay. 1995. *Sites of Memory, Sites of Mourning: The Great War in European Cultural History*. Cambridge University Press.

Wiseman, T. P. (ed.). 2002. *Classics in Progress: Essays on Ancient Greece and Rome*. Oxford: The British Academy/Oxford University Press.

Witt, Hubert (ed.). 1966. *Erinnerungen an Brecht*. 2nd ed. Leipzig: Reclam.

Wolf, F. A. 1985. *Prolegomena to Homer, 1795*. Tr. Anthony Grafton, Glenn W. Most, and James E. G. Zetzel. Princeton University Press.

Wollen, Peter. 1998. *Signs and Meaning in the Cinema*. 4th ed. London: British Film Institute.

1999. "Freud as Adventurer." In Bergstrom 1999: 153–170.

Wood, Robin. 1998a. "Man(n) of the West(ern)." *CineAction*, 46: 26–33.

1998b; rpt. 1999. *Sexual Politics and Narrative Film: Hollywood and Beyond*. New York: Columbia University Press.

2002. *Hitchcock's Films Revisited*. Rev. ed. New York: Columbia University Press.

2003. *Hollywood from Vietnam to Reagan . . . and Beyond.* New York: Columbia University Press.

Woodard, Roger (ed.). 2007. *The Cambridge Companion to Greek Myth.* Cambridge University Press.

Woodbury, Leonard. 1967. "Helen and the Palinode." *Phoenix,* 21: 157–176.

Wright, Evan. 2004; rpt. 2005. *Generation Kill: Devil Dogs, Iceman, Captain America, and the New Face of American War.* New York: Berkley Caliber.

Wuttke, Dieter (ed.). 2003. *Erwin Panofsky: Korrespondenz 1910–1968: Eine kommentierte Auswahl in fünf Bänden.* Vol. 2: *Korrespondenz 1937–1949.* Wiesbaden: Harrassowitz.

Wyke, Maria. 1997. *Projecting the Past: Ancient Rome, Cinema and History.* New York: Routledge.

1998. "Classics and Contempt: Redeeming Cinema for the Classical Tradition." *Arion: A Journal of Humanities and the Classics,* 3rd ser., 6.1: 124–136.

2003. "Are You Not Entertained? Classicists and the Cinema." *International Journal of the Classical Tradition,* 9: 430–445.

Zander, Peter. 2004. "*Deutscher* Härtetest: Wolfgang Petersen hat 'Troja' verfilmt – und fand in den Sagen Parallelen zu George W. Bush." *Berliner Morgenpost* (May 5); http://morgenpost.berlin1.de/archiv2004/040512/feuilleton/story677622.html.

Zanker, Graham. 2000. "Aristotle's Poetics and the Painters." *American Journal of Philology,* 121: 225–235.

2004. *Modes of Viewing in Hellenistic Poetry and Art.* Madison: University of Wisconsin Press.

Ziolkowski, Jan. 1990a. *On Philology.* University Park: Pennsylvania State University Press.

1990b. "'What Is Philology?': Introduction." In Jan Ziolkowski 1990a: 1–12.

Ziolkowski, Theodore. 2000a. "The Fragmented Text: The Classics and Postwar European Literature." *International Journal of the Classical Tradition,* 6: 549–562.

2000b. *The Sin of Knowledge: Ancient Themes and Modern Variations.* Princeton University Press.

# Index